Louisette Bertholle was brought up in a family of gourmets in France. As a child she spent her summers at Talloires, at the Auberge du Père Bise, where some of the recipes in this book come from, and it was there that her 'palate' was formed. In collaboration with Simone Beck, and Julia Child, with whom she founded the École des 3 Gourmandes, Madame Bertholle wrote *Mastering the Art of French Cooking*. She is also the author of *250 Recettes de Sologne et d'Ailleurs*.

Secrets of the Great French Restaurants

Nearly 400 recipes from famous restaurants starred in the Michelin Guide

Selected and edited by

LOUISETTE BERTHOLLE

author of the Introduction, Appendices and Glossary

Translated by Carole Fahy and Bud MacLennan

SPHERE BOOKS LIMITED
30/32 Gray's Inn Road, London WC1X 8JL

Note to the Paperback Edition

Since the publication of the hardback edition of this book there have
been changes in some of the stars awarded to the restaurants. It has
been decided, nevertheless, that the recipes would not be changed
accordingly, not only because they are excellent recipes individually
but also because they form a coherent whole.

The changes in the Michelin stars are as follows:

Restaurant unstarred in 1973 but given one star in 1974

Relais des Pyrénées *, Paris 20e.

Restaurant with one star in 1973 and two stars in 1974

La Bonne Auberge **, Antibes.

Restaurants which lost their stars in 1974

Chez Garin, Paris 5e (formerly **; restaurant closed).
Laurent, Paris 8e (formerly *; not listed).
Dagorno, Paris 19e (formerly *; not listed).
Le Diable Vert, Raphèle-les-Arles (formerly *).
Auberge du Gué des Grues, Gué des Grues, near Dreux (formerly *).
La Colombière, Etables-sur-mer (formerly *).
Restaurant de Paris, Lille (formerly *).
Sainte-Marie, Rocamadour (formerly *).

In addition the restaurant Le Galant Verre *, Paris 7e, has changed its
name to Le Petit Coin de la Bourse * and moved its premises to 16 rue
Feydeau, Paris 2e.

LOUISETTE BERTHOLLE

CONTENTS

ACKNOWLEDGEMENTS

The editor and publishers would like to express their gratitude to the chefs and restaurants who generously divulged their precious recipes. They would also like to thank M. Raymond Oliver for his recipes from Le Grand Véfour taken from his book, *La Cuisine*.

Design and picture research by Jean François Pinto Rousseau.

The engravings illustrated in this book belong to the collection of Editions Albin Michel, 22 rue Huyghens, Paris 14e. The jacket photographs are by Gian-Carlo Bonora of Rizzoli Editore, Milan.

WEIGHTS AND MEASURES

$100g = 3 \cdot 5$ oz
$1kg = 2 \cdot 2$ lb
$1l = 1\frac{3}{4}$ pt
$1dl = 4$ fl oz
$1cl = \frac{1}{3}$ fl oz

OVEN TEMPERATURES

Centigrade	Fahrenheit	Gas Regulo
120–140	250–275	$\frac{1}{4}$–$\frac{1}{2}$
150–160	300–325	1–2
180–190	350–375	3–5
190–200	375–400	5–6
200–220	400–425	6–7
230–250	450–475	8–9

INTRODUCTION

This is an original and unique collection of recipes from famous French restaurants which have been awarded stars by the Michelin Guide. The book contains about 400 recipes from more than 200 restaurants. Every 3-star restaurant is represented, nearly all 2-star restaurants are included, many with 1 star, and a few restaurants which are unstarred in the 1973 Michelin Guide but whose contributions are outstanding.

In France, the expression 'trois étoiles' (three stars) has but one meaning, immediately understood by all, as designating outstanding restaurants based on their listing in the Guide Michelin. This justly famous travellers' guide started using them in 1926, with a single star, *, which simply meant, in their own words: '*bonne table dans sa catégorie*', which may be freely translated as 'good food for the price'. Only in 1931 did there appear two stars, **, explained as: 'excellent fare, worth a detour', and three stars, ***: 'one of the best in France, worth the trip'.

During the Second World War both the Guide and the stars disappeared. The Guide reappeared in 1945 but single stars not until 1947, two stars in 1948 and three in 1951, which is a perfect indication of the enormous care which goes into the selection.

As every traveller in France learns, these stars are an extraordinarily reliable and respected measure not only of quality but also of consistency. This implies that a starred restaurant must without fail, day in and day out, serve a speciality worthy of the detour made by the passing client and the meal worth the particular expense incurred by its habitués. This requires the greatest effort and above all, constant attention on the part of the chef, as outstanding quality and service never become a routine. If there is any weakening this will quickly become known and the loss of a star may follow with the next edition of the Guide. Even if one star is lost, however, there remains the merit of having obtained it and the possibility of recovering it. For this reason the recipes in this book come from restaurants which had earned their stars in 1969, 1970 and 1971, even if since then one or two of them have lost a star.

The recipes were very carefully chosen to present the widest range of dishes and the specialities from each region of France. They were given to me directly by the chef who created or developed each dish. For this English version certain recipes of local interest, requiring rare ingredients difficult to find, have been omitted.

For centuries the art of cooking has been studied and perfected in France. The greatest years of French cooking were those between 1905 and 1915 and between 1920 and 1939 but the basis of classic French cooking was established at the end of the last century. Since then no new techniques have been discovered although traditional methods have been adapted and improved. I should like to pay a special tribute to Fernand Point, who had a tremendous influence on the cooking we know today and who brilliantly adapted the methods of those great masters before him: Escoffier, Montagne and Pellaprat. Fernand Point passed on to his pupils his techniques of subtle simplicity and especially his masterly light sauces, the *jus liés* in which the reduced stock is thickened with butter or cream or both. Many detailed recipes following Fernand Point's principles will be found in this book.

There is no mystery in the cooking of great restaurants. The only requirements are will and enthusiasm and I have tried to explain each recipe in this book in a way that can easily be followed by the most inexperienced cook. This book gives everyone the chance to enjoy the cooking of great restaurants at home, which is quite a novelty. The simplest are suitable for a family meal, and the more elaborate ones for a festive occasion when friends are invited to try the speciality of a famous restaurant. Some hostesses must admit to running short of imagination but they should find here an inexhaustible source of inspiration. There is so much choice that there is no longer any reason to repeat oneself.

I think with special sympathy of the many men and women who love cooking and cook themselves, not only of necessity but also for the sake of sharing the pleasure of tasting good food. I wish them all the joy I experienced when trying many of the recipes in this book, with an impression of breaking away from routine and of travelling by changing menus.

Culinary terms not in common usage are marked with an asterisk and are explained in the glossary at the end of the book. Each recipe is indexed both alphabetically and in the regional index. General directions for making the basic sauces, pastries and creams referred to in the text are given in the appendices.

An American author once wrote: 'Cooking is a sport without a season.' It is a sport which should be approached with spirit and enthusiasm. It is not a dreary chore but an exciting occupation which brings its rewards at each meal and in every season.

The cooking of great restaurants should not frighten anyone; it contains no mystery and anyone can try it who is willing to give it the proper care. One has to have the courage to take advantage of this book, which makes great cooking available to all who desire it.

It was not an easy task to write the recipes of the greatest French restaurants in French. Professional chefs have their own culinary language which had to be made completely clear. Now to present this book for practical use by English speaking cooks therefore required interpretation far beyond a simple translation.

But then, truly fine cooking can never be contained in recipes, however perfectly formulated, and the unique savour of each dish will always depend on the flair, the humour, the hard work and love, the proportions of which ingredients I must leave to each of my dear readers.

LOUISETTE BERTHOLLE

SOUPS

AU VIEUX PORT
LA ROCHELLE (CHARENTE-MARITIME)

LA POTÉE 'AU VIEUX PORT'
*A bouillabaisse from the Atlantic coast. The delicious mixture
of stock, vegetables and fish is a meal in itself.*

For 6 people

Vegetables
4 good potatoes, finely sliced
3 onions, finely sliced
4 leeks, the white parts only,
  finely sliced
6 cloves garlic
2 tomatoes
4 tbs olive oil

Fish (cleaned, prepared and
  cut in half)
3 *rascasses*, each weighing 500g

3 red gurnards, each weighing
  500g
3 fine weevers
500g angler fish (*lotte*) cut into
  large dice
6 fillets sole

Seasoning
salt, whole black peppercorns
a pinch cayenne
a pinch powdered saffron
a sprig thyme
1 bay leaf

To cook Gently sauté the vegetables in the olive oil in a tall
stew-pot for 5 to 6 minutes until they are soft. Stir during cooking
to prevent colouring.

Put all the fish except the sole fillets on top of the vegetables
in the pan. Add 3 litres of cold water, bring to the boil and simmer,
covered, for 30 minutes. Season while cooking. Ten minutes
before the end add the fillets of sole.

To serve Serve the bouillabaisse, having removed the herbs, in
piping hot soup bowls and hand round a dish of croûtons freshly
fried in oil and rubbed with garlic at the last moment.

Suggested wine Muscadet or a Loire wine, red or white.

MICHEL *
Brasserie des Catalans
MARSEILLE (BOUCHES-DU-RHÔNE)

BOUILLABAISSE

This soup, one of the glories of Mediterranean cooking, consists of a dish of fish and a soup served separately, but at the same time, with rouille *and* aïoli *sauces and croûtons rubbed with garlic.*

For 4–6 people

about 3kg of a mixture of *rascasse*, weevers, John Dory, wrasse (*rouquier*), conger eel, gurnard, crawfish and Mediterranean prawns
1dl olive oil
2 onions, finely sliced
2 leeks, white parts only, roughly chopped
4–6 cloves garlic (to taste)

2 large tomatoes, peeled, seeded and roughly chopped
parsley, dried fennel, small hot red pepper
cayenne pepper
4 potatoes, sliced
pure saffron (essential), threads or powdered
$2\frac{1}{2}$l hot water
12 slices bread, lightly dried in the oven, browned in oil and rubbed with garlic

To cook Gently soften the vegetables and seasonings in the oil, in a deep heavy saucepan, stirring to prevent colouring. Add the fish with firm flesh, reserving the soft fish such as the wrasse, as well as the crawfish and the prawns. Add the potatoes and hot water, bring to the boil and let the soup bubble fiercely for 10–15 minutes, depending on the size of the largest fish. Add freshly milled black pepper and a light sprinkling of salt. Put in the crawfish, add the prawns 5 minutes later and the soft fish a few minutes after the prawns. The soup should cook for a further 15–20 minutes after the crawfish has been added. Add a pinch of saffron just before the end of the cooking time.

When the crawfish is cooked, remove the fish and potatoes from the pan and arrange them on a large dish, preferably a metal one which will retain the heat. The prawns should be served whole and the crawfish cut in two down the length of its body, with the tail cut in sections, unshelled. Very small crawfish should be left whole.

To serve Strain the soup into a tureen. Arrange the pieces of fried bread on greaseproof paper in a bread basket and serve at the same time as the soup and fish.

Hand the *rouille* (see p. 346) and *aïoli* (see p. 354) sauces separately.

Suggested wine A rosé from Provence or any well chilled dry rosé or dry white wine if rosé is not available.

ERMITAGE MESSONNIER ★ ★
BELLEVUE-LES-ANGLES (GARD)

BISQUEBOUILLE À L'AVIGNONNAISE

A very special fish soup using both fresh-water and salt-water fish, lightly flavoured with anis and with a very subtle taste of garlic. The soup is thickened with eggs, cream and aïoli.

For 10 people

Fish
500g red gurnard
500g angler fish (*lotte*)
500g conger eel
500g pike
300g eel
20 crayfish, gutted
olive oil for the marinade
salt, freshly milled black
    pepper
thyme, parsley, bay leaf
saffron
measure Ricard or Pastis

For thickening the sauce
3 egg yolks
5 tbs double cream
½ cup *aïoli* (see p. 354)

Stock
1kg any small fish, cleaned
heads, bones and remains of
    the large fish
2l water

Mirepoix★
onions
1 leek, white part only
stick of celery
fennel root
shallot

Garnish
bread croûtons

aïoli
sauce ardente (*aïoli* with
    harissa)[1]

To prepare the fish Fillet the large fish; chop the fillets into pieces each weighing 50g and season well with salt and pepper. Put the crayfish aside.

To marinate Put 4 tablespoons of olive oil into a tall enamelled stew-pot; spoon in a layer of vegetable *mirepoix*, a bouquet garni of thyme, parsley and a bay leaf and a sprinkling of saffron.

Arrange the pieces of fish on the *mirepoix* and sprinkle with a good measure of Ricard or Pastis.

Put a piece of greaseproof paper on top of and touching the fish, put the lid on the pan and leave in a cool place for about 3 hours.

To make the stock Make a fish stock with the heads, bones and remains of the large fish, the whole small fish and the water. Bring to a boil, skim and boil rapidly for 20 to 25 minutes or until thickened. Keep warm until required.

To cook Put the crayfish on the fish in the marinade. Add the hot stock and a little extra boiling water if necessary to achieve the right consistency. Boil fiercely for 15 minutes, remove the fish and crayfish and drain. Strain the stock, discarding the whole small fish and bind with the egg yolks and cream, stirring continuously with a wooden spoon over very low heat. It must not boil. Finally, stir in the *aïoli* away from the stove.

To serve Arrange the fish in a glazed earthenware dish, using the crayfish as decoration. Coat with a third of the stock, which should have the consistency of a thin custard. Serve the rest of the stock in a tureen. The fish and the soup should be eaten together in large shallow bowls, with the croûtons spread with *aïoli* and served with a bowl of *Ardente* sauce (*aïoli* with *harissa*).

Suggested wine Tavel rosé.

---

[1] *Harissa* (or arissa): an African spice made into a paste with Chile peppers, garlic and tomato pulp. It should be used in very small quantities: a very tiny pinch to spice *rouille* or *aïoli*.

LA RÉSERVE ★ ★
BEAULIEU-SUR-MER (ALPES-MARITIMES)

MARMITE BERLUGANE

A mixture of turbot, John Dory, rascasse, mussels and scallops cooked in stock made from small rock fish. The soup is served with croûtons, a rouille *sauce and parmesan cheese.*

For 4 people

Stock
1kg small rock fish
1dl olive oil
3 onions, sliced thinly
2 medium-sized leeks, white parts only
1 stick celery
2 sticks fresh fennel
5g saffron
2 tbs tomato purée
5 cloves garlic
thyme, bay leaf, parsley stalks
salt, freshly milled black pepper
3l cold water

Fish
250g turbot
250g John Dory
300g *rascasse*, cut into large cubes
½l mussels
4 fresh scallops, with their coral

Tomato purée
500g good ripe tomatoes, peeled, seeded and pulped
2 tbs mixed herbs (parsley, chervil, tarragon, chives), finely chopped
oil

Rouille
2 cloves garlic
2 egg yolks
red pepper (to taste)
1dl olive oil
salt, freshly milled black pepper

Garnish
1 dish croûtons, browned in oil
1 bowl *rouille* (see p. 346)
1 dish grated parmesan or Gruyère cheese

To make the stock Put all the ingredients into the cold water. Bring to the boil and cook rapidly, covered, for 30 to 35 minutes to extract all the flavours. Press lightly through a sieve. Leave the strained stock to cool.

To make the tomato purée Cook the tomatoes in the oil, over a very moderate heat, for 20 to 25 minutes. Add the herbs. You should have about 3 tablespoons of purée by the end. Keep warm in the soup tureen which is to be used for serving the soup.

To cook the fish Put the fish in a tall stew-pot and add the cooled stock. Heat and boil for 7 to 8 minutes. Keep the pieces of fish warm in the tureen with the reduced tomato. Add the mussels and halved scallops to the remaining stock and boil for 7 to 8 minutes. Strain the stock into the tureen, stir with a wooden spoon and decorate with the mussels and scallops, making sure that the corals can be seen.

To serve Make the rouille by pounding the cloves of garlic, adding the egg yolks, red pepper, salt and pepper and lastly the olive oil, beaten in drop by drop as for a mayonnaise.

Serve the soup very hot with a dish of croûtons, fried in oil until golden and rubbed lightly with garlic, a bowl of *rouille* and a dish of parmesan or Gruyère cheese.

Suggested wine Blanc de blancs, domaine d'Ott.

**RELAIS DE
PARME** *
Biarritz Airport
ANGLET (PYRÉNÉES-ATLANTIQUES)

SOUPE DE POISSONS BASQUE

One of the most delicate fish soups from the south-west of France. The fish are filleted and served in a fish stock bound with egg yolks and cream. The dish is decorated with mussels and prawns and served with croûtons fried in oil and rubbed with garlic.

For 6 people

3kg fish, a mixture of *rascasse*, angler fish (*lotte*), red gurnard, weever, hake, John Dory; mussels and large prawns

Stock
oil and unsalted butter
trimmings and bones of the fish
1 large onion, finely sliced
1 leek, finely sliced

1l good dry white wine
1½l water
2–3 cloves garlic, crushed
thyme and bay leaf
2 tbs tomato purée
pinch of saffron
4 egg yolks
5 tbs double cream
1 pinch *espelette* pepper[1]
1 dish croûtons, fried in oil and rubbed with garlic

To prepare Fillet the fish. Put the fillets aside with the mussels and prawns.

Prepare a good stock by softening the onion and leek in the oil and butter, adding the fish trimmings and bones, the water and the white wine. Bring to the boil, add the crushed cloves of garlic, thyme, bay leaf and tomato purée; simmer for about 1½ hours. Press through a conical sieve into a bowl covered with muslin to ensure that no bits of fish are left in the stock. Reduce if necessary.

To cook Put the fish fillets into a heavy-bottomed pan; add the stock, a pinch of saffron, a very little tomato purée and a few drops of oil. Bring to the boil; add the mussels and prawns. Boil rapidly for a few minutes to cook the fillets, but do not over-cook: they should remain whole. Remove from the stove and leave, covered, for 5 minutes.

Strain most of the stock through a sieve into a bowl, leaving a little stock with the fillets, mussels and prawns in the pan. Keep warm. Beat the egg yolks and cream together with a fork in a fireproof soup tureen. Add the stock, a very little at a time, beating it in with a wire whisk over very gentle heat. Correct the seasoning and add the *espelette* pepper[1].

Carefully lower the fish fillets into the stock and arrange the mussels and prawns on top of the fish. The stock should be well-blended, creamy and rich.

To serve Heat for 2 minutes and serve in warmed soup bowls with a dish of croûtons, fried in oil and rubbed with garlic.

Suggested wine Muscadet or Chablis, well chilled, or a local wine such as Irouléguy.

[1] Remember that we are on the Spanish frontier; *espelette* pepper is a small red Spanish pepper, very hot, dried and pounded into a powder or preserved in oil (*editor's note*).

MICHEL *
Brasserie des Catalans
MARSEILLE (BOUCHES-DU-RHÔNE)

BOURRIDE

This dish from Marseilles is the best of the Provençal bourrides. It is a creamy fish soup enriched and thickened with aïoli *and flavoured with crawfish.*

For 4–6 people

3kg white Mediterranean fish (sea bass, bream, *pageau, sar, fiela* etc.)
1 small live crawfish, weighing at most 800g
1dl olive oil
2 onions, finely sliced
5–6 cloves garlic (to taste)
2 sticks fennel

1 small red pepper
1 pinch cayenne pepper
1 medium potato per person, sliced
2l hot water
salt, freshly milled black pepper
2 small slices toasted French bread per person

Gently stew the vegetables and flavourings in the oil, turning them, until they are soft but not coloured. Add the fish and potatoes and 2 litres of water. Bring to the boil, add salt and pepper and the live crawfish, having first stunned it with a blow on the head. Adjust the heat so that the liquid is just shuddering and cook for about 15 minutes.

Remove the fish and keep hot on a metal dish, surrounded by the vegetables.

Split the shell of the crawfish lengthways. Remove the flesh and slice thickly allowing at least one slice per person. Add to the fish.

To make the aïoli Make the *aïoli* at the same time so that the fish is not kept waiting. Thicken about ½ litre (2 cups) of *aïoli* with the garlic crushed and pounded with 1 tablespoon of olive oil, 6 egg yolks, salt, freshly milled black pepper and ½ litre of pure olive oil. (For the method see page 354.)

To bind the soup Put 2 tablespoons of *aïoli* per person, plus 1 extra, into a conical sieve. Reserve the rest. Strain 2 tablespoons of the fish stock into an enamelled saucepan. Gradually pour the rest of the stock over the *aïoli* and press through the sieve into the strained stock in the saucepan, beating the mixture as it comes through the sieve. When all the stock and *aïoli* are blended together in the saucepan, heat slowly, still beating continuously. Do not let it boil.

To serve Serve in individual warmed soup bowls. Put 2 small slices of toasted French bread in each bowl, spread with a little *aïoli*, and pour the stock over the toast. Serve the fish at the same time and hand the rest of the *aïoli* separately.

Suggested wine Well-chilled rosé or very dry white wine.

RESTAURANT DROUANT * *
PARIS 2e: PLACE GAILLON

POTAGE BISQUE DE HOMARD
When made with live lobsters this is the most wonderful of all soups.

For 6 people

1½kg small live lobsters
100g carrots
150g onions
bouquet garni
salt, freshly milled black
  pepper
100g rice

5 fresh tomatoes, peeled,
  seeded and pulped
25g tomato purée
200g unsalted butter
1dl double cream
1dl cognac
3dl white wine
2l fish or chicken stock (see
  p. 352)

To prepare Stun the lobsters by giving them a sharp blow on the head and split them in two, separating the body from the tail. Squeeze the creamy parts, liquid and coral from the body, into a bowl, press through a fine sieve and reserve.

To cook Dice the carrots and onions, soften them in half the butter, add the lobsters, season and cook gently until the lobsters turn a nice red. Flambé with the cognac, pour in the white wine, reduce slightly and add the fish or chicken stock, the tomato purée, fresh tomato pulp, and the bouquet garni. Season and cook, covered, for 20 minutes. Remove the lobsters, reserving the tails. Pound the bodies and add, with the rice, to the stock. Cook for about 30 minutes. Press through fine, taut muslin; bring the strained stock to the boil, and let it bubble for a few moments.

To serve Add the strained creamy parts of the lobsters and coral, the rest of the butter and the cream. Sprinkle lightly with cayenne pepper. Remove the tail shells, take out the intestinal gut and cut the flesh into large dice. Add to the stock. Serve very hot.

Suggested wine Very dry champagne.

MAXIM'S ★ ★ ★
PARIS 8e: 3 RUE ROYALE

POTAGE BILLY BY
Cream of mussel soup, served, very hot, in individual bowls. In summer it may be served chilled.

For 4 people

2l large mussels, tightly closed
2 medium onions, very finely
   chopped
sprigs of parsley
1 small stick celery

black peppercorns, crushed
1 wineglass very dry white
   wine
1 cup or ¼l fish stock
   (preferably made from sole
   trimmings) (see p. 352)
¼l double cream

Put the mussels, onion, parsley, celery and pepper in a saucepan with a lid. Pour over the white wine and the stock, cover and place over a lively heat. Shake the pan, keeping the lid on, until the mussels open. Cook for 5 to 6 minutes. Strain the liquid through a very fine cloth to eliminate any trace of sand and reduce by half. Add the cream and bring to boiling point, stirring continuously with a wooden spoon.

   Taste and adjust the seasoning if necessary.

To serve Serve very hot in soup bowls. Decorate each dish with finely chopped parsley or chives very finely cut with scissors.

HÔTEL DU GRAND CERF *
EVREUX (EURE)

SOUPE AU CRESSON DES VIKINGS

A deliciously fresh cream of watercress soup that can be served at the grandest dinner party.

For 4 people
- 1 dish small croûtons fried in butter until golden
- 1 bunch fresh watercress
- 60g unsalted butter
- 1 egg yolk

Cream sauce
- 3 tbs unsalted butter
- 3 heaped tbs flour
- 1l veal or chicken stock (see p. 352)
- salt, freshly milled black pepper

To make the cream sauce Make a white *roux* with the butter and flour in a heavy-bottomed saucepan, preferably of enamelled cast-iron. Remove from the stove and gradually beat in the heated stock, using a wire whisk. Return to the stove and simmer gently for 20 minutes, skimming at intervals.

To prepare the watercress Meanwhile plunge the watercress into a large pan of boiling water, add salt and boil rapidly for 5 minutes. Remove the cress, drain, run under cold water, drain again and dry on absorbent paper. Pound in a mortar or thick bowl with the butter and the egg yolk. Press through a colander into a saucepan.

To finish Using a wire whisk, beat a ladle of cream sauce into the watercress mixture in the pan. Gradually beat this into the rest of the cream sauce, away from the stove. Heat, stirring all the time, and correct the seasoning if necessary.

To serve Serve very hot in a tureen with a bowl of diced fried croûtons.

PAUL BOCUSE * * *
LYON (RHÔNE)

SOUPE DE COURGE À LA CRÈME

The pumpkin is a vegetable that is too often neglected. In this recipe for a delicious soup, the whole pumpkin is used as a tureen, filled with golden croûtons, grated Gruyère cheese and enriched with well-seasoned cream. After lengthy cooking the pumpkin flesh is soft and tender. The dish looks and tastes utterly delectable.

For 8–10 people
- 1 pumpkin, weighing 3–4kg
- 100–150g Gruyère cheese, grated

enough very fresh single cream to fill the pumpkin or fresh double cream, boiled for 5 to 6 minutes with one-third the quantity of fresh creamy

milk, salt, freshly milled black pepper, grated nutmeg	3–4 cups small croûtons

Cut off the top of the pumpkin so that it will make a tureen. Keep the lid. Carefully scoop out the seeds and stringy fibres with a spoon. Make sure that the flesh is completely cleaned by feeling it with your fingers.

Put alternate layers of croûtons and Gruyère cheese into the pumpkin until it is three-quarters full.

Season the cream filling with salt, pepper and grated nutmeg, and pour into the pumpkin until it is full. Cover with the lid and cook in a moderate oven, 165°C, 325°F, for two hours. Stir gently with a ladle from time to time to obtain a smooth consistency taking care to replace the lid.

To serve Carry the covered pumpkin to the table. Pour a ladle of cream into each heated soup bowl, adding some croûtons sprinkled with cheese and a piece of the pumpkin flesh, scooped out with a spoon.

LE GRAND VÉFOUR ★ ★ ★
PARIS 1er: 17 RUE DE BEAUJOLAIS

SOUPE AU PISTOU

This soup from the south-east of France is made in Provence and along the Mediterranean coast from Marseilles to Nice. It is particularly delicious in the spring, when green vegetables are at their most tender and basil is young and fresh. It is almost a meal in itself.

For 8 people

500g French beans, cut into 2cm lengths
3 large potatoes, diced
100g fresh white haricot beans (dried ones may be substituted)
3 tomatoes, skinned, seeded and pulped
4 small courgettes, diced (or the same quantity of marrow or pumpkin)
3 tbs vermicelli (optional)
1 bare tbs rock salt
2½l water
freshly milled black pepper

Pistou
the leaves of 8 sprigs basil
3 garlic cloves, peeled
3 tbs olive oil

If dried haricot beans are being used, put them into a saucepan of cold water, bring to the boil, cook for 5 minutes and drain. They will continue cooking in the soup. Follow the same procedure if the fresh beans are not sufficiently tender.

Put the haricot beans into a large saucepan filled with water. Bring to the boil, add the green beans and the potatoes; season with salt and cover. The soup will take about 40 minutes to cook. Half way through cooking time add the tomatoes. The courgettes should be added a little later, a few minutes before the vermicelli, which should be put in 5 or 6 minutes before the end of the cooking time.

To prepare the pistou Just before serving pound the basil in a mortar together with the finely chopped garlic until you obtain a smooth paste. Add the oil drop by drop, continuing to pound with the pestle; work the mixture vigorously with a wooden spatula or spoon to obtain a thickish cream.

To serve Put the *pistou* in a soup tureen, beat in the liquid part of the soup little by little, then add the rest. Taste for seasoning; a turn of the pepper mill is nearly always needed.

No wine.

RELAIS DES PYRÉNÉES
PARIS 20e: 1 RUE DU JOURDAIN

OUILLAT or TOURRI

A delicious and satisfying soup from the Pyrenees, made with tomatoes, onions, garlic and goose fat. It is served strained and thickened with vermicelli or slices of bread.

For 4 people

4 tbs goose or pork fat
2 onions, finely sliced
2 cloves garlic, crushed
4 good ripe tomatoes, seeded
   and quartered

1 small leek
1 stick celery
parsley stalks, ½ bay leaf
2l boiling water
2 tbs vermicelli *or* bread

Soften the onion in the goose fat in an earthenware frying-pan, add the garlic and tomatoes and cook gently, stirring continuously, for a few minutes. Pour in the water, bring back to the boil, add the leek, celery, parsley and bay leaf and boil for about 30 to 35 minutes.

Press through a sieve or purée in a blender, then put back in the same pan to heat through.

If you are using the vermicelli, add it to the soup at this point, as soon as it comes back to the boil. If you prefer bread, put some small slices at the bottom of the tureen. The soup bowls should be hot.

Suggested wine Madiran or a bordeaux.

HORS D'OEUVRES AND FIRST COURSES

LA POTINIÈRE * *
SOLRE-LE-CHÂTEAU (NORD)

TARTE AUX POINTES D'ASPERGES

An excellent seasonal tart. It should be made from asparagus with very green tips.

For 6–7 people

Rich short-crust pastry (see p. 356)
200g sifted flour
200g unsalted butter, cut into pieces
1 egg
1–2 tbs water
a pinch salt

Filling
1kg fresh green asparagus, cooked but still firm and with the green tips cut 5–6cm from the end and reserved

Sauce
3 tbs unsalted butter
3 tbs flour
4 tbs boiling milk
1½ cups fresh double cream
salt, freshly milled white pepper
grated nutmeg

75g grated Gruyère cheese

a 25–28cm flan tin

Make some light, rich short-crust pastry with the ingredients listed (see p. 356). Leave to rest for 1 hour in the refrigerator, then roll out and line the flan tin. Prick the pastry base and bake blind in a moderate oven (about 190°C, 375°F) for 10 to 15 minutes.

Make a very creamy white sauce with the ingredients given above. Arrange the asparagus tips on the pastry, cover with the sauce and sprinkle with the grated cheese. Return to the oven and cook for another 8 to 10 minutes at the same temperature, until the surface is golden.

To serve Turn out the tart on to a serving dish and serve warm, but not too hot, cut into triangular wedges.

Suggested wine Muscadet or Sancerre.

AUBERGE DE L'ILL ★ ★ ★
ILLHAEUSERN (HAUT-RHIN)

TARTE À L'OIGNON ALSACIENNE
An excellent winter first course. If it is made in the form of several little tarts, it may be served with cocktails. If it is to be a light meal in itself it may be served with a green salad.

For 6–8 people

250g rich short-crust pastry (see p. 356)
1 good cup onion, finely chopped
3 tbs unsalted butter
1 tbs oil

Filling
¼l double cream
¼l creamy milk, scalded and cooled
3 whole eggs + 2 yolks
salt, freshly milled black pepper
small pinch cayenne

To make the tart Line a 20–22cm flan tin with the pastry very thinly rolled out. Prick the surface with a fork, cover with a piece of greaseproof paper cut to size, fill with dried beans and bake blind in an oven preheated to 200°–205°C, 375°–400°F for 12 to 15 minutes.

To make the filling Cook the onions gently in the oil and butter, stirring from time to time until they are tender and turn golden. Do not let them brown. Put all the ingredients for the filling into a large bowl and beat well with a fork until the mixture foams. Add the chopped onions.

To cook the tart Place the pastry case on a baking sheet as near as possible to the front of the oven. Pour the filling very carefully into the case without moving it so that it doesn't spill.

Cook the tart in an oven preheated to 175°–190°C, 350°–375°F for 20 to 25 minutes. The surface should be golden.

Serve hot, cut into triangular wedges.

Suggested wine A white Alsatian wine such as Gewürztraminer.

NB The tart can be reheated, in which case it will be slightly less creamy.

LA BOULE D'OR *
PARIS 7e: 13 BOULEVARD DE LATOUR-MAUBOURG

QUICHE LORRAINE

This classic and satisfying first course is a delicious mixture of Gruyère cheese, bacon and cream baked in a pastry case.

For 6 people

250g rich short-crust pastry or half-puff pastry (see page 356)
150g Gruyère cheese, cut into very small pieces
150g lightly smoked belly of pork

8 egg yolks
½l fresh double cream
a little salt
freshly milled black pepper
grated nutmeg

1 flan tin about 28cm in diameter and 4cm high

To prepare Cut the belly of pork into small strips, blanch them, then leave to cool and dry on absorbent paper. Roll out the pastry to a thickness of 4mm. Line the flan tin with the pastry, scallop the edge and prick the surface lightly. Arrange the cheese and strips of pork on the pastry, pressing them gently into the base. Place on a baking sheet on a rack half pulled out from the oven, which should be preheated to 190°C, 375°F.

Beat the egg yolks, cream, salt, pepper and nutmeg together for 2 minutes with a hand whisk. Pour the mixture carefully into the tart without removing the tin from the oven and slide the rack carefully back into the oven.

To cook Cook for 40 to 45 minutes, lowering the heat after 20 minutes and again towards the end of the cooking time, if necessary. The quiche should be a golden colour and the pastry should be well done (but not dark), tending to come away from the edges of the tin.

Suggested wine It must be dry and white, perhaps an Alsatian wine, Traminer, Sancerre or Chablis.

LA FLAMICHE *
ROYE (SOMME)

FLAMICHE AUX POIREAUX

This dish from northern France makes a lovely first course in winter. It is a tart made of puff pastry filled with a mixture of cream and leeks stewed in butter. It is sometimes served with ham.

For 5 to 6 people

500g cleaned leeks
100g unsalted butter
3–4 tbs water
salt, freshly milled black pepper
double cream equal in weight
   to $\frac{1}{4}$ of the cooked leeks

500g puff pastry (see page 356)
1 egg yolk mixed with a little
   water

The leeks Chop the leeks finely, using all the white part but very little of the green. Stew gently in the butter, starting with half the total amount of butter and adding the rest a little at a time during the cooking. Moisten with the water, cover and cook gently until the leeks are completely soft and all the liquid has been absorbed. They should not be allowed to brown. Add the cream and season well.

The pastry Divide the pastry in two. Roll out one half on a damp baking sheet into a thin round. Place the leek mixture in the middle, leaving a border of 3cm all round. Brush the border with water. Roll out the rest of the pastry in the same way and place on top of the leek mixture. Press the edges firmly together so that they are well sealed. To help the pastry to rise, feather the edges with a sharp knife. Glaze the surface by brushing with the diluted egg yolk and make a trellis-work pattern with the point of a knife.

To cook Put the tart into a hot oven, 210°–220°C, 400°–425°F, for 10 minutes, then lower the heat to 165°–170°C, 325°–350°F for another 20 to 25 minutes. The surface of the pastry should be evenly golden with no dark spots.

To serve The tart must be served very hot, but may be cooked in advance and reheated.

Suggested wine A light red burgundy or Chinon.

AU VERT BOCAGE ⋆
PARIS 7e: 96 BOULEVARD DE LATOUR-MAUBOURG

TARTE À LA TOMATE
A light and savoury tomato tart.

For 10 people

6 eggs
200g double cream
60g softened unsalted butter
3kg ripe tomatoes, peeled,
   deseeded, with all the juice
pressed out and roughly
   chopped
200g grated Emmenthal cheese
salt, freshly milled black
   pepper
300g puff pastry (see page 356)

To prepare Beat the eggs in a deep bowl, as for an omelette. When they are foaming, add the cream and the butter a little at a time. Mix well, then add the chopped tomatoes and the cheese. Taste and season well.

Line a 25cm flan tin with the pastry.

To cook Add the filling and transfer immediately to a fairly hot oven, 200°–210°C, 400°–450°F. Lower the heat after 8 minutes, letting the temperature drop to 175°C, 350°F, or even 165°C, 330°F, and continue to cook for another 28 to 32 minutes. If the pastry starts to brown too quickly cover with buttered greaseproof paper. The surface of the filling should be golden.

To serve Serve very hot, straight from the oven. It should not be kept waiting.

Suggested wine A good rosé from Provence or Sancerre.

BEAUSÉJOUR ⋆ ⋆
LÉRY (EURE)

TARTE AUX MOULES
A delicate and savoury first course which would also make a lovely main dish for a light meal. It may be made without first cooking the pastry blind in which case it will have a softer texture.

For 6 people
Rich short-crust pastry (see p. 356)
250g flour
a pinch salt
100g unsalted butter
3 eggs yolks
2–3 tbs milk

Mussels
2l mussels
2dl dry white wine (Muscadet or Sancerre)
salt, freshly milled black pepper

Filling
½l double cream
3 eggs
salt, freshly milled black pepper

To prepare Cook the pastry case blind for about 12 minutes at 170°–175°C, 340°–350°F, in a tart tin with a removable base.

Place the cleaned mussels in a large pan with the white wine, put on the lid and cook over a lively heat, shaking the pan, until they open. Add the onion, shallot, parsley and pepper. Put back the lid and finish cooking the mussels; taste to make sure that they are ready. Remove all the shells and beards. Strain, and reduce the cooking liquid by half. Meanwhile arrange the mussels on the pastry case.

To cook Beat together the cream, eggs, salt and pepper in a bowl. Add the reduced mussel liquid and gently pour the mixture into the tart, which should have been placed on a baking sheet near the oven door to lessen the risk of spilling any of the filling. Cook in an oven preheated to 175°–190°C, 350°–375°F for 20 to 25 minutes. The filling should have risen and be golden brown. Remove the tart from the tin, keeping it on the base, and serve cut into triangular wedges.

Suggested wine Sancerre, Pouilly fumé or Pouilly Fuissé.

NANDRON ★ ★
LYON (RHÔNE)

SAUCISSON CHAUD LYONNAIS
This is a delicious and unusual first course – spicy Lyonnais[1] pork sausage, served with hot potato salad.

For 4 people

1 Lyonnais pork sausage, moist and not too salty; if necessary soak in cold water for 2 or 3 hours and wipe dry before cooking; it will have swelled a bit

1kg potatoes put into cold water and cooked in their skins

oil

Dijon mustard

a little dry white wine

salt, freshly milled black pepper

wine vinegar

1 small onion

1 tbs chopped parsley

To cook the sausage Put into cold water and bring to the boil. Simmer very gently indeed for 20 to 25 minutes. Reserve in the cooking liquid.

Potato salad Peel and slice the cooked potatoes. Season while still hot with the oil, mustard, dry white wine, salt, pepper, a drop or two of vinegar and 2 squeezes of raw onion pressed in a garlic press. Sprinkle with the chopped parsley.

To serve Slice the sausage and arrange the slices on a serving dish. Do not remove the skin. Serve with the hot potato salad and bread and fresh butter.

Suggested wine Beaujolais, Côtes-du-Rhône or a rosé.

[1] Lyonnais sausage is a large, spiced pork sausage which is served sliced and will feed several people. It is sometimes truffled (*translator's note*).

LE CHAPON FIN * *
THOISSEY (AIN)

GÂTEAU DE FOIES DE VOLAILLES À LA BRESSANE

A delicate and light first course. The livers are cooked in a terrine and served with Nantua or tomato sauce. The livers of Bresse birds are darker than other chicken livers and have the most delicate of flavours.

For 4–6 people

300g chicken livers, preferably from Bresse birds
75g flour
4 whole eggs and 4 yolks
3 tbs double cream
$\frac{3}{4}$l milk

salt, freshly milled black pepper
a small pinch grated nutmeg
a large pinch parsley, very finely chopped
$\frac{1}{2}$ clove garlic, squeezed through a garlic press, then crushed

To prepare Press the chicken livers through a sieve into a large bowl. Beat in the sifted flour with a wire whisk. Add the whole eggs one by one, working them in with a wooden spoon, then add the extra yolks in the same way. Using the whisk again, beat in the cream, then the milk, seasonings, parsley and garlic. Work well until the mixture is nicely thickened and all the ingredients are perfectly blended.

Check the consistency and seasoning: take a small piece of the mixture, roll it into a ball the size of a marble, poach it in boiling water and taste for seasoning.

To cook Pour the mixture into a round or rectangular terrine. Place the terrine in a pan of water, letting the water come halfway up the sides. Bring to simmering point on top of the stove, then transfer to an oven preheated to 160°–165°C, 320°–325°F. Cook gently for 40 to 45 minutes. Test by piercing with a trussing needle, which should come out cleanly. The gâteau should start coming away from the sides of the mould, another sign that it is cooked.

If the gâteau is not required immediately it will stay hot for 10 to 12 minutes if you leave it in the pan of water away from the heat.

To serve Turn out on to a warmed dish and serve with Nantua or tomato sauce.[1] Coat with several spoonfuls of sauce, serving the rest separately.

[1] An Aurora sauce moistened with good chicken stock and coloured with sieved and reduced fresh tomatoes goes very well with this dish (*editor's note*).

LE CHANZY *
ARRAS (PAS-DE-CALAIS)

AVOCAT FERMONT
This is a delicious and original first course of hot halves of avocado pear filled with poached eggs and coated with Béarnaise sauce.

For 2 people

1 avocado pear
wine vinegar

2 very fresh eggs
1 cup Béarnaise sauce (see p. 353)
salt, freshly milled black pepper

To prepare Make the Béarnaise sauce and keep it warm in the top of a double saucepan. Do not leave over the heat. Cut the avocado pear in two lengthways. Remove the stone and any of its outer skin that clings to the cavity. Place the two halves in a pan of warm water over moderate heat and bring to simmering point. If the avocado is not quite ripe leave it to simmer for several minutes, then drain on a clean cloth.

Lightly poach the eggs in water with a little vinegar. Drain and trim.

To serve Spoon 1 tablespoon of Béarnaise sauce into each avocado, slide in the egg, season with salt and pepper and coat it with another tablespoon of the sauce. Serve with the rest of the sauce in a small sauceboat.

Suggested wine White burgundy, for instance Chablis or Beaune.

LE PETIT VATEL *
ALENÇON (ORNE)

OEUFS POCHÉS AUX MOULES

An attractive first course. The eggs are poached in the liquid in which the mussels were cooked and served on croûtons. They are decorated with the shelled mussels and coated with a delicate sauce flavoured with the mussel liquid and enriched with a proportion of Hollandaise sauce.

For 4 people

3 tbs carrots, onions and celeriac (or celery), finely chopped for a *mirepoix**
unsalted butter
2l fine mussels, scrubbed and cleaned
8 very fresh eggs
8 slices bread, cut in squares with the crusts removed, fried in butter until golden and reheated when the dish is ready to serve

¼l good dry white wine
½dl water
2 shallots, finely sliced

Sauce
2 tbs unsalted butter
2½ heaped tbs flour
a pinch of saffron

Hollandaise sauce (see p. 352)
3 egg yolks
1 bare tbs water
2 tbs lemon juice
freshly milled black pepper
100g unsalted butter

Heat the mussels in a covered stewpan over a lively heat with the shallots, wine and water, shaking the pan until they open. They should cook for 6–8 minutes. Shell them and keep warm in a saucepan in 2 tablespoons of the cooking liquid.

Stew the vegetables for the *mirepoix* of carrot, onion and celeriac in butter with a little oil until transparent and tender. Season with salt and pepper and reserve.

Strain the cooking liquid from the mussels into a saucepan through a fine sieve lined with muslin. Bring to simmering point and poach the eggs for 3–3½ minutes. Drain and place them on the croûtons arranged on a heated oval metal serving dish. Reserve the liquid.

To make the sauce Make a white *roux* with the butter and flour. Stir in the mussel liquid, strained a second time to remove any flecks of egg white and beat vigorously with a wire whisk to obtain a smooth sauce. Add the *mirepoix*, bring to the boil, cook for a few minutes and strain through a conical sieve into a saucepan, preferably of enamelled cast-iron. Taste for seasoning and add a good pinch of saffron.

Make some Hollandaise sauce with 2 of the egg yolks, the lemon juice and water. Season with pepper. Thicken the sauce by whisking in the butter, cut up into walnut-sized pieces. Add a little salt, the third egg yolk and a dash of lemon juice.

Using a wire whisk, blend the Hollandaise sauce with the sauce reserved in the pan, beating it in a little at a time. Heat through, whisking continuously, and coat the eggs and mussels with all the sauce.

Suggested wine A dry white wine such as Chablis, Muscadet or Sancerre, served well chilled.

LA MÈRE BRAZIER *
LYON (RHÔNE)

FONDS D'ARTICHAUTS AU FOIE GRAS

A delicious classic hors d'oeuvre from Lyons.

For 4 people

4 large fresh artichokes, with good bases
4 slices *foie gras*, slightly smaller than the artichoke bases
4 slivers truffle
4 good lettuce leaves

Dressing
2 egg yolks
1 small tsp Dijon mustard
salt, freshly milled black pepper
the juice of half a lemon
groundnut oil
a dash of wine vinegar

Cook the artichokes in salted water with a little lemon juice. Cool, then pull off the leaves and cut out the chokes. Trim the bases. Make the dressing in a bowl, using very little vinegar; beat for 2 minutes. Dip the artichoke bases in the dressing for a few seconds, coating each side. Drain carefully, turning them over on absorbent paper, if necessary.

Arrange the lettuce leaves on a round metal dish, put an artichoke base on each leaf, fill each with a slice of *foie gras* and decorate with a sliver of truffle.

Suggested wine To remain in the Curnonsky[1] tradition a chilled Sauternes or a good white Côte-de-Beaune such as Montrachet or Meursault.

[1] A friend, well known in the cookery field, and I once promised Curnonsky never to serve *foie gras* with dressed salad: he believed that the dressing, particularly the vinegar content, ruined the delicacy of the *foie gras*. This is why I have substituted plain lettuce leaves for the dressed salad of the original recipe. I apologize to Mme Brazier while expressing my admiration for her (*editor's note*).

CAFÉ DE PARIS * *
BIARRITZ (PYRÉNÉES-ATLANTIQUES)

TRUFFES À LA SERVIETTE

All the delicious scent of the truffle is concealed beneath the napkin. . . .

For 4 people

4 fine fresh truffles, washed, scrubbed and lightly peeled
4 tbs unsalted butter
1 tbs shallot, very finely chopped

2½dl champagne or port
1 cup *demi-glace* sauce (see p. 352)
flour and water paste
4 small rounds of toast, 4–6cm in diameter

Sweat the truffles in the butter in a small copper sauté-pan over moderate heat. Add the chopped shallot. Moisten with the champagne or port, bring to boiling point and add the *demi-glace* sauce. Simmer, partly covered, for 10 minutes. Lift out the truffles and put them in a small ovenproof china terrine with a lid. Add the sauce and seal the lid with a flour and water paste. Place in an oven preheated to 165°–175°C, 330°–350°F, and cook for 5 minutes. The flavour of the truffles will permeate the sauce in the most delicious way. Place the truffles on the pieces of toast laid on a round serving dish between the folds of a white napkin. Serve the sauce separately.

Suggested wine Very dry champagne or a Blanc de blancs.

LA MÈRE GUY * *
LYON (RHÔNE)

TRUFFES FRAÎCHES SOUS LA CENDRE
Everyone should taste this magnificent dish once in a lifetime.

For 4 people

4 fine fresh truffles
½ bottle good light tawny port
300g half-puff pastry, divided into four (see p. 356)

100–120g *foie gras*
4 squares greaseproof paper and 4 squares silver foil, cut to the same size

Wash, brush and peel the truffles. Simmer in the port in an enamelled saucepan for 20 minutes. Leave to cool in the cooking liquid.

Roll out the pastry into circles the size of a small side plate. Mash the *foie gras* with 2 tablespoons of the cooking liquid and spread some on the centre of each round of pastry. Place a truffle on top of each portion. Brush the edges of the pastry with water. Draw the edges together in four folds to make an envelope shape. Press together so that the edges are tightly sealed.

Roll each round of truffled pastry in a piece of oiled greaseproof paper. Twist the ends together to seal. Roll in the silver foil and twist the ends as before.

The truffles may be cooked in two ways:

(1) In a fireplace beneath the cinders from a log fire. The truffles are cooked when the greaseproof wrapping turns brown.

(2) On a baking-sheet in the oven with enough hot cinders to cover the truffles completely. Cook in an oven preheated to 200°–205°C, 375°–400°F. After 25 minutes reduce the heat to 175°–165°C, 350°–330°F, then continue cooking for another 20 minutes.

To serve Remove the silver foil and serve in the greaseproof paper case, which will be lightly browned. Serve a Périgueux sauce separately (see p. 350).

Suggested wine Châteauneuf-du-Pape of a good vintage.

LA MÈRE GUY * *
LYON (RHÔNE)

TRUFFES DU VALROMEY EN SURPRISE

Foie gras *blended with butter, flavoured with cognac and rolled in powdered truffle. This is something exceptional, superb for a very special party.*

For 30–35 '*foie gras* truffles', depending on size

1kg cooked *foie gras*
300g best unsalted butter
1dl cognac or port

4 fresh truffles, washed, scrubbed, peeled and chopped as finely as possible with a knife
salt, freshly milled black pepper

Mash the *foie gras* with the butter and season with salt and pepper. Flavour with the cognac or port.

Knead the mixture in a bowl until it is perfectly blended.

Shape into balls the same size as truffles, each weighing about 40–50g. Place in the refrigerator. When very cold roll in the powdered truffle. They will look exactly like fresh truffles.

Suggested wine Meursault Goutte d'Or.

EGGS

OEUF COCOTTE AUX TRUFFES

Egg cooked in cream with chopped truffle. An elegant and delicate first course.

For each person

1 very fresh egg
a nut of butter

1 tbs fresh double cream
1 small tsp chopped truffle
salt, freshly milled black
    pepper

Melt the butter in an individual china or earthenware ramekin with a lid. Tilt the ramekin so that the sides are buttered, spoon in the cream and carefully break in the egg. Cover with the truffle, season with salt and pepper and put on the lid.

Place in a pan of boiling water, bring to the boil on top of the stove and simmer for about 8 minutes. Serve very hot.

Suggested wine A fruity white burgundy such as Meursault; it must not be too dry.

OEUFS BRAGANCE

Poached eggs served on fried halved tomatoes and coated with Béarnaise sauce.

For 4 people

4 good round tomatoes, halved
    and seeded
2 tbs unsalted butter
2 tbs oil
8 very fresh eggs
1 dl wine vinegar
2 dl water
bunches of parsley for the
    garnish

Béarnaise sauce (see p. 353)
1 dl wine vinegar
½ dl dry white wine
2 shallots, parsley and 2 sprigs
    tarragon, chopped
1 tbs cold water
3 egg yolks
180g unsalted butter

To cook the tomatoes Season the tomato halves and brown over a fairly high heat in the oil and butter for about 6 minutes, turning them over during the cooking. Keep warm.

To make the sauce Put the vinegar, white wine, shallots, tarragon and parsley into a small saucepan. Bring to the boil and cook over a lively heat until the liquid is reduced to a good tablespoon. Strain and cool.

Return the reduced base of the sauce to the saucepan with the cold water and egg yolks. Add a nut of butter and beat with a wire whisk for about 5 minutes until the mixture thickens to a cream froth. Add the rest of the butter, a little at a time, stirring very carefully until each piece is absorbed in the sauce.

To cook the eggs Heat the vinegar and water in a sauté-pan or a shallow saucepan. When the liquid is just shuddering, slide in the eggs and very carefully poach for three minutes. Remove the eggs and drain on a clean cloth.

To serve Arrange the tomatoes on a serving dish and put a poached egg on each half. Spoon three coatings of Béarnaise sauce over each egg. Decorate with fresh parsley, putting little bunches between each egg.

Suggested wine Sancerre, Muscadet or a young Beaujolais.

LA BOURGOGNE *
PARIS 7e: 6 AVENUE BOSQUET

OEUFS EN MEURETTE

Meurette *was originally a Burgundian dish; it is a cross between a soup of fresh-water fish and a* matelote *or fish stew. Following this principle, eggs* en meurette *are poached in a wine sauce, garnished with lardoons and mushrooms, decorated with garlic-flavoured croûtons and sprinkled with parsley.*

For 4 people

8 very fresh eggs

Meurette sauce
a *mirepoix** of 1 carrot and 1 onion, each very finely chopped
1 bouquet garni (parsley, thyme, bay leaf)
1 tbs unsalted butter, if necessary
4 cloves garlic, crushed
¾ bottle red Burgundy
50g pork fat, finely diced
1 cup good chicken or meat stock

*Beurre manié**
1 tbs unsalted butter
1 tbs flour

Garnish
100g fresh belly pork, cut into lardoons and sautéed in 2 tbs unsalted butter
100g mushrooms, sautéed in 2 tbs unsalted butter
salt, freshly milled black pepper
a dash of lemon juice
8 slices French bread to make 8 croûtons browned in butter and rubbed with garlic
2 tbs parsley, very finely chopped

To make the sauce Melt the bacon in a small copper sauté-pan or a small enamelled cast-iron casserole, and sweat the *mirepoix* in the fat, adding a little butter if necessary. Add the bouquet garni, cover and cook gently for 10 minutes, stirring from time to time. Add the wine, bring back to the boil, add the stock and garlic and cook for 20 minutes over a fairly lively heat.

Press the stock on the vegetables through a fine strainer into a deep round metal fireproof dish. Thicken by beating in the butter and flour, previously mashed together with a fork. Correct the seasoning.

To cook the eggs Heat the sauce in the metal fireproof dish over very gentle heat until it is just shuddering. Carefully break the eggs straight into the sauce. Poach them gently, without touching, for about 4 minutes. The yolks should be very soft.

To serve Decorate with the lardoons and mushrooms and surround with the reheated croûtons, sprinkled with parsley.

Suggested wine A good red burgundy.

HÔTEL-RESTAURANT DES VANNES * *
LIVERDUN (MEURTHE-ET-MOSELLE)

OEUFS FRITS À LA NEW YORKAISE

A delicious light lunch or supper dish. It should be made with small eggs, which look more appetizing than large ones. The eggs should have been kept at room temperature, not in the refrigerator.

For each person	*Garnish*
2 very fresh small eggs	2 small slices cooked ham, warmed through in butter
groundnut oil	2 tomato halves, grilled
a very little salt, freshly milled black pepper	2 tbs thick Béarnaise sauce (see p. 352)
	1 small bunch watercress

Pour oil into a small frying-pan until it is three-quarters full. Heat until it is very hot but not smoking. Carefully break the eggs into the pan. Fry them gently, keeping them round and compact. Drain on greaseproof paper, then add pepper and a light sprinkling of salt.

To serve Arrange the slices of ham on a heated metal dish. Lay the tomato halves on top and put a fried egg on each. Coat each egg with Béarnaise sauce. Decorate with the bunch of watercress between the eggs.

Suggested wine Dry white wine such as Muscadet or Sancerre.

JAMIN *
PARIS 16e: 92 RUE DE LONGCHAMP

OEUFS BROUILLÉS AU HOMARD

A rich and delicious dish, which can be made with left-over lobster. It should be served with fresh bread but nothing else.

For 5–6 people

1 lobster weighing 800g–1kg, cooked in a court-bouillon
15–18 eggs (3 eggs per person)
1½dl American sauce or bisque (see page 348)
60g unsalted butter, cut into pieces

1 tbs fresh tarragon, finely chopped (this adds flavour but is not absolutely necessary)
salt, freshly milled black pepper

Cut the lobster into large dice and place in a buttered round dish, preferably metal. Stir in the American sauce or bisque and keep warm. Beat the eggs in a saucepan, or in a bowl set in a pan of hot water, with the butter, salt and pepper. Heat, stirring continuously with a wooden spoon and scraping all the little bits of egg from the side of the pan. As soon as the mixture starts to thicken, transfer to the dish containing the lobster and sauce and work rapidly with a wooden spoon over very low heat, so as to blend the ingredients without further cooking. Taste for seasoning and transfer to a metal vegetable dish. Sprinkle with tarragon and serve immediately as scrambled eggs have a tendency to continue to cook and harden even after they have been removed from the heat.

Suggested wine A light white Sancerre, well chilled.

RELAIS BASQUE *
ORGON (BOUCHES-DU-RHÔNE)

PIPERADE

A light and delicious concoction of eggs blended with tomatoes, peppers and ham.

For 4 people

150g Bayonne ham, diced
200g sweet peppers, red or green, diced
1·5kg tomatoes, skinned, seeded and pulped

3 tbs unsalted butter
2 tbs oil
8 eggs, separated
salt, freshly milled black pepper

Soften the ham and peppers for 5–6 minutes in the oil and butter in a large frying-pan. Add the tomatoes, salt and pepper and continue to cook.

Beat the egg whites until stiff. Mix with the egg yolks and add to the cooked vegetable mixture. Stir quickly with a wooden spoon over moderate heat until the mixture thickens and is well

blended, with a light and foamy mousse-like consistency.
Serve immediately.

Suggested wine Dry white Jurançon.

OMELETTE DE LANGOUSTE À L'ARMORICAINE

This dish has a very subtle flavour. The omelette must be made slightly runny because it will continue cooking during the browning process.

For 4–5 people

1 red Brittany crawfish, weighing 1–1·5kg
4 tbs unsalted butter
1 tbs shallot, finely chopped
salt, freshly milled black pepper

1 pinch cayenne pepper
1dl Fine Champagne or cognac
10 eggs
1½ cups *sauce à l'Américaine* (see p. 348)
4 tbs double cream

To cook the crawfish Cook the crawfish in a court-bouillon, drain and cool. Separate the body from the tail, scoop out all the flesh from the body and legs and dice. Cut the meat from the tail into 8 small fillets and reserve.

Heat the butter in a frying-pan, add the diced crawfish, shallot, salt, pepper and cayenne. Mix well, cook for a few minutes and flambé with the Fine Champagne or cognac. Keep warm.

To cook the omelette Make an omelette in the usual way. When it is half-cooked add the crawfish mixture, well-drained. Put the tail fillets in the frying-pan, cover and heat through, without cooking.

Fold the omelette and slide on to a heated metal dish. Arrange the crawfish fillets in a row, overlapping, along the length of the omelette. Coat with the *Américaine* sauce mixed with cream. Glaze under a very hot grill for 1 minute and serve.

Suggested wine A very good Muscadet or white burgundy.

SAINTE-MARIE ⋆
ROCAMADOUR (LOT)

OMELETTE AUX TRUFFES

A lovely, foamy omelette in which the egg whites are separated from the yolks and whisked until stiff and snowy. It is served with a garnish of truffles, flavoured with madeira.

For 4 people

10 eggs, separated
2 truffles, fresh or tinned, finely sliced at the last moment, *or* truffle skins, with their liquid

10 drops madeira
a pinch salt, very little freshly milled black pepper
2 tbs unsalted butter

To prepare Put the egg yolks in a bowl, add the truffles and their juice and the madeira. Season.

Whisk the egg whites with a pinch of salt until stiff. Beat the egg yolks, truffles and madeira with a fork and fold into the egg whites.

To cook Heat the butter in a heavy cast-iron frying pan. When it is very hot (bubbling but not brown) pour in the egg mixture and stir with a fork very quickly indeed. It should cook no longer than 30 to 40 seconds and the finished omelette should be smooth and runny. Fold and turn on to a heated dish.

Serve immediately, on hot plates.

Suggested wine A dry white wine such as Muscadet, Sancerre or Chablis.

LE RELAIS DE L'EMPEREUR ⋆ ⋆
MONTÉLIMAR (DROME)

MARQUISE DE SÉVIGNÉ or OMELETTE AUX TRUFFES

An exceptional and subtle dish. The Marquise de Sévigné's château is near here at Grignan, where, from mid-December to February, the most beautiful and scented truffles are also to be found. The omelette, made with eggs beaten with thick cream, is particularly light. It is garnished with slivers of truffle and surrounded by truffle sauce flavoured with madeira.

For 2 people

6 very fresh eggs
salt, freshly milled black pepper
2 bare tbs fresh double cream
2 tbs fresh truffles, cut in *brunoise*⋆ sticks

4–5 tbs unsalted butter
5 slivers truffle, for decoration
1 cup veal stock
madeira
truffle skins, very finely chopped

Beat the eggs, seasonings, cream and diced truffles with a fork. Heat the butter in a smooth, shallow omelette-pan until it bubbles and then add the egg mixture. Cook the omelette quickly without letting it take colour; it should remain runny. Fold and slide it on to a heated oval metal serving-dish. Have the truffled sauce ready: pour the veal stock thickened and flavoured with madeira into a small saucepan. Add the truffle skins and a few more drops of madeira. Correct the seasoning and keep very hot. Spoon the sauce round the omelette and serve immediately.

Suggested wine Wine should not really be drunk with this dish but a light and fruity red Côtes-du-Rhône or a Saint-Joseph is acceptable.

PÂTÉS

AUBERGE DU PÈRE BISE ★ ★ ★
TALLOIRES (HAUTE-SAVOIE)

MOUSSE DE FOIES DE VOLAILLES
This is the lightest and most delicate of all mousses.

For 6 people

300g trimmed chicken livers
150g pork fat, diced
400g *foie gras*

2 tbs double cream

Marinade
1½dl dry red port
a sprig thyme
a small bay leaf
salt, freshly milled black
    pepper

To prepare Marinate the chicken livers and pork fat in the marinade.

Remove the livers and pork fat pieces and cook rapidly in butter. Lift out the livers when they are still pink. Add the port and reduce. Remove the herbs.

When the livers and pork fat have cooled reduce to a purée with their cooking juices, using a blender or a fine sieve.

Mix the *foie gras* with the purée and bind with the cream. Check the seasoning. Press the mousse into a small terrine or into individual ramekins and chill.

To serve Turn out of the mould and cover with some well-seasoned chicken jelly flavoured with port.

Suggested wine Dry white Savoy wine or a good white burgundy.

HÔTEL MODERNE *
CHAROLLES (SAÔNE-ET-LOIRE)

TERRINE DE FOIES DE VOLAILLES

An excellent cold first course which may be served with a green salad.

For 10 people

500g lean pork
500g fresh fat belly of pork
200g pig's liver
500g very fresh, cleaned
  chicken livers

Marinade
1dl good, very dry white wine
½dl madeira
½dl cognac
salt, freshly milled black
  pepper
fresh or dried tarragon
2 whole cloves garlic
½ onion, finely chopped

Forcemeat
2 eggs
1 bare level tbs flour
3 tbs strained marinade
salt, freshly milled black
  pepper
a pinch nutmeg
½ bay leaf
a sprig thyme
peppercorns
3 sheets back pork fat

1 *oval ovenproof terrine*
  with a lid

To prepare Roughly chop all the meat except the chicken livers, and put into the marinade omitting the madeira and cognac. Add 300 grams of the chicken livers, which should be left whole and chopped only after they have been marinated. The marinade should just cover the meat. Leave for 48 hours.

The remaining chicken livers are treated separately; they are kept whole and go in the centre of the pâté. Trim them and let them marinate for two or three hours in the madeira and cognac seasoned with freshly milled black pepper.

Remove the herbs and seasonings from the first marinade. Drain and wipe the meat and mince or chop finely. Roughly chop the marinated chicken livers. Blend the stuffing ingredients, first mixing the eggs, flour and the strained marinade, then adding the salt, pepper and nutmeg.

To prepare the terrine Cut one sheet of pork fat into two oval-shaped pieces to fit the terrine. Line the bottom of the terrine with one of the oval-shaped pieces, reserving the other, and line the sides of the terrine with the remaining sheets, letting the ends extend over the edge. Divide the stuffing into two equal parts. Press one half into the terrine until it is nearly half full. Add the whole chicken livers in a row along the middle of the terrine. Sprinkle with salt and a iittle of their marinade. Cover with the rest of the stuffing pressed well down, then fold the ends of the strips of pork fat over the top of the pâté. Cover with the reserved oval-shaped piece. Arrange the half bay leaf, the sprig of thyme and a few whole peppercorns on top of the pork fat. Seal the lid of the terrine with a flour and water paste, using 150–180 grams of flour.

To cook Put the finished pâté into a pan of water. Start the cooking on the top of the stove until the water starts to simmer, then transfer to a moderate oven (165°–170°C, 330°–340°F) and cook slowly for 2 hours. The water in the pan should be simmering all the time. Check the level after an hour and add some boiling water if necessary, maintaining the simmering.

When the pâté is done, remove the terrine, wipe dry and place on a rack to cool. Let it stand for 2 or 3 hours, then transfer to the refrigerator. It can be eaten after two days, but it will keep, refrigerated, for 7 or 8 days.

Suggested wine A well-chilled Beaujolais rosé or a Mâcon.

LES FRÈRES TROISGROS ★ ★ ★
ROANNE (LOIRE)

MOUSSE DE GRIVES AU GENIÈVRE

In October at the time of the grape harvest the flesh of the thrushes which feed among the vines has a particularly delicious flavour.

For 8 people

8 birds [1]
the same weight of fat from a *foie gras* or ordinary lard

salt, freshly milled black pepper
12 juniper berries

Pluck the birds and cut off the heads and feet. Take out the crop and part of the gut. Chop and mince very finely, adding salt, pepper and juniper berries and one-third of the fat.

Work the pâté in an enamelled cast-iron saucepan until the ingredients are well blended. Put the pan in a roasting-tin half filled with hot water and place in a moderate oven, 170°–175°C, 325°–350°F maximum. Heat, stirring with a wooden spoon from time to time, until the mixture changes colour and the meat turns from red to pale, clear grey.

Remove the pan from the oven and press the mixture through a very fine sieve or through the finest mesh of the vegetable mill. Leave to cool completely. Blend in the rest of the fat, slightly softened. Season.

Spoon the pâté into little earthenware terrines or individual ramekins. Serve well chilled with warm toasted country bread.

Suggested wine Red burgundy.

---

[1] A French proverb runs: 'If you haven't any thrushes, blackbirds will do . . .'. But we advise our readers to substitute pigeons instead (*editor's note*).

L'AUBERGE ★
L'ÎLE ROUSSE (CORSICA)

PÂTÉ DE MERLES

A unique pâté made with the Corsican blackbirds that are very common in the wild brushland of the island. Their flesh acquires a very special flavour from the berries they eat. Their dark brown plumage distinguishes them from the blackbirds of the mainland and their flesh is also far more tender and tasty. During the shooting season they are killed by the hundred, hence the exceptionally large quantities given in the recipe.

For 100 boned birds take the same weight of chicken livers and a piece of neck of pork equal to two-thirds of the weight of the birds.

4dl madeira	freshly grated nutmeg
chopped truffles	50g cornflour
7g salt per 500g meat	$\frac{1}{2}$dl cognac
1g freshly milled black pepper	$\frac{1}{2}$dl spirit of myrtle
7 juniper berries	

To prepare Stew the birds for 3 or 4 minutes in 3 decilitres of the madeira, turning them in the liquid. Leave to get cold, then bone them. Very finely chop the flesh of the birds and the chicken livers. Roughly chop the pork and the truffles, keeping the two separate. Put all the ingredients into a large bowl, add the seasoning, the cornflour diluted in the rest of the madeira, the cognac and the myrtle spirit. Mix well.

To cook Cook by steaming in tightly sealed containers. Give the pâté two cookings of one hour each, with an interval of 48 hours in between.

The pâté may also be cooked in little glazed earthenware terrines sealed with a flour and water paste between the containers and the lid. Put the terrines in a pan of lightly boiling water and cook in an oven heated to 175°C, 350°F, then reduced to 165°C, 330°F, so that the water simmers gently. The pâté should cook for $1\frac{1}{4}$ hours per 500 grams of the meat.

Suggested wine Patrimonio.

HÔTEL DU MIDI ★
LAMASTRE (ARDÈCHE)

PÂTÉ DE CANARD LUCULLUS

A galantine, cooked in the oven. It should be served cold, sliced.

For 15 people

1 plump duck weighing at least
  1·5kg
the duck's liver marinated in
  2 tbs cognac and freshly
  milled black pepper and
  diced
1 piece caul pork fat washed in
  lightly salted cold water and
  wiped dry
1kg very fresh pork fillet,
  trimmed
200g *foie gras*, mashed
salt, freshly milled black
  pepper
a pinch allspice

a tiny pinch curry powder
a tiny pinch Cayenne pepper
2 eggs
75g *foie gras*, diced
1 truffle, scrubbed, peeled and
  cut into strips
5 rashers barding bacon

Using a very sharp knife cut the duck open along the back. Detach the skin from the meat, being careful to keep it in one piece. Bone the duck completely. Cut the bones of the drumstick close to the feet, which should remain attached to the skin. Wash, scrub and dry the feet.

Dice the duck and pork meat and mince finely. Pound the minced meat in a large bowl together with the mashed *foie gras*, the seasoning and spices. Add the beaten eggs and work with a spatula for 5 minutes to lighten the mixture.

To prepare the pâté
Spread out the duck's skin on a board, with the outside downwards, and sprinkle with salt and pepper. Put the caul fat flat on to the skin. Spread half the forcemeat all over the fat. Add the diced *foie gras* and duck's liver in a row along the middle of the forcemeat, then add a row of slices of truffle. Cover with the rest of the forcemeat and pull the caul fat over the top and round the sides. Stitch the duck's skin together with a trussing needle and fine thread until you have a large sausage, with duck's feet. Wrap the 5 rashers of bacon round the pâté and tie a piece of string round each as for a joint of meat for roasting.

To cook the pâté Put the pâté into a buttered oven-proof dish and cook in a moderate oven, 175°C, 350°F, basting with the juices during the cooking, which will take about 50 minutes. Test with a needle or the point of a sharp knife to make sure that the juice is clear and transparent and no longer pink. Remove from the oven and leave until cold and firm. Keep refrigerated until required.

To serve Slice the pâté and arrange the slices on a serving dish. Serve if liked with a green salad.

Suggested wine A Côtes-du-Rhône, such as Hermitage or a dry Saint-Péray.

PAUL BOCUSE ★ ★ ★
COLLONGES-AU-MONT-D'OR, NEAR LYON (RHÔNE)

PÂTÉ PANTIN FERDINAND WERNERT

A pâté baked in a pastry crust but not moulded. It is made with veal, ham, pork and forcemeat, flavoured with madeira or cognac. It may be enriched with truffles, foie gras, chicken or game. It is one of the most remarkable gastronomic feats of French cuisine and also combines the art of pastry-making.

For 10 people

Rich short-crust pasty (p. 356)
500g flour
15g salt
150g unsalted butter
50g lard
1 egg
1½–2dl cold water (enough to be absorbed by the flour)

Pâté
500g veal fillet (cut 8 strips from it 15cm long and ½cm thick; reserve the rest of the meat)

500g fat bacon (cut 2 large slices 30cm long and 20cm wide and 8 lardoons the same size as the veal strips)
250g raw ham (cut strips similar to the others; reserve the rest)
2dl cognac

Stuffing
180g pork fillet, the rest of the veal, pork fat and ham, all finely minced
2 eggs
11–15g spiced salt
freshly milled black pepper
a pinch each thyme and bay leaf, powdered

To prepare the meat Put the strips of veal, ham and lardoons in a deep china pâté dish and season with the spiced salt, pepper, thyme and bay leaf. Knead by hand to impregnate the meats with the spices and moisten with the cognac.

To prepare the stuffing Pound the minced pork, veal, bacon, and ham in a mortar. Mix well. Add the eggs, the salt and the cognac from the meat marinade. Leave to macerate until required, stirring from time to time. To prepare the lining pastry make the pastry according to the instructions given on p. 356, in the proportions given above. Roll out three-quarters of the pastry to form a rectangle 35cm long, 25cm wide and 8mm thick. Put on a pastry slab or board.

To make the pâté Put one of the bacon slices on the centre of the undercrust leaving a border all round. Spread over a layer of stuffing, then a layer of the veal strips, bacon and ham alternately, then a second layer of stuffing and so on until it is all used up; end with a layer of stuffing and the second bacon slice. Press down firmly.

Dip a pastry brush in water and moisten the edges of the reserved pastry. Lift up the two long sides of the rectangle and lay them over the top layer of the pâté so that they join in the middle. Roll out the two ends of the undercrust. Lift them over the sides of the pâté and seal the edges by pressing with your fingers. Brush the whole surface of the pâté with a damp brush and place over it a rectangle of pastry of exactly the same size, made with the remaining quarter of the pastry. This layer must be feathered all round the edge with a knife so that it will become flaky during the cooking. Pinch the edge of the crust between the thumb and index finger. Glaze the top with the egg beaten with a drop of water. Use a knife to trace a surface pattern on the pastry and make two small funnels (1cm) in the centre. Insert into each funnel a little cylinder of buttered greaseproof paper to allow the steam to escape.

To cook the pâté Put into a moderate oven, 165°–175°C, 325°–375°F. When the pastry is brown protect with a fresh piece of greaseproof paper so that the pâté can't absorb any other smells. It will take $1\frac{1}{4}$ to $1\frac{1}{2}$ hours to cook. After about an hour juices should start to seep out of the pâté and form a sort of meat glaze. This shows that the cooking is almost finished.

To serve hot Take the pâté out of the oven, let it stand for 10 to 15 minutes, then, using a knife with a serrated edge, slice very carefully.

Suggested wine A really good burgundy or a Beaujolais of good vintage.

RESTAURANT DE LA PYRAMIDE ★ ★ ★
VIENNE (ISÈRE)

PÂTÉ DE MADAME BOURGEOIS

This pâté baked in pastry was a speciality of a famous cook from Priay (Ain), after whom it is named. Mme Bourgeois, whose spectacular pâté was a feast for gourmets in the Bresse area, was a close friend of Fernand Point's mother.[1]

For 12 people

750g fresh lean pork
1 chicken weighing about
   1·5kg
a few thin rashers bacon
salt, freshly milled black
   pepper

Marinade
2 carrots, diced
3 or 4 shallots, roughly
   chopped
a few sprigs parsley
peppercorns
3 tbs unsalted butter
2dl madeira
$\frac{3}{4}$l chicken stock

Forcemeat
the chicken liver
150g *foie gras*
2 truffles, scrubbed, peeled and
   chopped

Pastry
1kg sifted flour
$\frac{1}{2}$ tsp salt
250g unsalted butter
1dl cold water
5 eggs

Glaze
1 egg yolk diluted with a few
   drops of water

Marinade Gently stew the carrots, shallots and parsley in the butter. Moisten with the madeira and chicken stock. Add the peppercorns. Leave to cool. Cut the pork and the chicken into small pieces and leave in the cooled marinade for an hour or two.

To prepare the forcemeat Work together in a deep bowl the chopped chicken liver, the *foie gras* and the truffles until you have a thick mixture. Keep in a cool place.

To make the pastry Cut the butter into small pieces and crumble with the flour and the salt. Make a well in the middle of the mixture. Break the eggs into the well and blend all the ingredients without handling too much. Form into a ball and leave in a cool place.

To prepare the meat Bone the chicken, discarding the skin, nerves and any hard parts. Cut the flesh into strips or cubes. Remove the fat and nerves from the pork and chop finely. Mix with the chicken, add a sprinkling of salt and freshly milled pepper.

To prepare the terrine Line a large rectangular terrine first with the bacon rashers, then with the pastry rolled out into a rectangular shape large enough to allow the ends to extend over the outside of the terrine. Cover the undercrust with half the chicken and pork mixture, lay the forcemeat on top, and cover with the rest of the chicken and pork mixture. Fold the pastry over the top of the pâté, starting with the ends, so that the meat is hermetically sealed. Seal the edges with a pastry brush moistened with water. Glaze with the diluted egg yolk.

To cook Cook in a moderate oven, 175°C, 350°F, for about $1\frac{1}{2}$ hours. Reduce the heat during the second half of the cooking.

This pâté should preferably be served hot.

Suggested wine A red burgundy such as Côte-de-Nuits, Chambolle Musigny or Gevrey-Chambertin.

[1] Fernand Point was the great chef and proprietor of the world-famous Pyramide restaurant in Vienne (*translator's note*).

L'ESCALE ★ ★
VARCES, NEAR GRENOBLE (ISÈRE)

PÂTÉ DE SAUMON FRAIS

*A perfect summer dish which can be kept in the refrigerator
for several days. The mayonnaise should be made just before
the pâté is to be eaten.*

For 8 people

600g fresh salmon flesh
300g pike flesh, chopped and
   finely minced
salt, freshly milled black
   pepper

Panada
100g sifted flour
1dl milk

3 egg yolks
salt, freshly milled black
   pepper, nutmeg
40g unsalted butter
40g crayfish butter (see p. 355)
1 egg
40g blanched pistachios
30g chopped truffles
½dl cognac
½dl dry white wine

Mix the flour, milk and egg yolks in a saucepan, off the heat. Add
the salt, pepper and nutmeg. Heat gently, whisking continuously.
When the mixture thickens take the pan off the heat and add the
butter and crayfish butter. Blend with a spatula, then allow to
solidify over a very gentle heat for 2 or 3 minutes. Leave to cool
for 30 minutes. Add the whole egg, the pistachios, the truffles,
cognac, white wine and the minced pike flesh. Put the bowl on ice
and work with a spatula for 10 minutes until you have a smooth
paste.

The salmon Cut the salmon into fillets about 1cm square, then
season with salt and pepper.

To prepare the pâté Spread a layer of the panada in a buttered
rectangular pâté tin lined with greaseproof paper, then cover
with a layer of salmon fillets. Fill with alternate layers of the
panada and the salmon. Cover with greaseproof paper, then with
silver foil. Pierce the two layers of paper in two places with a trussing needle, letting the needle penetrate to the bottom of the pâté.

To cook Put the pâté tin in a pan of water and cook in a moderate
oven (165°–175°C, 330°–350°F) for about 1¼ hours. Remove from
the oven, leave to cool, then refrigerate for several hours.

Serve sliced, with Andalusian mayonnaise (see p. 346).

Suggested wine Sancerre or Pouilly fumé.

TAILLEVENT ★ ★ ★
PARIS 8e: 15 RUE LAMENNAIS

TERRINE DE BROCHET CURNONSKY

A delicate quenelle of pike cooked in a terrine. It can be kept for several days in the refrigerator and is equally good hot or cold.

For 5–6 people

Panada
¼l milk
salt, freshly milled black
  pepper
125g sifted flour
100g unsalted butter
4 egg yolks

Quenelle
200g very white mushrooms
3 tbs unsalted butter
200g pike flesh, diced
3 tbs shallots, finely chopped
1 tbs chopped parsley

1½dl dry white wine
600g pike flesh
salt, freshly milled black
  pepper
4 egg whites
½l fresh double cream

Accompaniment
white butter sauce if served
  hot (see p. 355)
green sauce if served cold (see
  p. 355)

To make the panada Boil the milk and season with salt and pepper. Whisk the flour, butter and egg yolks in a saucepan, then draw off the heat and add the boiling milk. Return the pan to the heat and work the mixture with a spatula over low heat, as for choux pastry, until it becomes thick and solid. Remove from the heat and leave to cool.

To make the quenelle Finely slice the mushrooms and stew them gently in the butter in a small frying-pan. Remove and stiffen 200g of the diced pike flesh in the same butter. Remove the pike. Add the shallots and parsley to the butter. Deglaze with the white wine, reduce and pour the liquid over the pike. Reserve.

Season the remaining 400g of pike flesh with salt and pepper and pound in a mortar, or put twice through the foodmill. When the mixture has become a smooth paste, spoon it into a bowl. Put the bowl inside a larger, shallow container filled with ice cubes and work the mixture with a spatula, over the ice, adding the cooled panada little by little, then, one at a time, the 4 egg whites, unbeaten. After about 5 minutes beat in the cream a little at a time until it has been completely absorbed. Finally, add the diced pike and mushrooms.

Line a buttered china terrine with greaseproof paper cut to fit. Fill with the quenelle mixture, pressing it well down so that there are no gaps, cover with buttered greaseproof paper and the lid. Put the terrine in a pan filled with boiling water and cook in a moderate oven (160°–170°C, 325°–350°F) for about 1¼ to 1½ hours.

To serve Serve hot in the terrine with white butter sauce served separately, or cold with a green sauce.

Suggested wine Sancerre or Pouilly Fuissé.

RESTAURANT MÔME *
JENZAT (ALLIER)

PÂTÉ BOURBONNAIS

A potato pie, flavoured with onions, shallots and garlic and enriched with cream. It makes a delicious simple meal, served with a green salad.

For 8 people

1kg half-puff pastry (see p. 356)
1kg potatoes, peeled and sliced
   thinly
2 onions
3 shallots
1 clove garlic
1 tbs parsley, very finely
   chopped

salt, freshly milled black
   pepper
50g unsalted butter
200g fresh double cream
1 egg yolk

an 18–20cm pie dish

To prepare Chop the onions, shallots, parsley and garlic and put in a bowl with the potatoes. Season with salt and freshly milled black pepper, stir with a wooden spoon and leave for 15 to 20 minutes to allow the flavours to be absorbed and the bitter juices to emerge. Wrap in a clean cloth.

Roll out the pastry into two thin rounds, one slightly larger than the other. Line the pie tin with the larger crust, leaving a border 3cm wide.

Spoon the potato mixture on to the pastry base and scatter the butter over the top, cut into small pieces. Cover the potatoes with the second round of pastry, brushing the edge with water. Brush the edge of the undercrust and join carefully to the top layer. Press well together to seal. Glaze with the egg-yolk diluted with water.

To cook Put the dish in an oven preheated to 200°–220°C, 400°–425°F. After 20 to 25 minutes reduce the heat to 175°–165°C, 350°–330°F, if the outside of the pastry is colouring too quickly. The pie will take about 45 to 50 minutes to cook.

Remove from the oven. Cut round the pastry lid and lift off; pour the cream over the potatoes, put back the pastry lid and return the dish to a hot oven for 6–8 minutes, to bring the cream to boiling point.

To serve Serve very hot, cut into wedges like a tart.

Suggested wine A rosé from Provence or from the Auvergne.

FOIE GRAS

Foie gras is one of the wonders of French gastronomy. Its flavour is incomparable and its very subtle, slightly bitter taste makes it one of the most sought-after of all culinary preparations.

Foie gras is produced in two regions of France: Alsace and the South-West. Alsatian *foie gras* is always served fresh and is therefore eaten between October and March, while *foie gras* from the South-West is usually tinned, except for the type prepared in the Landes, which is served fresh in season, often hot and *aux raisins*. In Perigord it is often served with a coating of the yellow fat produced during the cooking. Perigord liver is particularly delicately flavoured and highly-regarded.

The geese for *foie gras* are fattened solely with boiled yellow maize, which is forcibly fed to them with a funnel. This over-feeding gives them steatosis or penetration of fatty cells into the liver, hence the name *foie gras*, 'fatty liver'. The livers react in different ways to this treatment; the ones that are small and hard because they are affected by cirrhosis or fatty degeneration are discarded.

Ducks are fattened for their livers in the same way.

To choose a foie gras In the *foie gras* regions the livers are sold at markets and fairs from 15 November to the end of December – sometimes even until 15 January. In towns they may be found in specialist shops. Medium-sized livers that are firm but still relatively supple are excellent; they should be pink and spotless. Livers weighing 700–800g melt less in cooking than other sizes and it is worth taking trouble to find them.

To prepare foie gras Carefully remove the gall and any greenish traces it leaves, as well as any bloody threads, the skin and any other pieces that cling to it. The day before cooking add salt and freshly milled black pepper and leave the liver to rest in a cool place for 24 hours.

The liver can be studded with little sticks of fresh truffle or one or two whole truffles may be inserted into it to impart a delicate flavour. It may also be flavoured with port or armagnac, but as it absorbs alcohol very rapidly it must not be left to marinate for too long. The liver should be put into a terrine for an hour or two at the most and basted two or three times with a few table-spoons ($\frac{1}{2}$dl) of armagnac or port. Afterwards it should be carefully wiped dry.

To cook foie gras Cook the liver in the oven in a covered terrine placed in a pan of water. Seal the lid with a flour and water paste. Livers weighing 600 to 800g will take 30 to 40 minutes from the moment when the water in the *bain-marie* starts to simmer. If you cook them for too long the fat will separate from the flesh and the liver will become dry and chalky. The oven must be only moderate and the water should just simmer gently. *Foie gras* from Alsace is traditionally served pink and is therefore cooked for a shorter time than the kind from the South-West of France.

To serve foie gras *Foie gras* is eaten cold but not iced; if it is too cold it loses its flavour. It is most important to serve it at the beginning of a meal when the palate is fresh. The habit of serving it at the end of a meal, with a salad with a *vinaigrette* dressing which kills the taste of the liver as well as the wine, has now fortunately gone out of fashion.

The question of which wine to serve with *foie gras* has been argued about endlessly. In a *foie gras* region the local wines should be drunk. Some people will consider only a full-bodied red wine, while others prefer a dry white burgundy or champagne. A sweet vintage wine such as sauternes, well chilled, is the perfect accompaniment and a fine port served chilled is also good. But whatever the wine, it must be a good one.

Foie gras may be served either with toast or with fresh bread. Toast should be served warm rather than hot and must not be overdone, as the taste of burnt toast spoils the subtle flavour of the *foie gras*. Various types of bread may be served, such as very fresh French bread or a cottage loaf.

JAMIN *
PARIS 16e: 32 RUE DE LONGCHAMP

FOIE GRAS DE CANARD AUX RAISINS DE SMYRNE

A hot dish of sliced duck's liver flavoured with armagnac and gently cooked in butter, served with a rich sauce of sultanas previously steeped in Sauternes. The combination of flavours is particularly successful.

For 3 or 4 people

1 fine duck's liver (500–600g),
  sliced
salt, freshly milled black
  pepper
4 tbs armagnac
flour
4 tbs unsalted butter (for
  cooking the liver)

2 tbs unsalted butter (to finish
  the sauce)
100g sultanas
1dl white bordeaux wine,
  preferably Sauternes
½dl concentrated veal stock
3 or 4 slices bread lightly
  browned in butter

To prepare Soak the sultanas in the wine. When they have swelled simmer them for 5 minutes in the liquid. Remove and reduce the liquid by half. Season the thin slices of *foie gras* with salt and pepper and sprinkle with the armagnac. Leave for a few minutes, then wipe dry and flour lightly.

To cook Cook the liver for a few minutes in a small frying-pan in the butter. Keep the heat very low and turn the slices so that they cook evenly. Remove them from the pan when they are still pink and under-done. Stir into the butter in the pan the wine in which the sultanas were steeped and the armagnac from the liver. Deglaze with the veal stock and cook for 5 to 6 minutes, then add the slices of liver and the sultanas and heat through. Check the seasoning and finish the sauce by adding 2 tablespoons of fresh butter. Do not let it boil.

To serve Arrange the liver on the pieces of fried bread in a warmed serving dish and serve covered with the hot sultana sauce.

Suggested wine Sauternes.

HÔTEL-RESTAURANT DES VANNES ★ ★
LIVERDUN (MEURTHE-ET-MOSELLE)

TERRINE DE FOIE GRAS À LA GELÉE DE XÉRÈS

A terrine in which a whole goose liver is wrapped in forcemeat made of chicken livers and pork and served with chicken jelly flavoured with sherry.

For 10 people

1 fresh goose liver weighing
  500–600g
port
salt, freshly milled black
  pepper
allspice

a few very thin slices larding
  bacon, seasoned with salt
  and pepper

Forcemeat
200g chicken livers
200g fresh pork fat
200g lean pork

salt, freshly milled black pepper	1 beaten egg
3 tbs cognac	
3 tbs port	
3 tbs madeira	

Trim the liver, keeping the ends for the forcemeat. Marinate for an hour or two in the port with the seasonings.

Forcemeat Finely mince the chicken livers, the pork and the trimmings of the liver. Season with salt and pepper and blend with the cognac, port, madeira and beaten egg.

To prepare the terrine Line the sides and bottom of the terrine with the bacon. Cover the bacon with a layer of forcemeat, using two-thirds of the mixture. Place the liver on top and cover it with the rest of the forcemeat; lay a slice of bacon over the top. Seal the lid with a flour and water paste and put the terrine in a pan of water. Cook for about $1\frac{3}{4}$ hours in a moderate oven (175°C, 350°F). Leave to cool and keep in the refrigerator.

Prepare at the same time some good concentrated chicken jelly flavoured with sherry.

To serve Turn out the pâté, cut it into slices and arrange on a serving dish surrounded by a ring of the chopped chicken jelly. Serve the rest of the jelly separately.

Suggested wine Meursault or Château Chalons.

HÔTEL D'ALSACE *
RÔTISSERIE DES DUCS DE LORRAINE
SARREGUEMINES (MOSELLE)

FOIE GRAS DES DUCS DE LORRAINE

Foie gras cooked by the method used in Alsace. It is pounded until it is soft and tender, marinated, truffled, pressed into a terrine *and cooked in a* bain-marie. *It is particularly juicy and delicate when cooked this way.*

For 6 people	a pinch allspice
1 fine pink *foie gras*	200g fresh truffles, scrubbed, washed, dried and peeled
1dl armagnac	
½dl kirsch	
salt, freshly milled black pepper	

To prepare Knead the *foie gras* on a slab with the palm of your hand; remove the nerve fibres. Marinate for 12 hours in the spirits with the spices. Salt the liver, insert the truffles and press into the terrine to mould it. Seal the lid tightly with flour and water paste.

To cook Place the terrine in a pan of water and cook gently in a moderate oven for 1 hour 20 minutes. The temperature of the water must not rise above 90°C, 195°F. Leave the dish to cool and then chill for 12 hours.

To serve Serve with warm toast.

Suggested wine Pinot noir.

HÔTEL DE FRANCE * *
AUCH (GERS)

FOIE GRAS FRAIS DU GERS
This dish should be made with a fine fresh foie gras, *firm and pink, weighing 500–600g.*

> *Stock*
> the meaty carcases of 1 or 2
>   cooked chickens
> chicken giblets
> salt, freshly milled black
>   pepper

To prepare Trim the liver and wrap in a clean, damp linen cloth. Just before cooking sprinkle with a little salt and a generous amount of freshly milled black pepper.

The day before make some good stock with the chicken carcases and giblets. Simmer for at least 3 hours. Add a good seasoning of salt and a light sprinkling of pepper and reduce to about $\frac{3}{4}$l. Strain the stock through a strainer lined with a double layer of muslin. Leave to cool and degrease carefully. Pour into a thick earthenware casserole.

To cook Heat the stock gently. When the temperature reaches 60°C, 140°F, add the seasoned liver. The temperature must not be higher than 65°C, 150°F, during the cooking. When the liver is cooked it should not be hard but remain tender with a soft pink centre.

To serve Let it cool completely and chill for an hour or so before serving it in its jelly.

Suggested wine Sauternes.

HÔTEL DE FRANCE ★ ★
MONTMORILLON (VIENNE)

FOIE GRAS FRAIS POCHÉ DANS LA GRAISSE D'OIE

The foie gras *is cooked in a generous amount of goose fat, then flavoured with cognac and moulded. It should be served, well chilled, with chicken aspic flavoured with port and flambéed cognac.*

For 8 people

1 liver weighing 800g–1kg
salt, freshly milled black
    pepper, thyme, spices
1dl cognac

2kg goose fat
chicken aspic flavoured with
    2 tbs flambéed cognac and
    3 tbs good red port

To prepare Soak the liver in cold water for 2 hours. Drain, wipe dry, cut out the nerves and all the bloody bits. Season well, outside and in, and leave in a cool place for 2 hours.

To cook the liver Put the goose fat in a casserole, preferably earthenware, though an enamelled cast-iron one will do. Heat to 80°C, 175°F, add the prepared liver and cook for 30 minutes. Stir the fat frequently and keep the temperature even.

Drain the liver and when it has cooled sprinkle generously with cognac. Transfer to a pâté mould or a round terrine, pressing it down lightly with your hand or with a weighted board. Leave to cool before placing in the refrigerator.

To serve Serve well chilled with well-spiced concentrated chicken aspic flavoured with flambéed cognac and port.

Suggested wine White Sauvignon, Neuville de Poitou or Sauternes.

LE RELAIS BISSON ★
PARIS 6e: 37 QUAI DES GRANDS-AUGUSTINS

TERRINE DE FOIE DE CANARD FRAIS

A very delicate, but natural tasting dish. The livers are cooked whole in a terrine and flavoured with armagnac.

For 4 people

2 duck livers

1dl armagnac
salt, freshly milled black
    pepper
streaky bacon

Cut open the livers (but do not cut them right through) and very gently remove the veins and hard core so as to preserve their appearance. Put the livers well opened out on to a large dish, season with salt, pepper and sprinkle with the armagnac. Cover the dish and leave in the refrigerator for 2 to 3 hours. Transfer the livers to an ovenproof terrine, lined with finely sliced streaky bacon. Do not press the livers down too hard. Add more bacon to cover the livers, seal the lid and cook in a moderate oven, 165°–170°C, 325°–350°F for about 30 minutes. Leave to cool, then put in the refrigerator. Serve well chilled.

Suggested wine Sauternes, well chilled.

CONFITS

A *confit* is pork, goose, duck or turkey meat cooked in its own fat and preserved in an earthenware jar. In Gascony, Béarn, the Basque country, Quercy, Périgord and in the Rouergue, *confits* of pork, goose and duck, preserved in stoneware jars, are widely used in family kitchens. Commercially *confit* is preserved in tins by the Appert method.

Confit d'oie, preserved goose, is one of the oldest French traditional dishes. It was invented before the days of refrigeration to fill the need to preserve for a whole year birds bred to be fattened and killed at the end of the autumn, from mid-November to mid-December, or as late as the beginning of January in some areas. *Confit d'oie* was originally eaten hot in middle-class homes; in peasant homes solid goose fat spread on slices of country bread, eaten with a very little cold meat, provided the staple diet for months.

Confit d'oie
Procedure – preparation – cooking – use and method of reheating.

Procedure Kill the goose when the fattening is completed and it is ready to eat. Pluck, singe and allow to become completely cold before cutting up. Open the goose along the back from top to bottom, gutting it carefully. Remove the plentiful yellow fat which conceals the intestine, reserving it in a cool place. Remove the liver, being very careful not to damage or break it. It will be used in other dishes.

Preparation Goose is usually divided into quarters. Cut the bird into quarters, keeping the bones attached to the flesh so that the meat does not lose shape during cooking. Salt the quarters, using 30g of salt to each kilo of flesh. Place in a large bowl, cover with a cloth and leave in a cool place, 4°–8°C, 40°–50°F, for 20 to 24 hours. Shake off the salt and wipe carefully.

To cook Put a generous amount of goose fat into a large saucepan. Melted pork fat can be added later if necessary. Let the goose fat melt very gradually. As soon as it is three-quarters melted and warm, add the quarters of goose. The meat should not brown, but it must be completely covered by the fat.

Proportions
For 5l goose fat add muslin bag containing:
6 cloves garlic, unpeeled
25 whole white peppercorns
12 cloves

Bring to the boil very slowly and cook gently. The cooking time will vary from $2\frac{1}{4}$ to 3 hours depending on the texture of the goose flesh. Stir continuously with a long wooden spoon or spatula. Test the meat with a trussing needle: the needle should pierce the meat easily without being forced and the juice that escapes should be completely clear. When the meat is cooked remove the quarters from the pan and drain them. Remove the bones. The fat, which is yellow when raw, becomes white when cooked. Prepare the stoneware jars by lining them with melted goose fat so that the quarters of meat do not touch the sides of the jar. Arrange the meat in the jars and cover with warm fat. Leave for two days, then add a little hot goose fat to fill any empty spaces. As soon as the new layer of fat has set trickle over the surface a layer of melted pork fat. When the pork fat has set properly lay on top a sheet of greaseproof paper cut to the size of the top of the jar, pressing down so that it sticks to the fat. Then tie a double piece of strong greaseproof paper firmly round the neck of the jar. The *confit* is now made and can be kept from one season to another: usually from December to October of the following year.

Use and method of reheating Allow 1 or 2 quarters of *confit* for 4 people according to whether it is to be served as a first course or main dish. *Confit* is not improved by being served with complicated sauces. It should be served as it is, with the fat removed so that it is not too rich and heavy.

Reheat the pieces of *confit* covered with their fat in a dry frying-pan or in a fireproof earthenware dish in a moderate oven so that the *confit* 'sweats' off the fat and becomes a light golden colour. Reheating *confit* is a delicate art which requires practice.

To serve Serve the *confit* with the skin lightly browned and the meat soft with one of the traditional accompaniments: a dish of white haricot beans, buttered *petits pois*, fried cepes with a touch of garlic or potatoes *à la Sarladaise* (see below). The *confit* may also be served cold with a green salad.

Confit d'oie is an essential ingredient for authentic *cassoulet*.

Recommended wine Earthy wine: Madiran, a young bordeaux, Cahors, or even a young Beaujolais.

SPLENDID HÔTEL *
BORDEAUX (GIRONDE)

CONFIT D'OIE SARLADAISE

Preserved goose, reheated in the oven and served with potatoes cooked in the fat of the goose.

For 4 people	4 tbs fat from the *confit*
1 quarter of goose *confit*	salt, freshly milled black pepper
1kg very good potatoes, with yellow flesh	Périgueux sauce (see p. 350)

Put the quarter of *confit*, enveloped in a light layer of its fat, in a dry roasting-tin. Place in a moderately hot oven, 175°–185°C, 350°–375°F, for 10 to 12 minutes; drain off the fat. Reduce the heat and return the *confit* to the oven for another 15 minutes until the skin turns a light golden colour. Meanwhile cook the potatoes. Peel and slice them evenly. Sauté them for 10 to 12 minutes in 4 tablespoons of the fat from the goose. Transfer the frying-pan to the oven for 8 to 10 minutes to brown the surface of the potatoes. Remove and season with salt and pepper.

To serve Cut the *confit* into four serving pieces and arrange them on top of the potatoes in a serving dish. Serve with Périgueux sauce.

Suggested wine Saint-Émilion.

RELAIS DES PYRÉNÉES
PARIS 20e: 1 RUE DU JOURDAIN

CONFIT D'OIE COMME EN BÉARN

A preserved leg and wing of a goose; reheated and served with sauté potatoes. The people of Béarn claim that the art of reheating confit *demands great skill and practice; in fact it is simply a matter of care and patience.*

For 4 people	goose fat
1 leg and 1 wing potted preserved goose	a little salt and freshly milled black pepper
1kg potatoes, peeled and finely sliced	garlic, peeled and squeezed through a garlic press
	parsley, finely chopped

Leave the preserving fat on the goose pieces. Using a sauté-pan, reheat the goose in its fat over very moderate heat until the fat melts. Turn the pieces over and simmer, covered, for a few moments. Keep the pan warm. Meanwhile sauté the sliced potato in 3 or 4 tablespoons of the goose fat. Add a further tablespoon of fat if necessary while cooking. Add garlic and parsley to taste and season with salt and pepper.

To serve Carefully drain the fat from the pieces of goose. Arrange on a serving dish and garnish with the potatoes.

Suggested wine Madiran or a fairly full-bodied red wine.

RELAIS DES PYRÉNÉES
PARIS 20e: 1 RUE DU JOURDAIN

CONFIT D'OIE À LA BASQUAISE
Preserved goose served with cèpes *sautéed in oil and flavoured with garlic.*

For 4 people	3 tbs goose fat
1kg *cèpes*, carefully cleaned, washed and chopped	salt
	a little freshly milled black pepper (too much pepper will ruin the taste of the *cèpes*)
1 quarter goose *confit*, or a preserved goose leg and wing	
3 tbs oil	1 tbs parsley, finely choppe
	1 clove garlic, finely chopped

Gently heat the *confit* in its fat. Keep warm in the fat. Sauté the *cèpes* in a mixture of oil and goose fat. When the *cèpes* are cooked stir in the chopped parsley and garlic; season.

To serve Carefully drain the *confit* of all fat, carve into serving pieces, arrange in a serving-dish and garnish with the *cèpes*.

Suggested wine Irouléguy or a red wine served at room temperature.

Tinned goose liver and confit are widely used in French family kitchens and in restaurants. Good brands of tinned goose liver and *confit* are available all over France in specialist shops, grocers and in charcuteries specializing in luxury foods.

Goose liver and *confits* may be preserved if you buy fresh livers and legs and wings of goose at the beginning of December. In the south-west of France many people prepare *confits* and *foie gras* in tins and take the tins to be sealed by a local *sertisseur*. The tins will last indefinitely if properly sealed and are perfect for special occasions or impromptu meals. They must be stored in a cool place; make sure that there isn't a hot pipe near, as that will turn the fat rancid.

Here are two recipes which are perfectly simple but need to be cooked with care.

LE RÉGENT *
RODEX (AVEYRON)

CONFIT D'OIE GRAND-MÈRE
A luxury preserve which has an infinite number of uses.

Bone a fat goose and cut out what is known as the *manteau*, the 2 legs and the 2 wings in one piece. The *manteau* may be bought ready cut in the Périgord, in the Landes and in Béarn. Cut into 4 pieces and trim them to round off the edges. Sprinkle lightly with fine salt and pepper and leave to stand. Just before cooking wipe the pieces with a cloth to remove any salt that has not dissolved.

To cook Put the goose fat into a heavy pan, preferably a copper one, with the goose trimmings. Add 1 glass (12 centilitres) of water. If there is not enough fat to cover the pieces, add more goose fat or very white pork fat. Heat the fat and when it has almost melted, put the goose pieces into the pan on top of the trimmings. The goose should be completely covered by the fat. Bring to the boil and simmer very gently for about 3 hours, stirring frequently with a wooden spoon or spatula. Remove the pieces of goose and leave to cool.

The tinning process Put 1 or 2 pieces of goose into each well-dried tin, according to size. Add a little cold fat if necessary; the goose should be well covered. Seal the cover mechanically according to the instructions provided with the equipment.

To cook Put the tins into a large pan and cover with enough cold water so that it will not have to be replenished during cooking. Bring the water to the boil and boil rapidly for $2\frac{1}{2}$ hours from the moment the water starts to boil. Remove the tins and store in a cool place.

To use hot Tinned *confit* is reheated in the way described on p. 54 for potted *confit*. It may be served with *petits pois*, white haricot beans, sorrel or potatoes.

To use cold Chill the tin for 24 hours before opening. Serve with a crisp green salad.

Suggested wine Cahors or Côtes-du-Rhône.

LE RÉGENT *
RODEZ (AVEYRON)

FOIE D'OIE EN BOÎTE

This should be made with fresh goose livers bought at the beginning of December. It is important to use livers weighing 700 to 800g because they melt less than other sizes. Duck livers should not be tinned as they would shrink in the tin to half their original volume.

To prepare the liver Carefully remove the gall, bloody veins and all waste matter. The day before cooking season the liver with salt, pepper and a pinch of mixed spice and leave in a cool place. The following day, carefully wipe the inside of the tin and lid, cut the liver to fit and press well into the tin. Do not fill too full or it will be difficult to seal it. Bury some pieces of truffle in the middle of the liver, using 2 medium-sized truffles to each 1kg tin. Use fresh truffles if possible.

Seal the lid according to the instructions given with the equipment.

To cook Put the tins in a large copper preserving pan. Cover with plenty of cold water, enough to ensure that the tins will remain covered during cooking and that no water will have to be added. Heat and boil rapidly and continuously for 1 hour from the moment when the water is boiling well. Continuous boiling is important to ensure that the liver is properly preserved.

To use Leave the tins for at least 2 months, or preferably 3 to 4 months, before using.

Chill the tins, unopened, in the refrigerator for at least 24 hours before using.

Suggested wine Jurançon.

BROCHETTES

FLAVIO *
CLUB DE LA FORÊT
LE TOUQUET (PAS-DE-CALAIS)

BROCHETTES D'AGNEAU DE PRÉ-SALÉ

Cubes of tender meat from a leg of baby lamb, arranged on a skewer alternately with smoked pork and green peppers, brushed with oil and aromatic herbs. The meat and peppers are grilled, wrapped in grilled Parma ham and served with Creole rice and grilled tomatoes. Buttered French beans are served separately.

For 8 people (2 skewers per person)

1 well-hung leg of lamb, weighing 2½kg
250g smoked belly of pork, cut into very thin squares
4 green peppers, seeded and cut into small squares the same size as the pieces of pork
groundnut oil

dried mixed herbs (basil, thyme, bay leaf, marjoram, oregano, savory)
16 very thin slices Parma ham

Garnish
200g rice, cooked *à la Créole* (see p. 293)
8 tomatoes, halved, sprinkled with mixed herbs and grilled
500g fresh French beans, blanched for a few minutes and finished in butter

Bone the leg of lamb, remove the nerves and cut the meat into cubes 2cm square. Thread the meat, pork and green peppers alternately on the skewers. Brush with oil and roll each filled skewer in the herbs. Grill, using high heat, either over a charcoal fire, or on an electric or gas spit, or under the grill of the cooker, turning the skewers round gradually so that the meat and peppers cook evenly.

Grill the slices of ham separately. When the meat on the skewers is cooked roll each skewer in a piece of ham.

To serve Spoon the rice on to a large serving-dish and arrange the skewers on top, using the grilled tomatoes for decoration. Serve the French beans separately.

Suggested wine Beaujolais Villages.

HÔTEL DU ROY RENÉ
AIX-EN-PROVENCE (BOUCHES-DU-RHÔNE)

BROCHETTES DE ROGNONS ET DE FOIE DE VEAU À LA PROVENÇALE
A dish of kidneys, calves' liver, mushrooms and bacon, threaded on skewers, grilled and brushed with herb butter.

For 6 people

3 veal kidneys (or 6 lambs' kidneys)
100g calves' liver
12 mushroom caps
50g bacon

Provençal butter
100g best unsalted butter
3 tbs mixed parsley and chervil, finely chopped
2 shallots
2–3 cloves garlic, according to taste, very finely chopped and squeezed through a garlic press

Chop the kidneys, liver, bacon and mushrooms into pieces of roughly the same size. Thread alternately on to 6 skewers until they are all well filled. Grill, preferably over charcoal, or under the grill of the cooker, for 12 to 15 minutes. Turn the skewers during cooking.

Arrange the skewers on a heated metal dish and brush with the Provençal butter. Put the dish in the oven for a few minutes to melt and warm the butter but without further cooking.

Suggested wine Côtes-du-Rhône rosé.

LA RÉSERVE *
PESSAC (GIRONDE)

BROCHETTES DE RIS DE VEAU À LA DIABLE

Sweetbreads gently cooked in butter and cut into cubes which are threaded on skewers with squares of sweet peppers and bacon and grilled. A spicy devilled sauce goes well with the delicate sweetbreads.

For 2 people

2 veal sweetbreads, blanched for 3 to 5 minutes, dipped into cold water, dried, skinned and trimmed
1 large red pepper, cooked or tinned
100g fresh lean belly of pork, cut into squares, blanched and dipped into cold water
3 tbs unsalted butter

Devilled sauce
1 tbs shallot, chopped
1 liqueur glass cognac
1 tbs tomato purée
4 tbs *demi-glace* sauce (see p. 352)
a pinch cayenne pepper
2 dsp Worcester sauce, to taste
2 tbs butter

To prepare Braise the sweetbreads very gently in the butter. Cut into cubes when cooked and thread on the skewers, alternating them with pieces of pepper and pork. Reserve.

To make the sauce Soften the shallot in the butter, pour over the cognac and reduce by half. Add the tomato and *demi-glace* sauce, simmer for 5 minutes and finish by whisking in the Worcester sauce and cayenne pepper.

To cook Grill the skewers for about 5 minutes, turning them, until the meat is lightly browned but not dry. Arrange on a dish and coat each skewer with 2 tablespoons of the sauce. Serve the rest of the sauce separately.

Suggested wine Devilled sauce would kill a fine wine. A very dry rosé is suitable.

AUBERGE DE SAVOIE *
ANNECY (HAUTE-SAVOIE)

ROGNONS DE VEAU EN BROCHETTES À L'ESTRAGON

The tarragon sauce and rice are delicious with the kidneys. This recipe is for fried kidneys but they are just as good grilled.

For 4 people

4 veal kidneys
4 tbs unsalted butter
salt, freshly milled black
 pepper

Sauce
1 dl veal stock, reduced
½ dl madeira
1 tbs tarragon, very finely
 chopped

Carefully remove the fat from the kidneys and cut them in half lengthwise. Skewer them, threading two halves on to each skewer. Sauté in butter in a heavy frying-pan over a moderate heat, keeping them lightly pink. Remove to a serving-dish and keep warm.

The sauce Deglaze the buttery juices from the kidneys with the veal stock and madeira. Add the chopped tarragon and strain the sauce over the kidneys.
  Serve very hot with a bowl of rice pilaf (see p. 294).

Suggested wine A local wine such as Roussette de Frangy or Corton Charlemagne.

LE RELAIS BRENNER *
LÉZARDRIEUX, NEAR PAIMPOL (CÔTES-DU-NORD)

BROCHETTES DE SAINT-JACQUES

Scallops gently cooked in butter, flambéed with cognac and enriched with cream. They are cut in two, skewered, bread-crumbed and grilled, then served with their creamy cooking juices, sprinkled with parsley.

For 2 people

12 scallops in their shells

4 tbs unsalted butter
½ glass (1·2dl) cognac
2 tbs cream

| salt, freshly milled black pepper | 1 tbs chopped parsley |
| powdered saffron | dried golden breadcrumbs |

Open the scallops on a baking sheet over high heat. Clean, wash to remove any trace of sand, discard the beards and reserve the corals. Cut each scallop into two equal rounds. Heat the butter in a thick metal frying-pan and gently sauté the scallops in very hot butter for a few minutes. Flambé with the cognac, add the cream and saffron, put on the lid and boil for about 3 minutes.

Thread 12 scallop pieces on to each skewer. Arrange on a heated metal dish, pour the cooking juices from the pan over the scallops and sprinkle with breadcrumbs. Brown under the grill for about 3 to 5 minutes.

Sprinkle with parsley and serve. The corals may be sautéed in butter and used as a garnish.

Suggested wine Muscadet or any other very dry white wine.

LA JETÉE *
SAINT-ELME (VAR)

BROCHETTES DE MOULES, SAUCE PROVENÇALE

A distinctive dish from the Var coast, in the midst of the Riviera. It is very easy to make and delicious to eat. The mussels are softer and juicier if they are coated with fresh rather than dried breadcrumbs.

For 4 people

1l mussels
4 rashers bacon, each cut into 4 squares
1 egg yolk beaten with 1 tbs milk
fresh or dried breadcrumbs
olive oil
a sprig thyme
salt, freshly milled black pepper
1 lemon

Provençal sauce
1kg tomatoes, peeled, seeded and pulped
3 tbs olive oil
a bouquet garni* (thyme, bay leaf, parsley)
1 clove garlic

Put the mussels in a deep enamelled cast-iron saucepan and let them open over high heat without adding any liquid. Cover the pan but do not let the mussels cook. Shell them as soon as they open and thread on skewers two at a time, inserting a piece of bacon between each pair. Each skewer should consist of 4 pieces of bacon and 10 mussels. Dip the skewers in the diluted egg yolk and roll in the breadcrumbs. Leave for 10 minutes.

To cook Brush with a sprig of thyme dipped in olive oil and cook under a very hot grill, turning to cook evenly. Do not let the mussels blacken. They should be dry and well browned.

To make the sauce Cook the pulped tomatoes in the olive oil with the bouquet garni for 35 to 40 minutes. Before serving add the crushed clove of garlic.

To serve Transfer to a heated metal dish, add salt and pepper and decorate with lemon quarters. Serve the sauce separately.

Suggested wine A rosé from Provence, well cooled.

AUBERGE GOURMANDE *
VELAR-SUR-OUCHE (CÔTE-D'OR)

BROCHETTES JURASSIENNES

*Gruyère cheese wrapped in ham and fried in oil. Excellent cheese and the famous yellow wine (*vin jaune*) are to be found in the Jura.*

For 6 people

500g Gruyère cheese
6 slices juicy ham (York or Paris)
2 eggs, beaten with 1 tbs olive oil

1 cup dried white breadcrumbs
½l oil
parsley
salt, freshly milled black pepper

Cut the cheese into 30 cubes each measuring 2cm. Cut each slice of ham into 5 long strips and wrap each cheese cube in a strip of ham. Thread 5 wrapped cubes on to each 20cm skewer. Dip the skewers in the beaten egg mixture and roll in the breadcrumbs. Fry in very hot oil in a heavy frying-pan until golden but not too brown. The cheese should be half melted.

Drain carefully and arrange on a serving-dish. Season with salt and pepper and decorate with little bunches of fried parsley.

Suggested wine White Arbois or a yellow local wine served well chilled.

CHEESE DISHES

ANDROUET *
PARIS 8e: 41 RUE D'AMSTERDAM

FEUILLETÉS AU ROQUEFORT

Flaky pastry cases filled with a Roquefort cheese paste. They may be served warm as a first course or made half the size given in the recipe and served with drinks before a meal.

For 10 individual cases to be served as a first course

300–400g Roquefort cheese
80–100g unsalted butter

2 tbs flour
1 egg yolk
2 turns of the pepper mill
800–900g puff pastry (see p. 356)

To prepare Work the butter into the flour with a fork, add the egg yolk and Roquefort and work with a spatula or wooden spoon to obtain a smooth paste. Divide into 10 small sausage shapes.

Cut the pastry into 10 rectangles. Spoon some of the Roquefort mixture on to one half of each rectangle, fold over the other half of the pastry, moisten the edges with water and seal. Glaze the surface with egg yolk diluted with water.

To cook Cook on a baking-sheet in an oven preheated to 190°–200°C, 380°–400°F, for 12 to 15 minutes. Reduce the heat if the pastry browns too quickly.

Suggested wine As a first course Châteauneuf-du-Pape; before a meal, sherry or port.

RESTAURANT DE LA PYRAMIDE * * *
VIENNE (ISÈRE)

SOUFFLÉ AUX OEUFS POCHÉS

Lightly poached eggs presented in a cheese soufflé. The soufflé should be slightly underdone so that the inside is a bit runny, in keeping with the soft texture of the eggs.

6 very fresh eggs, poached and
  carefully drained

Soufflé mixture

¼l boiling milk
2 tbs unsalted butter
3 tbs flour

100g Gruyère cheese, grated
grated nutmeg
3 egg yolks
5 egg whites, stiffly beaten
  with a pinch of salt
25g Gruyère cheese, grated, for
  the top of the soufflé

To prepare Spoon a layer of the prepared soufflé mixture into
a buttered oven dish 20–21cm in diameter, 5–6cm high. Arrange
the poached eggs on top and cover with the rest of the mixture.
Mark the position of each egg with a pinch of grated cheese to
help you in serving.

To cook Cook in an oven preheated to 205°C, 400°F, lowering
the temperature to 190°C, 380°F, when cooking starts. Serve as
soon as the soufflé has risen and the surface is golden. It should
cook for no more than 9 to 12 minutes, so that the eggs remain
soft.

Suggested wine A white, fruity Côte-de-Beaune, such as
Meursault or Bâtard-Montrachet.

SAINT-MORITZ *
NICE (ALPES-MARITIMES)

SOUFFLÉ AU FROMAGE BRIOCHÉ

*A particularly delicious Gruyère soufflé using hardly any flour
but a little beer as the rising agent and for lightness.*

For 6 people

100g unsalted butter
a pinch salt
1dl light lager beer

1 dsp flour
freshly milled black pepper
10 eggs
100g Gruyère cheese, cut into
  very small dice

Whisk the butter, salt and beer together in an enamelled saucepan
over high heat. Remove from the stove as soon as the mixture
begins to froth. Stir in the flour away from the stove, and beat
for 3 minutes over very moderate heat. Remove the pan from the
stove and beat in the whole eggs one at a time. Return to the
stove and, over very gentle heat indeed, stir in the cheese until it
melts. Do not let it cook.
  Pour the mixture into a buttered soufflé dish and cook for
about 10 minutes in an oven preheated to 205°C, 400°F, lowering
the temperature to 190°C, 380°F, as soon as cooking starts.

Suggested wine A very dry and fruity white wine, such as
Blanc de blancs (preferably domaine d'Ott).

ANDROUET *
PARIS 8e: 41 RUE D'AMSTERDAM

STEAKS DE FROMAGE

Thick slices of Gruyère or Swiss Comté cheese coated with batter and fried, then covered with a frothy omelette cooked in the oven until it rises like a soufflé.

Batter
500g sifted flour
2 eggs
1½–2dl lager beer
salt, grated nutmeg
1 tbs oil
2 egg whites, stiffly beaten

Cheese fritters
1 thick slice cheese per
  person, each weighing 150g
  and 15mm thick

a very little salt
freshly milled black pepper
grated nutmeg
¾l groundnut oil

Omelette mixture
1½ eggs to each cheese fritter
salt, freshly milled black
  pepper, grated nutmeg

To make the batter Mix the flour and beer together in a bowl; make a well in the middle, break in the eggs, then fold them in. Stir in the oil and seasoning. Whisk to obtain a smooth paste. Fold in the beaten egg whites and leave for 1 hour before using. The mixture should be well blended and not too runny.

To prepare the fritters Sprinkle each side of the cheese fritters with salt, pepper and grated nutmeg. Dip them one at a time into the batter so that they are completely and evenly coated.

Meanwhile heat the oil in the frying-pan and drop in the cheese fritters one at a time. They should be completely covered with oil and must not touch. Fry for 3 minutes on each side, without browning. Drain thoroughly.

To make the omelette Beat the eggs until they are foaming. Season. Put the cheese fritters in an oven dish and pour over the beaten eggs. Slide the dish immediately into an oven preheated to 175°C, 350°F. The eggs will swell and lift up the cheese steaks, which should be soft and melting inside. The dish is done when the omelette has risen and is lightly browned.

Suggested wine Neuchâtel or Crépy.

HÔTEL DE LA GARE *
MONTBARD (CÔTE-D'OR)

GOUGÈRE BOURGUIGNONNE

A quite exceptional cheese pastry which can be made in one large crown or in individual shapes. It should always be served hot. It is indigestible if eaten cold and loses much of its subtle taste and texture. If it has to be made in advance, reheat in a low oven for 8–10 minutes before serving.

For 8 people	4 eggs
¼l water	100g Gruyère cheese, half
125g unsalted butter	grated and half cut into
5g salt	small cubes
125g flour	1 egg yolk, for glazing

Bring the water, butter and salt to boiling point in a saucepan. Add the flour, stir with a wooden spoon or spatula until the mixture will come away from the side of the pan and form a film at the bottom. Stir for a few seconds until it stiffens and dries. Remove the pan from the stove and fold in the eggs one at a time, working each one in very thoroughly before adding the next. Then add the cheese, half grated and half cubed. Arrange the mixture to form a crown on a baking-sheet and glaze the surface with the egg yolk. Cook in a very hot oven, about 200°C, 400°F, for about 25 minutes. The *gougère* should have puffed up and be a nice golden brown.

Check that the pastry is sufficiently dry; if it is too soft it will sink rapidly as it cools.

To serve Serve hot or warm, either at the beginning of a meal or after the cheese.

Suggested wine A *gougère* deserves the best wine. Serve either a good white Alsatian wine, such as Gewürztraminer, or a really good Côtes-du-Rhône.

HOSTELLERIE LENOIR *
AUVILLERS-LES-FORGES (ARDENNES)

FONDUES AU PARMESAN

A delicious cheese dish which should be served very hot as a first course.

For 10 or 12 people	¾ cup double cream
240g unsalted butter	4 egg yolks
100–110g flour	salt, freshly milled black
1l warmed milk	pepper, grated nutmeg
75g parmesan cheese, grated	1 egg yolk for the coating
	breadcrumbs

Make a white roux with the butter and flour. Stir in the hot milk and bring to the boil. Beat well with a wire whisk to obtain a smooth white sauce (see p. 347). Add the parmesan while the sauce is cooling. Work well and thicken with the egg yolks and cream. Turn the mixture out on to an oiled board ½cm thick. Leave to cool overnight or place for 2 hours in the refrigerator. Cut into squares or diamond shapes. Dip in flour, shake off the excess, dip into an egg yolk beaten with a little water, then into the breadcrumbs. Fry in oil hot enough to colour lightly. They should be golden but not brown. Serve on a dish covered with a napkin and decorate with fried parsley.

NB Before the mixture is left to cool, 150g Ardennes ham, cut into thin strips, can be added.

Suggested wine Pouilly Fuissé or Arbois.

ANDROUET *
PARIS 8e: 41 RUE D'AMSTERDAM

SALADE BERNOISE

An unusual cheese salad which may be served as a dish on its own. It is also excellent with roast pork or cold roast veal.

For 4 people

300g Emmenthal cheese
2 hard-boiled eggs, thinly
   sliced
2 tbs grated horseradish

75g double cream
2 tbs wine vinegar
1 dsp Dutch Carvi (small black
   caraway seeds)
salt, freshly milled black
   pepper

Cut the Emmenthal into strips or small cubes. Arrange in a shallow dish with the eggs and horseradish.

Mix the cream and vinegar together in another bowl, add the Carvi, salt and pepper. Coat the salad with this dressing, leave to stand and toss before serving. Decorate with sliced radish.

Variation Strips of celery or grated celeriac may be added and Dijon mustard used instead of the horseradish.

Suggested wine Schaffiser or Muscadet.

SHELLFISH

HÔTEL-RESTAURANT DES VANNES ★ ★
LIVERDUN (MEURTHE-ET-MOSELLE)

SAINT-JACQUES EN COQUILLES DE GALA

Fresh scallops cooked in pastry shells and coated with white butter sauce. The result is perfectly delicious.

For 4 people	a pinch of finely chopped parsley for each shell
12 fresh scallops	salt, freshly milled black pepper
250g thin short-crust pastry	
4–5 tbs unsalted butter	white butter sauce (see p. 355)
1 tsp shallots, very finely chopped	

Open the scallops and detach the edible parts (the white muscle and the coral). Reserve the corals and cut each white part into two rounds. Choose the best deep, well-marked shells, butter them and line them with the pastry, rolled out very thin. Cook for 10–12 minutes in an oven preheated to 190°C, 375°F. Allow to cool and turn the pastry case out of the shell. While the pastry is cooking gently sauté the scallops in the butter until they are cooked and very lightly coloured. The corals will take less time to cook than the white parts and should be added a few minutes later. Add the shallot at the end of the cooking time and sprinkle with salt and pepper.

To serve Arrange the scallops in the reheated pastry shells, using the corals as decoration. Coat each shell with 2 tablespoons of white butter sauce and sprinkle with very finely chopped parsley.

Suggested wine Sancerre, well chilled.

AUX PETITS PÈRES *
PARIS 2e: 8 RUE NOTRE-DAME-DES-VICTOIRES

COQUILLES SAINT-JACQUES SAUTÉES PROVENCALE

A simple and excellent dish of scallops flavoured with garlic and shallots and sautéed with mushrooms and fresh tomato purée. It can be served with Creole rice.

For 4 people

3kg fresh scallops
flour
salt, freshly milled black
  pepper
3 tbs oil
3 tbs unsalted butter

150g button mushroom caps,
  washed and cut into four
2 cloves garlic
2 shallots, very finely chopped
1 tomato, peeled, seeded and
  pulped
1 tbs chopped parsley

Open the scallops, separate and discard the beard. Rinse in several changes of water and dry in a clean cloth. Reserve the corals and cut each white part into two rounds. Season with salt and pepper and flour lightly.

Heat the butter and oil in a large frying-pan, add the floured white parts of the scallops and sauté gently, turning the pieces in the pan. When the edges start to turn golden, add the corals and mushrooms and sauté for a few minutes longer. Add the garlic, shallot, parsley and tomato pulp. Cover the pan and cook for a further 5 minutes, adding 1 more tablespoon of oil or butter if necessary. Arrange the scallops in a deep round heated china or metal dish with the corals arranged on top to look decorative.

Suggested wine A rosé from Provence well chilled.

CHEZ MÉLANIE *
RIEC-SUR-BELON (FINISTÈRE)

PALOURDES FARCIES GRILLÉES

Two names are associated with this clam dish: that of Mélanie and that of Curnonsky, the famous gastronome and writer. It is still one of the most inspired and most delicious ways of eating these little molluscs.

For 4 people

48 clams
6 shallots, very finely chopped
2 tbs parsley, very finely
  chopped
a few tarragon leaves, finely
  chopped

a pinch mustard powder
200g best unsalted butter
freshly milled black pepper
very little salt
dried breadcrumbs

To make the stuffing Soften the butter slightly and place in a bowl with the shallots, parsley, tarragon, mustard powder, pepper and salt. Work all the ingredients carefully and slowly together with a fork, so that all the herbs and spices are thoroughly incorporated into the butter.

To prepare Open the clams by placing them side by side in a large shallow roasting-tin containing just enough water to produce steam, over a very high heat. When the shells open, remove the empty halves and press a little stuffing into each of the half-shells containing the clams. Sprinkle each clam lightly with the breadcrumbs.

To cook Put the clam dish in a hot oven, 190°–200°C, 375°–400°F, for about 5 minutes.

Suggested wine Muscadet, well cooled, or any dry white Loire wine.

L'ESCALE * *
CARRY-LE-ROUET (BOUCHES-DU-RHÔNE)

MOULES GRILLÉES À LA PROVENÇALE

This dish could be called mussels à l'escargot, since the butter sauce is virtually the same as that used for snails. The mussels must be good ones, hand-picked. This is a particularly tasty first course requiring 6 to 12 mussels per guest, depending on how much they like garlic.

For 6 people

2kg good mussels, carefully cleaned and washed
1 glass white Cassis wine
2 very dry rusks, crushed
salt, freshly milled black pepper

Provençal or garlic butter
3–5 cloves garlic, according to size and taste
1 dsp olive oil
2 tbs parsley, very finely chopped
2 tbs chervil, very finely chopped

Open the mussels by putting them in a large pan and shaking them over a high heat for 6 to 8 minutes. Remove them from the pan, shell them and leave them to drain on a board covered with absorbent paper. Reserve half the shells, choosing the best ones, and discard the rest.

Provençal butter Chop the garlic and pound in a mortar with the oil, parsley and chervil. Cream the butter in a bowl. Work in the garlic and herb mixture with a fork. Season with salt and pepper. Put in the refrigerator for a few minutes to solidify without hardening.

To arrange the dish Put one or two mussels on each shell. Using a knife with a broad rounded blade, fill each shell with the garlic butter, levelling off with the knife.

Arrange the prepared mussels on snail dishes, if possible, or in a flat oven dish. Sprinkle each mussel with a pinch of the rusk crumbs. Put the dish under the grill until the butter softens and bubbles.

This dish should be served very hot, straight from the grill.

Suggested wine Blanc de blancs from Cassis, or a rosé from Provence.

LE CHALET *
ROYAN (CHARENTE-MARITIME)

LA MOUSCLADE D'AUNIS

This is a famous recipe from that part of the Atlantic coast where names such as Vendée, Aunis and Saintonge evoke the lovely woods and islands, mysterious narrow inlets and especially the beautiful coastline, a true fisherman's paradise. In this traditional dish the mussels are served in their half-shells coated with a sauce made from the cooking juices, plus white wine and cream. Serve it with Creole rice for a more substantial dish.

For 6 people

2kg mussels
1½l dry white wine
½dl olive oil
½dl groundnut oil
2 onions, finely sliced
1 sprig thyme, 1 bay leaf, 1 sprig parsley

a pinch curry powder
a pinch cayenne pepper
salt, freshly milled black pepper
1dl milk, heated to boiling point
flour
4 tbs fresh double cream
juice of half a lemon

Clean the mussels very carefully, scrape and scrub them. Rinse thoroughly.

Put the mussels in an enamelled cast-iron casserole with the white wine, thyme, bay leaf and parsley. Heat, cover the casserole and shake it. Sauté the mussels, without removing the lid, until they open. Cook for 5 minutes. Take the mussels out of the casserole and remove the empty half-shell from each.

Arrange the opened mussels in a serving-dish, preferably a metal one, side by side and touching each other, cover with paper and a lid. Keep hot.

Strain the mussel stock into another container and reserve.

To make the sauce Soften the onions in the oil in a saucepan; do not let them take colour. Sprinkle in a little flour and stir over the heat for 2 minutes. Pour in the hot milk and the strained stock still stirring. Season with a little salt, pepper, curry powder and cayenne. Add the lemon juice and simmer for about 10 minutes. Strain the sauce, add the cream and reheat. The sauce should be fairly thin.

Remove the paper and lid from the mussels and coat them with the sauce. Sprinkle with parsley and serve very hot on warmed plates.

Suggested wine Muscadet or Entre-Deux-Mers, or any other dry white wine, well chilled.

RELAIS BRENNER *
LÉZARDRIEUX, NEAR PAIMPOL (CÔTES-DU-NORD)

HUÎTRES GRILLÉES DU RELAIS
A simple recipe in which the oysters keep their full flavour.

For 2 people

12 good flat oysters
100g unsalted butter, blended
   with parsley and garlic

juice of 1 lemon
$\frac{1}{2}$ cup breadcrumbs, sieved
50g Gruyère cheese, grated

Open the oysters. Leave them attached to the deep half-shell with the juice and arrange them in an oven dish. On each oyster put 1 large nut of the prepared butter, a few drops of lemon juice and a sprinkling of breadcrumbs and grated cheese. Transfer the dish to a moderately hot oven, 165°–170°C, 325°–350°F, and serve as soon as the surface is golden.

Suggested wine Tavel rosé.

CHEZ DENIS
PARIS 17e: 10 RUE GUSTAVE-FLAUBERT

BOUCHÉES D'HUÎTRES DENIS
Small puff-pastry vol-au-vents filled with diced foie gras and raw oysters and served hot. They are a delicious appetizer, fresh and rich, and each is eaten in one mouthful.

For 4 people

12–16 very small puff-pastry
vol-au-vent cases (5cm
maximum diameter)

150g goose or duck *foie gras*
cut into large dice
12–16 fine oysters, kept very
cold

To assemble the vol-au-vents Do not loosen the oysters from their shells until the last minute. Warm the pastry cases until very hot. Put a cube of *foie gras* in each and slide a raw oyster on top.

Suggested wine Puligny Montrachet or Château d'Yquem, well chilled.

LA TOUR D'ARGENT ★ ★ ★
PARIS 5e: 15 QUAI DE LA TOURNELLE

HUÎTRES À LA BROLATTI

The oysters are poached and sautéed in butter. They are served in their shells, coated with a sauce made from white wine, shallots and the oyster stock, thickened with butter.

For 2 people

12 fine flat oysters, preferably
Marennes or Belon
2 shallots, finely chopped
2 tbs unsalted butter
2 tbs very dry white wine

the oyster stock, strained
through muslin
100g best unsalted butter, for
the sauce
2 tbs best unsalted butter, to
sauté the oysters
lemon juice (optional)

To prepare Open the oysters and detach them from their shells. Poach them in their own juice in a small enamelled saucepan for about 2 minutes or until the edges curl. Keep the stock. Drain the oysters, beard them and reserve the beards.

To make the sauce Soften the shallots in the 2 tablespoons of butter, without letting them take colour. Add the oyster beards, the white wine and 2 to 2½ tablespoons of the oyster stock and reduce. Whisk in the 100g of butter. Season with salt and pepper and add a few drops of lemon juice to taste.

To cook Strain the sauce into a small enamelled saucepan and keep warm. Put the deep halves of the oyster shells in the oven to heat and dry them out. Sauté the oysters in 2 tablespoons of butter, turning them for 2 minutes. Put an oyster in each heated half-shell and coat with about 2 tablespoons of the sauce.

To serve Arrange 6 oysters on each plate and serve very hot.

Suggested wine Champagne, Blanc de blancs, or a very dry Anjou, chilled on ice.

HÔTEL RITZ *
PARIS 1er: 15 PLACE VENDÔME

HUÎTRES MORNAY

A rare first course in France, where oysters are nearly always served raw and alive in their natural juice. Huîtres Mornay *were popular at the turn of the century and are still greatly appreciated today.*

For 2–3 people

12 fine flat oysters
unsalted butter
freshly milled black pepper

Mornay sauce
¼l Béchamel sauce (see p. 347)
1dl double cream
2 egg yolks
40g grated parmesan cheese
50g unsalted butter

To cook the oysters Open the oysters and detach from their shells. Strain all their juices into an enamelled saucepan. Wash and scrub the deep half-shells, dry and put them aside.

Poach the oysters in their juice for 2 to 3 minutes, or until the edges start to curl. Drain, reserve the cooking juice, and sauté in butter for about 2 minutes, without colouring them. Season with pepper and put aside. The cooking juice will replace salt in the sauce.

To make the sauce Stir the cream into the Béchamel and reduce to two-thirds of the original quantity. Add the egg yolks and parmesan cheese away from the heat and whisk in the butter. Strain the sauce through muslin or a fine sieve. Taste for seasoning and then add as necessary, several spoonfuls of the oyster stock, tasting after each addition. Add pepper to taste.

To serve Put the oysters in the half-shells, coat each with a little of the sauce, sprinkle with grated parmesan and brown in a hot oven, 215°–225°C, 425°–450°F, for a few minutes.

Suggested wine A dry, fruity and fairly full-bodied white wine such as Alsace Traminer or a white Jura wine such as Château-Chalon.

AUX LYONNAIS *
PARIS 2e: 32 RUE SAINT-MARC

COQUILLES SAINT-JACQUES À LA NAGE

The scallops can be cooked in advance, reheated and served warm in the white wine stock. Mayonnaise is served separately.

For 4 people

5kg fresh scallops, in their shells

Court-bouillon
1l water

¼l very dry white wine
1 carrot, cut into 3 sticks
1 onion, cut into 3 slices
1 bouquet garni
salt, black peppercorns

To cook Boil the court-bouillon for about 20 minutes in an enamelled pan. Add the shelled scallops to the stock and simmer for about 15 minutes. Remove the scallops and reduce the liquid by half.

To serve Serve the scallops in the stock in a large bowl. Hand separately a mayonnaise flavoured with lemon juice or a mustardy Remoulade sauce.

Suggested wine Sancerre or Muscadet.

LA COLOMBIÈRE*
ÉTABLES-SUR-MER (CÔTES-DU-NORD)

COQUILLES SAINT-JACQUES AU NATUREL

A classic recipe and still one of the best ways of cooking scallops.

For 4 people

16 scallops, alive and closed
3 tbs oil
4 tbs unsalted butter
flour

salt, freshly milled black pepper
2 shallots, very finely chopped
1 lemon
1 dsp parsley, finely chopped

To prepare Open the scallops, remove the gristly fibre and dark brown parts. Detach the edible white parts and the corals, rinse thoroughly and wipe dry. Reserve 4 good deep shells. Cut the white parts of the scallops into two or three pieces according to size and sprinkle lightly with flour. Put the orange corals aside.

To cook Heat the oil and 3 tablespoons of the butter in a frying-pan or sauté-pan, preferably a copper one, add the white parts of the scallops and sauté for several minutes, turning them and taking care not to let them go hard. Add the corals and continue cooking until the white parts of the scallops turn lightly golden.

Melt a nut of butter with a pinch of chopped shallot in each reserved shell. Put the white parts of the scallops back in the shells, decorate with the coral and strain the buttery cooking juices over the scallops. Reheat in a moderate oven for 3 minutes.

To serve Squeeze lemon juice over each scallop. Decorate with a pinch of finely chopped parsley and serve very hot.

Suggested wine Muscadet, well chilled.

HÔTEL DE LA MARINE★
CAUDEBEC-EN-CAUX (SEINE-MARITIME)

COQUILLES SAINT-JACQUES HAVRAISES

This dish is made with fresh scallops sautéed in shallot butter, garnished with the corals and shelled prawns and served in their shells. The sauce is made with white wine and dry vermouth and enriched with cream. The decoration, of unshelled prawns, little crescents of puff pastry and bunches of parsley, makes the dish look colourful and elegant.

For 4 people

12 fine scallops
16 prawns, cooked and shelled
parsley

Shallot butter
4 shallots, very finely chopped
75g unsalted butter

Sauce
½dl white wine
½dl Noilly Prat vermouth
4 tbs thick Normandy cream
salt, freshly milled black
  pepper

To cook Shell the scallops, reserving the corals and cutting the white parts into 2 rounds. Choose the 4 best deep shells and wash, scrub and dry them. Rub them with butter. Melt the shallot butter in a small copper sauté-pan, add the white parts of the scallops and sauté for 3 to 4 minutes over moderate heat, turning them. Add the corals and cook for another 2 minutes. Remove the white parts and the corals from the pan and reserve.

To make the sauce Deglaze the buttery juices in the pan with the white wine and vermouth, scraping any little bits off the bottom and sides of the pan with a wooden spoon or spatula and letting the liquid reduce until there is almost nothing left. Add the cream, bring to the boil, stirring continuously, and strain the sauce into a saucepan. Season with salt and pepper.

To serve Reheat the scallops in the sauce with the shelled prawns. Heat the buttered shells. Put 6 white pieces of scallop, 4 prawns and 3 corals into each shell. Coat with the sauce and decorate each shell with a little crescent of puff pastry, an unshelled prawn and a small bunch of parsley. Serve very hot on a heated metal dish.

Suggested wine Dry white such as Sancerre or Muscadet.

À L'HUITRIÈRE *
LILLE (NORD)

COQUILLES SAINT-JACQUES À LA BERCY

Scallops cooked in a concentrated stock of white wine, mushrooms and shallots, thickened with cream and butter. The dish is garnished with little crescents of puff pastry and the corals of the scallops.

For 5 people

700g fresh scallops, shelled
and sliced, with their coral

Sauce
2dl dry white wine
1dl fish *fumet*
½l mushroom *fumet*
5 shallots, very finely chopped

salt, freshly milled black
pepper
parsley stalks
2dl fresh double cream
125g unsalted butter

Garnish

6 crescents puff pastry
1 tbs parsley, finely chopped

To cook Put the white wine, fish and mushroom *fumets*, chopped shallots and parsley into a sauté-pan, bring to the boil and reduce by half. Add 2 tablespoons of the butter, the scallops and their corals, season with salt and pepper and cook for about 8 minutes. Half way through cooking add the cream. Remove the scallops and the corals and keep hot.

To finish the sauce Strain the stock into a saucepan. Bring to the boil and reduce for 3 minutes. Add the remainder of the butter, starting over very gentle heat, then moving the pan away from the stove, beating the butter in with a wire whisk to thicken the sauce. Taste for seasoning.

Reheat the white parts of the scallops in the sauce, reserving the corals.

To serve Transfer the scallops in their sauce to a serving-dish. Garnish with the corals and little crescents or *fleurons* of puff-pastry. Sprinkle with parsley.

Suggested wine Pouilly Fuissé.

LE VIVARIOS ★ ★ ★
PARIS 16e: 192 AVENUE VICTOR-HUGO

TIMBALE DE COQUILLES SAINT-JACQUES AU NOILLY

The scallops are poached in a mixture of dry Vermouth and a sole fumet. *They are served in a sauce enriched with cream and butter.*

For 2 people	Sole fumet
	the bones and trimmings of 2

For 2 people

2kg fine live scallops
2dl Noilly Prat vermouth
1 shallot, very finely chopped
salt, freshly milled black
    pepper

Sole fumet
the bones and trimmings of 2
    sole
2dl water
$\frac{1}{2}$ onion, finely sliced
1 small bouquet garni

Sauce
4 tbs double cream
125g unsalted butter

Open the scallops and remove the shells. Discard all the brown fringe, keeping the white parts and corals. Wash carefully to remove any trace of sand. Dry them and if they are large, cut them in half across.

Marinate the scallops with the shallots for 10 to 15 minutes in the vermouth, stirring from time to time. Meanwhile make the sole *fumet*. Cook the *fumet* for 30 minutes and strain the liquid through a conical sieve into a large saucepan, preferably enamelled cast-iron.

Remove the scallops from the marinade and add the marinade and shallots to the *fumet*. Put the scallops and their corals into the *fumet*, bring the liquid to the boil, season with salt and pepper and poach the scallops for 6 to 7 minutes.

Transfer the scallops to a silver mould or a round metal dish, cover and keep hot.

To make the sauce Reduce the contents of the pan almost to a glaze and strain into a small thick-bottomed saucepan. Add the cream, bring to the boil and bubble for 2 to 3 minutes. Whisk in the butter a little at a time, away from the stove, until the sauce is light and fluffy. Correct the seasoning, add a few drops of Noilly Prat, a few drops of lemon juice, if desired, and pour the sauce over the scallops. Heat the dish without letting the contents boil and serve on very hot plates. Creole rice (see p. 293) is a good accompaniment for this rich sauce.

Suggested wine A very dry white Champagne, Mesnil or Crémant, or a fruitier wine, such as Blanc de blancs from the south, domaine d'Ott.

CHEZ MICHEL ★ ★
PARIS 10e: 10 RUE DE BELZUNCE

POTIQUET DE MOULES FARCIES

A potiquet *is a little individual stoneware dish. Here the mussels are served with a sauce of butter and mushrooms lightly flavoured with garlic.*

For 4 people

2l fine mussels
½dl good dry white wine

Stuffing
500g best unsalted butter

125g parsley
25g garlic
40g button mushrooms
1 slice cooked ham
salt, freshly milled black
  pepper
4 cubes white bread, 3–4cm
  each side

To prepare Clean the mussels thoroughly: scrape, scrub, wash carefully and dry them. Open them in a casserole over high heat, with the white wine. Drain carefully and remove the shells. Strain the stock into a bowl and reserve.

Finely chop all the stuffing ingredients. Mix together in a bowl and work in the butter with a fork until it is properly blended. Divide the butter stuffing into 4 equal parts.

To cook Put 5 or 6 mussels into each little dish and fill with the stuffing. Put a bread cube on top of each and moisten with 2 table-spoons of the mussel stock. Transfer to a moderate oven, 165°C, 325°F, for about 10 minutes.

To serve Serve the mussels very hot in their individual dishes, with a little basket of very fresh bread, cut into cubes.

Suggested wine Sancerre or Muscadet.

LE CHALUT *
PARIS 17e: 94 BD DES BATIGNOLLES

TIMBALE NORMANDE

Mixed fish fillets and Dublin Bay prawns poached in mussel stock. The sauce is thickened with cream and the dish is served with croûtons fried in butter until golden.

For 4 people

750g fine mussels, carefully washed and cleaned
2dl dry white wine
600g sole, filleted
300g red mullet, filleted
600g John Dory, filleted
8 fine Dublin Bay prawns, shelled

Sauce

1½ cups fresh double cream
1 bare dessertspoon arrowroot or potato starch
2 tbs fresh double cream
1 tbs mixed parsley and chervil, very finely chopped
salt, freshly milled black pepper
8 triangular bread croûtons, crusts removed and fried in butter until golden

To cook Heat the mussels in a covered casserole with the wine until they open. Cook over high heat, shaking the pan without removing the lid, for about 6 to 8 minutes. Remove the mussels from the pan and shell them. Strain the mussel stock through a piece of cloth into a saucepan. Poach the fish fillets and prawns in the mussel stock for about 8 minutes. Transfer the fish and prawns to a timbale mould, add the shelled mussels and keep hot.

To make the sauce Strain the fish stock into a heavy saucepan and let it boil for 2 to 3 minutes. Add one cup of cream away from the stove. Thicken with the arrowroot diluted with the remaining half-cup of cream. Heat, whisking continuously, until the sauce thickens. Season with salt and pepper and pour the hot sauce into the timbale mould. Sprinkle with the chopped parsley and chervil and garnish with the croûtons.

Suggested wine White Pouilly fumé, well chilled.

HÔTEL DES ROCHERS *
'Chez Justin'
PLOUMANACH-EN-PERROS-GUIREC (CÔTES-DU-NORD)

HOMARDS GRILLÉS 'BÉBÉ JUSTIN'
A savoury dish of grilled lobsters with snail butter. The garlic is not too dominant and the butter is delicious with the lobster.

For 2 people

1 lobster, weighing 800g *or*
  2 young lobsters, each
  weighing 400g
about 4 tbs olive oil
salt, freshly milled black
  pepper

Snail butter
150g unsalted butter
30g powdered almonds
30g shallots, very finely
  chopped
30g parsley, very finely
  chopped
30g garlic, squeezed through a
  garlic press and pounded
  with a nut of butter
salt
freshly milled white pepper

Sauce
2dl fresh double cream
1 tbs tarragon mustard
1 tbs mixed herbs (chervil,
  chives, tarragon), very finely
  chopped
1 tsp arrowroot, blended with
  a very little cold water
a pinch cayenne pepper
salt
½dl old calvados

To make the snail butter Soften the butter in a small bowl. Work it vigorously with a small wooden spoon or spatula and beat in all the other ingredients until they are well distributed and the mixture is perfectly smooth. Put in a cool place.

To prepare the lobster Give the lobster a sharp blow on the head so that it will suffer as little as possible. Take it by the back and split it in two, using a knife with a serrated edge. Remove the coral and creamy parts from the head and reserve them in a bowl in a cool place.

To cook the lobster Season with salt and pepper and oil the flesh on the half-lobsters. Put them in an oiled roasting dish and transfer to a hot oven, 215°–225°C, 400°–425°F, to seal. Reduce the temperature to 165°–175°C, 325°–350°F, and cook for a further 5 minutes. Remove the lobsters from the oven and butter their flesh with half of the snail butter. Replace the lobsters in the oven and cook for another 5 minutes at a temperature of 165°C, 325°F.

  Meanwhile work the rest of the snail butter with the reserved coral and creamy parts from the head of the lobster. Take the dish out of the oven and spread this mixture over the buttered lobster. Cook under the grill another 5 minutes, to glaze the surface.

To make the sauce Put the cream, mustard, herbs, calvados, cayenne pepper and salt in a saucepan, preferably enamelled cast-iron. Add the diluted arrowroot and whisk over a low heat until the sauce reaches boiling point.

To serve Serve the lobsters in the oven dish and hand the sauce separately in a heated sauceboat.

Suggested wine Muscadet or Blanc de blancs.

RELAIS GASTRONOMIQUE PARIS-EST ★
PARIS 10e: COUR D'HONNEUR (FIRST FLOOR OF THE GARE DE L'EST)

HOMARD À LA NEW-BURG
A dish of lobster cooked in chunks, shelled and served in a sauce containing cognac, madeira, cream and lobster butter.

For 4 people

2 live lobsters, each weighing about 1kg
5–6 tbs olive oil
salt, freshly milled black pepper
2dl cognac
2dl madeira
4dl fresh double cream

2dl strong, reduced fish *fumet*

Beurre manié
2 tbs unsalted butter
the coral and creamy parts from the bodies of the lobsters (+the roe if the lobsters are female)
2 tbs flour

To prepare Give the lobsters a sharp blow on the top of their heads to anaesthetize them and cut them in sections as quickly as possible.

To cook Heat the oil in a sauté-pan, preferably a copper one, add the pieces of lobster and sauté rapidly, stirring and turning them. Season with salt and pepper, remove the lobsters and drain off the oil completely. Shell the pieces of lobster, crack and shell the claws and keep the meat hot in a timbale mould.

To make the sauce Deglaze the oil and juices in the pan with the cognac and madeira. Reduce by two-thirds. Add the cream and fish *fumet* away from the stove. Cover the pan and cook over moderate heat for 15 to 20 minutes at the most. Work together with a fork the ingredients for the *beurre manié* until you have a smooth paste. Put a small piece of the *beurre manié* on the end of a wire whisk and whisk it into the sauce over moderate heat until it melts and is absorbed into the sauce. Repeat the process two or three times until all the *beurre manié* has been absorbed. Let the sauce simmer for 5 to 8 minutes.

Press the boiling-hot sauce through a strainer on to the pieces of lobster.

To serve Serve with a small dish of rice pilaf (see p. 294).

Suggested wine White Chassagne Montrachet.

RESTAURANT DE L'OCÉAN *
FROMENTINE (VENDÉE)

HOMARD AU PORTO

Half-lobsters served in a sauce of port and cream, spiced with cayenne pepper.

For 2 people

1 live lobster, weighing
750–800g
olive oil
2–3 tbs unsalted butter

a sprig of thyme, bay leaf,
parsley stalks or root
salt, a dash of cayenne pepper
2dl good ruby port
¼l fresh double cream
freshly milled black pepper

To make the dish Strike the lobster on the head above the eyes, where the nerve centres are to be found, using a mallet, pestle or the blunt edge of a chopping knife. Cut very quickly in half from head to tail. Coat the lobster flesh in the half-shells with olive oil and put the shells into a very well-buttered sauté-pan. Add the herbs and brown the lobster for 10 minutes, shaking the pan and turning the lobster. When the flesh stiffens and the shell is a nice red, deglaze the cooking juices with the port, season with salt and cayenne and let the liquid reduce for about 5 minutes to one-third of the original quantity. Remove the lobster, split the claws and transfer the lobster halves and claws to a covered timbale mould.

To finish the sauce Strain the reduced cooking liquid into a heavy saucepan. Leave for a few minutes until the oil rises to the surface, skim off the oil and add the cream, stirring it in over very low heat without cooking. Tilt the pan from side to side until the sauce thickens slightly.

Coat the lobster halves with the sauce and serve very hot.

Suggested wine A Muscadet or a good light bordeaux, according to taste.

AUBERGE DE LA ROUGE *
SAINT-LÉONARD - FÉCAMP (SEINE-MARITIME)

HOMARD À L'AMÉRICAINE

A classic lobster recipe and one of the best. Furthermore it is not complicated.

For 2 people

1 live lobster, weighing 1kg
4 tbs olive oil
1 tbs onion, finely chopped

1 dsp shallot, finely chopped
2 medium-sized tomatoes,
peeled, seeded, squeezed
and roughly chopped

1 clove garlic, peeled, squeezed and pounded with 1 dsp olive oil	3 tbs unsalted butter
2 tbs fresh parsley and tarragon, crushed	salt, freshly milled black pepper
1½dl good dry white wine	a squeeze lemon juice
2 tbs good cognac	3 tbs unsalted butter, in small pieces
2 pinches cayenne pepper	

Stun the lobster by giving it a sharp blow on the head with a heavy instrument and proceed as quickly as possible: cut the tail into sections, following the marks on the joints; then cut the head in half lengthways; discard the pocket containing the gritty substance. Scoop out the inside creamy parts from the head and the coral and reserve. Season the lobster pieces with salt and pepper.

To cook Heat the olive oil in a heavy sauté-pan, preferably a copper one. Seal the lobster pieces by turning them over high heat. Remove the lobster pieces and reserve. Add the chopped onion to the oil in the pan. Let it soften for 2 to 3 minutes then add the shallot. Stir thoroughly with a wooden spoon or spatula and add the tomato, crushed garlic and 1 tablespoon of the crushed parsley and tarragon. Arrange the lobster pieces on top and pour in the white wine and cognac. Do not flambé. Add a pinch of cayenne pepper.

Bring to the boil and cook, covered, either on top of the stove or in the oven, for 20 minutes. Drain the lobster pieces. Shell the tail pieces and the claws. Arrange the lobster pieces with the half-shells in a timbale mould. Keep hot while finishing the sauce.

To finish the sauce Reduce the cooking liquid by half. Meanwhile blend the reserved creamy parts of the lobster and the coral with the butter. Season with salt and pepper and blend with a fork. Add the lobster butter to the reduced cooking liquid away from the stove, taking a little piece at a time on the end of a wire whisk and whisking it in over low heat. Beat continuously and work as quickly as possible. Season the sauce with a little more cayenne pepper and a few drops of lemon juice. Whisk in the small pieces of fresh butter away from the heat until the sauce is absolutely smooth.

To serve Pour the very hot sauce over the lobster. Sprinkle with 1 tablespoon of the mixed parsley and tarragon, finely chopped, and serve.

Suggested wine There are several theories: Muscadet, Sancerre rosé or a light red bordeaux (*not* warmed to room temperature).

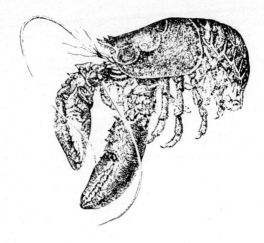

LEI MOUSCARDINS ✳
SAINT-TROPEZ (VAR)

LANGOUSTES À LA CRÈME

*Grilled crawfish with cream. Simple to make, rich and sumptuous,
this recipe is the finest of all grilled crawfish dishes.*

For 4 people

4 live crawfish, each weighing
  400g
1dl armagnac
100g unsalted butter, melted
  without boiling
salt, freshly milled black
  pepper

Sabayon
1 egg yolk
1dl fresh double cream
1 tbs chervil, tarragon and a
little parsley, mixed and
finely chopped

To prepare Place the crawfish on a board and stun them with a
sharp blow on the head with a heavy instrument so that they will
suffer as little as possible during the cooking. This is essential.

To cook Roast the crawfish for 12 minutes in an oven preheated
to 175°–180°C, 325°–350°F. Remove from the oven.

To make the sauce While the crawfish are cooking, prepare the
sabayon. Beat together the egg yolk and cream over very low heat
until the mixture thickens, without letting it boil. Add the herbs.

To finish Cut the crawfish in two from head to tail and remove
the intestinal gut. Sprinkle the crawfish halves with the armagnac
and cover with the *sabayon*. Put the crawfish back in the oven,
at the same temperature as before, until they turn a beautiful red.

To serve Serve very hot, arranged on a serving dish. Hand the
seasoned melted butter in a sauceboat and serve a dish of Creole
rice separately (see p. 293).

Suggested wine A very good dry white wine, either a burgundy or Blanc de blancs.

HÔTEL DE FRANCE *
MONTMORILLON (VIENNE)

GRATIN DE LANGOUSTINES

Dublin Bay prawns, cream and mushrooms, sprinkled with grated Gruyère cheese and browned in the oven.

For 8 people

1·2kg shelled Dublin Bay
  prawns
unsalted butter
300g button mushrooms,
  cleaned, finely sliced and
  sprinkled with lemon juice

¾l fresh double cream
salt, freshly milled black
  pepper
2 small pinches nutmeg
a small pinch cayenne
50g Gruyère cheese, grated

Sauté the prawns and mushrooms in a plentiful amount of butter and transfer to a buttered ovenproof dish.

Heat the cream with the salt, pepper, cayenne and half the nutmeg. Coat the prawns with the hot seasoned cream, sprinkle with the cheese and another pinch of nutmeg.

Put the dish under a hot grill for 5 to 6 minutes, until the surface is browned.

Suggested wine Muscadet.

LA CROIX BLANCHE *
ABLIS (YVELINES)

CRÊPES DE LANGOUSTINES À L'AMÉRICAINE

Prawn pancakes with sauce à l'américaine. A delicious first course, but also substantial enough for a light meal.

For 4 people

8 thin pancakes

Batter (see p. 357)
150g flour
a pinch salt
2 eggs + 1 yolk
2 tbs light lager beer and
  enough water and milk, in
  equal quantities, to make a
  smooth and semi-liquid
  paste

Filling
48 medium-sized Dublin Bay
  prawns
4 tbs oil
4 tbs unsalted butter

Sauce à l'américaine (see p.
  348)
the heads and shells of the
  prawns
½dl cognac
1dl fresh double cream
4 tbs Gruyère cheese, grated

To cook the prawns Sauté the unshelled prawns in the butter and oil, pour over the heated cognac and set light to it. Cover the pan and cook, turning the prawns, for 4 to 5 minutes. Remove the prawns and shell when cool.

To make the sauce Make the sauce as described on p. 348, in the prawn pan, using the remains of the cooking juices. Remove the meat from the heads of the prawns and add to the sauce. Boil the shells and remains of the heads in just enough fresh water to cover, for 10 minutes. Press all the shells through a sieve with a pestle to extract the juices and add the juice to the sauce together with the cooking stock. Reduce the sauce if necessary and strain. Add the cream, being careful not to let the sauce boil again. Keep the prawns hot in a little of the sauce.

To cook the pancakes Make the pancakes with the ingredients listed. Arrange 6 prawns on each cooked pancake and fold or roll. Arrange the filled pancakes on a buttered ovenproof serving-dish. Coat generously with the sauce, which should come halfway up the sides of the pancakes. Sprinkle with the grated cheese and put the dish under a hot grill for about 2 minutes to glaze the surface. Serve on very hot plates.

Suggested wine Dry white wine, such as Sancerre or Muscadet.

LA BRISE
ÎLE-AUX-MOINES (MORBIHAN)

CRÊPES DES MOINES

Pancakes stuffed with a seafood mixture, coated with American, Aurore or Hollandaise sauce and glazed in the oven.

For 6 people

Classic pancake batter (see p. 357), lightly salted
1 tbs fresh tarragon, finely chopped *or*
1 tsp dried powdered tarragon

Filling (for each pancake)
2 small rounds lobster meat *or*
1 scallop, white part and coral, whole or sliced *or*

5 prawns *or*
2 or 3 Dublin Bay prawns *or*
2 or 3 mussels, according to size

Sauce
½ l *sauce à l'américaine* (see p. 348)
or Aurore sauce (see p. 347)
or Hollandaise sauce (see p. 352)

Add the tarragon to the batter. Make 12 pancakes and spoon some of the filling into the middle of each. Cover the filling with 1 or 2 tablespoons of the chosen sauce, and fold the pancakes.

To serve Arrange the pancakes on a lightly buttered metal dish. Coat each pancake with sauce and glaze for a few minutes in a very hot oven or under the grill.

Suggested wine Muscadet or Anjou rosé.

LE GRAND VÉFOUR ★ ★ ★
PARIS 1er: 17 RUE DE BEAUJOLAIS

TOAST DE CREVETTES À LA ROTHSCHILD

A particularly delicate and savoury first course. A hollow case of toast, filled with shrimps in a cream and brandy sauce and browned in the oven. The dish should be decorated with a fine slice of truffle.

For 2 people

2 slices bread, cut from a tin
   loaf, 3cm thick
3 tbs unsalted butter
2 tbs oil
Gruyère cheese, grated

Shrimp filling
250g large shrimps
1 tsp sea salt
12 whole black peppercorns
3 tbs unsalted butter
1 tbs cognac

Sauce
2 shallots, finely choppéd
1 carrot, finely chopped
1 onion, finely chopped
2 tbs unsalted butter
2 tbs oil
1dl dry white wine
1 tsp tomato purée
1dl water
1 very small bouquet garni
1 tbs cognac, flambéed
1 tbs double cream
1 tbs butter, cut into small
   pieces
potato starch

To prepare the toast Carefully scoop out the crumbs from the middle of the slices of bread without spoiling the shape. Trim the outside with a knife. Toast in the oven and then brown on top of the stove in the oil and butter mixture. Drain on absorbent paper and reserve on a metal serving dish. Keep hot.

To cook the shrimps Cook the shrimps in boiling water seasoned with sea salt and whole peppercorns. Leave to cool, shell and reserve, keeping the heads and shells for the sauce.

To make the sauce Soften the shallots, carrot and onion in the butter and oil. Heat the white wine and tomato purée in another pan and reduce slightly. Strain the reduced liquid over the softened vegetables, add the water and the bouquet garni, bring to the boil and boil lightly for 20 minutes. Strain the liquid through a conical sieve into another saucepan, reduce slightly, then add the flambéd cognac, the cream and the pieces of butter. Whisk until all is absorbed and adjust the seasoning. Heat through and thicken the sauce with a small pinch of potato starch, diluted in 1 teaspoon of cold water.

To finish Gently sauté the shrimps in the butter and cognac. Drain and fill each case with an equal quantity of shrimps. Stir the butter and cognac mixture into the sauce and pour the sauce over the shrimps. Sprinkle lightly with grated cheese and glaze under a hot grill.

To serve Garnish each toast case with a sliver of truffle.

Suggested wine A really good dry bordeaux, such as Château Haut-Brion Larrivet.

CRAYFISH

Crayfish are small fresh water crustaceans with a particularly light and delicate flavour. They must be cooked alive. They resemble the lobster in appearance but are very much smaller and have a far more subtle taste. They are seldom used in British cooking although they are plentiful in some rivers. Unfortunately few British cooks are willing to take the trouble to prepare them.

To choose crayfish The best crayfish are those with dark brown, almost black shells which turn a bright red when cooked. Those with grey or bluish shells will turn a dull pink during cooking.

Small and medium-sized crayfish weighing up to 50 grams are used mainly for soups, sauces and garnishes. The choicest crayfish are those weighing about 75 grams, which are becoming so scarce in French rivers that they now often have to be imported. These large crayfish are prepared *en buisson*, which means cooked in a court-bouillon, served piled high in a dome, or with a Bordelaise sauce (see p. 350).

To keep crayfish Crayfish should be kept alive in a deep basket filled with grass or nettles and covered with nettles, in a cool larder or cellar. This way they will live for 4 to 5 days, or up to a week in cold weather. Females are generally preferred to males. Their roe is used for crayfish butter and in sauces.

To prepare crayfish The black intestinal gut must always be removed. It has a bitter taste which is particularly strong and unpleasant in spring during the breeding season.

The gut may be removed in two ways:
1. Pull out the middle section of the tail by twisting quickly and pull gently from above so that the gut comes out in one long thread.
2. This is a more difficult operation but it keeps the tail intact: insert the point of a small knife beneath the end of the gut in the very small opening near the end of the tail and pull gently on the gut, drawing it out between the end of the knife and the tip of your thumb, being careful not to break it.

Crayfish must be cooked immediately after they have been gutted or else their juices will run out through the hole left by the intestine.

Wash the crayfish in cold water and drain them in a sieve or colander. Plunge each one into a pan of bubbling court-bouillon or a pan of sizzling butter (according to the recipe) as soon as it is gutted and cleaned.

Some French restaurants do not gut crayfish. This does not matter provided the crayfish have been left to starve in running cold water for 24 hours.

To cook crayfish Put the live crayfish into the cooking liquid and cook very quickly at a high temperature so that they do not dry out. The braising-pan or sauté-pan in which they are cooked must be wide enough to allow all of them to be close to the heat, which means that you can sauté them without removing the lid. Crayfish should not be cooked in too much liquid. In the old days, the grandest chefs would specify 'a glass' of liquid, or 1·2 decilitres, 'for 24 crayfish'. Never cook crayfish in red wine; it turns them black. Allow 6 crayfish per person.

HÔTEL DE FRANCE *
NANTUA (AIN)

ÉCREVISSES À LA NAGE AUX AROMATES

A simple dish of crayfish served in their cooking liquid. This is still one of the best ways of eating crayfish.

For 6 people

48 medium-sized live crayfish (about 2kg)

Court-bouillon
1½l water
2 carrots, cut into rounds
6 cloves garlic, peeled
15g rock salt

15g black peppercorns
sprigs of parsley, with stalks
thyme
10 mint leaves
5 sage leaves
1 bottle good very dry white wine (Pouilly, Chablis, Mâcon or Seyssel)

Leave the crayfish under running water for 1 hour. Meanwhile, put the vegetables, seasonings and herbs into a large stewpan with the water and boil for 30 minutes. Add the wine, bring back to the boil and continue boiling for a further 5 to 6 minutes. Drain the crayfish, plunge them into the fast-boiling liquid and boil rapidly, covered, for 5 minutes at the most. Remove the pan from the stove and leave to cool, keeping the pan covered.

To serve Arrange the crayfish in a dome, one on top of the other, in a deep soup tureen or salad bowl. Remove the herbs and garlic from the court-bouillon, leaving the carrots and peppercorns. Reduce and pour over the crayfish. Serve warm.

Suggested wine Whatever wine you have used to cook the crayfish, well chilled.

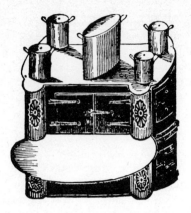

BARRIER ★ ★ ★
TOURS (INDRE-ET-LOIRE)

ÉCREVISSES DU PAYS AU VOUVRAY

*The crayfish are flambéed with cognac, cooked in Vouvray wine
and served in a light and frothy cream and butter sauce.*

For 8 people

50 fine live crayfish
150g unsalted butter
200g fresh double cream
4 tbs *mirepoix bordelaise*
  (shallots stewed in butter
  moistened with red
  burgundy, reduced to a
  glaze and sieved to produce
  2 tbs)[1]

½dl good champagne or cognac
1dl very good dry white
  Vouvray
salt, crushed black peppercorns, small pinch of
  cayenne pepper

To cook Clean the crayfish carefully, freshen under running
water and gut them. Heat 100g of the butter in a large copper or
heavy enamel saucepan, add the crayfish and sauté them over
high heat for 2 to 3 minutes. Pour over the cognac and flambé,
stirring the crayfish. Pour in the Vouvray to put out the flames.
Stir in the seasonings and the *mirepoix*, put the lid on the pan
and boil briskly for 5 minutes. Crayfish should always be cooked
quickly. Transfer the crayfish to a warmed deep serving-dish and
keep hot while you finish the sauce.

To make the sauce Add the cream to the liquid in the pan and
reduce over a high heat until the mixture thickens slightly. Strain
into a small saucepan, place over low heat and whisk in the
remaining 50g of butter, a piece at a time. Adjust the seasoning,
which should be fairly peppery, and coat the crayfish with the
very hot sauce.

Suggested wine Dry Vouvray or Pouilly fumé.

[1] Although a technique from Bordeaux burgundy is used because with its higher degree of
alcohol it retains both colour and flavour better than bordeaux wine (*editor's note*).

HÔTEL DE FRANCE *
SÉZANNE (MARNE)

ÉCREVISSES AU CHAMPAGNE

Champagne gives a delicious flavour to the stock and goes very well with crayfish.

For 4 people

24 good crayfish
1 bottle still champagne
2 carrots, finely sliced
2 onions, finely sliced

2 cloves garlic, unpeeled
whole black peppercorns
salt
1 bouquet garni (thyme, bay
   leaf, parsley, chervil, fresh
   tarragon and 1 sprig fennel)

Wash and drain the crayfish. Do not gut them[1]. Put the champagne in an enamelled stewpan with the carrots, onions, pepper, salt and the bouquet garni and boil for 10 minutes. Plunge the crayfish into the liquid and boil rapidly for 12 to 14 minutes. Leave the crayfish in the liquid until they are lukewarm.

Arrange them in a dome, one on top of the other, in a deep soup tureen or salad bowl. Reduce the cooking liquid slightly and pour over the crayfish.

Suggested wine Still champagne, chilled.

[1]We are not responsible for this direction (*editor's note*).

ROSTANG * *
SASSENAGE NEAR GRENOBLE (ISÈRE)

GRATIN DE QUEUES D'ÉCREVISSES

This dish, one of the supreme achievements of Dauphiné cooking, seldom appears on restaurant menus nowadays. This classic recipe is a great favourite.

For 4 people

1kg live crayfish (24–28)
4–5 tbs unsalted butter
a *mirepoix* of carrots and
   shallots, very finely chopped
1dl good cognac
1dl good dry white wine
tomatoes

1 sprig thyme
½ bay leaf
salt, freshly milled black
   pepper
2 cups fresh double cream

Beurre manié
1 tbs flour
1 tbs unsalted butter

To cook Wash the crayfish and leave for a few minutes in very clean water; gut them. Heat the butter in a large saucepan, preferably copper, and add the carrots and the shallots. Stew gently, stirring, for 2 minutes. Add the crayfish, cover and sauté for 5 minutes, shaking the pan. Pour the cognac into the pan and set alight, stirring it well into the crayfish so that the flavour is thoroughly absorbed. Put out the flames by pouring in the wine, then add the tomato and herbs.

Put the lid back on the pan and cook for a further 5 minutes.

To make the sauce Detach the heads from the bodies. Put the heads back in the pan, crush them lightly and cook for a few more minutes to reduce the sauce. Add the cream, bring slowly back to the boil and strain the sauce through a wire sieve lined with muslin into a small enamelled cast-iron saucepan, pressing on the crayfish and twisting the muslin towards the end of the operation to extract all the juices. Heat the sauce and thicken with the *beurre manié*. Whisk the sauce with a wire whisk until it thickens. It should be rich and smooth.

To serve Shell the crayfish. Spoon a layer of the hot sauce into the bottom of a copper or enamelled cast-iron oven dish. Arrange the crayfish on top, cover with the rest of the sauce, and glaze the dish under a very hot grill for about 2 minutes. Serve immediately.

Suggested wine A very dry white wine with a good bouquet, such as Côte-de-Beaune, Meursault or Chassagne Montrachet.

LUCAS-CARTON ★ ★
PARIS 8e: 1 PLACE DE LA MADELEINE

CASSOLETTE DE QUEUES D'ÉCREVISSES À LA NANTUA

A delicious dish of crayfish cooked in white wine and brandy, served with sauce made from the crayfish stock and enriched with cream, then browned under the grill.

For 4 people

3kg live crayfish
1½dl cognac
½ bottle good dry white wine
3 tomatoes, peeled, seeded and
   pulped
2 tbs tomato purée
3 tbs fresh double cream
3 tbs unsalted butter
1 sprig thyme, bay leaf
salt, freshly milled black
   pepper
a pinch cayenne pepper

Mirepoix
1 carrot
1 onion
1 slice celeriac
½ fennel bulb, finely chopped
3 tbs unsalted butter

Beurre manié
1 tbs unsalted butter
1½ tbs flour

Garnish (optional)
a few slivers of truffle
puff-pastry crescents

To cook the crayfish Finely chop all the vegetables for the *mirepoix*, stew them in the butter and oil for a few moments in a sauté-pan and add the crayfish. Season with salt and pepper and sauté. Pour over the cognac and set light to it, shaking the pan. Add the white wine, bring to the boil, add the tomato pulp and purée, the thyme and the bay leaf. Cover the pan and cook gently for 10 minutes. Remove the crayfish and allow to cool before shelling. Discard the heads, reserving the creamy parts inside and the juice but removing the little sack, which is bitter. Put the tails in an oven dish and cover.

To make the Nantua sauce Add the creamy parts and the liquid from the heads to the juices in the pan. Bring to the boil and then press them through a conical sieve into another pan. Reduce this sauce to half the original quantity. Thicken slightly with the *beurre manié*.

Add the cream and whisk in the butter until the sauce thickens, but do not let it boil. Correct the seasoning and add a small pinch of cayenne pepper.

To serve Coat the crayfish with the sauce and glaze under a very hot grill for a few moments. Garnish with finely sliced truffles and little puff-pastry crescents if desired.

Suggested wine Crépy, Seyssel or Meursault.

LA TOQUE BLANCHE *
MEGÈVE (HAUTE-SAVOIE)

OMELETTE ROYALE

This crayfish and truffle omelette is a true gourmet's delight. It is coated with a sauce made from the heads and shells of the crayfish flavoured with cognac and white wine and thickened with cream. The filling and sauce may be prepared in advance.

For 4 people

Omelette
12 eggs
salt, freshly milled black pepper
1 tbs cold water
5 tbs unsalted butter

Filling
16 medium-sized live crayfish, ready for cooking
1–2 truffles, peeled and very finely sliced

Sauce
the shells and heads of the crayfish (with the gut removed)
4 tbs unsalted butter
2 tomatoes, peeled, seeded and pulped
2 shallots, very finely chopped
½dl cognac
1dl very dry white wine
1dl water
1½dl fresh double cream

Cook the crayfish in a court-bouillon for 10 minutes. Remove, shell the tails and put them aside.

Cook the heads and shells very gently in the butter, shaking the pan. Add the shallots and tomatoes and stew with the lid on the pan for about 5 minutes. Pour in the cognac to deglaze the juices, reduce for 1 minute and add the wine and water. Cook, covered, for 15 minutes. Strain the liquid through a conical sieve into a thick saucepan, pressing down the shells to extract all the juices. Reduce the liquid by half, add the cream and correct the seasoning. Keep the sauce very hot while you cook the omelette.

To make the omelette Break the eggs into a bowl, add salt, 2 turns of the pepper mill and the water and beat with a fork. Melt the butter in a large omelette pan and when it starts to bubble add the beaten egg mixture. As soon as the bottom starts to set add the meat from the crayfish tails and sliced truffle and scramble lightly with a fork. The omelette should remain slightly runny in the centre. Fold and roll, then slide on to an oval heated serving dish.

Coat the omelette with the hot sauce and serve.

Suggested wine Puligny Montrachet.

LE CHAPON FIN ★ ★
PAUL BLANC, SON OF LA MÈRE BLANC OF VONNAS (AIN)
THOISSEY (AIN)

SALADE DE QUEUES D'ÉCREVISSES
A lovely hors d'oeuvre, deliciously fresh and beautiful to look at.

For 3 or 4 people

20–24 fine crayfish
1l court-bouillon, well seasoned and cooked for 20 minutes

Mayonnaise

2 egg yolks
Dijon mustard
salt, freshly milled black pepper
groundnut oil

juice of about ½ lemon (to taste)
a few drops vinegar

Vinaigrette dressing
Dijon mustard
a very little wine vinegar
juice of ½ lemon
salt, freshly milled black pepper
groundnut oil
a large pinch chervil, very finely chopped
a large pinch tarragon, very finely chopped

Clean the crayfish, gut and wash them under running water. Boil them in the court-bouillon for 5 minutes. Remove the pan from the stove, leaving the crayfish in the court-bouillon. Shell them when they have cooled sufficiently, leaving 3 or 4 unshelled to use as decoration.

Season the shelled tails with lemony mayonnaise or vinaigrette dressing.

To serve Arrange 3 or 4 young lettuce leaves per person in the shape of a flower, removing the central rib. Put a portion of dressed crayfish in the middle of each flower. Decorate each portion with a whole unshelled crayfish. Lay out on a serving-dish. Serve very cold.

Suggested wine Crépy, Seyssel or white Ermitage, well chilled.

FROGS AND SNAILS

FROGS

Frogs are a very great delicacy and it is a pity that they are still unpopular in Britain. They are highly regarded in France where they appear on restaurant menus all over the country and are sometimes prepared at home. Only the hind legs are eaten and in France these are sold skewered, usually by the dozen. If they are small allow 10 to 12 per person; a skewer of 12 large ones will serve two people.

Whole frogs should be prepared as follows: skin the frogs, joint them at the top of the thighs, leaving the two hind legs joined in one piece. Cut off the toes with scissors. Leave the legs to soak for 2 or 3 hours in a large bowl of cold water, chilled with ice cubes, to rid them of all traces of bloody fibres. Wipe them and soak in cold milk. Dry carefully before cooking. They will take about 10 minutes to cook.

LA MÈRE BLANC ★ ★
VONNAS (AIN)

GRENOUILLES SAUTÉES À LA MEUNIÈRE

A deceptively simple recipe. The incomparable flavour of freshly caught frogs from the Bressan marshes is enhanced by Madame Blanc's culinary skill. The quality and quantity of the butter used is one of the reasons for its success.

For 4 people

4 dozen frogs
sifted flour
250g unsalted butter
salt, freshly milled black
   pepper

2 cloves garlic, squeezed
   through a garlic press and
   crushed
2 tbs parsley, finely chopped

Cut off the frogs' heads and feet. Tie up the legs and soak them in cold water for 1 hour. Drain and dry in a cloth.

To cook Dust the frogs lightly with flour, shaking off any excess. Heat the butter gently in a frying pan and add the frogs when it is very hot but not brown. Cook quickly for 10 to 12 minutes, turning over half-way through. Season with salt and pepper. As soon as the frogs are an even golden brown, transfer them to a deep round serving-dish, preferably a metal one. Mix the garlic and parsley together with your fingers and sprinkle the mixture over the frogs. Strain over the very hot buttery cooking juices.

Suggested wine Pouilly Fuissé, well chilled.

RESTAURANT DEMORNEX *
SAINT-JEAN-DE-GONVILLE (AIN)

CUISSES DE GRENOUILLES SAUTÉES AUX FINES HERBES
The frogs' legs are simply sautéed in butter flavoured with garlic and sprinkled with fresh herbs.

For 4 people

about 30–32 frogs' legs, well dried
flour
6 tbs unsalted butter
2 small cloves garlic, squeezed through a garlic press

1 tbs oil
2 tbs parsley and chervil, finely chopped
1 tbs chives, finely cut with scissors

Sauté the frogs in a frying-pan containing 2 tablespoons of very hot butter and add another 2 tablespoons while they are taking colour. Meanwhile, pound the garlic with the olive oil. When the frogs are cooked and golden, taking about 8 minutes, reduce the heat, add the garlic mixture, the remaining 2 tablespoons of butter and 1 tablespoon of the chopped mixed herbs, stirring to mix well with the frogs. The mixture should be very hot but should not boil. Taste and correct the seasoning.

To serve Arrange the frogs in a wide shallow dish. Pour the cooking juices over them and sprinkle with the rest of the herbs. Lemon juice may be added, according to taste.

Suggested wine Pouilly Fuissé or Mâcon blanc.

AUBERGE DE L'ILL * * *
ILLHAEUSERN (HAUT-RHIN)

GRENOUILLES AU RIESLING
Frogs from Alsace are cooked in Alsatian Riesling, which is also drunk with the dish.

For 4 people	salt, freshly milled black pepper
30 frogs' legs	1 clove garlic, crushed
5 tbs unsalted butter	1 tbs *beurre manié*★
3 shallots, very finely chopped	1 tbs mixed herbs, chopped
1dl Alsatian Riesling	2 tbs fresh double cream
4 tbs chicken stock	

To cook Heat 2 tablespoons of the butter in a sauté-pan; soften the shallots in the butter without colouring, add the frogs' legs and another 2 tablespoons of butter. Sauté, then add the wine and stock, which should cover them. Season with salt and pepper, add the garlic and cook for 10 minutes. Transfer the frogs' legs to a heated metal serving-dish.

To serve Reduce the cooking liquid and bind and thicken with the *beurre manié*. Using a wire whisk, beat the cream and the remaining tablespoon of butter into the sauce.

Coat the frogs' legs with the sauce and sprinkle with the mixed herbs.

Suggested wine Alsatian Riesling, well chilled on ice.

SNAILS

Snails hibernate from October to March; this is the best time to eat them. From the end of spring until the beginning of autumn snails roam among hedges and fields, feeding voraciously off grass and weeds. This continuous search for food toughens their flesh. At the end of the summer, sensing the approaching winter, they eat more and more and in October, fat and replete, they retire into their shells behind a fine layer of plaster-like material. They discard for the winter the hard substance they have amassed round their 'collar'.

In France, where snails are very popular, two main types are eaten, known as *escargots de Bourgogne* or *de vignes* and *petits gris*.

HÔTEL DE PARIS ET DE LA POSTE ★ ★
SENS (YONNE)

ESCARGOTS À LA BOURGUIGNONNE

The snails are cooked in a court-bouillon containing white burgundy and garnished with parsley butter flavoured with garlic and shallot.

For 4 people

4 dozen snails, their shells closed for the winter
1 cup rock salt
1 cup wine vinegar
½ cup flour

Court-bouillon
1 bottle white burgundy and the same amount of well-flavoured stock
2 carrots, finely chopped
2 onions, finely chopped

1 bouquet garni (parsley, bay leaf and a strong flavouring of thyme)
salt, crushed white peppercorns

Burgundy butter
2 tbs parsley, very finely chopped
1 dsp garlic, very finely chopped
1 tbs shallot, very finely chopped
1 tbs table salt, freshly milled black pepper to taste

To prepare the snails Remove the hard covering which seals in the snail. Wash the snails thoroughly under running water and leave them for 2 hours in a good amount of water with the rock salt, vinegar and flour. Wash the snails again in plenty of water and blanch them for 5 minutes in a large stewpan filled with boiling water. Drain them and run them under cold water. Take each snail out of its shell and cut off the black part at the end of its body.

To cook Put the snails in a pan with the white wine and stock. The liquid should completely cover the snails. Add the carrots, onion, bouquet garni, salt and pepper and simmer over very low heat. The small variety known as *petits gris de Bourgogne* should be cooked for 3 hours and large snails for 4 hours.

Leave them to cool in the cooking liquid.

To prepare the burgundy butter Work all the ingredients together with a fork to obtain a smooth, well-blended paste.

To arrange the dish Press a nut of burgundy butter into each shell. Add a well-drained snail to each shell, and another nut of butter, smoothing off with the flat of a knife so that the butter is level with the shell.

Arrange the snails on special snail dishes or any ovenproof serving-dish. Heat through in a moderate oven, 165°–170°C, 325°–350°F, without letting the butter boil. Serve immediately with very fresh bread, which should be used to soak up the butter that escapes from the snails.

Suggested wine A good white burgundy.

FRESH-WATER FISH

TRUITES À LA CRÈME

Trout cooked in butter enriched with mushroom stock and cream.

For 4 people

4 trout, each weighing 180–
200g, ready for cooking,
salted and floured
200g cultivated mushrooms

7 tbs unsalted butter
salt, freshly milled black
pepper
lemon juice
a small pinch cayenne pepper
½l fresh double cream

To cook Cut the stalks off the mushrooms, slice the caps finely, soften them in 3 tablespoons of the butter and season with salt, pepper and lemon juice.

Warm the rest of the butter in an ovenproof dish and when it is very hot but not browned add the trout. Cook them quickly on both sides and when they are a light golden colour add the mushrooms and their cooking juices, the cream and a small pinch of cayenne pepper. Bring to the boil and put under the grill for 7 to 8 minutes to finish the cooking and brown the trout.

Serve as soon as the surface is evenly browned, in the dish in which they were cooked.

Suggested wine Pouilly Fuissé or white Seyssel.

PETIT VATEL *
ALENÇON (ORNE)

TRUITES FARCIES SAUCE NORMANDE

Trout stuffed with whiting and mushrooms, poached in white wine and shallots, served in a sauce thickened with cream and egg yolk, flavoured with calvados.

For 2 people

2 trout, each weighing 200g
1 dl white wine
1 dl cold water
2 shallots, finely chopped

Stuffing
100g whiting, flesh only
125g mushrooms

2 tbs double cream
1 egg white
salt, freshly milled black
  pepper

Sauce
2 tbs double cream
1 egg yolk
2 tbs calvados
a few drops lemon juice

To prepare Carefully clean, wash and gut the fish, remove the backbone and dry them in a cloth.

To make the stuffing Pound the ingredients in a mortar or put them through a blender. Press half the stuffing into the space left by the backbone in each trout, between the two fillets and tie up both ends of the trout.

To cook the trout Arrange in a deep fireproof dish. Pour over the white wine and cold water and add the chopped shallots. Poach the trout for about 10 minutes.

To make the sauce Strain the cooking liquid into a small saucepan. Reduce to one-third of the original quantity. Add the egg yolk, cream, calvados and lemon juice. Check the seasoning.

To serve Untie the trout and remove the skin. Arrange them on a serving dish. Coat with the sauce and serve very hot.

Suggested wine Muscadet.

HOSTELLERIE DE LA FUSTE *
LA FUSTE-PAR-VALENSOLE (NEAR MANOSQUE) (ALPES-DE-HAUTE-PROVENCE)

TRUITES AUX AMANDES
The trout are cooked in oil until they are golden, flavoured with lemon juice and covered with almonds browned in butter. The dish is decorated with shaped half lemons.

For 6 people

6 live trout, each weighing
  250g
flour
1 dl groundnut oil
the juice of 2 lemons

6 half lemons, fluted and cut
  into basket shapes
250g flaked almonds, half
  bitter, half sweet
salt, freshly milled black
  pepper
3 tbs unsalted butter

Stun the trout, make sure that they are completely lifeless, gut them through the gills, rinse and dry them. Sprinkle them with salt and coat them lightly with flour.

To cook Pour the oil into a large frying-pan and heat it until it is very hot but not smoking. When the oil starts to sizzle add the trout and cook them over a lively heat for 5 minutes on each side. Drain all the oil from the frying-pan, sprinkle the trout with lemon juice and transfer them to an oval metal dish. Keep warm.

To serve Put the butter into the same frying-pan, let it melt and add the almonds. Stir the almonds over a lively heat until they turn golden; season with salt and pepper. Coat the trout with the butter and almonds, decorate with the half lemons and serve immediately.

Suggested wine A dry white wine from Provence.

RESTAURANT DE LA CÔTE-D'OR ★ ★
CHÂTILLON-SUR-SEINE (CÔTE-D'OR)

TRUITES CHABLISIENNES
The trout are very simply cooked in the oven with butter, good Chablis wine, completely reduced, and cream.

For 4 people

4 trout, each weighing 200g
salt, freshly milled black
   pepper
3 tbs unsalted butter

3 tbs shallots, finely chopped
1½dl good dry Chablis
¾l fresh very thick double
   cream

To prepare Gut the trout, clean them well but don't wash them, and season with salt and pepper. Lay them in a very well buttered oven dish and put a few knobs of butter on top of the trout.

To cook Bake for 5 minutes in an oven preheated to 175°C, 350°F. Sprinkle the trout with the shallot and return the dish to the oven for 3 minutes. Pour in the white wine and let it reduce in the oven until the liquid is all but dried up. Add the cream and simmer the trout in the oven for 10 minutes. The cream will have reduced by about half, the sauce will be smooth and deliciously flavoured.

Serve very hot indeed on hot plates.

Suggested wine Chablis.

ALBERT 1er ET MILAN ★
CHAMONIX (HAUTE-SAVOIE)

TRUITE AUX NOISETTES
The trout is rolled in powdered almonds, fried in butter, baked in the oven and served in a butter sauce with grilled hazelnuts and decorated with parsley and lemon.

For each person

1 trout, weighing 180–200g
1 egg, beaten with a fork
50g powdered almonds
2 tbs clarified unsalted butter
1 tbs fresh butter

lemon juice
20g hazelnuts, chopped and
  grilled
1 slice lemon
salt, freshly milled black pepper
1 tbs parsley, chopped

To prepare Gut the trout and salt the inside. Wipe, dip in milk and drain off the excess liquid. Flour lightly, dip in the beaten egg and roll in the powdered almonds.

Blend together the remaining egg and the rest of the powdered almonds and press the mixture into the inside of the trout.

To cook Fry the trout in the clarified butter, colouring each side. Finish cooking in a moderate oven, about 150°C, 300°F. Melt the butter in a small saucepan, add the hazel nuts and let them become lightly golden. They must not brown.

To serve Arrange the trout on a serving-dish, pour the butter and hazelnuts over, then sprinkle in the lemon juice to make the butter foam. Season with salt and pepper and decorate with the lemon slice and chopped parsley.

Serve with potatoes, trimmed and rounded and steamed.

Suggested wine Crépy de Savoie.

HÔTEL DE CRO-MAGNON *
LES EYZIES-DE-TAYAC (DORDOGNE)

TRUITES FARCIES AUX FINES HERBES

The stuffing is a simple one of breadcrumbs and very finely chopped fresh herbs.

For 4 people

4 river trout
2 tbs dried white breadcrumbs
1 tbs tarragon, very finely
  chopped
1 tbs parsley, very finely
  chopped

1 tbs chives, finely cut with
  scissors
groundnut oil
1½dl dry white wine
lemon juice (optional)
salt, freshly milled black
  pepper

To prepare Gut the trout through the gills and carefully clean the insides. Dry with a cloth, inside and out, and season with salt.

Prepare the stuffing by mixing together in a bowl the breadcrumbs and herbs. Bind with a few drops of oil and season very lightly with salt and pepper. Insert some of the stuffing into each trout, through the gills.

To cook Roll the trout in the oil, arrange them in a well buttered oven dish and cook in a hot oven, 200°–215°C, 375°–400°F, for about 10 minutes.

To serve Deglaze the juices in the cooking dish with the white wine and lemon juice to taste. Serve straight from the oven.

Suggested wine Dry white Bergerac.

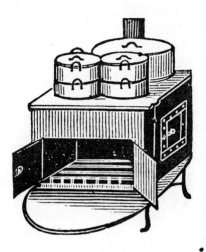

HÔTEL PÉGURIER *
AVÈNE-LES-BAINS (HÉRAULT)

TRUITES AU LARD
These taste like smoked trout and the sauce, strongly flavoured with lemon, is delicious.

For 4 people

4 trout, each weighing 150g, gutted and salted
4 rashers smoked bacon, very thinly sliced
2 tbs shallots, finely minced

juice of 2 lemons
¼l dry white wine
4 level tbs fresh butter, to finish the sauce
½ cup white breadcrumbs
salt, freshly milled black pepper

Sprinkle the shallots into a buttered ovenproof dish. Interlard the trout with the bacon and put them into the dish. Half cover them with the wine and cook in a hot oven 200°C, 400°F, for 10 to 12 minutes. Take out of the oven, remove the bacon and set it aside. Arrange the trout in an ovenproof oval serving dish.

To make the sauce Pour the liquor in which the trout was cooked into a saucepan. Add the bacon and lemon juice and boil to reduce by about half. Add the butter bit by bit, in little pieces, stirring the sauce continuously with a wooden spoon to prevent lumps forming. Adjust the seasoning. Pass the sauce through a fine strainer. Reheat.

To arrange the dish Sprinkle the trout with breadcrumbs, garnish with the bacon rashers and cover with the sauce, taking care not to wash off the breadcrumbs in the process. Put the dish under the grill for 2 minutes and serve immediately.

Suggested wine Dry white, the same as used for the sauce; Chablis or Pouilly Fuissé or a rosé from Provence, well chilled.

CHEZ GARIN * *
PARIS 5e: 9 RUE LAGRANGE

TRUITES SOUFFLÉES DE CHEZ GARIN

A dish of great subtlety. The trout are stuffed with a mousseline *of pike flavoured with truffle, which rises like a soufflé during the cooking. Crayfish butter, fresh cream and a few sultanas are added to the cooking juices to make the sauce.*

For 4 people

4 trout, each weighing 250g
100g unsalted butter

Pike mousseline
200g pike flesh
2 egg whites
2dl fresh double cream
1 truffle, chopped

salt, freshly milled black
  pepper, grated nutmeg
2 tbs crayfish butter
2dl fresh double cream
2 tbs seedless sultanas,
  steeped in lukewarm tea
  until they swell, and then
  drained

To prepare Remove the central bone of the trout by cutting along the back. Do not slit along the stomach. Gut, dry the insides and season with salt and pepper.

To make the pike stuffing Press the pike flesh through a very fine sieve or put through the blender. Gradually work in the egg whites with a wooden spoon or spatula, using half an egg white at a time. Fold in the cream a little at a time and, stirring vigorously all the time, add the truffle, salt, pepper and nutmeg. Chill in the refrigerator.

To cook the trout Stuff the trout with the pike *mousseline*. Arrange in a well-buttered oven dish, letting them rest on their stomachs. Spoon the rest of the butter between the trout and season with salt and pepper. Cover with a piece of buttered greaseproof paper and cook for 16 to 20 minutes in a moderate oven, 165°–170°C, 325°–350°F.

To serve Add to the dish in which the trout have been cooked the crayfish butter, the cream and sultanas. Heat the dish under the grill for a few moments and serve very hot.

Suggested wine A white burgundy of good vintage, such as Meursault or Montrachet.

BARRIER ★ ★ ★
TOURS (INDRE-ET-LOIRE)

MOUSSELINE DE TRUITE AU COULIS D'ÉCREVISSES

A classic, very delicate mousseline *of trout, moulded in little individual moulds and coated with crayfish sauce. The crayfish heads, stuffed with some of the* mousseline *and poached, are used to decorate the dish.*

For 8 people

1 very fresh trout, weighing 1kg
500g double cream
1 egg white, unbeaten
salt, freshly milled black pepper
3 tbs fresh unsalted butter
12 live crayfish, washed and gutted
¼l double cream

Mirepoix
1 carrot, finely chopped
1 onion, finely chopped
3 or 4 shallots, finely chopped
3 tbs unsalted butter
¼l dry white wine
tarragon, parsley

Beurre manié
2 tbs flour
2 tbs unsalted butter

To prepare Fillet the trout and purée the flesh in a blender. Put into a terrine resting in a larger container filled with ice cubes and work it with a wooden spoon or spatula with the egg white and a seasoning of salt and pepper. Add the cream, a little at a time, working it in vigorously with a spatula until the mixture becomes light and swells. Leave in the refrigerator for at least 1 hour.

To make the crayfish sauce Stew the vegetables for the *mirepoix* gently in the butter until they are transparent and tender. Add the crayfish and sauté them in the *mirepoix* until they turn a good bright red; season with salt and 2 turns of the pepper mill. Add the herbs, moisten with the wine and cook for 10 minutes, tossing two or three times. Leave the crayfish to cool, then shell them. The tails will be added to the sauce. Empty the heads, reserving both them and the juices and white parts inside them but discarding the little stomach pouch containing sand.

Pound the juices and meat from inside the crayfish heads with the tail shells and 3 tablespoons of butter, press through a sieve and reserve the resulting crayfish butter.

To assemble the basic ingredients of the sauce Reduce the crayfish cooking liquid in a small saucepan, preferably an enamelled cast-iron one. Whisk in the crayfish butter.

To cook the mousseline Press most of the *mousseline* of trout into individual buttered moulds, reserving a little. Cover them and poach them very gently for 15 minutes in a pan of simmering water. Turn out on to a heated plate.

The shells of the crayfish heads are filled with the rest of the *mousseline* and poached separately.

To serve Finish the sauce just before serving. Reheat, beat in the cream with a wire whisk and thicken with the *beurre manié*. Whisk the sauce, add the crayfish and coat the individual *mousselines* with the very hot sauce.

Decorate with the stuffed crayfish heads.

Suggested wine A very good dry Vouvray or dry Montlouis, well chilled.

AUBERGE DU PÈRE BISE * * *
TALLOIRES (HAUTE-SAVOIE)

TRUITE AU PORTO

An outstanding recipe from an exceptional chef. It is a lake salmon trout stuffed with a mixture of celery, carrots, truffles and button mushrooms, bound with diced quenelle *of trout. It is moistened with a very little Noilly Prat and equal proportions of port, sherry and very dry white wine. The sauce is light and enriched with cream, then finished with a very little Mousseline sauce — Hollandaise sauce thickened with cream. The dish is decorated with slivers of truffle and fluted mushrooms.*

For 2 people

1 trout from Lac d'Annecy, preferably a salmon trout, weighing 450–500g
2 shallots, very finely chopped
2 tbs Noilly Prat vermouth
½dl port
½dl sherry
½dl good very dry white wine
salt, freshly milled black pepper

Stuffing
3 tbs *julienne* of celery, carrot,

truffle and fresh mushrooms
2 tbs diced *quenelle* of trout*

Sauce
1 cup fresh double cream
2 tbs Mousseline sauce (see p. 353)
a few drops lemon juice

Garnish
2 slivers truffle
2 mushrooms, fluted

To make the stuffing Gently stew, separately, each of the vegetables for the stuffing, in butter. Add the diced *quenelle* of trout and mix all the ingredients very carefully together.

To cook the trout Gut the trout carefully, removing the back bone without spoiling the shape of the trout and without opening it completely. Season with salt. Insert the stuffing into the trout. Do not tie it up.

Sprinkle a well-buttered ovenproof dish, preferably enamelled cast-iron, with the chopped shallots. Lay the trout in the dish and pour over the vermouth, port, sherry and white wine. Cover with buttered greaseproof paper. Bring the liquid to simmering-point on top of the stove, then put the dish into a moderately hot oven, 175°C, 350°F, and cook for about 20 minutes. Keep the trout hot under the paper.

To make the sauce Strain the cooking liquid from the trout through muslin into a good small saucepan, enamelled cast-iron if possible, reduce the liquid to a glaze, beat in the cream to thicken the sauce and finish by beating in the *mousseline* and a few drops of lemon juice. Adjust the seasoning. Strain the finished sauce through muslin and heat it through without letting it boil.

To serve Carefully transfer the trout to a heated and lightly buttered silver serving-dish and coat with the sauce, which must be very hot.

Decorate with the slivers of truffle and fluted mushrooms. Serve immediately on heated plates.

Suggested wine A dry white bordeaux such as Château Larrivet.

HÔTEL ROYAL *
ÉVIAN (SAVOIE)

TRUITE DU LAC LÉMAN À LA ROYALE

A truly regal dish if the trout and the sauce are perfectly cooked. The recipe requires very rare ingredients and should preferably be made and eaten on the spot.

For 4 people
- 1 salmon trout, weighing 1kg, seasoned with salt, and prepared for cooking
- 2 tbs shallots, finely chopped
- 125g mushrooms, very finely sliced
- 2dl good cognac
- 1 bottle Crépy or Seyssel wine or, if unavailable, Chablis
- salt, freshly milled black pepper

Sauce
- ½l double cream

Garnish
- 12 crayfish, cooked *à l'américaine* (see p. 348), with their sauce
- 6 mushrooms, fluted and cooked
- 6 puff-pastry crescents
- 1 truffle, very finely sliced

To cook the trout Sprinkle a well-buttered oven dish with half the shallots and half the mushrooms. Lay the trout on top and spread the rest of the shallots and mushrooms over and round it. Pour over the cognac and the wine, which should come no more than two-thirds of the way up the sides of the trout. Season with pepper and a very little salt, cover with a piece of buttered grease-proof paper and heat gently on top of the stove. When the liquid begins to shudder, transfer the dish to an oven preheated to a moderate temperature, 170°–175°C, 325°–350°F and cook for about 25 minutes, basting the trout frequently. Remove the dish from the oven, skin the trout and transfer it to an oval serving-dish. Cover with fresh greaseproof paper and keep hot.

To make the sauce Strain the cooking liquid from the trout and from the crayfish through a conical sieve into a good small saucepan. Reduce to a quarter of its original quantity over fairly high heat, add the cream and reduce again for several minutes over a moderate heat until you have $\frac{1}{2}$ litre of sauce. Check the seasoning.

To arrange the dish Arrange the shelled crayfish round the trout and put the fluted mushrooms on top. Coat with all the sauce and decorate with the slivers of truffle. Decorate the edge of the dish with the crayfish shells and pastry crescents.

Suggested wine A first-class Crépy or a very good Seyssel; alternatively, a fine Chablis.

PAVILLON DE L'ERMITAGE *
CHAVOIRE (HAUTE-SAVOIE)

OMBLE CHEVALIER DU LAC D'ARGENT

Char is the rarest and finest of fresh-water trout. In this recipe the char is cooked very carefully in butter.

For each person

1 char[1] (from Lac d'Annecy, if possible) weighing 250–300g, which is the best weight for this type of fish
unsalted butter

salt, freshly milled black pepper
1 lemon, fluted and sliced
parsley, very finely chopped
lemon juice

To prepare the fish Gut and wash the fish, remove the fins and sprinkle the inside with salt. Dip the fish into milk, then dust with flour and leave for a few moments. Heat a generous amount of butter in a metal ovenproof dish, or a frying-pan, until it turns the colour of hazelnuts. Add the char, fry it quickly on each side over high heat and then transfer the dish to an oven preheated to 175°C, 350°F. Cook for 8 to 10 minutes, depending on the size of the fish. Drain off all the cooking butter, transfer the char to a heated metal serving-dish and season with salt. Heat another large amount of fresh butter until it turns a pale nut-brown, add lemon juice, season with salt and pepper and pour over the fish.

To serve Decorate the fish with one or two fluted lemon slices and dust the lemon with a pinch of parsley. Serve very hot.

Suggested wine White Crépy from Savoy.

¹The char may be replaced by a lake trout, preferably a salmon trout (*editor's note*).

AUBERGE SAINT-JACQUES ✱
ORLÉANS (LOIRET)

SAUMON DE LOIRE GRILLÉ, BEURRE MAÎTRE D'HÔTEL

A grilled fresh-water salmon with parsley butter; it may be served with small steamed potatoes sprinkled with parsley.

For 8 people

8 slices, each weighing about 200g, from a fine Loire salmon weighing 5–6kg
salt, freshly milled black pepper
4 lemons, cut in half and fluted
2 bunches curly parsley

Maître d'hôtel butter
250g best unsalted butter
2 tbs parsley, *very* finely chopped
salt, freshly milled white pepper
juice of 2 lemons

To cook Trim the slices of salmon, season with salt and freshly milled white pepper, but do *not* oil them. Lay them straight on to a grill over a live charcoal fire, cook them for 5 or 6 minutes and then turn to cook the other side. Remove the slices of salmon from the grill and mark them with a crisscross pattern on both sides, using a red-hot skewer. When the salmon steaks are cooked the central bone will come out easily. Remove it, arrange the steaks on a heated serving-dish and decorate with the half-lemons and little bunches of parsley.

To make the Maître d'hôtel butter While the salmon is cooking melt the butter in a heavy saucepan, preferably an enamelled cast-iron one. Add the chopped parsley, salt, pepper and lemon juice. Beat with a wire whisk over very moderate heat, without letting it boil. Pour the parsley butter into a sauceboat. It is the best accompaniment for grilled salmon.

Suggested wine Sancerre or Loire wine, well chilled.

HÔTEL DU BÉARN *
OLORON-SAINTE-MARIE (PYRÉNÉES-ATLANTIQUES)

DARNE DE SAUMON DU GAVE GRILLÉ AU BEURRE BLANC BÉARNAIS

Grilling is by far the best way to cook fresh salmon. White butter sauce, enriched with fresh cream, is the perfect accompaniment.

For 2 people

1 fresh salmon steak, 3–4cm thick, weighing 300–400g
1 lemon, cut into quarters
salt, freshly milled black pepper

White Béarnaise butter sauce
100g unsalted butter, chilled
and cut into small cubes
1 glass dry white Jurançon wine
2 shallots, very finely chopped
2 or 3 tbs double cream
lemon juice

To cook the butter sauce Put the wine and shallot, seasoned with pepper, into a small saucepan and bring to the boil. Cook for a few moments. Before the liquid evaporates completely, add 1 tablespoon of the cream and thicken the sauce over very moderate heat, by whisking in first one cube of butter until it is completely absorbed, then whisking in the rest of the butter, a small piece at a time and working rapidly until all is absorbed. If the mixture heats too quickly lift the pan off the heat. When all the butter has been absorbed add the rest of the cream, stirring it in well with the wire whisk. Season with salt and lemon juice.

To cook the salmon Salt and oil the thick piece of salmon, place it on a very hot grill until it begins to take colour, turn and make

a crisscross pattern on the cooked, golden surface with a red-hot skewer. Grill the second side and turn it over to make the same pattern. Remove the central bone.

To serve Serve very hot on a dish lined with a napkin, decorated with the lemon quarters. Serve the butter sauce separately in a sauceboat and garnish with steamed potatoes, trimmed and rounded.

Suggested wine White Jurançon, well chilled on ice.

LA MARÉE
PARIS 8e: 1 RUE DARU

AIGUILLETTES DE SAUMON TURENNE

A rich and elegant dish which would enhance any dinner. Thick slices of salmon are covered with a fish mousseline, *while the garnish of mushrooms, cucumbers and tomatoes is a perfect complement.*

For 10 people
- 1 fresh salmon weighing 3kg, the fillets cut into thick slices
- 1 tbs shallots, very finely chopped
- 1½dl dry white wine
- 1½dl reduced fish *fumet**

Garnish
- 250g button mushrooms, sliced, sautéed in butter with salt, pepper and a few drops of lemon juice
- 200g cucumbers, peeled, sliced and blanched
- 4 tomatoes, peeled, sliced and seeded

Mousseline of fish
- 400g pike or sole flesh
- 4 egg whites
- 400g fresh double cream
- salt, freshly milled black pepper, pinch of cayenne

Sauce
- 1 cup Hollandaise sauce (see p. 352)
- 1 cup fresh double cream

To prepare the fish mousseline Put the fish through a mincer or blender, then press it through a fine sieve. Spoon into a bowl placed in a larger container filled with ice and season with salt, pepper and a pinch of cayenne. Add the egg whites one at a time, working each one in vigorously with a wooden spoon or spatula before adding another, so that the fish is given body by absorbing the eggs. Fold in the cream in the same way, working it in little by little to obtain a light mass in which all the elements are completely blended.

To cook the salmon Spread a layer of chopped shallot over the bottom of a well-buttered sauté-pan. Lay the seasoned slices of salmon on top and, using a knife, spread each one with a good layer of the fish *mousseline*. Put a layer of mushrooms, one of cucumber and one of tomato on top.

Pour in the white wine and fish *fumet*. Heat on top of the stove until the liquid begins to shudder, then transfer to an oven pre-heated to 190°–205°C, 375°–400°F. Bake for 10 to 12 minutes.

Carefully drain the salmon slices and arrange them on a long, lightly buttered metal serving-dish. Cover with a piece of grease-proof paper until ready to serve.

To prepare the sauce Reduce the cooking juices from the salmon until you have a *demi-glace* (see p. 352). Thicken this with the cream and the Hollandaise sauce. Coat the dish with the sauce and glaze for 1 minute under a hot grill or in a very hot oven.

Suggested wine Alsatian, Riesling or Puligny Montrachet.

RESTAURANT TROISGROS * * *
ROANNE (LOIRE)

ESCALOPES DE SAUMON À L'OSEILLE

The salmon scallops are cooked in oil until golden and served on a bed of sauce made of reduced fish fumet, *white wine and vermouth, thickened with cream and butter. The sorrel that is served with the fish is barely cooked in the sauce so that it retains its fresh and slightly bitter taste.*

For 4 people

1 tail piece of salmon, weighing 1kg
3–5 tbs oil
salt, freshly milled black pepper

Sauce
1dl very dry white wine
½dl Noilly Prat vermouth
1dl fish *fumet**, made with the bones and trimmings of 2 sole and the usual vegetables and herbs
¼l double cream
2 handfuls fresh, tender sorrel
lemon juice

To prepare Remove the skin and bones from the salmon, which should leave you with 800 grams of salmon flesh; cut this into 4 slices, each weighing 200 grams, place these between 2 sheets of oiled greaseproof paper and flatten them with the flat of a carving knife.

Remove the stalks from the sorrel and cut the leaves into very thin ribbons with a pair of scissors.

To make the sauce Reduce the wine, vermouth and fish *fumet* in a thick enamel or enamelled cast-iron saucepan[1] until you have only 4 tablespoons of liquid. Add the cream and continue reducing until the sauce is the right consistency. Whisk in the shredded sorrel so that is just very lightly poached, taking the pan off the heat as soon as the sauce starts to boil. Thicken the sauce with the butter, adding it a little at a time either over very low heat or in a pan of hot water away from the stove. Check the seasoning and squeeze a few drops of lemon juice into the sauce.

To cook the salmon Sauté the salmon slices in the oil in a copper sauté-pan over high heat, turning them over half way through; take care not to let them become dry. Remove the slices from the pan and drain them.

To serve Pour all the sauce, which should have been kept very hot, into a round, shallow serving-dish and arrange the slices of salmon on top of the sauce.

Suggested wine A good Mâcon blanc or rosé.

[1] Do not make the sauce in a metal saucepan because the acid in the sorrel would react to the metal, making the sauce taste bitter and turning it a grey colour; even if it is made in an enamel pan it may turn a dull colour, in which case beat in an egg yolk, which will improve it (*editor's note*).

HOSTEN *
LANGEAIS (INDRE-ET-LOIRE)

BROCHET AU BEURRE BLANC
The pike is poached in a court-bouillon and served with white butter sauce. It is one of the best ways of cooking this delicate fish.

For 6 people

1 fine pike, weighing about 1·5kg

White butter sauce
2dl very dry white Loire wine such as Muscadet

50g shallot, finely chopped
salt, freshly milled white pepper
juice of half a lemon
200g best unsalted butter, softened
pinch of cayenne

To cook the pike Gut it, but to help remove the skin after cooking, do not scale it. Poach it in about 2 litres of well-flavoured court-bouillon, which should be barely simmering, for about 25 minutes.

To make the white butter sauce Put the wine, shallot, salt and pepper into a saucepan, copper if possible. Let it reduce until the liquid has all but evaporated, add 2 tablespoons of water and whisk in the butter, a little at a time, over very moderate heat, until the sauce is smooth and perfectly blended. Add the lemon juice, cayenne pepper and 1 tablespoon of the court-bouillon.

To serve Arrange the pike on a large serving-dish and serve the white butter sauce separately in a sauceboat.

Suggested wine Any of the dry white wines from the Loire valley such as Vouvray, Muscadet or Sauvignon.

AUBERGE SAINT-JACQUES *
ORLÉANS (LOIRET)

BROCHET À L'ORLÉANAISE

A large pike baked in the oven and coated with a sauce made of reduced vinegar and shallots thickened with egg yolks and butter.

For 6 people

1 pike, weighing 1·75–2kg
2 tbs oil

Sauce
3 tbs Orléans vinegar
1 tbs shallots, chopped

2 turns freshly milled white pepper
2 egg yolks
2 tsp cold water
200g unsalted butter, cut into pieces

To cook Gut and trim the pike; make a few slanting incisions with the point of a knife, season with salt and pepper and flour lightly. Lay in a well-buttered oven dish and spoon over the oil. Lightly colour the pike in a moderately hot oven, 175°–185°C, 350°–375°F, then continue cooking for 40 to 45 minutes, basting every 10 minutes. Reduce the heat slightly half-way through the cooking and if the pike is browning too quickly cover it with greaseproof paper.

To make the sauce When the pike is almost ready, reduce the vinegar, chopped shallot and white pepper to a glaze in a thick saucepan. Thicken with the egg yolks and the cold water, beating with a wire whisk over very low heat indeed so that the yolks do not curdle, then add the butter, whisking it in piece by piece over moderate heat until it begins to foam. Check the seasoning.

To serve When the pike is cooked transfer it to a heated metal serving-dish and strain over the sauce. Serve immediately.

Suggested wine Sauvignon de Bué-en-Sancerrois.

AUBERGE BRESSANE * *
BOURG-EN-BRESSE (AIN)

QUENELLES DE BROCHET SAUCE NANTUA

Quenelles of pike with Nantua sauce, the most famous sauce of Bresse and Bugey. It is a cream sauce enriched with crayfish butter and often garnished with crayfish.

For 12 *quenelles* (serving 12 people as a first course or 6 people as a main dish)

Panada
250g flour
½l milk
3 egg yolks
salt, freshly milled black
    pepper, grated nutmeg

Quenelle mixture
1 pike, weighing 500g
salt, freshly milled black
    pepper, nutmeg

125g unsalted butter
6 eggs
2–3 tbs fresh double cream

Nantua sauce
½l Béchamel sauce (see p. 347)
6 tbs fresh double cream
60g crayfish butter for each ½l
    sauce

Garnish
12 crayfish, heads removed

To make the panada The panada will bind the pike flesh. Thin down the flour with the cold milk, whisking it in with a wire whisk. Add the eggs and seasonings and continue to beat. Bind these ingredients over the heat, working them vigorously with a wooden spoon or spatula to dry the mixture. Leave to cool completely before using.

Quenelle mixture Remove the skin and bones from the pike; you should have 250 grams of flesh. Pound this with the salt, pepper and nutmeg or put it twice through the vegetable mill. Work 250 grams of panada and the butter into the pounded pike flesh. When the mixture is smooth and well blended put it through the vegetable mill or blender and spoon into a bowl resting on ice cubes in a large container. Add the eggs one at a time, working the mixture vigorously with a wooden spoon or spatula after adding each egg. Finally, to lighten the mixture, work in the cream in the same way.

To cook the quenelles Shape the *quenelles* with a spoon; do not flour them. Poach them in boiling salted water for 7 to 8 minutes. They are cooked when they rise to the surface.

To make the sauce Make the sauce by adding the cream to the Béchamel and, away from the stove, beating in the crayfish butter in the proportions indicated.

To serve Pour half the sauce into a gratin dish large enough to hold the *quenelles*. Drain the *quenelles* with a skimmer or perforated spoon and lay them on top of the sauce. Cover with the rest of the sauce and garnish with the crayfish. Warm over moderate heat and serve.

Suggested wine Roussette de Seyssel or a very dry white wine.

BRASSERIE DU NORD *
LYON (RHÔNE)

MATELOTE D'ANGUILLES À LA LYONNAISE

One of the best of eel matelotes, *made with red and white wine.*
Steamed potatoes are good with this dish.

For 8 people

2kg very fresh medium-sized
  eels
100g unsalted butter
salt, freshly milled black
  pepper
1dl cognac

Fumet
2 carrots, roughly chopped
2 onions, roughly chopped
thyme, bay leaf, parsley stalks,
  all tied together

250g fat belly of pork, cut into
  large lardoons)
1½l red Beaujolais
½l dry white wine such as
  Pouilly Fuissé

Garnish
2 tbs parsley, very finely
  chopped
8 triangular croûtons, fried in
  butter

To prepare the eels Skin and cut into chunks; cut off the heads, tails and fins and reserve them for the *fumet*.

To prepare the fumet Lightly colour the carrots, onions, lardoons and herbs, in a large heavy-bottomed saucepan over low heat; add the heads, tails and fins of the eels. Stir well with a spatula or wooden spoon, pour in the red and white wine, season lightly with salt and pepper and let the *fumet* simmer for 2½ to 3 hours. Strain through a conical sieve into a saucepan, pressing a little on the eel heads to extract all the juices. Put this excellent *fumet* back on the stove to continue simmering.

To cook the eels Quickly sauté the eel chunks in butter in a frying-pan. Season with salt and pepper, pour in the cognac and set light to it, turning the eel pieces as you do so. Remove them before they can start to cook and toss them into the *fumet*. Rinse out the pan with a little of the *fumet* and add the resulting liquid to the contents of the saucepan. Let it simmer very gently for a few moments, cover and place in a moderate oven preheated to 165°C, 325°F, for about 10 to 12 minutes to finish cooking the eels. Remove the pan from the oven, taste the sauce and adjust the seasoning if necessary. Add 2 tablespoons of butter.

To serve Arrange the eel pieces in a deep serving-dish with all their sauce, sprinkle with parsley and decorate with the reheated croûtons.

Suggested wine White Graves or Sauternes; or Saint-Estèphe, Saint-Julien or Saint-Émilion.

CLOS DES BERNARDINS *
PARIS 5e: 14 RUE DE PONTOISE

ANGUILLES AU VERT

A beautifully simple dish with an exquisite flavour. The pieces of eel are browned in oil, finished in an infusion of herbs and puréed green vegetables and served covered with the green sauce.

For 6 or 8 people

3kg eels
4 tbs oil
lemon quarters

Vegetables and herbs
500g spinach, cooked
500g sorrel, melted in butter
½ bunch watercress, stewed in
   butter

3 tbs tarragon, chervil and
   parsley, very finely chopped

Infusion of green herbs
2 tbs white nettles
2 tbs burnet leaves
1 tbs green ginger

To prepare Blanch the herb infusion for 5 minutes in 2 litres of water. Leave for 20 minutes to infuse, then strain the liquid through muslin.

Put the green vegetables twice through the finest mesh of the vegetable mill, or purée them in a blender. Pour over the herb infusion. Season with salt and pepper, bring to the boil in a saucepan and reduce by a third.

To cook the eels Cut the eels into chunks 5 or 6 centimetres in length. Heat the oil in a frying-pan and colour the eels in it for about 5 minutes. As soon as the pieces have stiffened and are starting to turn golden brown, put them into the green sauce and cook them for about 10 minutes. Check the seasoning.

To serve Arrange the pieces of eel on a serving-dish, cover with the green sauce and garnish with lemon quarters. Serve hot or cold.

Suggested wine White wine from the Saône district.

SALT-WATER FISH

SOLES ISIDORE

A very simple recipe. The method of cooking the whole sole in the oven with butter, shallots, tomatoes and white wine preserves its full flavour.

For 4 people

4 sole, each weighing 250g
100–125 g unsalted butter
2 tomatoes, peeled, seeded and
    finely sliced
2 tbs shallot, very finely
    chopped

½ bottle Muscadet
1 large tbs dried white bread-
    crumbs and a little extra
    salt, freshly milled black
    pepper

Remove the black skin from the sole, wipe them well and season with salt. Generously butter a large ovenproof dish in which the sole can also be served. Lay them in this dish, sprinkle with salt and pepper, dot with little pieces of butter, then add the tomatoes mixed with the chopped shallot and season again lightly. Pour over the wine, sprinkle with the breadcrumbs and transfer to a moderate oven, about 165°–175°C, 325°–350°F.

Bake for 18 to 20 minutes, then dot with some more butter and sprinkle over another layer of breadcrumbs. Return to the oven and bake for another 12 to 15 minutes, the total cooking time being about 30 minutes.

To serve Serve in the dish in which they were cooked, straight from the oven.

Suggested wine Sancerre or Muscadet.

AU VERT BOCAGE *
PARIS 7e: 96 BOULEVARD DE LATOUR-MAUBOURG

FILETS DE SOLE VERT BOCAGE

A simple dish flavoured with herbs. The sole fillets are served in the dish in which they were cooked and covered with the reduced cooking liquid enriched with cream.

For 4 or 5 people

3 sole, weighing 600–700g
salt, freshly milled black
   pepper
½ bottle very dry white
   burgundy or Sancerre
1 or 2 shallots, depending on
   size, very finely chopped

150g mushrooms, finely sliced
2 large tbs chervil and
   tarragon, finely chopped
200g fresh double cream

To prepare Fillet the sole, season the pieces with salt and pepper, trim them and fold them in two, from the outside to the inside. Strew the shallots over the bottom of an oven-proof dish, lay the sole fillets on top, sprinkle the mushrooms over the fillets and then add the chopped herbs. Moisten with the wine, which should just cover the fillets, and season with salt and pepper.

To cook Start cooking the fillets on top of the stove. Allow the liquid to simmer for 2 minutes, then add the cream off the heat and cover the dish with a piece of buttered greaseproof paper. Finish the cooking in a moderate oven, about 170°C, 325°F, for 8 to 10 minutes, depending on the size of the fillets.

To serve Pour the liquid into a saucepan and let it reduce for about 2 minutes. Cover the sole fillets with this delicious juice and serve in the dish in which they were cooked. Serve with small steamed potatoes, sprinkled with parsley.

Suggested wine Sancerre or a dry white burgundy, chilled on ice.

DAGORNO *
PARIS 19e: AVENUE JEAN-JAURÈS

FILETS DE SOLES DAGORNO

A simple and delicious dish in which the fillets are garnished with duxelles *of mushrooms and served with a sauce made from the cooking liquid, enriched by a little Hollandaise sauce.*

For 2–3 people

2 sole weighing 300–340g,
  filleted and salted
2 shallots, finely chopped
1dl dry white wine
1dl stock made with the skins
  and bones of the soles and
  reduced
4 tbs *duxelles* of mushrooms,
stewed gently in 2 tbs of
unsalted butter blended with
2 tbs fresh double cream

*beurre manié**
1 tbs plain flour
1 tbs unsalted butter

2 tbs Hollandaise sauce
2–3 crescents puff pastry

Sprinkle the bottom of a sauté pan (a copper one if possible) with the chopped shallots, then lay on top the fillets of sole. Moisten with the white wine and stock. Heat gently until the liquid is gently shuddering and cook for 5–6 minutes. Lift out the fillets, arrange on a serving dish and cover with the heated creamed *duxelles*.

Keep the dish warm while reducing the cooking liquid in a saucepan by three-quarters. Bind with a little *beurre manié* made with the butter and flour and add the Hollandaise. Adjust the seasoning and pour the sauce over the fillets, then put the dish under the grill for a few minutes.

To serve Decorate the dish with hot crescents of puff pastry.

Suggested wine A dry white wine, such as Sancerre, Muscadet or Chablis.

DU GUESCLIN *
RENNES (ILLE-ET-VILAINE)

SOLES DORÉES DU GUESCLIN

A beautiful-looking dish and simple to make. The sole are cooked in butter until golden, sprinkled with flaked almonds browned in butter and served with an original garnish of Dublin Bay prawns croque monsieur.

For 4 people

4 sole each weighing 225–250g
150g unsalted butter

Garnish
8 slices of bread cut from a tin
  loaf, crusts removed and
  lightly toasted on one side
  only
250g Dublin Bay prawns
  cooked in a court-bouillon

6 slices lemon, fluted
4 thin slices Gruyère cheese

To finish the dish
4 tbs double cream
3 tbs unsalted butter
100g flaked almonds
salt, freshly milled black
  pepper

To cook the sole Melt 100 grams of the butter in a large frying-pan, put in the sole and cook them slowly over moderate heat without letting the butter turn brown. Do not turn the fish. Half-way through cover with the remaining butter, melted and very hot, and put the pan under the grill to colour the surface. Remove when the fish are a nice golden colour.

To prepare the garnish Place a slice of Gruyère on the un-cooked sides of 4 of the pieces of toast; arrange the shelled prawns on top. Cover with the other 4 pieces of toast, the cooked side on the outside. Press the pieces of toast well together so that the filling won't fall out and brush the outsides with melted butter. Put the 4 *croque-monsieur* on a baking-sheet and cook in an oven preheated to about 175°C, 350°F, until they are heated through and the Gruyère has melted. Cut each *croque-monsieur* diagonally in half to make 8 small triangles.

To finish the dish Melt the cream in a heated oval serving-dish and season it with salt and pepper. Lay the sole in it and keep the dish warm while you fry the almonds in the butter until they turn golden. Drain the almonds carefully and sprinkle them over the fish.

To serve Arrange the triangular *croque-monsieur* and the fluted lemon slices alternately round the edge of the dish.

Suggested wine Meursault.

LE RABELAIS
CAEN (CALVADOS)

FILETS DE SOLE À LA FAÇON NORMANDE

A Norman dish, but still very French. It is the classic recipe for serving fillets of sole. It is now very often simplified and is rarely served with the full garnish as described in this recipe.

For 4 people

2 sole, each weighing 500g
a little salt, freshly milled black
    pepper
¼l semi-dry white wine

Fumet
the reserved sole bones and
    trimmings
1 onion, finely sliced
1 leek, white part only, finely
    sliced
3dl water
1 bouquet garni*
2 tbs unsalted butter

Garnish
4 large button mushroom caps
a few drops lemon juice
a walnut butter
salt, freshly milled black
    pepper
100g cooked mussels, with
    cooking liquid reserved
100g cooked prawns, shelled

4 oysters, poached in their
    juices, with juices reserved

Sauce
cooking juices from the sole,
    mushrooms, oysters, mussels
    and crayfish
3 egg yolks
¼l double cream
salt, freshly milled black
    pepper
1 lemon

Decoration
4 crayfish, cooked in a court-
    bouillon,* with cooking
    liquid reserved
4 slivers truffle
4 triangles bread, cut from a
    tin loaf
3 tbs unsalted butter, for
    frying the croûtons

To make the fumet Fillet the soles, reserving the bones and trimmings. Soften the onion and leek in the butter in a saucepan but don't let them take colour. Add the water, the bones and trimmings of the fish and the bouquet garni and cook for 15 minutes. Strain the liquid and reserve the *fumet*.

To cook the sole Season the fillets with salt and pepper and lay them in a deep, lightly buttered roasting-tin. Pour over the reserved *fumet* and the wine and season again with salt and pepper. Cover with a piece of buttered greaseproof paper. Bring to the boil on top of the stove, then transfer to a moderate oven, 165°–175°C, 325°–350°F, and bake for 10 minutes, making sure that the liquid is simmering gently all the time.

Meanwhile, cook the mushroom caps in a very little water flavoured with lemon juice, plus a knob of butter and a seasoning of salt and pepper. Reserve the juices.

Remove the fillets from the roasting-tin and lay them down the centre of a long serving-dish. Arrange the mussels, prawns, mushroom caps and oysters alternately round the fillets and cover with a piece of greaseproof paper. Keep hot.

To make the sauce Strain the liquid in which the sole were cooked and reduce it slightly until you have about $\frac{1}{4}$ litre. Make a *velouté* sauce (see p. 347) and stir in the reduced cooking liquid. Add the mushroom juices, the oyster juices and 3 tablespoons each of the stock from the mussels and the crayfish, all strained.

To thicken the sauce Beat the egg yolks and cream together in a bowl and season with salt and pepper. Whisk into the sauce for a minute or two over the heat. Squeeze in a few drops of lemon juice and correct the seasoning if necessary.

Coat the sole fillets and their garnish with plenty of the sauce.

To decorate the dish Lay the slivers of truffle on the mushrooms and arrange the mushrooms and reheated croûtons down the sides of the dish, with the shelled crayfish at either end.

Suggested wine Muscadet or Blanc de blancs.

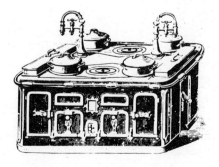

LEDOYEN * *
PARIS 8e: CARRÉ CHAMPS-ÉLYSÉES

SOLES SOUFFLÉES À LA MOUSSE DE HOMARD

Soles stuffed with a mousseline *of pike and lobster flesh, souffléed in the oven and coated with* sauce à l'américaine.

For 10 people

10 sole, each weighing 220–250g
½l good dry white wine
¼l very reduced sole *fumet*, made from the bones
a squeeze lemon juice
salt, freshly milled black pepper
10 small thick pieces lobster meat

Lobster mousse
350g pike flesh
350g lobster flesh
the lobster coral
2 egg whites
700g double cream
a pinch cayenne pepper
salt, freshly milled black pepper
sauce à l'américaine (see p. 348)

To make the lobster mousse Prepare the lobster mousse in advance, leaving enough time for it to chill in the refrigerator. Pound the pike and lobster flesh and the lobster coral finely together, in a mortar if possible, or in a bowl. Alternatively put it through the finest mesh of the mincer and then through the finest mesh of the vegetable mill to get rid of all the little pike bones and to obtain a smooth paste. Put the bowl containing the paste into a larger container filled with ice cubes and season the mixture with salt, pepper and cayenne. Holding the bowl firmly over the ice, work the egg whites into the mixture, little by little, with a wooden spoon or spatula until they are well absorbed. Add the cream, working it in vigorously a spoonful at a time until it is completely absorbed. The mixture should froth up and become lighter. Correct the seasoning and leave in a cool place for at least 1 hour before stuffing the sole.

To prepare and cook the sole Clean the sole. Remove the black skin and scrape off the white skin. Remove the central bone by slitting the sole right down on the side from which the black skin has been removed. Lift off the 2 fillets on the same side, being careful not to detach the head and tail. Stuff each sole with some of the lobster mousse and press the fillets back into place. Arrange the stuffed soles in a well buttered enamelled cast-iron roasting-tin. Pour over the white wine and the fumet. Add a squeeze of lemon juice, salt and pepper, cover with a piece of buttered grease-proof paper and cook in a moderate oven, 175°C, 350°F, for about 6 to 8 minutes. The liquid should be just shuddering. The stuffing will turn coral pink.

To serve Carefully remove the sole from the dish, using 2 wooden spoons or spatulas, and trim off all the little bones from the sides. Arrange on 2 long, heated metal serving-dishes, 5 soles to each dish. Coat each sole with 4 tablespoons of the *sauce à* *l'Américaine* and decorate with a little round of lobster flesh. Spear each sole head with an ornamental silver skewer and serve very hot.

Suggested wine Still champagne, well chilled on ice or a white burgundy such as Meursault.

HÔTEL DE PARIS ET DE LA POSTE * *
SENS (YONNE)

FILETS DE SOLES HOMARDINE

A very effective dish for a special meal. The sauce is delicious and looks beautiful; it is a pink sauce à l'américaine, *enriched with Hollandaise and sweetened with fresh cream.*

For 6 people

3 fine sole, each weighing 600–700g
2dl very dry white wine (Chablis)
salt, freshly milled black pepper
unsalted butter
2 small lobsters, each weighing 850–950g

1 cup *sauce à l'américaine* (see p. 348)
4 tbs Hollandaise sauce (see p. 352)
4 tbs fresh double cream
6 little puff pastry crescents (optional)

To cook the sole Fillet the sole and salt the fillets. Make a fish *fumet* using the sole bones and reduce the liquid to a quarter-litre. Poach the fillets in the concentrated *fumet* diluted with the white wine and seasoned with salt and pepper. Drain the fillets, arrange them on a buttered metal serving-dish, cover with a piece of buttered greaseproof paper and keep hot. Reduce the cooking liquid to 4 tablespoons.

To prepare the lobster Meanwhile, cook the lobsters *à l'améri-caine*, or you can do this in advance. Shell the lobsters, cut the tails into small thick chunks and arrange on top of the sole fillets.

To prepare the sauce Put the *sauce à l'américaine* into a sauce-pan and add the reduced cooking liquid from the soles. Shell the lobster claws and add the meat to the saucepan, with the creamy parts and coral from the heads. Add the thickened Hollandaise sauce (see p. 352). Check the seasoning, beat the sauce and then add the cream, without beating but stirring it in gently so that it makes pretty pink marblings in the sauce.

To serve Coat the sole fillets with the sauce and serve immediately. The dish may be garnished with 6 little puff-pastry crescents.

Suggested wine A Chablis, Preuses or Vandesir, of a really good vintage.

LA POULARDE BRESSANE *
GRENOBLE (ISÈRE)

FILETS DE SOLE WALEWSKA
A lavish dish famous at the beginning of this century. The combination of sole and crawfish in a bisque sauce decorated with truffle produces a harmony of pink and black.

For 4 people

1 very fresh sole, weighing about 1·2kg
¼l very good dry white wine
2 shallots, chopped
salt, freshly milled black pepper
1 small crawfish, weighing 800–900g, cooked in a court-bouillon cooled, shelled and cut into thick chunks
3 tbs unsalted butter

1dl cognac
1 small truffle, peeled and finely sliced
puff-pastry crescents (optional)

Sauce
3 tbs unsalted butter
3 tbs flour
a squeeze lemon juice
1dl double cream
2 tbs lobster bisque
2 egg yolks

To cook the sole Fillet the sole. Put the fillets in a buttered fireproof dish and poach them in the white wine with the shallots, and a seasoning of salt and pepper for 6 to 7 minutes. Drain the fillets, arrange them on an oval metal serving-dish, cover with buttered greaseproof paper and keep hot. Strain the cooking liquid into a saucepan.

To cook the crawfish Stew the pieces of crawfish gently in the butter in a sauté-pan and deglaze the juices with the cognac. This will bring out the full flavour of the crawfish. Arrange the pieces on top of the sole fillets. Add the deglazed juices to the pan containing the sole stock and heat through.

To make the sauce Make a roux with the butter and flour, pour in the contents of the saucepan, whisk vigorously and cook for 2 to 3 minutes. Add a squeeze of lemon juice, the cream and the lobster bisque. Beat the egg yolks in a bowl until they foam and add them to the sauce away from the heat. Put the sauce back over very low heat.

Beat the sauce until it reaches boiling point, check the seasoning and pour over the sole fillets and crawfish pieces. Lay a sliver of truffle on each piece of crawfish. The dish may also be garnished with little crescents of puff pastry.

Suggested wine A Blanc de blancs or a Meursault would be appropriate with this dish.

DOMAINE DE LA TORTINIÈRE *
MONTBAZON (INDRE-ET-LOIRE)

PAUPIETTES DE SOLE SOPHIE

Paupiettes of sole stuffed with smoked salmon butter, served on a bed of mushrooms and coated with the reduced cooking liquid thickened with egg yolks and cream.

For 8 people

16 fine sole fillets
2dl very dry white wine
(Chablis or Sancerre)

Mushroom duxelles
500g very fresh mushrooms,
very finely chopped
4 tbs unsalted butter
salt, freshly milled black
pepper
a squeeze lemon juice
2 tbs double cream

Smoked salmon butter
125–160g smoked salmon
50g softened unsalted butter
a squeeze lemon juice
freshly milled black pepper,
salt if necessary

Sauce
2 egg yolks
3 tbs double cream

To make the smoked salmon butter Put the smoked salmon through a small vegetable mill. Using a fork, work the salmon into the butter on a plate, add a squeeze of lemon juice and pepper; taste, and add a little salt if necessary.

To cook the sole Lay the sole fillets on a board and season lightly with salt and pepper. Spread them right down the middle with a thin layer of the smoked salmon butter, roll them into paupiettes and arrange them side by side in an ovenproof dish. Cover with a piece of buttered greaseproof paper.

Moisten the paupiettes with the wine and start the cooking on top of the stove. When the liquid begins to shudder, transfer to a moderate oven, 165°–175°C, 325°–350°F, and cook for a maximum of 10 minutes with the liquid gently shuddering. Drain and keep hot.

To make the duxelles of mushrooms Gently stew the mush-rooms in the butter for 3 to 4 minutes. Remove the pan from the heat and add salt, pepper, a squeeze of lemon juice and the cream. Keep hot.

To make the sauce Reduce the liquid in which the sole were cooked by half, then heat through in a saucepan. Beat the egg yolks and the cream together in a bowl; remove the saucepan from the heat and, using a wire whisk, beat in the egg and cream mixture. Heat to thicken the sauce, stirring with a wooden spoon or spatula. Do not let it boil. Taste and adjust the seasoning if necessary.

To serve Spread a good layer of the mushroom *duxelles* over the bottom of a lightly buttered metal serving-dish, arrange the well-drained paupiettes on top and coat with the sauce. Decorate each paupiette with a small piece of smoked salmon, cut into an attractive shape. Serve very hot.

Suggested wine Blanc de blancs or a still champagne.

NANDRON * *
LYON (RHÔNE)

SUPRÊMES DE TURBOT AU VIN DE POUILLY

The cooking in this restaurant· is perfect and its secrets are equally well kept. After a good deal of coaxing, this recipe for suprêmes de turbot *was eventually divulged. They are light and quite delicious. The proportions were given for one person, so multiply as required.*

For 1 person

1 escalope of turbot, weighing 60g and cut from a whole turbot weighing 1·5kg
salt, freshly milled black pepper
½dl sole *fumet*,* made with bones and trimmings
½dl Pouilly Fuissé
½dl water
salt, freshly milled black pepper, mixed herbs and spices
1 tbs Hollandaise sauce (see p. 352)

Pike mousse
pike flesh
1 tomato
unsalted butter

*duxelles** of button mushrooms
unsalted butter
½ shallot, very finely chopped

Garnish
1 sliver truffle
whole cooked crayfish, shelled
puff-pastry crescents

To make the mousse Put the pike flesh through the vegetable mill or purée it in the blender. Peel the tomato, crush it, draining off all the liquid, and sweat it gently in butter. Work the pike with the tomato over ice.

To prepare the turbot Lay a large sheet of greaseproof paper (foolscap size) on a board and butter it. Spoon 1 tablespoon of the pike mousse into the middle, lay the slice of turbot on top and cover with 2 more tablespoons of the mousse. Fold over the paper so that the contents are completely wrapped up and press the ends firmly together to make a little rectangular packet. Put the packet into the cold sole *fumet* in an ovenproof dish, add the white wine, water and seasonings and poach for 10 to 12 minutes in a moderate oven. Remove the packet and keep warm on a metal serving-dish.

To make the sauce Strain the cooking liquid into an enamelled saucepan and reduce by half. Thicken with the Hollandaise sauce.

To serve Unwrap the packet and drain off any liquid that has seeped out into the dish. Arrange the *suprême* on the dish and coat with the sauce. Garnish with a sliver of truffle and decorate with whole cooked crayfish and little puff-pastry crescents. Serve very hot.

Suggested wine This dish deserves the best Pouilly Fuissé or a good Mâcon; if it is to be served in the evening, choose instead a very dry champagne.

L'OASIS * * *
LA NAPOULE (ALPES-MARITIMES)

FILETS DE SOLE AU NOILLY
A very simple recipe for sole fillets. It is always a pleasing dish.

For 4 people
1 fine sole weighing 1kg, divided into 4 fillets with bones reserved
salt, freshly milled black pepper
1dl Noilly Prat vermouth

Fish fumet
the sole bones
¼l dry white wine
¼l water
1 onion
thyme, bay leaf, parsley stalks

salt, freshly milled black pepper

Garnish
125g mushrooms
3 tbs water
unsalted butter, cut into pieces
juice of half a lemon
salt, freshly milled black pepper
puff-pastry crescents (optional)

Sauce
4dl double cream
3 egg yolks

To make the fish fumet Boil the ingredients listed until the liquid has reduced to half its original quantity. Strain.

To cook the sole Put the 4 sole fillets into a buttered sauté-pan. Pour in the vermouth and the reduced fumet. Poach the fillets gently for 10 minutes, then remove and keep hot on a metal serving-dish.

To garnish Finely slice the mushroom caps and cook them over high heat for about 3 to 4 minutes in the butter melted in the water and the lemon juice, seasoned with salt and pepper. Strain the liquid through a fine sieve into a small saucepan. Drain the mushrooms and add them to the sole fillets as a garnish.

To make the sauce Reduce the strained juices from the mushrooms until you have only 2 tablespoons. Reduce the cooking liquid from the sole by half, then add the reduced mushroom liquid and the cream. Bring to the boil, remove from the heat and, using a wire whisk, beat in the egg yolks. Warm over very low heat, taking great care not to let the sauce boil, and stirring with a wooden spoon or spatula.

Correct the seasoning and add, according to taste, a few drops of fresh lemon juice.

To serve Coat the sole fillets with very hot sauce and if desired decorate the dish with little puff-pastry crescents.

Suggested wine Dry burgundy, such as Chablis or blanc de blancs.

RESTAURANT DROUANT * *
PARIS 2e: PLACE GAILLON

SOLES AU CHAMPAGNE
The soles are garnished with quenelles *and mushrooms, but it is the champagne in which they are cooked that makes the sauce so delicious.*

For 4 people

4 sole, each weighing 350g
2 shallots, finely chopped
¼l very dry champagne
¼l fish fumet
salt, freshly milled black
  pepper

Sauce
1 tbs meat glaze
4dl double cream
200g unsalted butter

Quenelles
100g raw pike flesh

salt, freshly milled black
  pepper, grated nutmeg
½ beaten egg
100g double cream

Garnish
8 mushroom caps, fluted and
  stewed in seasoned butter
  with lemon juice
4 slivers truffle
4 little puff-pastry crescents

To make the quenelles Work the pike flesh with a pestle over ice, season, beat in the egg with a wooden spoon or spatula and blend in the cream a little at a time. Work the mixture vigorously until the texture is firm but light. Shape 4 little *quenelles* with a spoon, poach them in water which is just simmering, and keep them hot.

To cook the sole Sprinkle a well-buttered fireproof dish with the chopped shallots and lay the sole on top. Pour the champagne over the fish and add the lightly seasoned *fumet*. Poach the sole for 20 minutes, without letting the liquid quite boil. Lift out the sole and keep them hot.

To make the sauce Reduce the cooking liquid by half, add the meat glaze and the cream and reduce by one-third. Whisk in the butter, at first over low heat, then away from the heat, until the mixture thickens.

To arrange the dish Trim the sole, cutting away the little bones from each side, and arrange them on a buttered silver serving-dish. Put 2 mushrooms and 1 *quenelle* on each sole. Coat with a film of sauce, glaze under the grill, then arrange slivers of truffle on top and the pastry crescents round the edges.
Serve the rest of the sauce separately.

Suggested wine Champagne.

MAXIM'S ★ ★ ★
PARIS 8e: 3 RUE ROYALE

SOLE ALBERT

A sole quickly sautéed in butter, breadcrumbed and finished in vermouth in a very hot oven.

For 1 person

1 sole, weighing 250–300g
4 tbs unsalted butter
flour
1 egg yolk
2 tbs fresh breadcrumbs, made in a vegetable mill or blender

1–2 shallots, depending on size, very finely chopped
about 1 glass Noilly Prat vermouth

To cook Skin the sole on both sides, season with salt and pepper and make a shallow incision right along the back. Melt 3 table-spoons of the butter in a frying-pan and fry the sole quickly on both sides. Sprinkle the chopped shallot over the bottom of a buttered ovenproof dish and lay the sole on top. Pour the vermouth round the sides of the fish, and coat the top of the sole with flour, beaten egg yolk and finally the breadcrumbs.
Put the dish into a very hot oven, 215°–225°C, 400°–425°F, until the soles are cooked and the breadcrumbed surface is golden brown.
Lift out the sole, trim away the little bones from each side and remove the central bone. Reshape the sole, arranging the 4 fillets on a buttered serving-dish, and keep hot.

To serve Strain the sauce into a small saucepan, reduce a little and add the remaining butter, without letting the sauce boil. Spoon some of the sauce round the sole and serve the rest in a sauceboat. Serve with 2 small steamed potatoes.

Suggested wine A really good white burgundy.

PRUNIER-TRAKTIR *
PARIS 1er: 9 RUE DUPHOT

FILETS DE SOLES PRUNIER

One of the most appetising of sole dishes. The sole are poached in the oven and garnished with poached oysters. The oyster stock is added to the sauce, which is thickened with egg yolks and cream. Slivers of truffle add to the beauty of the dish.

For 4 or 5 people

24 Belon oysters
3 sole, each weighing 350–400g
1dl dry white wine
½dl water
a squeeze lemon juice
freshly milled black pepper
1 sprig thyme
2 tbs unsalted butter, divided
   into small knobs

Sauce
2dl double cream
2 egg yolks, beaten with a fork
2 tbs unsalted butter

Garnish
slivers of truffle

To cook the oysters Open the oysters; keep the juice and strain it through muslin. Poach the oysters for 3 minutes in their natural juices and keep the cooking liquid.

To cook the sole Fillet the sole and place the fillets in a lightly buttered ovenproof dish. Pour in the white wine, the water and the cooking juices from the oysters. Add a squeeze of lemon juice, freshly milled black pepper, thyme and butter. Do not add any salt. Bring the liquid to the boil on top of the stove, cover the fillets with buttered greaseproof paper and poach them in a moderate oven, 170°C, 350°F, for 8 minutes. Arrange the fillets on a metal serving-dish and decorate the edges of the dish with the oysters. Cover again with the greaseproof paper and keep the dish hot.

To make the sauce Reduce the cooking liquid from the sole in a good thick saucepan, preferably enamelled cast-iron. Add the cream. Let the mixture boil fairly briskly for 5 minutes. Remove the pan from the heat and whisk in the beaten egg yolks. Heat very gently indeed, whisking continuously, to thicken the sauce. Finally add the butter piece by piece, stirring continuously with a wooden spoon or spatula without letting the sauce boil. Check the seasoning.

To serve Coat the sole fillets with the sauce while it is still very hot. Decorate each fillet with a sliver of truffle.

Suggested wine Chablis or Pouilly.

HOSTELLERIE DU COQ HARDY *
BOUGIVAL (YVELINES)

DÉLICES DE SOLES EN CHAUD-FROID

Double fillets of sole, stuffed with creamed duxelles *of mushrooms coated with a* chaud-froid *sauce, glazed with jellied fish stock and served with pieces of lobster and artichoke bases and a* macedoine *of vegetables.*

For 4 people

2 sole, each weighing 800g (8 fillets)
1 lobster, weighing 1kg, cooked in a court-bouillon*
4 tbs *duxelles**of mushrooms, cooked in butter and cream
a squeeze of lemon juice, salt and freshly milled black pepper

½l *chaud-froid* sauce reduced jellied fish stock and cream (fish *velouté*, see p. 347)
½l jellied fish stock, well seasoned and flavoured with lemon juice
8 mushrooms, fluted

Fillet the soles. Make a well-seasoned fish *fumet** with the bones and equal amounts of white wine and water. Poach the sole fillets in the *fumet*. Leave them to cool in the cooking liquid, then drain them on a piece of cloth.

Arrange the fillets in pairs, putting a spoonful of *duxelles* of mushrooms between them.

Final presentation Arrange the stuffed sole fillets in a fan-shape on a round or oval serving dish. Coat with the *chaud-froid* sauce. Put a little piece of lobster at one end of each fillet and a fluted mushroom in the middle. When the sauce has set properly, glaze the fish and the garnish with the jellied fish stock.

To garnish Serve the dish with small artichoke bases filled with a *macédoine** of vegetables bound with mayonnaise (see p. 354) enriched with cream and well seasoned.

Suggested wine Chablis or any white burgundy.

ALLARD ★ ★
PARIS 6e: 41 RUE SAINT-ANDRÉ-ES-ARTS

POISSON AU BEURRE BLANC

*The white butter sauce is delicious with either sea or freshwater
fish cooked in a court-bouillon or grilled or roasted in the oven.*

For 6 people

1 fish, weighing 2·5kg, gutted,
trimmed and ready for
cooking
1 bunch parsley

White butter sauce
3 tbs shallot, finely chopped

2 tbs white peppercorns,
crushed
a pinch rock salt
2dl white wine vinegar
about 700g very fresh unsalted
butter, cut into pieces
a squeeze of lemon juice

To cook the fish Poach the fish in a court-bouillon★ or grill it
or toast it in the oven. Arrange on an oval serving-dish and garnish
with a little bunch of parsley.

To make the white butter Put the shallot, pepper, salt and
vinegar in a small saucepan, an enamel one if possible and let the
mixture reduce over a steady heat until the liquid has almost
evaporated. Now add the butter, beating it in with a wire whisk
a little piece at a time over *very* gentle heat, waiting for one piece
to be completely absorbed before adding another. Work quickly
and calmly, whisking continuously until all the butter has been
incorporated. The sauce must be foamy and *opaque*. Strain quickly
through a fine sieve to skim off the foam. Check the seasoning
and add a squeeze of lemon juice.

To serve Serve the sauce in a sauceboat as an accompaniment for
the fish.

Suggested wine A very dry white wine such as Muscadet,
Sancerre, Mâcon or Chablis.

RESTAURANT DEMONCY ★
DORMANS (MARNE)

TURBOT BRAISÉ MAURICE CHEVALIER

*Turbot cooked in the oven in still champagne. It is served with
a sauce enriched with eggs and cream and a little Hollandaise
sauce.*

For 8 people

1 turbot weighing 4–5kg
salt, freshly milled black
    pepper
unsalted butter
½ bottle still champagne.

Fumet★
trimmings of the turbot
sole bones
onion
carrot

bouquet garni
lemon juice
salt, freshly milled black
    pepper

Roux
2½ tbs unsalted butter
2½ tbs flour

To thicken the sauce
3 eggs yolks
250g double cream
3 tbs Hollandaise sauce (see p.
    352)

To cook the turbot Put the turbot in a very well buttered roasting-tin or oven-dish and season with salt and pepper. Pour over the still champagne and 1 litre of the reduced fish *fumet* and scatter a few small pieces of butter over the fish. Poach in a moderate oven, 165°–175°C, 325°–350°F, basting frequently.

To make the sauce Meanwhile make a white roux in a sauté-pan with the butter and flour. When the turbot is cooked, beat the cooking liquid from the turbot into the roux with a wire whisk.

To bind and finish the sauce Mix the cream and egg yolks together in a bowl and season with salt and pepper. Add this mixture to the sauce. Whisk well with a wire whisk and fold in the Hollandaise sauce over a very low heat.

To serve Remove the black and white skin from the turbot. Arrange on a heated oval metal serving-dish, cover with half the sauce and serve the rest in a sauceboat.

Suggested wine Still champagne.

À L'HUÎTRIÈRE ★
LILLE (NORD)

DARNES DE TURBOT À LA BRÉVAL
Thick slices of turbot braised in the oven on a bed of tomatoes and mushrooms, coated with the reduced cooking liquid enriched with cream and butter.

For 6 people

1 turbot, weighing about 3kg
2 tbs unsalted butter
2 tbs shallots, finely chopped
250g mushrooms, finely sliced
6 medium-sized tomatoes,
    skinned, seeded and diced
1 glass white wine

Fumet★
the turbot trimmings (or sole
    trimmings)
1 onion, finely sliced
parsley stalks, thyme, bay leaf
juice of half a lemon
2dl dry white wine
½l water
a little salt, freshly milled
    black pepper

To finish the sauce
3dl double cream
100g unsalted butter

Garnish
6 puff-pastry crescents

To prepare Divide the turbot in two lengthways. Cut it into thick slices and remove the black skin.

Cook the fish *fumet* for 30 minutes and strain through a fine sieve.

To cook the turbot Spoon a layer of chopped shallots, mushrooms and tomatoes into a well-buttered enamelled cast-iron casserole. Arrange the slices of turbot on top and pour in the wine and the *fumet*. Start cooking on top of the stove, then cover with a piece of greaseproof paper and continue cooking in a moderate oven, 160°C, 325°F, for about 25 minutes. The liquid should simmer gently but continuously. Lift the pieces of turbot out of the oven-dish, cover with a fresh piece of greaseproof paper and keep hot.

To finish the sauce Reduce the liquid in which the turbot was cooked, including the vegetable base, in a saucepan, add the cream and reduce once more by three-quarters. Remove the pan from the heat and beat in the butter with a wire whisk, adding a little piece at a time and letting each piece become completely absorbed in the sauce before adding another. Check the seasoning when all the butter is absorbed.

To serve Arrange the slices of turbot on a serving-dish, coat with the sauce and decorate the dish with little crescents of puff-pastry.

Suggested wine Puligny Montrachet.

LA MARÉE ★ ★
PARIS 8e: 1 RUE DARU

TURBOT À LA MOUTARDE
Mustard, aromatic herbs and tomatoes all add flavour to the sauce.

For 2 people

1 turbot, weighing 1·2kg, filleted
a pot strong Dijon mustard
1 dsp shallot, finely chopped
3 tomatoes, peeled, sliced and seeded
3 tbs fresh breadcrumbs, sieved

1 tbs parsley, chopped
1 tbs thyme flowers and bay leaves, crumbled together
olive oil
1dl dry white wine
1dl fish *fumet**, reduced
2–3 tbs unsalted butter
a squeeze of lemon juice

To cook Butter a sauté-pan and sprinkle in the chopped shallots. Dip a pastry brush into the mustard and coat the turbot fillets with it. Lay the fillets on top of the shallots and garnish with the sliced tomatoes. Sprinkle with the breadcrumbs and the crushed herbs, mixed with a few drops of olive oil. Pour in the wine and *fumet*, bring to the boil over a high heat and then put the pan into a hot oven, 190°–200°C, 375°–400°F, for 10 to 12 minutes.

To serve Drain the fillets well and arrange them on a long metal serving-dish. Reduce the cooking liquid a little if necessary, but do not strain it. Remove the pan from the heat and beat in the butter with a wire whisk, a little at a time, letting each piece become completely absorbed before adding another piece. Taste the sauce and adjust the seasoning if necessary. Pour the sauce, with the tomatoes, round the turbot fillets and serve.

Suggested wine A full bodied white burgundy.

BEAUSÉJOUR ★ ★
LÉRY (EURE)

TURBOT 'SAINT-JACQUES'
Turbot braised first in white wine, then in good thick cream with scallops and mussels and served in the dish in which they were cooked with the cooking juices thickened with egg.

For 6 to 8 people

1 turbot, weighing 3kg
1l mussels
2kg scallops
½l good very dry white wine
salt, freshly milled black
   pepper

parsley stalks
1l fresh double cream
1 tbs parsley, very finely
   chopped

To prepare the fish Gut and wash the turbot. Remove the head. Cut away the dark brown skin from the back of the turbot with a filleting knife.

Put the mussels in a large pan with a well-fitting lid and shake the pan, holding the lid on, over a high heat until they open. Shell and reserve the juice.

Open the scallops, remove the gristly fibre and dark brown parts, wash them thoroughly and wipe them dry. Cut them in two if they are large.

To cook the turbot Put the turbot into a well-buttered braising-dish. Pour over the white wine, season with salt and 3 turns of the pepper mill and add the parsley stalks. Cook in a low oven, 160°C, 325°F, with the wine gently shuddering, for about 30 minutes.

Take the dish out of the oven and add to the wine, which will have reduced, the cream, the mussels and their strained juices and the raw scallops. Return the dish to the oven and cook for a further 30 minutes. Place a piece of greaseproof paper over the turbot and hold it firmly with one hand while tilting the dish with the other hand to let the liquid drain through a fine sieve into a saucepan. Keep the scallops, mussels and turbot hot beneath the greaseproof paper.

To prepare the sauce Warm the juices in the saucepan over very moderate heat. Whisk together in a bowl the egg yolks and a ladleful of these juices. Pour the diluted egg yolk into the saucepan, whisking continuously over very low heat without letting the sauce boil until it thickens. Coat the turbot with the sauce, sprinkle with the parsley and serve in the dish in which it has cooked, with a separate dish of small steamed potatoes.

Suggested wine Puligny Montrachet or a dry Graves (Laville or Haut-Brion).

HÔTEL DE LA COURONNE *
ROUEN (SEINE-MARITIME)

BARBUE AU CIDRE
A Norman recipe with a fresh and unusual taste. The brill is cooked in cider and calvados.

For 4 people

4 fine large fillets or 8 medium-sized fillets of brill, trimmed
salt, freshly milled pepper
3 tbs unsalted butter
1 dsp shallot, very finely chopped
1 small ladle (4 tbs) calvados
½ bottle (3½dl) dry cider
1 cup double cream
squeeze of lemon juice

Hollandaise sauce (see p. 352)

the juice of half a lemon
1 tbs water
salt, freshly milled black pepper
2 egg yolks
100g unsalted butter

To cook the fish Sweat the shallot gently in the butter in a sauté-pan. Flambé the calvados in the ladle and pour it into the pan. Remove the pan from the heat and put in the seasoned brill fillets, turning them two or three times in the calvados. Pour in the cider immediately and poach the brill.

Remove the brill fillets, drain them well and arrange them on a long heated metal serving-dish.

To make the sauce Reduce the cooking liquid over high heat until you have just 4 tablespoons. Make some Hollandaise sauce with the ingredients listed and whisk in the cream. Add the reduced cooking liquid. Taste for seasonning and add a squeeze of lemon juice if desired.

To serve Warm the sauce thoroughly without letting it boil and spoon over the brill fillets. Serve with steamed potatoes sprinkled with parsley.

Suggested wine Bottled cider or Sancerre or Pouilly-sur-Loire.

RESTAURANT COCONNAS ⋆
PARIS 4e: 2 BIS PLACE DES VOSGES

MERLAN COCONNAS
Whiting cooked in the oven in equal quantities of fish stock and white wine, sprinkled with fresh breadcrumbs so that it will turn a nice golden brown.

For 1 person

1 fine whiting, weighing about 300–350g
unsalted butter
2 tbs shallot, finely chopped
1dl dry white wine
1dl fish *fumet* ⋆

1 sprig parsley
1 sprig thyme
salt, freshly milled black pepper
white breadcrumbs, dried in the oven

To prepare Slit the whiting right down the back and lift out the spine. Gut it carefully without opening up the stomach. Generously butter an ovenproof dish, preferably an enamelled cast-iron casserole, then sprinkle in the chopped shallot. Lay the whiting on top and pour in the wine and the *fumet*. Add the herbs and season with salt and pepper. The liquid must not cover the fish but should come half-way up the side.

To cook Put the dried breadcrumbs through a vegetable mill or blender and sprinkle over the fish; dot with a little butter and bring to the boil on the top of the stove. Transfer the dish to a moderate oven, 175°C, 350°F, for only 15 minutes, as the whiting is a rather delicate fish with flesh that flakes off easily.

When it is cooked the whiting should be a nice golden brown and the sauce, which will have reduced by half, will be thickish and smooth. Add a few drops of lemon juice if desired.

Recommended wine A dry white wine such as Muscadet or Pouilly, served very cold.

LE CAMÉLIA ★★
BOUGIVAL (YVELINES)

MERLANS DES BECS FINS
Fine whiting cooked in the oven with a little fish fumet, *finely sliced leeks, chopped shallots and a delicious seasoning containing saffron. The whiting are served in the reduced cooking liquid enriched with butter.*

For 6 people	*Fish fumet*★
6 fine, absolutely fresh whiting	sole bones, crushed
salt	unsalted butter
unsalted butter	parsley stalks, crushed
a pinch saffron	shallots, crushed
2 tbs shallot, chopped	a little salt, freshly milled
8 medium-sized leeks, white	black pepper
parts only, cut into very fine	mushroom stalks (optional)
strips	

To prepare Gut the whiting through the gills to prevent the flesh falling away during the cooking. Trim and season with salt.

To make the fumet Sweat the crushed sole bones in butter, with the other ingredients listed. Cover with water and cook over high heat for about 20 minutes. Strain through a conical sieve and leave to cool.

To cook the whiting Liberally butter an oven dish, sprinkle the bottom with the chopped shallot and lay the whiting on top.

Sprinkle with the saffron and add the finely sliced leeks. Pour over no more than $\frac{1}{2}$ litre of the cold *fumet*. Bring the liquid to the boil on top of the stove, then transfer the dish, uncovered, to a moderate oven, 170°C, 325°F, and cook for 25 minutes, basting frequently.

To serve Carefully lift out the fish and keep them hot on a metal serving-dish. Sprinkle the sliced leeks over them. Strain the cooking liquid into a small saucepan and reduce by about a third. Put the pan over very low heat and thicken the sauce by whisking in 2 tablespoons of butter, a small piece at a time, letting each piece become completely absorbed in the sauce before adding another.

Correct the seasoning and add a few drops of lemon juice if desired. Coat the whiting with the sauce and serve immediately.

Suggested wine White Jurançon.

HÔTEL DES ROCHERS *
'Chez Justin'
PLOUMANACH-EN-PERROS-GUIREC (CÔTES-DU-NORD)

STEAK DE LOTTE AU POIVRE

The flesh of the angler fish, firm as meat, is very suited to being cooked like steak au poivre *and can be flambéed. The result is delicious and original.*

For each person

250g angler fish flesh
mignonette pepper or white
   peppercorns crushed
salt
3–4 tbs groundnut oil
2 tbs unsalted butter
$\frac{1}{2}$dl cognac
$\frac{1}{2}$dl port

1dl reduced veal stock
or a little meat glaze
or a little veal stock thickened
   with potato starch or
   arrowroot

To finish the sauce

2 tbs unsalted butter
2dl double cream

To prepare Ask the fishmonger to cut you a steak of angler fish about 2·5cm thick and weighing about 250g. Season the steak with salt and dip it into the *mignonette* pepper or the crushed white peppercorns, pressing the grains well into the fish.

To cook Heat the oil in a thick sauté pan, preferably a copper one, seal quickly on both sides and then cook over a low heat for about 10 to 12 minutes turning it over so that both sides cook evenly. Remove the fish and keep hot. Clean the pan, add the butter, put back the steak and warm through over a lively heat. Pour the cognac over the fish and flambé it.

To make the sauce Pour in the port to deglaze the juices in the pan. Add the reduced veal stock, the meat glaze or the thickened veal stock. Transfer the steak to a small heated serving-dish.

To finish the sauce Put the butter into the sauté-pan, whisk in the cream, warm through and scrape in all the little particles from the sides and bottom of the pan with a whisk. Strain all the sauce over the steak.

Serve with steamed potatoes.

Suggested wine Muscadet.

CHARRETON *
LES HALLES (RHÔNE)

FILETS DE LOTTE AU GRATIN

A very simple dish of sliced angler fish cooked in the oven in a concentrated mixture of white wine and finely sliced mushrooms.

For 4 people

4 slices angler fish, each
  weighing 150–200g
salt, freshly milled black
  pepper
200g mushrooms

2 shallots, very finely chopped
2 tbs oil
2 tbs unsalted butter, diced
1dl dry white wine
50g fresh breadcrumbs
lemon juice (optional)

To prepare Cut off the stalks of the mushrooms level with the caps and slice the caps finely. Stew the chopped shallots gently in the oil for a few minutes. Sprinkle the stewed shallot over the bottom of an earthenware or metal oven dish and distribute the butter on top. Add the seasoned slices of fish and stiffen them quickly on both sides. Arrange the mushrooms round the fish, pour in the wine and sprinkle the breadcrumbs over the fish.

To cook Put the dish into a moderate oven, 175°C, 350°F, and cook for 25 to 30 minutes, by which time the breadcrumbed surface should be lightly golden.

Add lemon juice according to taste and serve.

Suggested wine Pouilly Fuissé or Pouilly fumé or Mâcon Viré.

LEI MOUSCARDINS *
SAINT-TROPEZ (VAR)

CAPOUM FARCI

A capoum, or scorpion fish, is a large, pink Mediterranean rascasse, with delicate and tasty flesh. This recipe for stuffed capoum may be used for any other fish weighing at least 1½ kilograms. The liver of the fish adds to the flavour of the stuffing.

For 4 people

1 *rascasse*, weighing 1·5kg,
　cleaned, with liver reserved

Stuffing
2 tbs mushrooms, chopped *en
　duxelles**
1 tbs onion, very finely
　chopped
2 tbs unsalted butter
salt, freshly milled black
　pepper
a squeeze lemon juice
2 slices ham, finely chopped
2 tbs mixed herbs (chervil,
　tarragon, parsley), very
　finely chopped

the fish liver, chopped
1 egg, beaten with 2 drops
　water

Vegetable base
2 onions, finely sliced
800g tomatoes, skinned,
　seeded and roughly chopped
2 tbs unsalted butter
2 tbs oil
$\frac{3}{4}$l very dry white wine
thyme, bay leaf
salt, freshly milled black
　pepper

To bind the sauce
$\frac{1}{2}$l double cream
50g unsalted butter

To make the stuffing Stew the chopped mushrooms and onion in the butter with salt, pepper and lemon juice. Put into a bowl with all the other stuffing ingredients, blend well together with a wooden spoon or spatula and stir in the beaten egg. Knead the mixture together in your hands, stuff the fish, wrap it in buttered greaseproof paper and tie it loosely.

To cook the fish Stew the vegetables for the braising base in the oil and butter for 2 or 3 minutes in a fish kettle or a deep oven dish, stirring them with a wooden spoon or spatula. Lay the fish on this vegetable base, pour in the wine and add the thyme, bay leaf and a little salt and pepper.

　Heat, and as soon as the liquid is boiling steadily transfer the dish to a moderate oven, 175°C, 350°F, and bake for about 40 minutes, basting during the cooking. Lift out the fish, keeping it in its paper wrapping, and place on a heated serving-dish.

To finish the sauce Strain the cooking juices and reduce in a saucepan on top of the stove by about two-thirds. Add the cream, bring to the boil, remove the pan from the heat and stir the fresh butter into the sauce, which should not boil.

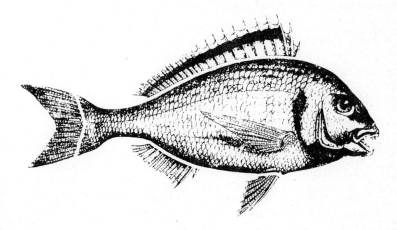

To serve Remove the paper from the *capoum* and serve with a dish of pilaf rice (see p. 294). Serve the sauce in a sauceboat.

Suggested wine A dry white wine, or a rosé from Provence, well chilled.

RÔTISSERIE ATLANTIC ★ ★
WIMEREUX (PAS-DE-CALAIS)

GRONDIN FARCI À LA BOULONNAISE

An unusual recipe in which a large gurnard is stuffed with a delicate mixture of pork and veal, breadcrumbs and herbs and braised in white wine.

For 4 people

1 large grey gurnard weighing 1·8kg, cleaned and seasoned with salt

Stuffing
250g pork and veal mixed and finely minced
2 small shallots, very finely chopped

2 tbs unsalted butter
2 tbs fresh breadcrumbs, sieved
2 tbs *fines herbes* (parsley, chervil and tarragon), finely chopped
1 egg, beaten
2dl good dry white wine
salt, freshly milled black pepper

To make the stuffing Melt the butter in a frying-pan and stew the shallot for a few moments in the butter stirring as you do so. Add the pork and veal and remove the pan from the heat as soon as the meat turns white. Put the contents of the pan into a bowl and leave to cool. Add the egg, breadcrumbs and herbs and season with salt and pepper. Work with a wooden spoon or spatula to obtain a smooth mixture. Shape the stuffing into a roll and press it into the prepared and salted fish. Do not sew or tie up the fish.

To cook the fish Put the fish into a buttered oven dish, pour over the wine and cover with buttered greaseproof paper or silver foil. Heat the dish on top of the stove until the liquid starts to shudder, transfer to a moderate oven, 170°C, 325°F, and cook for 30 minutes. Remove the paper 5 minutes before the end of the cooking time. Serve in the dish in which it was cooked.

Suggested wine Mâcon Viré or Sancerre.

ERMITAGE MESSONNIER ★ ★
BELLEVUE-LES-ANGLES (GARD)

LOUP DE LA MÉDITERRANÉE BRAISÉ AU RICARD

One of the finest of Mediterranean fish stuffed with finely sliced vegetables and herbs and braised in lettuce leaves. The reduced cooking liquid is blended with Béarnaise sauce well flavoured with tarragon. Ricard gives a pleasing taste of aniseed.

For 4 people

1 sea bass, weighing 1·2–1·4kg
  or 2 sea bass, each weighing
  600–700g
2–3 tender lettuces
3–4 tbs unsalted butter
½ cup shallots, very finely
  chopped
1 measure Ricard or other anis
  apéritif
½l fish *fumet*★, reduced
½l dry white wine
salt, freshly milled black
  pepper

Vegetables and herbs for the
  stuffing
1 celery heart
1 fennel bulb
1 leek, white part only
young parsley stalks
tarragon leaves, very finely
  sliced
3–4 tbs unsalted butter

Sauce
½l fish *velouté*★, well thickened
2 tbs unsalted butter, cut into
  small pieces
¼l Béarnaise sauce (see p. 353),
  well flavoured with tarragon

Gut and clean the bass and plunge them into simmering water for a few seconds. Remove all the skin and stomach and gills. Season with salt and pepper.

To make the stuffing Cut all the vegetables and herbs into very thin strips, then melt gently in the butter without letting them take colour. Season with salt and pepper, leave to cool and stuff the fish.

Plunge the very green lettuce leaves into a large pan of boiling water and leave for 1 minute. Run the leaves under cold water, then dry carefully in absorbent paper. Wrap the bass completely in the lettuce leaves.

To cook the bass Butter an oven-dish very generously, leaving a few knobs of butter on the bottom and sides. Sprinkle a layer of shallots over the bottom of the dish and lay the bass on top. Sprinkle the Ricard over the fish and leave the dish in a cool place for 1 to 2 hours.

Pour over the fish *fumet* and the wine, which should come half-way up the sides of the bass. Braise in a moderate oven, 175°C, 350°F, for 30 to 35 minutes at the most. The lettuce leaves should be soft and a light golden colour. Drain the cooking liquid into a small saucepan and reduce by half.

To make the sauce Add the fish *velouté* and the Béarnaise sauce to the reduced cooking liquid and finally the diced butter, stirring it in well, piece by piece, away from the heat. The sauce should be thick.

To serve Lay the fish on a long serving-dish and coat it with a few spoonfuls of the sauce. Serve the rest in a sauceboat.

Suggested wine White Châteauneuf-du-Pape.

LA RÉSERVE ★ ★
BEAULIEU-SUR-MER (ALPES-MARITIMES)

LOUP FARCI DE LA RÉSERVE
Sea bass, stuffed with herbs and mushrooms, cooked in white wine and fish fumet *and served in its cooking juices flavoured with herbs.*

For 4 people

1 sea bass, weighing about 1kg
salt, freshly milled black
   pepper
1 egg
1dl dry white wine
2dl fish *fumet**, reduced
1 shallot, finely chopped
1 sprig thyme
½ bay leaf
1 clove garlic, cut in half
100g unsalted butter
salt, freshly milled black
   pepper

Stuffing

100g mushrooms, very finely
   chopped
1 tbs unsalted butter
salt, freshly milled black
   pepper
100g fresh fine breadcrumbs
100g unsalted butter
2 hard-boiled egg yolks, sieved
1 tbs parsley, finely chopped
1 tbs chervil, finely chopped
1 tbs chives, very finely cut
   with scissors

To make the stuffing Wring the chopped mushrooms in a clean cloth to squeeze out their natural juice and stew them gently for 1 minute in the butter. Mix the mushrooms and their buttery cooking juice with all the other ingredients for the stuffing; add the egg and bind the mixture by working it with a wooden spoon or spatula.

To prepare the fish Cut the bass open along the back and lift out the central bone without damaging the fish and being careful not to leave any bones behind. Lay it on its back, season with salt and pepper. Spread the inside with the stuffing, press the sides together again and put into a buttered oven proof dish, preferably earthenware. Sprinkle the bass with the white wine and fish *fumet* and add the chopped shallot, thyme, bay leaf, garlic and butter.

To cook the stuffed bass Place the dish in a moderate oven and bake for 20 to 25 minutes, basting once or twice during the cooking. The bass should turn a light golden colour. Serve straight from the oven in the dish in which it was cooked accompanied by steamed potatoes.

Suggested wine White Bellet or Pouilly Fuissé.

LA PALANGROTTE
'Chez Lucienne'
SÈTE (HÉRAULT)

ROUGETS À L'ESCABÈCHE

Red mullet fried in oil and served with a sauce of reduced vinegar flavoured with mint.

For 4 people

8 red mullet, each weighing
about 200g
salt
flour
oil

100g dried mint, pounded with
a pestle in a mortar (or
crumbled)
1dl wine vinegar

To cook Salt the red mullet and flour them lightly. Cook in a frying-pan in very hot oil, which should come half-way up the sides of the fish. Watch carefully to see that they do not burn. Turn them over half-way through.

Transfer to a heated oval serving-dish. Carefully strain 4 tablespoons of the cooking oil into a small saucepan, preferably enamelled.

To make the sauce Boil the mint in the vinegar in another small saucepan. Strain the reduced mixture into the first saucepan, reheat and strain the sauce over the mullet. Sprinkle with very finely chopped parsley and serve hot or cold.

Suggested wine A rosé from Provence.

LA POULARDE *
'Chez Lucullus'
NICE (ALPES-MARITIMES)

ROUGETS À LA SAUVAGE

This is one of the best ways of cooking red mullet. The livers are kept whole and the mullet are delicately flavoured with local herbs.

For 4 people

1 large or 2 medium-sized red
mullet (200g of fish per
person)
1 branch fresh fennel, thyme,
marjoram and dried
rosemary

1dl olive oil, not too strongly-
flavoured
salt, freshly milled black
pepper
milk
flour
1 fluted lemon, sliced

To cook Scale and trim the mullet but do not gut them. Dip them in the milk and then in the flour.

Warm the oil in a frying-pan until it is hot but not smoking. Fry the mullet in the oil, carefully turning them from time to time so that they cook evenly. Watch carefully to see that the oil does not brown. The mullet should take 6 to 8 minutes to cook, depending on their size. Chop the herbs roughly, add them to the pan and spoon the cooking oil over the herbs and the mullet for 4 to 5 minutes.

To serve Arrange the fish on a serving-dish decorated with the fluted lemon slices. Season with salt and pepper and cover with the herbs.

Strain the hot oil over the mullet through a fine sieve covered with a cloth or a piece of muslin. Serve immediately with steamed potatoes, which will soak up the herb-flavoured oil in the most delicious way.

Suggested wine A dry white wine or a rosé from Provence. Never serve red wine with olive oil.

CHEZ MAX *
PARIS 8e: 19 RUE DE CASTELLANE

THON FRAIS BRAISÉ À LA TOMATE

A whole fresh tunny fish cooked in the oven with crushed tomatoes, carrots and onions and served cold with its garnish. An excellent summer dish, that may be prepared in advance.

For 10 people

1 tunny fish weighing 5kg
750g carrots, finely sliced
750g large onions, finely sliced
oil
750g fresh tomatoes, skinned, seeded and crushed
125g tomato purée

1 head garlic, each clove peeled and very finely sliced
1 bouquet garni*, strongly flavoured with thyme
1 tbs rock salt
a pinch cayenne pepper
freshly milled black pepper

To cook Carefully lift off the 4 fillets and reshape the fish. Lightly colour the carrots and onions in oil in a sauté-pan, stirring them with a wooden spoon or spatula. Add the fresh tomato and the tomato purée, the garlic, bouquet garni and seasonings and stew gently for 5 minutes, stirring. Put 3 tablespoons of oil into a large oven dish; cover the bottom with a layer of half the stewed vegetables, lay the tunny fish on top and arrange the rest of the stewed vegetables round the fish. Add the bouquet garni, cover with silver foil and cook in a moderate oven, 175°C, 350°F, for about 1 hour.

To serve Let the tunny fish cool and slice it thinly. Arrange the slices on a serving-dish surrounded by the tomatoes and other vegetables. Serve cold.

Suggested wine A rosé from Provence or Anjou.

LE VENDÔME *
AIX-EN-PROVENCE (BOUCHES-DU-RHÔNE)

BRANDADE À L'HUILE D'OLIVE

A mousse of salt cod, thickened with cream and olive oil, and flavoured with garlic.

For 8 people

1·5kg dried salt cod, seasoned with salt
thyme, bay leaf
black peppercorns
2 cloves garlic, squeezed through a garlic press and pounded with 1 tbs olive oil
1 lemon

2dl fresh double cream
3dl pure olive oil
freshly milled black pepper, salt, if necessary
2–3 tbs Béchamel (see p. 347), if necessary
8 triangular croûtons, fried in oil

Desalt the cod by leaving it overnight under running cold water. It will soften and swell. Scale and put the fish into a fish kettle full of cold water seasoned with thyme, a bay leaf and peppercorns. Heat and simmer for 6 to 8 minutes. Remove the fish kettle from the heat and leave the cod in the liquid for 10 minutes. Drain carefully and remove all the skin and bones. Flake the flesh into an enamelled cast-iron saucepan, add the garlic pounded with olive oil, and a little grated lemon peel.

Gently heat the cream and olive oil separately in 2 small saucepans. Pound the cod with a wooden pestle to help it absorb the cream and oil. Over very low heat incorporate alternately small amounts of cream and oil, working each amount in vigorously with a spoon or spatula until it has been absorbed and continuing until all the cream and oil are used up. The *brandade* should be a white mass, thick and mousse-like. Add a squeeze of lemon juice, freshly milled black pepper and a little salt if necessary.

If the *brandade* is not thick enough, work in 2 or 3 tablespoons of thick, well-seasoned Béchamel with a wooden spoon or spatula.

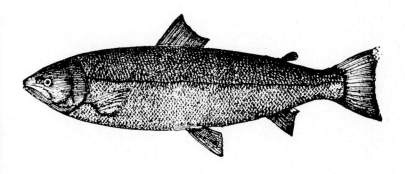

To serve Pile up the very hot *brandade* in a mound on a round heated serving-dish. Score down the sides with a fork, insert the *croûtons* at regular intervals and serve immediately.

Suggested wine Blanc de blancs, domaine d'Ott.

L'OUSTAU DE BAUMANIÈRE ★ ★ ★
LES BAUX-DE-PROVENCE (BOUCHES-DU-RHÔNE)

BRANDADE DE MORUE EN CROUSTADE

Poached egg in a pastry crust garnished with cod mousse lightly flavoured with garlic.

To cook Make a court-bouillon★ with the usual vegetables, herbs, slice of lemon, water, a glass of white wine and peppercorns (no salt). Leave to cool. Poach the cod fillets in the court-bouillon and drain them.

Purée the fillets in a mortar or blender. When the flesh has become mousse-like in texture blend in some fruity olive oil, working it in vigorously with a wooden spoon or spatula. Add a few tablespoons of fresh thick cream to lighten the mixture. Keep the *brandade* very hot.

Prepare some half-puff pastry (see p. 356) and shape it into individual vol-au-vent cases. Cook these pastry cases.

Poach one egg per person and keep the eggs warm.

To serve Put 1 tablespoon of *brandade* at the bottom of each pastry case, lay a poached egg on top and cover with another tablespoon of *brandade*.

Serve with Mousseline sauce (see p. 353) lightly flavoured with lemon juice, in a sauceboat.

Suggested wine A rosé from Provence.

POULTRY

VOLAILLE GRILLÉE HÔTEL DE PARIS

A simple recipe: breadcrumbed chicken, grilled and roasted and served with grilled bacon and Béarnaise sauce.

For 4 people

1 very tender chicken, weighing about 1·2kg
300g fine mushrooms
1 tbs parsley, chopped
a squeeze of lemon juice

100g fresh breadcrumbs, put through a small vegetable mill or blender
100g unsalted butter
8 thin rashers bacon

To cook Cut open the chicken along the back and bone it completely. Divide into 4 pieces. Put these on a baking-sheet and grill under fairly high heat for 5 to 6 minutes on each side. Transfer the chicken pieces to a roasting-tin with the skin side upwards. Clean the mushrooms, cut off the stalks level with the caps, slice, not too finely, and sprinkle with lemon juice. Strew the prepared mushrooms over the chicken pieces, then the chopped parsley and breadcrumbs. Melt the butter and pour half of it over the chicken and cook in a moderately hot oven, about 175°C, 350°F, for 20 to 25 minutes. Baste with the rest of the butter during the cooking.

The breadcrumbed surface of the chicken should be crisp and golden brown. Put the roasting-tin under the grill for a few minutes if the surface is not sufficiently crisp or coloured.

Grill the bacon while the chicken is cooking.

To serve Arrange the chicken pieces on a heated metal serving-dish with the bacon round it. Serve with fried potato chips or crisps and Béarnaise sauce (see p. 353).

Suggested wine A rosé from Provence.

LE CHAPEAU ROUGE *
DIJON (CÔTE-D'OR)

POULET DU MOUTARDIER, SAUCE DIABLE

This chicken grilled with a coating of mustard and bread-crumbs is quickly cooked. Served with Diable sauce and fried potatoes and perhaps grilled tomato halves, it makes a delicious meal for 4 people.

For 4 people

1 Bresse chicken *or* 1 very tender chicken weighing about 1·2–1·3kg
1 cup unsalted butter, just melted
salt, freshly milled black pepper
strong Dijon mustard
dried white breadcrumbs
watercress for the garnish

Diable sauce
3 shallots, finely chopped
black peppercorns, crushed
½dl dry white wine
½dl wine vinegar
1 cup veal stock
2 tbs tarragon, chervil and a very little parsley, very finely chopped
chives, very finely cut with scissors

To cook Split the chicken along the back without cutting it right through. Remove the breast bone and the small rib bones, flatten the chicken for grilling and season it with salt and pepper. Pour the melted butter into a deep dish and roll the chicken in the butter until it is completely coated.

Put the chicken in a pan under the grill, not too close, and cook for about 15 minutes, turning it over after 7 to 8 minutes, making sure that it doesn't become dry. Remove the chicken from the grill, brush it with mustard and dip it in the breadcrumbs. Finish cooking the chicken under the grill, adding a few knobs of butter when it starts to turn golden. It should cook for a total of 25 to 28 minutes.

To serve Carve the chicken into 4 pieces and arrange these on a heated metal serving-dish. Decorate with watercress at one end of the dish. Serve with fried potatoes and Diable sauce in a sauceboat.

To make the Diable sauce Put the chopped shallots, crushed peppercorns, dry white wine and vinegar in a saucepan over the heat and reduce to $1\frac{1}{2}$ tablespoons of liquid. Add the veal stock and boil for 3 minutes. Add the finely chopped *fines herbes* and strain the sauce into a sauceboat.

Suggested wine The Diable sauce would ruin a great wine. Choose a good very dry Sancerre rosé or a more fruity dry rosé from Provence.

CHÂTEAU D'ARTIGNY *
MONTBAZON (INDRES-ET-LOIRE)

POULETS FLAMBÉS
Roast chickens flambéed at table and served with a delicious herb butter flavoured with rum, gin and Chartreuse.

For 6 people

3 tender chickens, each
   weighing 900g–1kg
the chicken livers
salt, freshly milled black
   pepper

Stuffing
3 small onions, each stuck with
   a clove
6 thin slices carrot
3 small sticks celery
9 small sprigs parsley
1 bay leaf, divided into three
3 small sprigs thyme
unsalted butter
oil

Sauce
½ cup unsalted butter
1 tsp each tarragon, shallot and
   parsley, finely chopped
1 tsp chives, finely cut with
   scissors
300g mushrooms, finely sliced
2 tbs dark rum
2 tbs gin
2 tbs yellow Chartreuse
1 medium lump sugar

To cook the chickens Season the insides of the chickens with salt and freshly milled black pepper. Press the liver and a few pieces of butter into each bird and add the vegetables and herbs, equally divided between the chickens.

Truss the chickens. Lay them side by side in a buttered roasting-tin. Brush the surface with oil and cook them at the top of a hot oven at 200°–210°C, 375°–400°F, for 40 to 45 minutes, turning them over during the cooking. When they are cooked put them on a carving board and split them in two, down the back, with poultry shears. Keep the livers but discard the vegetables and herbs from inside the birds.

Arrange the chickens on a long metal serving-dish, add the livers, cover with silver foil and keep hot.

To make the sauce Make the sauce at table on a flamer or portable hotplate. Warm the butter in a small sauté-pan, add the herbs, bring the butter to the boil, add the mushrooms and cook for about 3 minutes. Soak the sugar lump in a little of the rum. Warm the rest of the rum with the gin and Chartreuse in a ladle. Set light to the sugar and rum mixture, pour it into the ladle and pour the contents, flaming, into the pan. Flambé and pour the sauce over the chickens. Baste the chickens and serve.

Suggested wine A light red bordeaux such as Médoc.

LE VERT D'EAU *
ANGERS (MAINE-ET-LOIRE)

FRICASSÉE DE POULET À L'ANGEVINE

A fricassée of chicken cooked in white Anjou wine garnished with little onions and mushrooms. The sauce is thickened with cream. This is an excellent recipe, simple and easy to make.

For 4 people

1 chicken, weighing 1·5kg, cut into 8 pieces
200g button onions, trimmed
100g unsalted butter
350g button mushrooms, quartered
1 bottle dry white Anjou wine
½l double cream

To cook Heat the pieces of chicken and onions in the butter in a small, deep earthenware or metal frying-pan, preferably copper, over very low heat until they are very slightly coloured. Add the mushrooms, pour in the wine and simmer, covered, until the chicken is cooked, which should take about 35 minutes.

Lift out the pieces of chicken and arrange them on the serving-dish with the onions and mushrooms. Cover and keep hot.

To make the sauce Reduce the cooking liquid in the frying pan by half. Add the cream and boil for a few moments. Correct the seasoning and pour the sauce over the chicken and its garnish.

Suggested wine Preferably a white Anjou wine such as Coulée de Serrant or a semi-dry La Roche aux Moines.

HÔTEL DE LA POSTE *
BEAUNE (CÔTE-D'OR)

POULET AU VIN DE BOURGOGNE

A particularly fine fricassée of chicken. The chicken is removed from the pan as soon as it is cooked but the sauce, made with two bottles of white Beaune, is given a long slow cooking. The chicken is coated with the sauce and garnished with little glazed onions, bacon, mushrooms and sliced truffles.

For 4 people

1 chicken, weighing 1·2kg, cut into 8 pieces
1 tbs chicken dripping
2 tbs unsalted butter
2 onions
2 heads garlic, the cloves peeled
1 bouquet garni
2 bottles young and fruity white Beaune of a good vintage, not more than 5 years old
2 tbs flour

Garnish
12 button onions, trimmed and cooked in water, butter, sugar and salt until they glaze

12 rashers larding bacon,
softened in butter
12 buttom mushroom caps,
sautéed in butter, seasoned
with salt, freshly milled
black pepper and a squeeze
of lemon juice

4 truffles, scrubbed, cleaned
and cut into fairly thick
strips

Melt the chicken dripping and the butter in a sauté-pan, preferably copper. Add the onion, garlic and chicken pieces and sauté quickly in the fat until they are very slightly coloured, stirring continuously.

Pour a glass of wine from one of the two bottles and put it aside. Pour all the rest of the wine into the pan, put it over high heat and set light to it as soon as it starts to boil. Stir and dissolve the flour in the reserved glass of wine and add it to the pan. Cook over a low heat for about 30 to 35 minutes until the chicken pieces are tender. Transfer the chicken to the serving dish, cover and keep hot. Strain the sauce into a good saucepan and let it cook and reduce for about $1\frac{1}{2}$ hours, skimming off all traces of fat during the cooking.

To serve Reheat the garnish and arrange it round the chicken, sprinkling the truffle on top so that it shows to good effect; coat the chicken and the garnish with the sauce.

Suggested wine A really good white Beaune.

ROYAL CHAMPAGNE *
CHAMPILLON (MARNE)

POULET SAUTÉ AU CHAMPAGNE
In the champagne country, the chicken is cooked in champagne and champagne is drunk with the dish.

For 4 people

1 fine Bresse chicken, weighing
1·8kg to 2kg
50g unsalted butter
1 glass champagne
¼l double cream
1 egg yolk
salt, freshly milled black
pepper

150g button mushrooms,
sliced and cooked in very
little water with a few knobs
of butter, a squeeze of
lemon juice, salt and freshly
milled black pepper
a squeeze lemon juice

To cook Cut the chicken into 8 pieces for sautéing. Stew these in the butter in a thick-bottomed sauté-pan for about 35 minutes, covering the pan during the last 15 minutes of cooking. By the end of the cooking time the pieces of chicken should be tender and a lovely pale golden colour. Transfer to another pan and keep them, covered, over very low heat.

To make the sauce Pour the glass of champagne into the pan to deglaze the juices and add two-thirds of the cream. Reduce the resulting sauce by a third.

Beat together in a bowl the rest of the cream and the egg yolk, season with salt and pepper and add to the sauce, away from the heat. Strain the sauce into a braising-pan of enamelled cast-iron. Put the pan over a very low heat and beat the sauce with a wire whisk until it thickens. Add the mushrooms and their juices. Check the seasoning and add a squeeze of lemon juice according to taste.

Put the chicken pieces into the sauce and reheat for about 10 minutes. If the sauce is not thick enough, whisk in some *beurre manié*.★

To serve Arrange the chicken pieces on a serving-dish and cover them with all the sauce.

Suggested wine A light champagne or a Blanc de blancs.

LA RÉSERVE ★
PESSAC (GIRONDE)

COQ SAUTÉ AU VIN DE GRAVES
An absolutely original coq au vin *in which the sauce is based on red and white bordeaux wine.*

For 4 people

- 1 farmhouse chicken, weighing 1·5–2kg
- 200g fresh belly of pork, cut into lardoons
- goose fat
- 2 carrots
- 2 onions
- 1 leek, the green part only, finely sliced
- 3 tbs sifted flour
- ⅓ bottle white Graves
- ⅔ bottle red Graves
- 6 cloves garlic, peeled
- 1 tbs tomato purée
- 1 small bouquet garni★

- 300g mushroom caps, quartered (keep the stalks) and cooked with 2 tbs unsalted butter, water, salt, sugar and a little freshly milled black pepper
- glazed onions (see p. 293)
- 6 triangular croûtons, fried in butter
- 1 tbs *fines herbes*, very finely chopped

Beurre manié
- 1 tbs unsalted butter
- 1 tbs flour

To prepare Cut off the neck of the bird and remove the wings, the breasts, and the legs. Put aside for the sauce base the neck, cut in two, the pinions and the carcase with the remaining flesh, chopped into pieces.

To cook the sauce base Brown the neck, wing tips and carcase of the chicken in the goose fat; add the lardoons, carrots, onions,

leeks and mushroom stalks. When the vegetables start to brown sprinkle the flour into the pan and stir it into the other ingredients until it begins to take colour.

Set light to the wine and pour it into the pan. Add the garlic, tomato purée and bouquet garni. Cook over very moderate heat, skimming the fat off the surface during the cooking.

When the sauce is cooked, there should be just over half a litre. Strain and skim the fat carefully off the surface with a spoon.

To cook the chicken Using the same sauté-pan, brown the legs and breasts, stirring the pieces into the goose fat, then add the sauce base and cook gently. Remove the chicken pieces when they are cooked and reserve them.

To make the sauce Strain the juices through a conical sieve and check the seasoning, adding salt and freshly milled black pepper if necessary. Add a pinch of sugar and the *beurre manié*, beating it into the sauce with a wire whisk.

To serve Put the chicken pieces back into the sauce, add the mushroom caps and glazed onions and reheat for a few moments. Transfer the chicken, vegetables and sauce to a round serving-bowl. Spike with croûtons, sprinkle with *fines herbes* and serve very hot.

Suggested wine Red Graves, Pape Clément or Bouscaut, or Haut-Brion.

HÔTEL DE FRANCE *
LA CHARTRE-SUR-LE-LOIR (SARTHE)

POULET AU VIN DE CHINON
A young chicken, cut into quarters, cooked like a coq au vin *with a concentrated sauce and served with button onions and mushrooms.*

For 4 people

- 1 chicken, weighing about 1·2kg, cut into 4 pieces
- 4 tbs *demi-glace* (see p. 352) *or* 1dl veal stock
- 125g unsalted butter
- 12 button onions
- 12 lardoons fresh fat belly of pork
- 12 small mushroom caps, cooked with very little water, butter, a squeeze of lemon juice, salt and freshly milled black pepper
- 1 small bouquet garni* (thyme, parsley, bay leaf)
- 1 bottle good Chinon wine, not more than 5 years old
- 1 tbs parsley, very finely chopped
- 2 tbs oil
- 2 cloves garlic, crushed
- 1 tbs flour

*Beurre manié**
- 1 tbs butter
- 1 tbs flour

Heat the butter and the oil in a sauté-pan, add the chicken pieces and sauté them for about 10 minutes over moderate heat. Add the onions and the lardoons and continue to cook until all the ingredients are golden. Add ½ litre of the wine and when it starts to boil add the bouquet garni. Cover the pan and continue cooking for 30 to 35 minutes, with the liquid simmering gently. Transfer the chicken pieces to a deep round serving-dish, cover and keep warm.

To make the sauce Add 2 decilitres of the wine and the 2 crushed garlic cloves to the liquid in the sauté-pan, let it reduce over a lively heat and moisten with the *demi-glace* or well-flavoured veal stock. Reduce a little more. Strain the sauce into a saucepan and add the *beurre manié*, beating it in with a wire whisk to thicken the sauce.

To serve Add the onions and mushroom caps to the sauce and reheat. Pour the very hot sauce over the chicken pieces and sprinkle with the parsley.

Serve with steamed potatoes or small fried potatoes.

Suggested wine The same Chinon.

AUX ARMES DE FRANCE ★ ★
AMMERSCHWIHR (HAUT-RHIN)

VOLAILLE AU VINAIGRE
A fricassée of chicken in which the cooking butter is deglazed with vinegar and white wine. The sauce is lightly flavoured with tomato purée and thickened with butter.

For 6 or 8 people

2 chickens, each weighing
  1·2kg
salt, freshly milled black
  pepper
150g unsalted butter
1dl wine vinegar

1dl white wine
1 tbs tomato purée
1dl stock
4 cloves garlic, crushed or
  squeezed through a garlic
  press

Cut each chicken into 8 pieces and season with salt and pepper. Heat 4 tablespoons of the butter in a sauté-pan and quickly colour the chicken pieces, turning them over so that they brown evenly. Pour in the vinegar and white wine to deglaze the juices in the pan, add the tomato purée and the stock and cook, covered, over moderate heat for 30 to 35 minutes.

To serve Arrange the chicken pieces on a heated serving dish. Skim the fat off the cooking liquid and add the rest of the butter, beating it in over very low heat a small piece at a time, letting each piece become absorbed before adding the next and taking care not to let the sauce boil. Check the seasoning and strain the sauce over the chicken pieces.

Suggested wine A good dry rosé.

MAXIM'S ★ ★ ★
PARIS 8e: RUE ROYALE

POULET AU VINAIGRE DE XÉRÈS

Chicken served cold with small blanched onions and coated with a delicate jelly flavoured with sherry vinegar which gives the dish a fresh and original taste.

For 4 people
1 fine chicken with good flesh
   weighing 1·7–1·8kg, cut into
   4 pieces
3 tbs unsalted butter
1 tbs oil
4dl sherry vinegar
1½l well-flavoured chicken
   stock, reduced
1 small bouquet garni* (thyme,
   bay leaf, parsley stalks)
salt, freshly milled black
   pepper

*Mirepoix**
2 onions
1 carrot
1 stick celery
3 tbs unsalted butter

Garnish
12 button onions, blanched
1 tbs chives, finely cut with
   scissors

To cook Bone the chicken carcase and crush it. Colour the pieces in the butter and oil in a sauté-pan. Remove them when they are an even light golden colour and reserve. Stew the vegetables for the *mirepoix* in the butter in another sauté-pan until they are soft and transparent, add the crushed chicken carcase and let it brown. Pour in the vinegar to deglaze the juices in the pan, add the chicken quarters and the bouquet garni and cook over very low heat, watching the chicken wings, which will be cooked and should be removed before the legs.

Drain the chicken pieces very carefully and arrange them on a metal serving-dish garnished with the blanched onions.

To make the jelly Reduce the vinegar by a third and add the chicken stock, skimming occasionally to obtain a clear reduction. Strain through a conical sieve or a fine wire sieve covered with muslin. Leave to cool, add the chives and place in the refrigerator to set. When the jelly has reached the consistency of oil, spoon it over the chicken pieces and onions. Put the chicken back into the refrigerator to let this coating of sauce set and then add another coating. Repeat the operation several times until the chicken is well coated with the jelly. Then refrigerate for 1½ to 2 hours and serve when the jelly is completely set.

Suggested wine Still champagne.

HOSTELLERIE DU COQ HARDY ∗
BOUGIVAL (YVELINES)

POULET À L'ESTRAGON, RÔTI À LA BROCHE AU FEU DE BOIS

A simple and delicious dish. The chicken is juicy and tasty, with a crisp skin and a wonderful flavour of tarragon.

For 4 people

1 fine chicken, weighing 1·5–1·8kg
5 sprigs fresh tarragon
2 tbs unsalted butter
3 tbs water

salt, freshly milled black pepper

To prepare Put the sprigs of tarragon inside the chicken and sew up the opening. If it has to be cooked on an electric spit, put the butter, water and an extra sprig of tarragon in a pan beneath the spit which will catch the juices that drip from the chicken.

To cook Secure the chicken firmly on the spit and let it turn over a good charcoal fire for 40 to 45 minutes. Season the cooked chicken lightly with salt and pepper and carve it into pieces. Collect the juices that will escape from the chicken while it is being carved, add them to the juices in the pan beneath the spit, plus a knob of butter, and check the seasoning.

Arrange the chicken pieces on a serving-dish and serve the juice separately, in a small sauceboat.

Suggested wine Château Beychevelle or any good red bordeaux.

AUBERGE DU PÈRE BISE ∗ ∗ ∗
TALLOIRES (HAUTE-SAVOIE)

POULARDE BRAISÉE À LA CRÈME D'ESTRAGON

Fried chicken, stuffed with fresh tarragon, and served in a cream sauce flavoured with tarragon.

For 4 people

1 fine chicken, weighing 1·5kg
the chicken giblets
4 tbs chicken stock

4 tbs double cream
1 bunch fresh tarragon
salt, freshly milled black pepper

Season the inside of the bird with salt and pepper and stuff it with the fresh tarragon. Truss the chicken and warm it in a thick, very well buttered stewpan, turning it over until it is lightly golden on all sides. Remove the bird, put the giblets at the bottom of the pan, replace the bird, add the chicken stock and cook, covered, over very low heat for 40 minutes. The juice should be pale gold. Remove the tarragon and continue cooking for a few moments. Add the cream. Strain the sauce through a fine sieve. It should be smooth, creamy, and rather thin. Cut the chicken into 4 pieces, coat each piece generously with the sauce and serve.

Suggested wine Romanée Saint-Avant or Musigny, or a red burgundy.

RESTAURANT DEMORNEX *
SAINT-JEAN-DE-GONVILLE (AIN)

FRICASSÉE DE POULET À LA CRÈME D'ESTRAGON

A famous recipe from the Ain in the Bugey area. It is a superb way of serving a tender young bird when fresh tarragon is available.

For 4 people

1 tender chicken, weighing 1·2kg, cut into 4 pieces (or one of 1·75kg cut into 8 pieces)
50g unsalted butter
2–3 sprigs fresh tarragon

2dl chicken stock
1dl white wine
2dl cream
salt, freshly milled black pepper, a pinch of cayenne
1 tbs tarragon leaves, very finely chopped

Lightly brown the pieces of chicken in the butter in a sauté-pan over low heat. Add the tarragon, deglaze with the white wine, then moisten with the stock. Season with salt and pepper. Cover and cook gently, turning the chicken pieces once or twice. When the bird is cooked and tender, which should take 20 to 25 minutes, lift out the pieces and arrange them on a heated serving dish. Cover with greaseproof paper. Add the cream to the juices in the pan and reduce over low heat until the sauce becomes smooth and will coat a spoon.

While it is still very hot press the sauce through a muslin strainer on to the chicken. Sprinkle with tarragon.

Serve with Creole rice (see p. 293).

Suggested wine Pouilly Fuissé or a drier Savoie wine such as Roussette de Seyssel or Crépy.

L'AUBERGADE *
PONTCHARTRAIN (YVELINES)

POULET SAUTÉ GRENOBLOISE

A simple, quickly made recipe for chicken sautéed with tomato.

For 4 people

1 fine chicken, cut into 8
   pieces, seasoned with salt
   and freshly milled black
   pepper
3 tbs unsalted butter
1 tbs oil
6 cloves garlic, peeled
1dl dry white wine

2 large or 3 medium-sized
   tomatoes, skinned, seeded
   and pulped
1dl veal stock *or* water
3–4 tbs unsalted butter to
   thicken the sauce
1 tbs parsley, finely chopped

To cook Heat the oil and butter in a sauté-pan, preferably a copper one. Add the chicken pieces, laying them side by side so that they touch. Lightly colour the chicken pieces, turning them over so that they become evenly golden. Add the whole cloves of garlic, cover the pan and continue to cook the chicken over low heat. When it is nearly cooked, drain off some of the butter, pour in the wine to deglaze the remaining juices in the pan, add the tomato, cover the pan and finish the cooking.

To serve Arrange the chicken pieces on a heated metal serving-dish. Remove the garlic and add the veal stock or water to the sauce. Add the butter, beating it in with a wire whisk over very low heat, a little piece at a time, letting one piece become completely absorbed before adding another and taking care not to let the sauce boil. Check the seasoning. Pour all the sauce over the chicken pieces and sprinkle lightly with parsley.

Suggested wine A dry rosé, such as Sancerre or Quincy.

ITHURRIA ★
AINHOA (PYRÉNÉES-ATLANTIQUES)

POULET SAUTÉ À LA BASQUAISE

*A typically Basque dish of chicken with tomatoes and peppers,
the sauce enriched with Bayonne ham and spiced with garlic.
It is served with a pilaff of rice.*

For 4 people

1 young chicken, weighing
   1·2kg
6–7 tbs oil
salt, freshly milled black
   pepper, a pinch of cayenne
flour
4 onions, thinly sliced
4 red peppers, finely chopped
4 cloves garlic, crushed and
   pounded with 1 tbs oil

10 tomatoes, skinned, seeded
   and pulped
2 tbs tomato paste
2 lumps sugar
1 bouquet garni★ (thyme,
   bay leaf, parsley, chervil)
1 small bone from a Bayonne
   ham *or* a piece of Bayonne
   ham weighing about 200g
1 tbs parsley, finely chopped
1dl water

Divide the chicken into 4 pieces. Trim away any bits from the
inside the carcase, salt and flour the pieces.

Heat 4 tablespoons of the oil until boiling in a sauté pan and
sauté the chicken pieces in it over a high heat. When they are
lightly browned all over, cover and leave to simmer for 10 minutes.
Take out the chicken pieces. Put another 2 tablespoons of oil
into the same pan and cook the onion for 2 to 3 minutes until just
coloured. Add another tablespoon of oil if necessary and then put
in the peppers. Add the garlic, pulped tomatoes and tomato
paste, the sugar, bouquet garni and ham and season with the salt,
pepper and cayenne. Moisten with about 1 decilitre of water, or
slightly more if necessary. Cook this sauce, covered, for about
15 minutes. Put in the chicken, cover and leave to simmer for
about 30 minutes or until the chicken is tender.

Serve in a fairly deep round dish, sprinkled with the finely
chopped parsley and with a dish of rice pilaf (see p. 294).

Suggested wine Château du Taillan, Médoc.

LA BONNE AUBERGE ★
ANTIBES (ALPES-MARITIMES)

COQUELET SAUTÉ PROVENCALE

*Quartered chicken pieces with tomato. A typical dish from the
South of France, simple, quickly cooked, a pleasing colour and
very tasty.*

For 2 people

1 chicken, weighing 1kg, cut
 into 4 pieces
4 tbs unsalted butter
4 tbs oil
8 button onions, trimmed
4 cloves garlic
6 button mushrooms, halved
thyme, bay leaf, stick of
 celery, tied together

½dl dry white wine
1 tbs *fines herbes*
a few black olives

Tomato base
8 tomatoes, skinned, seeded
 and crushed
2 tbs olive oil
2 tbs unsalted butter
salt, freshly milled black
 pepper

Prepare the tomato base by cooking the crushed tomatoes in the olive oil and butter mixture in a heavy pan for 15 minutes. Season with salt and pepper and reserve.

To cook the chicken Heat the butter and oil in a sauté-pan, preferably a copper one, add the chicken pieces and cook them, turning them to colour evenly, until they are lightly golden. Add the onions, garlic, mushrooms and bouquet garni and continue to cook until the vegetables turn a light golden colour, stirring almost continuously. When the vegetables have taken colour pour over the wine, reduce for a few moments and add the crushed tomato. Cook for 30 minutes. Correct the seasoning after tasting.

To serve Transfer the chicken pieces and their garnish to a deep serving-dish, sprinkle with the *fines herbes*, finely chopped, and decorate with the black olives.

Suggested wine A rosé from Provence would be very suitable.

LE PROVENÇAL *
JUAN-LES-PINS (ALPES-MARITIMES)

POLLO PÉPITORIA
A typically Provençal chicken fricassée. The chicken is sautéed and decorated with a mixture of garlic, almonds, bread soaked in vinegar and a bay leaf. The sauce is thickened with a strongly lemon-flavoured mayonnaise. The dish tastes fresh, original and delicious.

For 4 people

1 chicken, weighing about
 1·5kg, cut into 8 pieces

Provençal base
1 head garlic, each clove
 peeled
1 handful almonds
75–80g white bread in one
 piece, soaked in good wine
 vinegar

salt, freshly milled black
 pepper
½ bay leaf
4 tbs olive oil
1 cup chicken stock, reduced
¾ cup or 10 tbs mayonnaise,
 well-flavoured with lemon
 (see p. 354)

To cook Colour the ingredients for the base in the olive oil in a frying-pan for 2 or 3 minutes. Remove all the ingredients, carefully draining them to leave as much oil as possible in the pan. Put the chicken pieces into the pan and colour them for about 15 minutes, turning them from time to time so that they become an even light golden colour. Add 1 or 2 more spoonfuls of oil if necessary.

Meanwhile reduce the base to a paste by pounding the ingredients in a mortar or putting them twice through a small vegetable mill. Thin the paste by stirring in the reduced poultry stock with a wooden spoon or spatula. Add this sauce to the chicken pieces in the frying-pan, cover and finish cooking over moderate heat for 20 to 25 minutes. Remove the chicken pieces from the pan and keep them warm. Thicken the sauce by beating in the mayonnaise with a wire whisk, away from the heat, a little at a time.

Put the chicken pieces back into the sauce and keep the pan warm in a pan of boiling water. The sauce must not boil.

To serve Transfer the chicken and sauce to a deep round serving-dish and serve with steamed potatoes sprinkled with parsley.

Suggested wine A rosé from Provence, well chilled on ice.

HÔTEL DU GRAND CERF *
ÉVREUX (EURE)

POULET DE FERME AUX MORILLES

A fricassée of chicken with morels and cream, flavoured with flambéed calvados.

For 4 people	¾l fresh double cream
1 farmhouse chicken, weighing 1·2–1·4kg, ready to cook, cut into 8 pieces	*Garnish*
	200g morels, very carefully cleaned and washed to remove any trace of sand
4 tbs unsalted butter	
2 tbs oil	
salt, freshly milled black pepper	3 tbs unsalted butter
	1 tbs oil
1dl calvados, warmed in a ladle	2 tbs shallots, very finely chopped

To prepare Heat 3 tablespoons of butter and 1 tablespoon of oil in a frying-pan and sauté the morels. Add the shallots and cook for about 10 minutes. Reserve.

To cook the chicken Melt the butter and oil in an earthenware sauté-pan with a handle and gently sauté the chicken pieces over moderate heat, turning them, for 6 to 8 minutes. Season with salt and pepper. Pour in the calvados and set light to it, shaking the pan. Pour in the cream and cook, covered, for 25 to 30 minutes. Add the morel garnish 5 minutes before the end of the cooking.

To serve Serve the chicken and morels in the sauté-pan, with a small bowl of Creole rice (see p. 293).

Suggested wine White wine such as Pouilly fumé, or a red bordeaux such as Saint-Émilion.

LA MÈRE CHARLES * * *
MIONNAY (AIN)

POULARDE DE BRESSE MIREILLE

This is more than a simple fricassée of chicken with morels and cream: it is a special dish invented by la Mère Charles of Mionnay, which lies in the 'good triangle' that joins the Lyonnais, Bresse and Bugey.

For 4 people

- 1 chicken, weighing about 1·4kg, cut into 8 pieces
- 1kg fresh morels, very carefully cleaned and washed to remove all traces of sand, wiped and dried

unsalted butter
½dl good dry white wine
1l fresh double cream
salt, freshly milled black pepper
1 egg yolk

Heat 4 or 5 tablespoons of butter in a fairly large sauté-pan, preferably copper, add the chicken pieces and cook them quickly for a few minutes without letting them take any colour. Pour over the wine, let the liquid reduce until it has almost evaporated, then add the morels. Pour in the cream and continue to cook gently for 35 to 40 minutes.

Transfer the chicken pieces and morels to a deep metal serving-dish and keep hot. Reduce the cooking liquid to ½ litre. Beat in the egg yolk with a wire whisk, away from the heat, to thicken the sauce and strain the very hot sauce over the chicken.

Suggested wine A local dry white wine such as Saint-Joseph or white Ermitage.

HÔTEL DE LA CÔTE-D'OR * *
SAULIEU (CÔTE-D'OR)

POULARDE BELLE AURORE

A fricassée of Bresse chicken in a cream sauce. The chicken is cooked in white Meursault wine which gives the sauce a superb flavour and the garnish of morels in puff-pastry adds to the beauty of the dish.

For 4 people

1 fine chicken, weighing 1·5kg,
    cut into 8 pieces
unsalted butter
1½dl white Meursault
1 clove garlic
1 bouquet garni*

Sauce
½l very fresh double cream
5 egg yolks
juice of ½ lemon
salt, freshly milled black
    pepper

Garnish
4 puff pastry cases (see p. 356),
    filled with morels tossed in
    butter, lightly coated with a
    soupçon of sauce, kept hot
    until required

To cook Gently stew the chicken pieces in 4 or 5 tablespoons of butter in a covered sauté-pan for 15 minutes without letting them colour. Uncover the pan, add the wine, garlic and bouquet garni and cook the chicken gently in the liquid for about 40 minutes. Remove the garlic and the bouquet garni.

To make the sauce Beat together the cream and egg yolks in a bowl and add this liaison to the sauce, stirring it in vigorously over very low heat indeed, taking great care not to let the sauce boil. When the sauce has thickened add the lemon juice, 1 or 2 tablespoons of butter and correct the seasoning.

To serve Arrange the chicken in a deep serving-dish and cover with the sauce. Garnish the dish with the morel vol-au-vents.

Suggested wine Chambolle Musigny 'Amoureuses'.

HÔTEL-RESTAURANT INTERNATIONAL RIVOLLIER *
AIX-LES-BAINS (SAVOIE)

POULARDE À LA CRÈME AUX CÈPES DU REVARD

A delicious way of cooking chicken. The cèpes *that grow on Mont Revard, which dominates the Lac du Bourget, have a very strong and wonderful flavour. In this recipe they are sautéed separately from the chicken and are finished in a sauce made from reduced chicken stock, fresh milk and local cream. There is no garlic in the dish.*

For 4 people

1 fine chicken, weighing 1·2kg
unsalted butter
salt, freshly milled black
    pepper
1kg fresh *cèpes*[1]
2dl good dry white wine

½l very good chicken stock

Sauce
¼l fresh rich milk
¼l fresh double cream
100g unsalted butter
50g sifted flour

To cook the cèpes Break the caps off the stalks and peel with a vegetable parer. Keep the skins, which can be used later to flavour a sauce, minced meat or an omelette. Cut the *cèpes* into long fairly thick slices. Put them in a buttered sauté-pan, a copper one if possible, season with salt and pepper and sweat gently, covered, for 30 minutes, stirring occasionally and adding little pieces of butter if necessary. Remove the pan from the heat and reserve.

To cook the chicken Season the inside of the chicken with salt and freshly milled black pepper before trussing. Let it take on an ivory colour in an enamelled cast-iron casserole, then add 4 table-spoons of melted butter. Lay the chicken on its side and spoon the butter over it, then turn the bird on to the other side, adding more butter if necessary. Leave the chicken on its side and pour over the wine and stock.

Cook the chicken gently, covered, for 40 minutes, turning it two or three times. Lift out of the casserole, cut away the trussing string and keep warm in a copper or another metal casserole until ready to serve.

To make the sauce Quickly reduce the cooking liquid to 2 or 3 tablespoons. Add the fresh milk and cream and thicken the sauce with some *beurre manié**. Warm the sauce through beating vigorously until it reaches boiling-point, let it boil for 20 seconds, and strain through a conical sieve on to the reserved *cèpes*. Heat until the sauce is boiling steadily and the *cèpes* are very hot.

Pour the sauce over the chicken and serve immediately.

Suggested wine A light red burgundy from the Côte de Châlons: a Mercurey, for instance.

[1] If *cèpes* are not available, whole caps of small very white button mushrooms or quartered caps of larger mushrooms may be substituted. Either variety should be cooked for 10 to 12 minutes (*editor's note*).

AUBERGE DE L'EMPEREUR *
CHAILLY-EN-BIÈRE (SEINE-ET-MARNE)

COQUELET À LA CRÈME AUX CIBOULETTES

A very young cockerel cut in half and partly boned, for two people. The cream sauce with chives is very pleasing.

For 2 people

1 very young cockerel,
    weighing about 900g, ready
    for cooking
salt, freshly milled black
    pepper

3–4 tbs unsalted butter
$\frac{1}{2}$l double cream
2 rounded tbs chives, very
    finely cut with scissors

To prepare Split the cockerel in two lengthways. Remove the rib bones, and pull out the legs without actually detaching them. Season with salt and freshly milled black pepper.

To cook Melt the butter in a sauté-pan with a lid, preferably a copper one, and add the chicken halves with the inside downwards. Cook them quickly on each side until they become an even pale golden colour, add 2 or 3 tablespoons of hot water, cover the pan and cook over very low heat for 20 minutes. Remove the lid and add the cream away from the heat. Return to the heat and let the sauce reduce fairly rapidly until it becomes perfectly smooth and blended.

    Add the chives and heat through for a few moments without letting the sauce boil. Check the seasoning.

To serve Transfer the chicken halves to a deep, heated serving-dish and coat them with all the sauce.

Suggested wine A fairly full-bodied red burgundy, such as Pommard or Chiroubles.

PAUL BOCUSE * * *
COLLONGES-AU-MONT-D'OR (NEAR LYON) (RHÔNE)

CHAPON DE BRESSE, GROS SEL

This Bresse capon, cooked in coarse salt has an unexpected and delicious flavour. It is easy to make and very rewarding if the bird is a really good tender one. That is the reason the recipe specifies a capon from Bresse. The flavour of the bird, the delicious aroma of the truffle and the pungency of the salt make a sauce unnecessary.

For 6 people

1 fine capon, preferably from
    Bresse, weighing 1·75–1·9kg

1 fresh truffle, washed,
    scrubbed, peeled and finely
    sliced
10kg sea salt

To prepare Insert the slivers of truffle under the skin of the legs and wings of the bird.

To cook Put 3kg of the salt into a large cast-iron casserole and lay the capon on top. Fill the casserole with the rest of the salt and transfer, *uncovered*, to a very hot oven, about 190°–200°C, 375°–400°F. Cook for about 1¾ hours, watching the dish carefully during the cooking and reducing the heat if necessary.

To serve Turn out the chicken on to a carving board and crack open the block of salt that will have formed. The capon will emerge perfectly cooked and deliciously flavoured and seasoned by the salt and truffles.

Serve with a dish of fresh vegetables.

Suggested wine Côtes-du-Rhône.

HENRY *
LYON (RHÔNE)

VOLAILLE DU ROY HENRY TRUFFÉE AU GROS SEL

The chicken is truffled and cooked in a white poultry stock. When cooked, the bird has a beautiful white appearance, marbled with the little pieces of dark truffle which show through the skin. It is served with the usual vegetables for a pot-au-feu, a bowl of rock salt and another of pickled gherkins.

For 4 people

1 chicken, weighing 2kg, ready to cook
2 fresh truffles, scrubbed and finely sliced
salt, freshly milled black pepper

Garnish
12 small carrots, trimmed and rounded
12 small turnips, trimmed and rounded
8 leeks, white parts only
10 button onions, trimmed

White stock
3kg veal knuckle
chicken giblets
chicken carcase, crushed
1 onion
1 carrot
1 leek, white part only
1 stick celery
thyme, bay leaf, tied in a bouquet
1–2 tbs vinegar
salt, freshly milled black pepper

To make the white stock Cook the veal knuckles in salted water with a little vinegar for 12 to 15 minutes. Remove the veal, run it under cold water and dry it between 2 sheets of absorbent paper.

Put the veal knuckle, together with the other ingredients, into a stewpot and add water until it is three-quarters full. Add 15 grams of salt and cook for 3 hours over very gentle heat. Carefully skim the surface when the liquid starts to boil, adding 1 tablespoon of cold water after each skimming. Leave the stock to cool and strain it through a thick cloth or a fine strainer into a large enamelled cast-iron casserole.

To cook the chicken Insert the slivers of truffle beneath the skin of the chicken legs and breast. Put the chicken into the white stock, bring the liquid slowly to the boil and season with 2 turns of the pepper mill. Add the vegetables for the garnish and cook, covered, over moderate heat for 1 hour, taking care to remove the vegetables as soon as they are cooked. Reserve the vegetables in a saucepan, keeping the different ones apart, and moisten with a few tablespoons of stock. Reheat before serving.

To serve Joint the chicken, reshape it and arrange it in a fairly deep serving-dish. Surround with groups of the reheated vegetables and moisten with several spoonsful of the very hot stock.

Serve with a bowl of rock salt and a dish of pickled gherkins.

Suggested wine New Beaujolais, such as Fleurie, or a light red wine.

LA MÈRE BRAZIER * *
COL DE LA LUÈRE (NEAR LYON) (RHÔNE)

POULARDE POCHÉE DEMI-DEUIL

This chicken dish, generously truffled and cooked in an aromatic court-bouillon, has been made famous by one of the most celebrated of the Mères Lyonnaises. The Béarnaise with horse-radish is an excellent accompaniment.

For 4–6 people

2 chickens, each weighing 1kg, seasoned inside with salt and freshly milled pepper and trussed
4 medium-sized truffles, scrubbed, peeled and finely sliced

*Court-bouillon**
6 leeks, white parts only
8 small carrots
4 turnips
2 sticks celery
1 sprig thyme and 1 bay leaf
200g smoked belly of pork, soaked in cold water, diced, blanched for 5 minutes and run under cold water
2½l water
100g unsalted butter

To prepare Slit the skin of the chickens and insert a generous number of slivers of truffles between the flesh and the skin. Push them well in so that their flavour will permeate the inside of the birds.

Prepare a very well-flavoured court-bouillon with the ingredients listed and cook for 1 hour over moderate heat. Leave to cool.

To cook the chickens Poach the chickens in the court-bouillon for 15 minutes from the moment when the liquid starts to boil. Leave the chicken in the pan on the edge of the stove to keep warm without cooking.

To cook the vegetable garnish Remove the vegetables from the court-bouillon, stew them gently in a little butter and arrange them in a round serving-dish. Keep the dish warm. Strain the court-bouillon and reduce it to 3 or 4 tablespoons. Beat in the rest of the butter with a wire whisk away from the heat, a little at a time, letting each piece become thoroughly incorporated before adding another. Spoon the sauce over the vegetables.

Carve each chicken into 4 and serve with the vegetable garnish and a Béarnaise sauce (see p. 353), with horse-radish.

Suggested wine Champagne, well chilled on ice, or, for lovers of red wine, a château-bottled bordeaux.

PAUL BOCUSE ★ ★ ★
COLLONGES-AU-MONT-D'OR (NEAR LYON) (RHÔNE)

DINDE DE CRÉMIEU, TRUFFÉE
A family recipe for the winter. It may be made with very few truffles and will be succulent and fragrant.

For 6 or 8 people
1 turkey, weighing about 3kg
a few slivers of truffle

Stuffing
400g sausage meat
400g truffles, chopped

Court-bouillon★
5–6l cold water
1 veal knuckle
1 oxtail, cut into chunks
carrots, onions, leeks
2 cloves
salt, freshly milled black pepper

To prepare Insert a few slivers of truffle beneath the skin of the turkey before stuffing and trussing it. Wrap in greaseproof paper, then in a bag made of jute or some other coarse, loosely woven fabric.

Dig a fairly shallow hole in the garden and bury the turkey. The cold and dampness of the earth will bring out all the flavour of the truffles, which will permeate the turkey. Keep dogs and other animals away from the place where the turkey is buried. Leave for 2 days.

To cook Prepare the court-bouillon and cook it for 2 hours in a large stewpan. Remove the vegetables after 45 minutes or as soon as they are tender and reserve them. Strain the court-bouillon, leave to cool until it is lukewarm, then add the unwrapped turkey and poach for $1\frac{1}{2}$ hours in the gently simmering stock, turning it carefully during the cooking.

To serve Arrange the stuffing in the middle of a large, heated oval metal serving-dish. Carve the turkey and arrange it round and over the stuffing, pressing it well in. Reheat the vegetables from the court-bouillon and arrange them in little heaps of contrasting colours round the turkey.

Serve a pilaf rice (see p. 294) separately, with the bouillon, which won't need to be reduced, in a small soup-bowl.

Suggested wine A Côtes-du-Rhône or a really good vintage burgundy.

ROSTANG ★ ★
SASSENAGE (ISÈRE)

POULARDE DAUPHINOISE
Truffled chicken stuffed with its liver and foie gras, flavoured with cognac and madeira and cooked in a pig's bladder in a chicken stock.

For 4 people

1 young hen, weighing 1·3kg
1 pig's bladder
100g truffles, finely sliced
100g *foie gras*

$\frac{1}{2}$dl good cognac
$\frac{1}{2}$dl very good madeira
$\frac{1}{2}$dl truffle essence (optional)
4l chicken stock
salt, freshly milled black
    pepper

To prepare Soak the pig's bladder in fresh water for 8 to 10 hours before cooking the chicken. Wipe it dry before using. Insert slivers of truffle under the skin of the wings and legs of the bird. Lightly season the inside with salt and pepper and stuff with its liver, the *foie gras* and the rest of the truffles. Truss carefully and put it in the bladder. Season lightly with salt and pepper, pour in the cognac, madeira and truffle essence, and tie the ends of the bladder firmly together with string to seal.

To cook Pour the chicken stock into a deep stewpot or a large enamelled cast-iron casserole and put in the chicken in the bladder, being careful not to pierce the bladder. Bring the stock slowly to the boil and cook the chicken for 40 to 45 minutes. The bladder should remain intact and will have expanded. Lift it out of the stock, untie the string, remove the chicken and pour all the juices from the bladder into a bowl.

Spoon the stuffing out of the chicken and press it through a sieve.

To serve Joint the bird and arrange the pieces on a heated serving-dish. Thicken the juice from the bladder with the sieved stuffing, warm it through and pour into a sauceboat.

Serve the chicken with a dish of mixed vegetables, trimmed, blanched and buttered, each variety arranged in a separate bunch.

Suggested wine A red burgundy such a Volnay.

LE LIÈVRE AMOUREUX *
SAINT-LATTIER (ISÈRE)

POULET AUX ÉCREVISSES

The chicken and crayfish are cooked separately and combined in a sauce made from their cooking juices, flavoured with white burgundy and flambéed with cognac. Madeira and cream give the finishing touch. When you taste this dish you will realize that chicken and crayfish were made for each other.

For 4, 5 or even 6 people

Chicken
1 tender chicken, cut into 8 pieces
3–4 tbs unsalted butter
2dl good dry white wine
2 tomatoes, skinned, seeded and pulped
salt, freshly milled black pepper

Crayfish
1kg crayfish
4 tbs unsalted butter

1 tbs shallot, finely chopped
1 clove garlic, squeezed through a garlic press
1 glass cognac
2 tbs flour
1dl dry white wine
1dl chicken stock
salt, freshly milled black pepper
a pinch saffron

Sauce
1 small glass madeira
3 tbs fresh double cream
1 tbs chervil, chopped

To cook the chicken Melt the butter in a sauté-pan, add the chicken pieces and turn them in the butter until they become lightly golden. Season lightly with salt and add a third of the wine. Cover the pan and cook for 20 to 25 minutes, adding the rest of the wine in two equal parts, the first after 7 minutes and the second after 15 minutes. Add the crushed tomato 10 minutes before the end of the cooking time and finish cooking over moderate heat. Remove the pan from the stove and put it aside, covered, to keep hot.

To cook the crayfish Melt the butter in another larger sauté-pan, add the crayfish and cook them over high heat until the shells turn colour. Add the shallot and garlic, stir, pour in the cognac, and set light to it.

Sprinkle the flour over the crayfish, let it brown slightly, stirring with a wooden spoon or spatula and pour over the wine and chicken stock. Season with salt, pepper and a pinch of saffron.

Cook for 2 to 3 minutes, then add the chicken and its cooking juices. Cover, let the liquid reduce for several minutes and finish by stirring the madeira and then the cream into the sauce.

To serve Arrange the chicken pieces and the crayfish in a fairly deep serving-dish, reserving a few crayfish for decoration. Coat generously with all the sauce, without straining it, sprinkle with chervil, decorate with the remaining crayfish and serve very hot.

Suggested wine White Ermitage.

LE CHÊNE VERT *
SAINT-POURÇAIN-SUR-SIOULE (ALLIER)

POULET AU FROMAGE
A chicken cooked in stock made with the giblets and fresh vegetables. The bird is then cut into pieces, coated with a velouté sauce enriched with eggs and cream, covered with a thick layer of grated Gruyère cheese, and browned in the oven.

For 4 people

1 chicken, weighing 1·35–
  1·5kg, ready for cooking
3 tbs unsalted butter
1 tbs oil
150g Gruyère cheese, grated

Stock
neck and pinions of the
  chicken
claws of the chicken, scalded
  and skinned
2 carrots
2 onions
2 leeks, white parts only

1 stick celery
1 bouquet garni*
1 clove garlic
1 clove
2dl dry white wine (e.g. Saint-
  Pourçain)
1½l water
salt, freshly milled black
  pepper

Sauce
2½ tbs unsalted butter
3½ heaped tbs flour
2 egg yolks
2 tbs double cream
a squeeze lemon juice

To make the stock Make a stock with the ingredients listed and let it boil for 25 minutes. Leave to cool.

To cook the chicken Heat the chicken in the butter and oil, turning it until it turns an ivory colour. Drain well, then poach in the stock for about 35 minutes. Remove from the stock and cut into 4 pieces. Take out the rib bones and cut off the end of the drumstick. Arrange the chicken pieces in a shallow buttered oven dish. Reduce the stock by a third, strain it and carefully skim off the fat.

To make the sauce Make a *velouté* (see p. 347) by cooking together the butter and flour, then moistening with the reduced stock. Bring the sauce to the boil and whisk it with a wire whisk until it is smooth. Thicken the sauce with the egg yolks and cream, beating in the liaison with a wire whisk over very gentle heat. Check the seasoning.

Add a light squeeze of lemon juice, according to taste. Leave to cool.

To serve Coat the chicken pieces with the sauce, spooning it over each piece until it is well covered. Spread each piece with a thick layer of grated Gruyère cheese. Put the dish in a very hot oven, 210°–215°C, 400°–425°F, for a few minutes until the surface is crisp and golden. Serve immediately.

Suggested wine A local wine such as Saint-Pourçain, either white or rosé.

LA POULARDE *
'Chez Lucullus'
NICE (ALPES-MARITIMES)

CAPILOTADE DE POULET PAYSANNE

A variation of casseroled chicken which may be made in advance and reheated in a covered dish over very gentle heat. The chopped garlic and parsley cooked with the chicken give it a true country flavour. It is a simple and practical recipe, requiring only one serving-dish.

For 4 people

1 chicken, weighing about 1·7kg
100g unsalted butter, clarified
500g potatoes, new if possible
12 mushroom caps, finely sliced
2dl groundnut oil
2 cloves garlic, crushed
1 tbs parsley, finely chopped
1 tbs chervil, finely chopped

To cook Heat half the total amount of butter and half the oil in a sauté-pan with a lid. Add the chicken pieces and cook over moderate heat for about 15 minutes, turning the pieces during the cooking and keeping the pan half covered.

Cook the potatoes in the rest of the butter and oil in a smaller sauté-pan until they are very slightly coloured. Add the mushroom caps and cook for a further 2 minutes, mixing with the potatoes. Transfer the contents of the pan into the larger pan, with the chicken.

Cover the large pan and leave it over moderate heat until the chicken and potatoes are cooked and tender. Sprinkle the crushed garlic, parsley and chervil into the pan and heat for a few minutes, stirring so that everything becomes well flavoured.

To serve Transfer the chicken and vegetables to a serving-dish. Stir 4 tablespoons of water or stock into the pan to deglaze the juices, reduce for 1 to 2 minutes and strain the reduced sauce over the chicken.

Suggested wine A red wine from Provence or Beaujolais.

RESTAURANT DROUANT ★ ★
PARIS 2e: PLACE GAILLON

PAUPIETTES DE POULET LUCULLUS
Chicken paupiettes,* stuffed with diced foie gras, *garnished with slices of truffle and served with a sauce enriched with cream.*

For 4 people
- 1 fine chicken, weighing 1·5kg
- 1 truffle, with 4 slivers cut off it and the rest diced
- 100g pink *foie gras*, cut into 4 cubes
- 150g pork caul fat, to wrap round the paupiettes

Sauce
- 1 onion, roughly chopped
- the chicken carcase, crushed
- 3 tbs unsalted butter
- 1dl white wine
- ½l chicken stock or water
- 1 bouquet garni*
- ½l double cream
- salt, freshly milled black pepper

To prepare Divide the chicken into 4 pieces and bone it, keeping 2 centimetres of bone at the end of the pinions and drumsticks. Lift off a little of the flesh from the thickest part of each leg, and chop it very finely and season very lightly with salt and pepper.

To make the sauce Melt the butter in a saucepan, add the crushed chicken bones and let them turn golden over a gentle heat. Stir in the white wine to deglaze the juices, add the stock or water and the bouquet garni, bring to the boil and reduce by half. This should take about 30 minutes. Strain the stock.

To make the paupiettes Make the 4 paupiettes by cutting open the wings and legs and flattening them with the flat of a meat chopper. Put on to each flattened piece of chicken a little of the chopped seasoned meat from the legs, 1 cube of *foie gras* and 2 truffle dice. Roll up each piece of chicken into paupiettes so that the stuffing is well enclosed and wrap each paupiette in a piece of caul fat, letting the bones protrude.

To cook Generously butter a sauté-pan and lay the paupiettes in it so that they touch each other. Let them cook gently for about 10 minutes on top of the stove, pour the strained stock over into the pan, boil for 5 minutes, cover the pan and cook for about 35 minutes in a moderate oven.

To finish the dish Arrange the paupiettes of chicken in a heated serving-dish, strain the cooking juices through muslin or a fine sieve into a small saucepan, bring to the boil, and skim the surface to remove all the fat. Add the cream, reduce to the required consistency, check the seasoning and coat the paupiettes with the sauce.

Put a sliver of truffle on each paupiette and decorate each bone with a little paper frill.

Suggested wine Very dry champagne.

LE COQ HARDI *
BOUGIVAL (YVELINES)

POULET DES GOURMETS EN PIE
A stuffed quarter of chicken for each person, wrapped in puff pastry, served with Chasseur sauce flavoured with madeira and spiced with Worcester sauce.

For 3 people

1 very tender chicken
2 thin slices ham
2 tbs unsalted butter
3 slivers truffle
1 egg yolk
3 tbs double cream
half-puff pastry (see p. 356)

Stuffing
2 tbs double cream
1 tbs parsley, very finely chopped

salt, freshly milled black pepper

Chasseur sauce (see p. 348)
white roux
white wine
chicken stock
madeira
mushrooms
butter
lemon juice
salt, freshly milled black pepper

To prepare Roast the chicken and leave to cool. Cut into 4 pieces. Bone each piece and reserve 1 leg, which will be used for the stuffing.

To make the stuffing Finely dice the meat from the reserved leg and mix it with the cream and parsley; season with salt and pepper.

To make the pastries Make some half-puff pastry and cut into 6 10cm squares.

Sauté the ham for 2 minutes in the butter; cut into 3 squares slightly smaller than the squares of pastry. Arrange 1 square of ham on each of 3 of the pastry squares. Top with 1 tablespoon of the stuffing, a sliver of truffle and a boned chicken piece. Cover with a second square of pastry. Brush the edges of the pastry with water and fold over the edges to make a rim, pressing them together with your fingers. Glaze the surface with egg yolk, then make a crisscross pattern on the surface with the point of a knife and feather the rim. Make a chimney in the top of the pastry to let the steam escape during the cooking, insert a funnel into the chimney and pour in 1 tablespoon of the cream. Put the little pastries into an oven preheated to 190°–205°C, 375°–400°F and cook for about 30 minutes.

To make the sauce Slice the mushrooms finely, and cook with very little water, butter, a squeeze of lemon juice, salt and pepper. Make a white roux in the usual way, pour in the white wine and the chicken stock. Flavour with madeira, add the mushrooms and their juices and a dash of Worcester sauce. Check the seasoning.

Suggested wine A fairly full-bodied red wine: Chinon, Bourgueil.

DUCK AND OTHER BIRDS WITH DARK FLESH

RESTAURANT DROUANT ★ ★
PARIS 2e: PLACE GAILLON

CANARDS RÔTIS GARNIS DE NAVETS
Roast ducklings with turnips and little glazed onions.

For 6 people

2 tender ducklings, each weighing 1·5–1·7kg
200g unsalted butter
salt, freshly milled black pepper
1dl madeira
2dl *demi-glace* (see p. 352)
2dl brown veal stock (see p. 352)

a pinch mixed herbs, dried and pounded (basil, oregano or marjoram, savory, fennel seeds, rosemary)
400g turnips, trimmed to the size of olives and glazed (see p. 293)
18 button onions, trimmed and glazed (see p. 293)

To cook Rub the ducklings with butter, season and roast in a deep ovenproof dish in a moderate oven, 165°–175°C, 325°–350°F. They will take 35 to 40 minutes, depending on their age and quality. Lift them out of the dish and keep hot under greaseproof paper.

To make the sauce Spoon the fat from the dish and stir in two-thirds of the madeira to deglaze the cooking juices. Add the *demi-glace* and veal stock and reduce slightly. Boil together the rest of the madeira and the herbs and stir this infusion into the reduced liquid. Pour a little of this sauce over the turnips and onions and reheat, simmering lightly for 8 to 10 minutes.

To finish the dish Joint the ducklings and arrange them in a serving dish surrounded by the vegetables. Coat with the rest of the sauce.

Suggested wine Saint-Émilion or another red bordeaux.

HÔTEL MÉTROPOLE
LUXEUIL-LES-BAINS (HAUTE-SAÔNE)

CANETONS À L'ORANGE
Roast ducklings in orange sauce flavoured with Grand Marnier, garnished with slices of orange.

For 8 people

2 tender ducklings, each weighing 1·3–1·5kg, with their giblets
2 onions
2 medium-sized carrots, roughly chopped
6 tbs unsalted butter
2 whole oranges for the sauce

2 oranges for the garnish, thinly sliced
1 tbs caster sugar
½l chicken stock
½l dry white wine
1dl Grand Marnier
1 tbs tomato concentrate
1 tbs potato starch or arrowroot

Rub the ducklings with butter and sprinkle with salt and pepper. Put them in a lightly buttered roasting-pan, and add the vegetables and the reserved trimmed giblets from the ducks.

To cook Roast for about 35 minutes in an oven preheated to 175°C, 375°F, then turned down to 165°C, 325°F when the cooking starts. Baste from time to time with the fat from the pan and stir the vegetables and giblets.

While the birds are cooking prepare the sauce.

To make the sauce Finely grate the peel of the oranges and mix with the caster sugar. Put into a small saucepan with half the white wine, the Grand Marnier and the juice from the oranges and simmer for 10 minutes. Keep warm.

When the ducklings are cooked, remove them and skim the fat off the juices in the pan. Add half the stock and the tomato concentrate. Reduce over high heat until the liquid starts to thicken. Add the rest of the white wine and a very little stock. Reduce for a few more minutes. Strain into the reserved orange sauce.

Thin the potato starch with a little white wine. Bring the sauce to the boil, then pour in the diluted starch to thicken it, stirring vigorously all the time.

Carve each duck into 4 neat pieces and put into a sauté pan on top of the stove. Pour over the sauce and transfer to a fairly low oven, 140°–150°C, 275°–300°F, for about 10 minutes.

To serve Arrange the pieces of duck on a serving dish and cover them with the very hot sauce. Garnish with the orange slices.

Suggested wine Anjou de Cabernet or Côte-Rôtie.

HÔTEL DU DAUPHIN ★
L'AIGLE (ORNE)

CANETONS À LA BIGARADE

The ducklings are roasted, jointed and served in a Bigarade sauce (Espagnole sauce with bitter oranges and lemons cooked in a syrup made of sugar and vinegar). This recipe has more character than the usual canard à l'orange *and is more highly flavoured.*

For 10 people

3 ducklings, each weighing about 1·5kg
½ cup clarified butter

Bigarade
¼l white wine vinegar
250g sugar

6 small bitter oranges
2 lemons
½l dry white wine
1l Espagnole sauce (see p. 349)
the duck carcases, crushed
salt, freshly milled black pepper
½ cup boiling water if necessary

To cook the ducklings Rub the ducklings well with the clarified butter and put them side by side in a well-buttered deep enamelled roasting-pan. Cook them for 35 to 40 minutes in an oven preheated to 175°–185°C, 350°–375°F. They should be slightly underdone. Cut off the wings and legs and remove the breast in one piece. Keep the pieces of meat covered. Chop up the carcases and reserve them for the sauce.

To make the sauce Boil the vinegar and sugar in an enamelled cast-iron saucepan until the syrup turns a pale golden colour.

Meanwhile, carefully remove the zest from the oranges and lemon, using a potato peeler. Slice the zest into thin strips and blanch them in boiling water for 10 minutes. Run under cold water and dry on absorbent paper. Cook for 10 minutes in the syrup, then remove. Using a knife with a serrated edge, carefully cut away all the white pith and skin from the peeled oranges and lemons, divide them into their natural sections, add them to the syrup and boil for 5 minutes. Pour in the white wine and the Espagnole sauce, bring back to the boil and add the crushed duck carcases, which should be well covered with liquid. Add boiling water if necessary. Season with salt and pepper and simmer very gently for 2 hours, skimming the surface at frequent intervals. Check the seasoning, remove the orange and lemon sections and reserve.

Strain the sauce through muslin or a fine sieve into a sauté-pan, pressing on the carcases to extract all the juices. Cut the duckling breasts into long fillets and add them with the wings and legs to the sauce in the pan. Reheat, covered, for 5 minutes.

Reheat the orange and lemon sections separately in a little of the sauce.

To serve Arrange the pieces of duckling in a deep round serving-dish, coat with all the sauce and arrange the sections of orange on top.

Suggested wine A very good red bordeaux.

LASSERRE ★ ★ ★
PARIS 8e: 17 AVENUE FRANKLIN-ROOSEVELT

CANARD BRAISÉ À L'ORANGE

A recipe for duck with orange that is both simple and different. There is no orange peel, only orange juice and slices of peeled fresh orange. The sauce is light and exquisite.

For 3 or 4 people

1 duckling, weighing 2–2·2kg
6 fine oranges
200g unsalted butter
1dl Grand Marnier

Sauce
1 tbs wine vinegar

1 tbs caster sugar
1 small ladle orange juice
  (about 3 squeezed oranges)
1½dl brown stock (see p. 352)
salt, freshly milled black
  pepper
½dl Mandarin (orange apéritif)
½dl apricot liqueur

To prepare the oranges Peel the oranges and cut them into segments with a very sharp knife, removing any white pith or fibres.

To cook the duckling Fry the duckling in the butter in an enamelled cast-iron braising-dish or casserole, cooking it gently for 45 minutes. Add the Grand Marnier and simmer for a further

5 minutes. Remove the duck and keep it hot under a piece of greaseproof paper.

To make the sauce Strain the cooking juices from the duck into a good small saucepan. Add the vinegar, sugar, orange juice and brown stock. Simmer gently for 10 minutes, thoroughly skimming off the fat and impurities and strain through a conical sieve. Season with salt and pepper and add the Mandarin and the apricot liqueur.

Put half the orange segments into a small sauté-pan, moisten lightly with 4 or 5 tablespoons of the sauce, warm through and remove from the heat as soon as the liquid starts to boil.

To serve Joint the duckling and arrange the pieces on a long serving-dish. Surround them with the remaining orange segments and coat with the sauce. Serve the rest of the sauce separately.

Suggested wine Saint-Émilion, Tavel rosé or Arbois, according to taste.

LES BERCEAUX *
ÉPERNAY (MARNE)

AIGUILLETTES DE CANETONS MONTMORENCY

Only the breasts of the ducklings are used. They are cut into strips, flambéed with cognac and reheated in a sauce flavoured with port, orange juice, redcurrant jelly and sour Montmorency cherries.

For 4 people

2 ducklings, each weighing
   1·8kg
4–5 lbs unsalted butter
salt, freshly milled black
   pepper
½dl cognac
grated nutmeg

1½dl port
juice of 1 orange
¼l *demi-glace* or brown duck
   stock (see p. 352)
1 tbs redcurrant jelly
500g Montmorency sour
   cherries, stoned

To cook Lift off the meat from the breast of each duckling in 2 pieces by inserting a filleting knife on each side of the bone in the middle of the breast. Do not fillet the meat in advance or it will tend to become dry. Lightly salt the meat and sauté the pieces in the butter in a sauté-pan over fairly high heat, without letting them take colour and turning them during the cooking. The meat should be half-cooked and pink. Drain off the cooking butter, pour in the cognac and set light to it. Season with pepper and grated nutmeg. Remove the pieces of duckling and keep them warm.

To make the sauce Add the port to the pan, stirring it in to deglaze the juices, then add the orange juice and reduce by half.

Meanwhile heat the *demi-glace* or duck stock in a small saucepan, pour in the contents of the sauté-pan and mix well, stirring with a wooden spoon or spatula. Remove the pan from the heat and whisk in the redcurrant jelly with a wire whisk until it melts and is absorbed into the sauce. Add the cherries and warm over very low heat to poach the cherries slightly without letting them boil. Reheat the duckling breasts in the sauce, drain them, place them on a board and cut them into long fillets.

To serve Arrange the duckling fillets on a heated metal serving-dish, coat with half the sauce and garnish with half the cherries. Serve the rest of the sauce and cherries separately in a sauceboat.

Suggested wine A really good red bordeaux such as Bouzy.

EL BRAVO *
SAINT-JEAN-DE-LUZ (PYRÉNÉES-ATLANTIQUES)

CANARDS AUX PÊCHES
Peaches are delicious with duck. This dish may be served with Creole rice or fried potatoes.

For 6 people

2 ducklings, each weighing about 1·7–1·8kg, ready for roasting
2 tbs unsalted butter (if necessary)
salt, freshly milled black pepper
2 tins peaches in syrup, drained and sliced, the syrup reserved

Mirepoix *
2 tbs unsalted butter
1 tbs oil
2 carrots, finely sliced
2 onions, finely sliced
1 clove garlic, crushed
1 bouquet garni* (parsley, thyme and bay leaf, tied together)

Sauce
1dl dry white wine
3dl chicken or veal stock (see p. 352)
3 tbs wine vinegar
1dl peach syrup
½dl Fine Champagne or cognac

To cook the mirepoix Warm the butter and oil in a small sauté-pan, add all the ingredients for the *mirepoix* and stew them gently for 3 to 4 minutes without letting them take colour. Turn all the vegetables and juices into an oven dish or casserole, spreading them out to make a layer of vegetables on the bottom.

To cook the ducklings Arrange the ducklings side by side, touching each other, on top of the vegetables and roast them in a moderately hot oven, 165°–175°C, 325°–350°F, for about 45 minutes, turning them during the cooking. If necessary, add 2 to 3 tablespoons of water and 2 tablespoons of butter during the cooking. Season with salt and pepper. Lift out the ducklings, cover them and keep warm.

Add the white wine to the dish to deglaze the juices, scraping the bottom and sides with a fork. Bring to the boil, moisten with the veal or chicken stock, simmer for 6 to 8 minutes without reducing too much and strain the liquid through a fine sieve into a saucepan, pressing on the vegetables a little. Skim off the fat thoroughly, add the vinegar and peach syrup and bring to the boil. Add the sliced peaches, simmer steadily for 5 minutes, taste and correct the seasoning if necessary.

Set light to the cognac or Fine Champagne in a ladle and add it to the sauce.

To serve Joint the ducklings, arrange the pieces on a deep round serving-dish and coat them with the sauce and the sliced peaches.

Suggested wine Pomerol.

CHEZ DENISE *
ABBAYE DE PORT-ROYAL-DES-CHAMPS (YVELINES)

CANARD AU CIDRE
A dish that cannot hide its Norman origins. The sauce is made with cider, cream and apples.

For 4 people

1 Barbary duckling, weighing
    1·5–1·8kg
50g unsalted butter
½l cider
¼l double cream

salt, freshly milled black
    pepper

Garnish
1kg apples, peeled, cored and
    quartered
50g unsalted butter
½ lemon

To cook Season the inside of the duckling with salt and pepper and truss. Rub well with the butter, put it in a buttered ovenproof dish (preferably an earthenware one) and roast in an oven preheated to 190°C, 375°F, until the breast is golden brown. Turn the duck to cook first one side, then the other, basting at intervals. Add more butter if necessary and pour 2 tablespoons of hot water down by the side of the duck. Roast for 35 to 40 minutes, remove the duck, joint it and keep it warm.

To make the sauce Skim the fat off the cooking juices and add the cider to deglaze. Let the liquid reduce a little, then add the cream and reduce until the sauce will coat a spoon. Season with salt and pepper.

To cook the apples Rub the quartered apples with lemon juice, sauté them in butter and season lightly with salt and pepper.

To serve Arrange the pieces of duckling on a heated metal serving-dish. Surround the duck with the quartered apples and coast with the very hot sauce.

Suggested wine Bottled cider or Muscadet.

CENTRAL HÔTEL *
ROTISSERIE DE LA CRÉMAILLÈRE
NANTES (LOIRE-ATLANTIQUE)

CANETON AU MUSCADET ET AUX RAISINS MUSCATS

A fricassée of duck garnished with small glazed onions, sautéed mushrooms, muscat grapes and croûtons fried in butter.

For 4 people

1 duckling, weighing about 2kg, jointed into legs, wings, drumsticks and breast
5 tbs butter
50g shallots, finely chopped
1 large glass Muscadet
1 dl very good *demi-glace* sauce (see p. 352)
3 dl fresh cream
a pinch sugar
3 tbs eau-de-vie of Muscadet (or cognac)

6 triangular croûtons, fried in butter

Garnish
12–15 small glazed onions (see p. 293)
1 bunch large Muscat grapes, peeled and pips removed
200g very white button caps, sautéd in butter with salt and pepper

To cook Sauté the pieces of duck in 4 tablespoons of the butter in a frying-pan over moderate heat, beginning with the breast, which should be taken out when hardly cooked. Continue with the wings, then the drumsticks, then the legs, which should be cooked for a few minutes longer and be lightly browned. Remove and keep hot. Strain the cooking butter. Clean and wipe out the pan and put back the strained butter. Add 1 tablespoon of fresh butter. Put in the shallots and sweat them, then pour over the wine and reduce by a quarter. Add the *demi-glace* sauce and the cream and bring to the boil. Put the pieces of duck back into the sauce to finish cooking. Add the pinch of sugar and the eau-de-vie or cognac flambéed in a kitchen ladle. Adjust seasoning if necessary.

To serve Arrange the pieces of duck on a warmed round metal dish, surround with the garnish of glazed onions, grapes and mushrooms reheated in a little of the sauce and decorate with the reheated croûtons.

Suggested wine Gamay or Bourgueil rosé.

ALLARD ★ ★
PARIS 6e: 41 RUE SAINT-ANDRÉ DES ARTS

CANARD AUX OLIVES
Roast duck in a tomato and olive sauce with a little of the cooking juices from the duck.

For 4 people
1 duck weighing about 1·5kg, ready for roasting
500g stoned green olives
1l clear poultry stock, very lightly salted
1 cup ($\frac{1}{4}$l) spicy tomato sauce, with very little salt

To make the sauce Cook the olives in a saucepan in three-quarters of the stock and allow to simmer for about 1 hour. Add the tomato sauce and simmer for a further 20 to 25 minutes.

To cook the duck While the sauce is cooking, roast the duck in a well-buttered dish at 170°C, 340°F, basting from time to time. Cook for a total of 45 minutes, lowering the oven temperature for the last 20 minutes. Turn the duck and baste it with the remainder (about 1 cup) of the stock, which must be very hot, to obtain plenty of well-flavoured juices for the sauce.

To serve Slice the breast and cut off the legs and wings. Arrange on a well-heated metal serving-dish. Add the juices from the duck to the sauce after straining well and boil for 3 to 5 minutes. Cover the duck with about a third of the sauce and the olives, and serve the remainder in a sauceboat.

Suggested wine A red burgundy or a rosé de Sancerre.

AUX LYONNAIS *
PARIS 2e: 32 RUE SAINT-MARC

CANARD DANS LES CHOUX

A simple winter dish. Cabbage goes very well with duck and both are served in the same dish.

For 4 people

1 duck, weighing about 1·82kg,
  ready for roasting
2kg green cabbage
3 tbs unsalted butter
3 tbs water
salt, pepper

To cook the cabbage Remove the hard ribs and blanch the leaves in a large pan of boiling water for 10 minutes. Drain, rinse through under running water, chop the cabbage roughly and reserve.

To cook the duck Put the duck in a sauté-pan with a lid with half the butter and the water. Roast it in an oven preheated to 175°–185°C, 350°–370°F, basting three times and turning and seasoning at the same time. Cook for about 35 to 40 minutes until a pink juice appears if you insert the point of a knife into one of the thighs.

Carve the duck. Put the cabbage in the pan, and stir well to impregnate it with the duck juices. Season lightly, then add the pieces of duck and cover them with the cabbage. Put the lid on the pan and braise gently in the oven for 10 to 12 minutes, adding a few knobs of butter if necessary.

Serve the duck and cabbage together in a deep serving-dish.

Suggested wine A red Tain-l'Hermitage or Beaujolais.

LE RITZ *
PARIS 1er: 15 PLACE VENDÔME

CANETON EN COCOTTE ESCOFFIER

Cooked in this way the duck remains moist and the mixed vegetables add a fresh taste of spring.

For 4 people

1 tender duck, weighing about
  1·75–1·9kg, seasoned inside
  and out
1 sprig thyme
1 sprig rosemary
1 sprig savory
4 tbs unsalted butter
4 tbs water

Vegetables
1 bunch spring carrots
1 bunch turnips
10 small onions
10 small potatoes

Sauce
1dl champagne
2dl chicken stock (see p. 352)
salt, freshly milled black
  pepper

To cook Put the herbs inside the duck, truss it and place it into a casserole with a lid with 2 tablespoons of the butter. Place over medium heat to seal the duck without browning it at the start of cooking.

Now put the covered casserole into a medium oven, 165°–175°C, 330°–350°F. Baste after 15 minutes, turning and seasoning it. Spoon 2 tablespoons of the hot water round the duck. Add the rest of the butter and the water after another 10 minutes. The total cooking time is 40 to 45 minutes.

To prepare the vegetables Trim the turnips to the shape of olives. Cook them in butter with water, salt, sugar and pepper, until lightly glazed. Glaze the onions in the same way. Put the potatoes in a saucepan filled with cold water; cover, bring to the boil and boil steadily for 5 minutes. Drain and toss them in butter, without allowing them to take colour.

Arrange all the vegetables in an oval china serving-dish with a lid, enough to take the duck as well. Keep hot. When the duck is cooked take it out of the oven, put it in a saucepan so that all the juices drain off it. Remove and add to the pan the rest of the cooking juices from the casserole.

Place the duck on a carving-board and remove the carcase by carving off the legs, the wings and the breast in whole pieces. Don't slice it or else it will go dry. Keep hot, covered with a piece of paper and the lid.

To make the sauce Crush the carcase and put it together with the herbs from inside the duck in a well-buttered sauté-pan over high heat, turning and stirring. When the carcase begins to brown put the champagne in a ladle, set light to it and pour into the pan with the stock to deglaze the juices. Reduce, season with salt and pepper, then strain into the saucepan containing the duck juices. Leave until the fat rises to the surface, remove this very carefully and then simmer over low heat for about 10 minutes, skimming off the impurities with a spoon as they come to the surface.

To finish Meanwhile, lift the meat off the legs and arrange it in the dish containing the vegetables. Carve the breast into fillets and arrange in the middle, with the wings down the sides.

Spoon all the sauce over the duck and put the lid on the dish. At this stage, the dish can be kept waiting if necessary without spoiling.

When ready to serve, put the covered dish in a very low oven for about 10 to 15 minutes, so that the vegetables are fully flavoured with the sauce.

Serve in the same dish.

Suggested wine A red bordeaux such as Saint-Émilion of a good vintage.

HÔTEL DE FRANCE ★ ★
AUCH (GERS)

STEAK DE CANARD AU POIVRE VERT
Slices of duck breast from a duck which has been fattened for foie gras *or from a large Barbary duck, cooked like steak and coated with an interesting sauce in which green peppercorns are added at the end to give spiciness.*

For 2 to 3 people

2 fillets cut from the breast of a *foie gras* duck	1dl double cream
4 tbs goose fat	1 dozen green peppercorns (drained from their preserving liquid)
½dl Espagnole sauce (see p. 349)	4 tbs armagnac
	1dl white wine
	1dl veal stock

To cook In a heavy frying-pan, preferably copper, quickly brown the breast fillets over high heat in the goose fat, leaving them slightly pink. Flambé with the armagnac, then lift out and keep hot.

To make the sauce Lightly deglaze the juices in the pan with the white wine, then pour them into a heavy saucepan. Pour in the veal stock and add the Espagnole sauce. Reduce for about 25 to 30 minutes. Thin with the fresh cream and simmer for another 6 to 8 minutes; 5 minutes before the cooking is finished add the green peppercorns, well drained.

To serve Cut the fillets into escalopes, coat with the sauce and serve very hot.

Suggested wine Madiran or a full-bodied red wine.

AUBERGE DE CONDÉ ★ ★
LA FERTÉ-SOUS-JOUARRE (SEINE-ET-MARNE)

CUISSES DE CANETONS AU BOUZY
Bouzy is a red wine from the Champagne district made from grapes grown between the upland regions round Rheims and the valley of the Marne. It is particularly good with duckling.

For 4 people

2 plump tender ducklings
2 carrots, finely sliced
2 onions, finely sliced
3 tbs unsalted butter

Stock
the duckling carcases
3 tbs *mirepoix*★
¼l very dry white wine
¼l clear chicken stock
1 sprig parsley
1 sprig thyme

Beurre manié★
1 tbs flour
1 tbs unsalted butter

Stuffing
150g neck of pork, minced
the meat from the duck
    carcases, chopped
3 duck's livers, steeped in ½dl
    cognac, then chopped
a small piece garlic, crushed
1 tsp onion, very finely
    chopped
1 tsp parsley, very finely
    chopped
salt, freshly milled black
    pepper

Garnish
3 tbs grapes steeped in strong
    tea, drained and wiped

To prepare Carve off the breast, reserving the slices for use in another dish. Pull off the legs and bone them, leaving on the top of the feet 2 centimetres beneath the ankle joint. Crush the carcases, reserving the rest of the meat for the stuffing.

To make the stock Put the crushed carcases in a saucepan with the *mirepoix*. Soften gently in the butter, then pour in the wine and chicken stock. Add the herbs and season lightly. Simmer for 2 hours, then strain.

To make the stuffing While the stock is cooking, prepare the stuffing. Put the ingredients into a bowl, mix thoroughly, then sauté in the butter for 3 minutes. Leave the mixture to cool slightly before stuffing the duckling legs. Sew up the legs to hermetically hold the stuffing in, then put in the refrigerator for 1 hour.

To cook the legs The legs are cooked on a bed of vegetables in a heavy-bottomed braising-pan. Soften the carrots and onions in the butter without letting them take colour. Spoon them into the bottom of the braising-pan and lay the legs on top. Fry very gently with the duck stock, then cover the pan and place in a moderate oven 165°–170°C, 330°–340°F. When they are cooked, remove them.

To make the sauce Skim the fat from the juices left in the pan. Put the brandy in a ladle, set light to it and add to the pan. Pour the wine into the pan and reduce the sauce by a third, then put the legs back and cook for a further 20 minutes over low heat.

Thicken the sauce with the *beurre manié*, then reduce for a further 10 minutes. Check the seasoning.

To serve Arrange the legs in a deep round metal dish. Sprinkle the grapes and the liquid in which they were steeped over the legs, then cover with the sauce. Serve very hot on heated plates.

Suggested wine Bouzy or a champagne rosé.

CANARD ROUENNAIS

Also known as *canard au sang* ('duck with blood'). The term 'pressed duck', often used in English, is incorrect, since it is not the duck that is pressed, only the carcass.

Rouennais duck, a speciality of Rouen, the capital of Normandy, deserves special mention as it is one of the most famous dishes of this part of France. Innumerable tourists and drivers have made a happy detour to taste it!

Definition It is different from all other ducks because of its exceptional quality. It must be young, with plenty of flesh and extremely tender.

Method of killing The duck must be strangled, not bled. This is essential. While the duck is still warm, pluck the breast so that the blood flows into that part of the bird. Draw it, taking care not to spill any blood and catching any that does escape in a bowl.

To cook Remove the gall from the liver, then replace the liver in the cavity. Set aside the lungs and do not salt the inside. Truss the duck and roast on a spit for about 16 to 20 minutes, then remove and skin. Each of the different parts of the bird are treated separately. Cut off the legs; remove the thigh bones, keeping only the bones of the drumsticks. When ready to serve mark with a hot skewer, brush with melted butter and put under the grill to cook. Sprinkle with crushed, coarse salt. The cooking can be done while the breast is being served. The slices of breast are served 'pink', accompanied at one end of the dish by the wing tips rolled in breadcrumbs and grilled like the legs. The slices of breast are sprinkled with a sauce made from good bordeaux wine seasoned with shallots, flambéed cognac, the blood collected by pressing the carcase and the minced and sieved liver and heart. The whole of the sauce should be sieved through a fine strainer. The sauce is usually made in advance and gently reheated on a spirit heater at the table as it requires careful watching.

In restaurants where the various parts of the bird are served one after the other, the breast and wings first and then the legs, a very hot plate is provided each time. And in restaurants where the drumsticks are not served, one duck is the normal portion for two people.

This is a festive dish which has made the name of some of the great Normandy restaurants. The two recipes we have been given are exceptionally fine. The third, from a great Paris restaurant, is both excellent and rich.

DUCK PRESS In restaurants the carcase is pressed in a special press. At home a strong vegetable mill will do just as well; cut up the carcase with poultry scissors over the mill balanced over a large bowl, so that nothing is lost. Then give 2 or 3 turns backwards and forwards to press out the blood and juice.

HÔTEL DE LA COURONNE *
ROUEN (SEINE-MARITIME)

CANETON À LA ROUENNAISE

The very tender duck is cooked until rare and then carved into pieces. The breast is flambéed and the wings and wingtips are rolled in breadcrumbs and grilled. The carcase is pressed and the blood and juices are added to the sauce.

For 4–5 people

1 Rouen duck, strangled
unsalted butter
crushed coarse salt

Sauce
3dl good red burgundy
½dl good cognac or Fine
   Champagne

1 shallot, very finely chopped
coarse salt, pepper
mixed spices

For the giblets
1 egg white
white breadcrumbs
squeeze of lemon

To cook the duck Prepare according to the instructions on page 196. Truss, season with coarse salt and roast in a hot oven, 190°–200°C, 375°–400°F, for 12 to 15 minutes, turning on all sides.

Dust a long or oval buttered dish with crushed coarse salt and arrange the slices of breast down the centre. Flambé the cognac or Fine Champagne and sprinkle the breast slices lightly, turning them. Dust lightly with crushed salt.

Spread the wings and wing tips with mustard, brush with beaten egg white, then roll in the breadcrumbs and grill, together with the legs, turning them. Arrange the wing tips at the end of the dish, season them with coarse salt and squeeze a little lemon over. Arrange the legs around the slices of breast, then salt.

To prepare the sauce Boil up and reduce the wine and shallot in an enamelled cast-iron saucepan until you are left with 1½ decilitres. Chop up the carcase and press it to extract the blood through a fine sieve and add to the pan; slightly heat the sauce, whisking all the time, but without allowing it to boil. Strain through a fine strainer and then sprinkle over the pieces of duck, but not over the crumbed trimmings. Put the dishes in the oven for a few seconds to glaze lightly.

To serve Serve on a spirit heater at the table, gently stirring the sauce to a good consistency, without letting it coagulate or boil.

Suggested wine A red vintage burgundy.

HÔTEL DE DIEPPE *
ROUEN (SEINE-MARITIME)
CANETON ROUENNAIS *FÉLIX-FAURE*

This dish was eaten for the first time in 1937, on board a steamer called the Félix-Faure *in Le Havre. It has been highly regarded ever since.*

For 2–3 people

1 Rouen duckling weighing 2kg, strangled, with no blood let

Rouennais base
1 bottle (75cl) red Beaune
200g shallot, chopped
75cl veal stock

thyme
a pinch mixed spice
salt, pepper

Sauce
½dl brandy
1dl port
a squeeze lemon
200g unsalted butter
freshly milled pepper

To make the Rouennais base Reduce the wine with the shallot and a sprig of thyme until it forms a glaze, either in the oven or under the grill. Pour in the veal stock. Add a pinch of mixed spice, salt and freshly milled pepper. Cook the resulting sauce over medium heat for 1 hour, skimming frequently.

To prepare and cook the duck Clean the duck, chop up the heart and liver and put them into a conical sieve. Place the sieve over a saucepan and pour the Rouennais base through it, pressing well to extract the juices and flavour from the giblets.

Seal the prepared duck on a spit and cook for about 17 to 18 minutes. Carve the breast into long thin slices and arrange them on a buttered metal dish. Spread the wings and legs with mustard, roll them in breadcrumbs and grill them under a very hot grill. Add them to the dish. Press the carcase, letting the blood and juices drip into a bowl.

To finish the sauce Flambé the brandy in a small sauté pan over a table spirit heater. Pour over the Rouennais base, then the port and add a squeeze of lemon. Heat until nearly boiling, then draw off the heat and add the blood from the bowl. Beat with a whisk to bind the sauce, then add the butter in little pieces, beating all the time until the sauce thickens. Check the seasoning and spoon the sauce over the breast pieces. Heat the dish without allowing the sauce to boil. Serve on very hot plates.

Suggested wine A Hospice de Beaune of a good vintage.

LUCAS CARTON ★ ★
PARIS 8e: 9 PLACE DE LA MADELEINE

ROUENNAIS À LA ROUENNAISE

This is the personal recipe of Francis Carton, owner of the restaurant. The sauce is particularly rich.

1 good duck weighing 2kg, strangled (see p. 196)	2dl Bordelaise sauce (see p. 350)
2 tsp dry white wine	½ bottle good red burgundy
50g *foie gras*	peel of 1 lemon
50g best unsalted butter	peel of 1 orange
1 level tsp salt	1½dl good cognac
30 half-turns of the pepper mill	

Draw the duck, reserving the blood. Cut up the liver and lungs and press them through a fine strainer. Truss the duck and roast in a very hot oven for 20 minutes.

Meanwhile warm the burgundy in a saucepan with the lemon and orange peel. Reduce to a glaze,★ add the warmed cognac and flambé.

Mix the mustard in a bowl with the white wine and reserve. Using a fork, mash together the *foie gras*, butter, salt and pepper and the remains of the sieved liver and lungs. They must all be thoroughly blended together. Now cut up the duck. Cut the legs in two, separating thighs and drumsticks, carve the breast and wings into fillets, cut up the carcase and press through a 'duck press' to extract all the blood and juices.

To finish the sauce Add the Bordelaise sauce to the reduced burgundy in a heavy-bottomed saucepan, removing the orange and lemon peel. Then add, whisking in over very moderate heat, the *foie gras* mixture. The resulting sauce should be fairly thick. Now add the reserved blood and stir well with the whisk without allowing to boil.

To serve Coat the slices of the breast with the sauce and serve on very hot plates. Serve the legs separately after the breast has been eaten.

Suggested wine A really good red burgundy.

HÔTEL D'ESPAGNE ★
VALENÇAY (INDRE)

PIGEON-PIE

This is an exceedingly savoury and practical dish which may be cooked in advance and reheated. A green salad may be served as an accompaniment.

For 2 or 3 people	salt, freshly milled black pepper, paprika
2 pigeons	
6 thin slices smoked bacon	3 tbs parsley, finely chopped
4 hard-boiled eggs, chopped	250g half-puff pastry (see p. 356)
6 potatoes, peeled and sliced	

To prepare Cut the raw pigeons into four pieces and bone the carcases. Flatten the pieces with the side of a large meat cleaver.

To cook Make some stock from the carcases and reserve. Place in a buttered earthenware pie-dish a layer of bacon, one of pigeon, one of hard-boiled egg and one of potato. Fill the dish with alternate layers of each ingredient, seasoning each lightly with salt, pepper, paprika and chopped parsley.

Cover with a thin layer of pastry, make a hole in the centre and bake in a hot oven, 175°–185°C, 350°–370°F, for 1–1¼ hours, lowering the temperature half-way through the cooking. During the cooking pour the reserved stock into the pie through the hole in the top.

Take out of the oven and leave to stand for 6 to 8 minutes before serving.

Suggested wine A red Chinon.

LE CAMÉLIA ★ ★
BOUGIVAL (YVELINES)

PIGEONNEAUX AUX CONCOMBRES
This dish should be cooked in the spring when young pigeons are at their most tender and cucumbers have not yet formed their pips.

For 6 people

6 tender young pigeons salted, peppered and trussed
2 cloves garlic, unpeeled
unsalted butter
1 heaped tbs chives, very finely cut with scissors

Vegetables
1·5kg cucumbers, peeled and thickly sliced

24 small white onions, each with a cross cut deep into the base
3 tbs unsalted butter
salt, freshly milled black pepper
1 scant tbs caster sugar

Sauce
¼l fresh double cream
½dl Noilly Prat vermouth
salt, freshly milled pepper

To cook the pigeons Butter the pigeons well and place them in a very well-buttered oven dish with the garlic. Place in a moderate oven, 165°–175°C, 330°–350°F. As the pigeons begin to turn golden baste them from time to time. Make sure that the butter does not burn, and pour a little boiling water, 2 or 3 tablespoons at a time, round the side of the pigeons towards the end of the cooking time, which is about 30 minutes in all. At the end of the cookings time there should be a small amount of juice, well concentrated. When the pigeons are done lift them out of the baking-dish and place them in a deep serving dish with a lid. A small copper casserole would be ideal.

To cook the garnish Put the cucumbers and onions in a sauté-pan half full of water. Add 3 tablespoons of butter, salt and pepper.

Cover and cook over high heat for about 8 to 10 minutes, shaking the pan as the liquid evaporates. Remove the lid and sprinkle the sugar over the vegetables to caramelize them slightly. Keep hot.

To make the sauce Deglaze the juices from the pigeons with the fresh cream and allow to reduce until the sauce is thick enough to coat a spoon. Then pour in the vermouth through a conical sieve and bring to the boil. Check the seasoning and strain this over the pigeons.

To serve Arrange the vegetables round the pigeons, put back the lid and simmer for a few moments to allow the different flavours to blend. Sprinkle the chives over the birds and carry the dish to the table.

Suggested wine A red Chambolle Musigny.

ALLARD * *
PARIS 6e: 41 RUE SAINT-ANDRÉ-DES-ARTS

PINTADE AUX LENTILLES
A delicious winter dish. The guinea fowl are served with lentils and little squares of fat pork in a sauce made from chicken stock flavoured with tomato.

For 2 people

1 guinea fowl weighing about
  1kg ready to roast
salt, freshly milled black
  pepper
3 tbs unsalted butter
2 tbs chicken dripping *or* oil
1½dl clear chicken stock
500g lentils washed
1 large onion
a bouquet garni (thyme, bay
  leaf and parsley)

Sauce
100g fresh breast of pork,
  lightly salted
2 tbs chicken dripping
1 large onion, finely chopped
1 cup chicken stock
1 cup concentrated veal stock,
  flavoured with tomato

Garnish
1 bunch watercress, washed
  and drained

To cook the guinea fowl Season the guinea fowl and lay it on its side in a buttered roasting-tin. Coat well with a thick layer of butter mixed with the chicken dripping. Roast in a moderate oven, 170°–180°C, 340°–360°F. As the bird turns golden turn it over on to the other side. Finally lay it on its back until it is cooked. Cover the breast with a piece of silver foil for the rest of the cooking time if it is browning too quickly. Test the bird with the point of a knife. It is done when the juice that seeps out is white, not pink. The total cooking time will be 40 to 45 minutes.

To cook the lentils Put the lentils in a saucepan of cold water and bring to the boil. Add the onion and the bouquet garni. Season with salt and pepper to taste during the cooking and when the lentils are soft, drain and discard the onion and bouquet garni.

To make the sauce While the guinea fowl and the lentils are cooking cut the breast of pork into small squares, plunge them into boiling water, leave 5 minutes, rinse under running cold water, drain and wipe dry. Put them into a sauté-pan with the chicken dripping. When they are soft but barely taking colour add the onion. When the onion begins to turn golden deglaze the juices with the chicken stock. Then add the tomato-flavoured veal stock. Reduce the sauce by half, stirring occasionally with a wooden spoon or spatula.

To serve Carve the bird in half and place on a hot metal dish garnished with the watercress. Spoon over the rest of the juice from the roasting-tin. Put the lentils in a heated vegetable dish, pour the reduced sauce over and stir it in. Season to taste.

Serve the guinea fowl very hot with the lentils.

Suggested wine Beaujolais or a red burgundy.

HOSTEN ★ ★
LANGEAIS (INDRE-ET-LOIRE)

PINTADEAU FARCI AU PIED DE COCHON

The pig's trotter makes the guinea fowl, often a dry bird, pleasantly moist and juicy.

For 4 people

1 young guinea fowl, weighing
    about 1·5kg
unsalted butter
5 tbs water

Stuffing
the reserved heart and liver
    from the guinea fowl
150g breast of pork
150g breast of veal
1 pig's trotter, cooked and
    boned
$\frac{3}{4}$l water
1 heaped tbs flour
juice of half a lemon
salt

Marinade
$\frac{1}{2}$dl brandy
thyme, bay leaf, parsley
1 shallot, finely chopped
1 onion, finely chopped
1 clove garlic, finely chopped
a pinch mixed spice
black peppercorns

To prepare the stuffing Marinate the breast of pork and veal and the liver and heart of the guinea fowl in the marinade for 5 to 6 hours or overnight. Take out and wipe the meat dry. Put everything through the finest mesh of the mincer. Season the stuffing and work together in a bowl with a whole egg.

Important note Do not marinate the pig's trotter. Cook it in the water with the flour, lemon juice and salt only after the other meat has finished marinating. Bone completely.

Clean and prepare the guinea fowl, chop up the pig's trotter, mix with the stuffing and stuff the bird. Sew up with a trussing needle and truss the bird.

To cook the guinea fowl Spread the breast of the guinea fowl with butter and put in a small buttered casserole. Roast, uncovered, in a moderate oven, 170°–180°C, 340°–360°F, for 45 minutes, turning on all sides and basting half-way through. Add 4 tablespoons of hot water and continue the cooking.

When the guinea fowl is cooked carve it into four pieces. Spoon the stuffing on to a heated metal dish and arrange the pieces of guinea fowl round it. Deglaze the juices in the casserole with 1 tablespoon of water and 1 tablespoon of butter. Taste and season if necessary. Strain the juices into a bowl or a small heated sauceboat.

To garnish Guinea fowl goes very well with a *gratin dauphinois* (see p. 281) grilled tomatoes sprinkled with parsley or braised chicory.

Suggested wine A very good bordeaux, or, failing that, a Beaujolais, but don't choose one too young.

GIFFON *
GRANE (DRÔME)

PINTADEAU AUX GIROLLES

A young guinea fowl cut into 4 pieces, flambéed in brandy, served in a cream sauce flavoured with port and garnished with fresh chanterelle mushrooms.

For 4 people

1 young guinea fowl, weighing 1–1·2kg, cut into 4 pieces
6 tbs unsalted butter
3 shallots, very finely chopped
1dl cognac
1dl red port

1dl fresh double cream
250–500g *chanterelles* (or *girolles*)

To cook the guinea fowl Soften but do not brown the pieces of guinea fowl in a well-buttered frying-pan (with 4 tablespoons of the butter) turning them. Add the shallot and stir very gently for 5 to 6 minutes. Pour over the cognac and set light to it; deglaze with the port. Season with salt and pepper, pour over the cream, then replace the lid and cook for another 20 to 25 minutes or until tender. Take out the guinea fowl and reduce the sauce to a good consistency.

To cook the mushrooms While the guinea fowl is cooking, sweat the mushrooms in a buttered pan with the rest of the butter over moderate heat for 10 to 12 minutes, until all their liquid has evaporated, then add them to the guinea fowl. Cover and bring to the boil once more to blend the flavours. Transfer the guinea fowl to a deep heated metal dish, preferably a round one. Garnish with the *chanterelles* and pour the sauce over. Serve very hot.

Suggested wine A Tavel rosé.

LA CROIX-BLANCHE *
CHAUMONT-SUR-THARONNE (LOIR-ET-CHER)

COU D'OIE FARCI, SAUCE AUX RAISINS

A tasty and original first course of goose neck in a sultana sauce. Accompanied by a purée of chestnuts or potatoes it makes a meal on its own.

For 2 people

1 goose neck

Stuffing
250g good sausage meat
100g preserved goose confit or
    goose meat, finely chopped
1–3 truffles, peeled
150g *foie gras*, cut into small
    pieces
salt, freshly milled black
    pepper
1kg goose fat

Raisin sauce
100g good large raisins or
    sultanas

½ bottle dry white wine (e.g.
    Sauvignac)+4–5 lumps
    sugar *or*
½ bottle sweet bordeaux
    white wine (e.g.
    Monbazillac)
1 cup well-seasoned tomato
    sauce flavoured with dried
    herbs
salt, freshly milled black
    pepper, paprika
2 cups concentrated goose,
    duck or chicken stock
2 tbs goose fat
1dl water

To prepare Sew up the neck at the narrowest end. Mix the finely chopped sausage meat, goose meat, *foie gras* and truffles in a bowl. Knead by hand and season with salt and pepper. Stuff the neck and sew up the other end to seal hermetically.

To cook Heat the goose fat in a small cast-iron casserole or frying-pan; put in the neck, bring to the boil and cook for 45 minutes to 1 hour, depending on its thickness.

Cooked in this way the neck may be preserved, completely covered in goose fat, with 6 to 8 necks to a stone jar.

While the neck is cooking prepare the sauce:

To make the sauce Steep the raisins in the wine in advance. Then in an enamel saucepan reduce the wine for 5 to 7 minutes. Add the tomato sauce (also the peelings from the truffles if liked), the seasoning, the stock and the goose fat. Bring to the boil, then cook and reduce over moderate heat, skimming for at least the first 20 minutes. After 30 minutes add the cold water a spoonful at a time. The total cooking time is 1 hour.

When the sauce is ready, put the well-drained neck into the sauce to flavour it. It can be kept hot, if necessary.

To serve Slice the neck and serve with the sultana sauce in a separate sauceboat.

Suggested wine Sauvignon rosé or Chinon or red Bourgeuil.

LAMB AND MUTTON

RESTAURANT LYONNAIS *
TOURS (INDRE-ET-LOIRE)

CÔTES D'AGNEAU VILLANDRY

Lamb cutlets deliciously flavoured with tarragon. Their juices are deglazed with Vouvray and they are served with artichoke bases filled with a duxelles *of mushrooms.*

For 8 people

8 thick or 16 medium-sized lamb cutlets, from the best part of the rib, with the bones trimmed
1 wine glass Vouvray
2 tbs tarragon, very finely chopped
2 tbs thickened veal stock or 2 tbs meat glaze

salt, freshly milled black pepper
about 100g unsalted butter

Garnish
8 cooked artichoke bases, sautéed in butter and sprinkled with lemon
400g mushrooms

Clean wash and dry the mushrooms. Chop finely *en duxelles** and cook over high heat.

To cook the meat Brown the lamb chops over high heat in a buttered sauté-pan, turning them. Lift out, deglaze the pan with Vouvray, add half the tarragon, thicken with the veal stock or add the meat glaze. Reheat the cutlets in this sauce over moderate heat.

To serve Arrange the cutlets on a heated metal dish. Add 1 tablespoon of butter to the boiling sauce off the heat. Pour the sauce over the cutlets and dust with the rest of the tarragon

Garnish the dish with the artichoke hearts stuffed with the mushroom *duxelles*.

Suggested wine Vouvray.

L'OASIS ★ ★ ★
LA NAPOULE (ALPES-MARITIMES)

NOISETTES D'AGNEAU À LA DREUX

Prime lamb cutlets are boned and sautéed in butter, coated with a rich sauce containing madeira, foie gras, *cream and truffles if wished.*

For 4 people

8 fairly thick cutlets taken
    from the best part of the rib,
    boned
4 tbs butter
salt, freshly milled black
    pepper
1dl madeira
2kg veal bones
bones from the cutlets,
    chopped
1 carrot, chopped

1 onion, cut into quarters
1 sprig thyme
$\frac{1}{2}$ bay leaf
2dl dry white wine
1l boiling water

Sauce
the brown stock, reduced
deglazed juices from the
    cutlets
150g *foie gras*
2 tbs fresh cream

To make the brown stock Brown all the ingredients in a dripping tin in a moderate oven, 175°C, 350°F, turning them. They may also be sprinkled with a little melted butter to help the browning process. Then put them into a sauté-pan, pour in the wine and boiling water and cook for $1\frac{1}{2}$ hours, skimming for 20 minutes, occasionally removing any scum. The liquid should reduce by four-fifths. Strain through a sieve lined with a piece of muslin into a good heavy saucepan.

To make the sauce Heat the pan containing the reduced brown stock. Add the mixture or *foie gras* and cream, mashed together with a fork, and then cook the *noisettes* of lamb so as to be able to use their juices.

To cook the noisettes of lamb Heat the butter in a sauté-pan and cook the *noisettes* over high heat, turning half way through. They should remain pink and retain all their juices; overcooking will ruin them. Arrange on a metal dish and keep warm without further cooking for a moment.

To finish the sauce Deglaze the juices from the lamb with the madeira. Boil for a few seconds. Strain into the pan containing the sauce, whisk with a wire whisk and correct the seasoning if necessary. Heat the sauce, without boiling, and spoon over the *noisettes* of lamb. Garnish each with a sliver of truffle (optional).

Suggested wine A really good bordeaux, such as Pomerol.

LA TOUR D'ARGENT ★ ★ ★
PARIS 5e: 15 QUAI DE LA TOURNELLE

NOISETTES DES TOURNELLES

Thick noisettes cut from the fillet of a saddle of lamb. They are sautéed, covered with a little onion purée, then glazed under the grill and served in their cooking juices, deglazed with vermouth and sherry and enriched with butter.

For 10 people

2 good saddles of lamb, boned
½ cup clarified unsalted butter
½dl Noilly Prat vermouth
½dl sherry
1dl veal stock
6 tbs unsalted butter

Soubise purée
500g onions, peeled
4 tbs unsalted butter
4 tbs very thick Béchamel
    sauce (see p. 347)
salt, freshly milled black
    pepper
2 egg yolks

First bone the saddles and carve each into 5 thick steaks or *noisettes*.

To make the Soubise purée Blanch the onions for 5 minutes, then soften them gently in the butter in a saucepan, taking care that they do not take colour. Add the very thick Béchamel and stir thoroughly. Season with salt and pepper and leave to finish cooking over very gentle heat until the onions are very soft. Put through the finest mesh of the vegetable mill. Bind the purée with the egg yolks.

To cook the meat Heat the clarified butter in a sauté-pan and in it sauté the *noisettes* gently until they are golden, turning once. When they are still pink and not quite cooked, lift them out and arrange them on a metal dish. Keep hot.

To make the sauce Deglaze the juices in the pan with the vermouth and sherry, reduce, then add the veal stock. Reduce by half. Enrich the reduced sauce with the butter, whisking it in over gentle heat until it rises and taking care that it does not boil. Keep the saucepan hot by putting it in a pan of hot water off the heat.

To finish the dish Put a teaspoon of the Soubise purée on each *noisette*, but don't spread it over. Place the dish under a very hot grill for a minute or two to glaze. Serve with the hot sauce in a separate sauceboat.

Suggested wine The best is Château Gruaud Larose.

LA DIABLE VERT *
RAPHÈLE-LÈS-ARLES (BOUCHES-DU-RHÔNE)

CARRÉ D'AGNEAU GRILLÉ AU FEU DE BOIS

This may seem too simple to require a recipe, but there are rules for grilling over a wood fire, and it must be done with great care.

For 4 people
1 best end of neck of lamb
oil

dried sage leaves, crushed
salt, pepper
a brazier or barbecue

To prepare Remove only the main bone, keeping the tail bones. Cut away the skin and any excess fat. Oil the meat and dust all over with the powdered sage pressing it on with your hands.

To cook Prepare a fire of olive wood or charcoal, or use a barbecue. Once the fire is glowing, place the grill over it a little way away from the fire and put the meat on it. Keep the heat high at first so that the outside of the meat will be crisp. Cook for about 20 minutes, turning from time to time.

To serve Carve into thick cutlets.

Suggested wine A Côte-Rôtie or any other Côtes-du-Rhône.

LE PROVENÇAL
JUAN-LES-PINS (ALPES-MARITIMES)

GIGOT AU PISTOU

A small leg of lamb, strongly flavoured with herbs, boned and stuffed with a paste made from fat bacon, basil, garlic and parsley all chopped and mixed together. The leg of lamb is roasted, wrapped in pastry and returned to the oven to cook the pastry.[1]

For 4 people
1 small very tender leg of
   lamb, weighing under 1kg
about 350g half-puff pastry (6
   turns) (see p. 356) ready to
   use and kept in the
   refrigerator

Pistou
100–120g fat bacon, finely
   chopped

3 cloves garlic, finely chopped,
   then crushed
1½ tbs basil, finely chopped
1 tbs parsley, finely chopped

To glaze
1 egg yolk

To garnish
grilled tomatoes, dusted with
   parsley
small sautéed potatoes

To make the pistou Mix all the ingredients thoroughly with a fork forming them into a small ball.

To prepare the leg of lamb Bone the lamb without cutting through the meat by sliding the blade of a very sharp knife round the bone. Pull out the bone. Fill the cavity with the pistou. Draw the edges of the meat over the cavity and sew up with a trussing needle.

To cook Roast the meat in a very hot oven, 205°–210°C, 400°–425°F for 15 minutes to a maximum of 20 minutes, turning from time to time and basting with melted butter half way through. Take out of the oven.

Roll out the pastry, place on a baking sheet and wrap the leg of lamb in it, leaving the knuckle bone protruding. Seal the pastry carefully with a brush dipped in water. Glaze the surface by brushing with egg yolk diluted with 2 drops of water. Return the oven to 190°–200°C, 375°–400°F, to cook the pastry, about 15 to 20 minutes.

To serve Serve with grilled tomatoes dusted with parsley and small sautéed potatoes.

Suggested wine Red Côtes-de-Provence.

---

[1] The same stuffing may be used for a leg of lamb roasted without the pastry and simply sprinkled with melted butter, in which case one must cook for a further 7 to 8 minutes (*editor's note*).

L'OUSTAU DE BAUMANIÈRE ★ ★ ★
LES-BAUX-DE-PROVENCE (BOUCHES-DU-RHÔNE)

GIGOT D'AGNEAU FARCI EN CROÛTE

A delicious way of cooking spring lamb. A treat for a small number of guests, or else serve two legs for eight people.

4–5 people

1 tender leg of lamb, weighing about 1kg, from a spring lamb not more than 3 months old
350g puff pastry (see p. 356)
1 egg yolk, to glaze

stuffing
6 lambs' kidneys, diced
2 tbs unsalted butter
½dl madeira
100g mushrooms, chopped *en duxelles*★
75g truffles, chopped
a few leaves of dried thyme, rosemary and tarragon, powdered by rubbing between the palms of the hands
salt, freshly milled black pepper

To prepare Using a sharp knife, cut out the bone from the chump end of the leg. The stuffing goes into the cavity left by the bone.

Stew the diced kidneys very gently in butter for a few seconds, then leave for another minute or so over moderate heat, adding the herbs, mushrooms and truffle. Leave to cool, then stuff the cavity. Pull the edges of the meat together at the top and sew up the cavity with a trussing needle.

To cook Rub the leg of lamb with a little softened butter, then place in an ovenproof dish in a hot oven, 200°–210°C, 400°–425°F, for fifteen minutes to brown the meat on the outside and make the juices run. Take out of the oven and leave to cool, until the outside is nearly cold.

Wrap in the rolled-out puff pastry, then place on a baking sheet. Glaze the pastry by brushing it with the egg yolk beaten with 2 drops of water and make a crisscross pattern with the point of a knife. Put the lamb back into the oven, 180°–190°C, 350°–375°F, for 15 to 20 minutes, to finish the cooking and let the pastry turn a nice golden colour.

When the lamb is carved the delicious aroma sealed in by the pastry will waft out.

To serve Serve immediately either with a *mousseline* of fresh peas (see p. 284) or a *gratin dauphinois* (see p. 281), both recipes from the same restaurant.

Suggested wine A really good fairly full-bodied red wine such as Côtes-du-Rhône or Châteauneuf du Pape.

CAPUCIN GOURMAND *
NANCY (MEURTHE-ET-MOSELLE)

ROND DE GIGOT AUX HERBES DE PROVENCE

Thick slices of leg of lamb with the bone, flavoured with thyme, rosemary and savory, fried and served with fresh flageolet beans.

For 4 people

4 thick slices cut through a leg of lamb (ask your butcher to saw through the central bone and leave it in)

4 tbs unsalted butter
1 tbs oil
salt, freshly milled black pepper
thyme, rosemary, powdered savory

Season the slices of lamb with salt and pepper. Using a pastry brush, brush with oil, then press in the herbs.

To cook Heat the butter and the oil in a frying-pan until very hot. Cook the slices of lamb for five minutes on each side. Arrange on a dish. Garnish with a bunch of cress (optional).

Serve with fresh *flageolet* beans in a vegetable dish.

Suggested wine Côtes-de-Provence, either red or rosé.

LE TRINQUET *
SAINT-ÉTIENNE DE BAIGORRY (PYRENÉES-ATLANTIQUES)

SAUTÉ D'AGNEAU À LA NAVARRAISE

Lamb sautéed with onions, garlic, paprika and cayenne pepper. A quick and easy recipe, very typical of the south-west of France.

For 6 people

1 hindquarter spring lamb
3 tbs unsalted butter
2 tbs oil
2 onions, peeled and thinly sliced
6 sweet red peppers, seeded and diced

3 tbs oil
1 tsp paprika
1 clove garlic, crushed
a dash powdered cayenne or 1 small hot red pimento
a dash vinegar
salt, freshly milled black pepper

To cook Cut the piece of lamb into cubes each weighing about 40 grams and season them with salt and and pepper. Heat the butter and oil in a sauté-pan (copper if possible) over moderate heat and gently sauté the pieces of lamb until they are beginning to be lightly browned at the edges. Add the onion, cover the pan and cook for another 5 minutes, stirring. Add a dash of vinegar, stir and leave, covered, off the heat.

Sauté the peppers separately in the hot oil in a frying-pan, stirring with a wooden spoon. Stir in the garlic and cook gently for 7 to 8 minutes, then add the contents of the sauté-pan. Add a dash of cayenne; taste and correct the seasoning, then leave to stew gently, covered, for a few minutes.

To serve Arrange the sautéed lamb on a round, heated metal dish. Garnish with sautéed potatoes and *cèpes*, dust with chopped parsley and serve immediately.

Suggested wine A light red bordeaux.

VEAL

MILLION ★
ALBERTVILLE (SAVOIE)

RÔTI DE VEAU MILLION

The veal is cooked in the oven with its garnish. The cooking juices are skimmed of fat and carefully deglazed.

For 5–6 people

1–1·2kg loin of veal
salt, freshly milled black
    pepper
1 tbs oil
3 tbs unsalted butter

Garnish
3 large tomatoes, peeled,
    seeded and chopped into 4
    pieces
3 shallots, peeled
2 carrots, cut into sticks
1 clove garlic, crushed
6 small onions, peeled, with a
    cross cut deep into the base

Put the butter and oil into a roasting-pan and add the meat. Brown all over in a moderate oven, 170°C, 350°F, without crisping. Add the prepared vegetables. Continue cooking in a moderate oven for about 45 minutes, covering the meat and the vegetables with foil towards the end if necessary. Take out the meat and vegetables.

To make the sauce Spoon a very little of the fat out of the pan. Deglaze with 4–5 tablespoons of hot water and leave to boil for 2 to 3 minutes until reduced, scraping the meat drippings off the bottom of the dish with the flat part of the fork as soon as the juice becomes slightly syrupy.

To serve Carve the meat into slices and arrange them on a heated oval metal serving-dish. Arrange the vegetables round them. Serve the sauce in a sauceboat.

Suggested wine A white wine from Savoy, Roussette de Seyssel or Crépy.

BEAUSÉJOUR ★ ★
LÉRY (EURE)

ESCALOPE VALLÉE D'AUGE

Norman veal is 'white', tender and delicious. These escalopes are sautéed in the truly Norman way, flambéed in calvados and served with cream and apples. It is an unusual and subtle dish.

For 4 people

4 veal escalopes, each weighing
   150g
4 tbs unsalted butter
¼l fresh double cream

2 tbs calvados
2 Normandy or Golden
   Delicious apples, peeled,
   cored and sliced thickly
butter for cooking the apples

Cook the apples in butter in a frying-pan until they are soft but not pulped. Reserve.

To cook the meat Season the escalopes with salt and pepper and flour lightly. Melt the butter in a cast-iron or copper frying-pan over fairly high heat and sauté the escalopes for 3 minutes each side or until golden.

Pour over the calvados and set light to it. Pour in the cream to put out the flames, then reduce over very low heat for about 10 minutes.

Lift out the escalopes and keep them warm on a metal serving-dish. Meanwhile, rapidly reduce the cooking juices from the escalopes and the juices from the apple pan. Spoon this sauce over the escalopes, garnish with the apple slices and serve very hot.

Suggested wine A very good red bordeaux.

GRAND HÔTEL ★
TENCE (HAUTE-LOIRE)

ESCALOPES DE VEAU BRILLAT-SAVARIN

A simple dish and quick to make when all the ingredients are readily available. The escalopes are sautéed, flambéed with cognac and served in cream. The recipe has a famous name.

For 6 people

6 veal escalopes, each weighing
   150g
flour
6 tbs unsalted butter
½ glass cognac
¼l cream

250g button mushrooms,
   cleaned, sliced and cooked
   en fumet (in a very little
   water with little knobs of
   butter, a squeeze of lemon
   juice, salt and pepper)
salt, freshly milled black pepper

To prepare Dip the escalopes in the flour, shaking off any excess. Flatten well so that the flour sticks.

To cook Heat 4 tablespoons of the butter in a heavy frying-pan, put in the escalopes and cook gently until they are golden but not browned. Take out and place on a long heated metal dish. Add the rest of the butter to the pan, scrape the little particles off the bottom of the pan with a fork and strain the cooking butter over the escalopes. Heat the dish, pour over the heated cognac and set light to it.

Mix together the cream, the mushrooms and their cooking liquid in a bowl. Salt and pepper this mixture and cover the escalopes with it. Heat to boiling point then tilt the dish and spoon the juices over the escalopes.

Put the dish under the grill to glaze and serve very hot.

Suggested wine A red bordeaux, such as Saint-Émilion.

ALBERT 1er ET MILAN *
CHAMONIX (HAUTE-SAVOIE)

ESCALOPE SAVOYARDE
Fried escalope of veal with morels, sprinkled with Gruyère cheese and browned in the oven. The juices are deglazed with cognac and madeira and thickened with cream.

For each person

1 escalope of veal, weighing about 150–180g
20g dried morels or 125g button mushrooms
flour
4 tbs butter
1 slice cooked ham, trimmed
2 tbs cognac
3 tbs madeira
1dl veal stock
2 tbs fresh cream
salt, freshly milled black pepper
1 tbs Gruyère cheese, grated

To prepare Put the morels to soak in lightly salted water for 1 hour. Blanch for 5 minutes, wipe and reserve.

Dredge the escalope with flour, dusting off any excess; fry in half the butter in a heavy frying-pan, just colouring both sides.

Butter an oven dish with the rest of the butter, line the bottom with ham and lay the escalope on top. Keep warm.

Deglaze the juices in the pan with the cognac and madeira. Pour in the veal stock and thicken with cream. Add the morels and finish cooking them in this sauce. Taste and season with salt and pepper.

To finish cooking Coat the escalope with the sauce and the morels, sprinkle a thick layer of cheese on top and glaze under the grill or in a hot oven, 200°–205°C, 385°–400°F. Serve with Creole rice (see p. 293).

Suggested wine Pommard or Médoc or a red bordeaux.

FOUQUET'S *
PARIS 8e: 99 AVENUE DES CHAMPS-ÉLYSÉES

MÉDAILLONS DE VEAU ALEXANDRA

The veal médaillons *are fried in butter and their cooking juices are deglazed with brandy and marsala. They are decorated with a sliver of truffle and served with artichoke bases filled with morels (or button mushrooms if you cannot obtain morels).*

For 6 people

6 thick slices cut from 1kg
fillet of veal, trimmed
125g unsalted butter, clarified
6 slivers truffle

Garnish
6 medium-sized fresh artichoke
bases
¾l water
1 heaped tbs flour

salt, freshly milled black
pepper
juice of half a lemon
unsalted butter
60g dried morels
3 tbs double cream

Sauce
1 tbs cognac
1 tbs marsala *or* madeira *or*
sherry
3–4 tbs veal stock

To cook the garnish Start with the garnish. Cook the artichoke bases in the water with the flour, salt and lemon juice. Drain on absorbent paper and fry lightly in butter. Drain a second time.

To cook the mushrooms Soak the morels in cold water for 3 hours. Drain, trim and peel. Cut into small pieces and sauté in butter with salt and pepper. When they are cooked, add the cream, boil for a few minutes, then fill the artichoke hearts with the morels and keep warm on a metal serving-dish. (If you cannot get morels use button mushrooms, chopping the caps into quarters and sautéing them in butter with a squeeze of lemon juice and salt and pepper.)

To cook the veal Heat the butter in a copper frying-pan and cook the veal *médaillons* over low heat, turning half-way through. Cover, finish the cooking and transfer to the dish containing the artichoke bases. Arrange a sliver of truffle on each slice and keep warm.

To make the sauce Pour the butter in which the veal was cooked, into a bowl; it should be clear and it will be used later. Deglaze the pan with the cognac and marsala and reduce a little; then add the juice from the truffles (if they were tinned) and the veal juices. Heat the sauce and pour over the veal, then reheat the butter and strain it over the veal and its garnish.

The *médaillons* may be served with a dish of small trimmed potatoes fried in butter.

Suggested wine A red bordeaux such as Saint-Émilion.

HOSTELLERIE DU CHÂTEAU ★ ★
FÈRE-EN-TARDENOIS (AISNE)

GRENADIN DE VEAU LAGUIPIÈRE

The grenadin *is the veal equivalent of tournedos. The sauce and garnish have flavour and elegance.*

For 4 people

600g fillet of veal, boned, trimmed, larded and divided into 4 good *grenadins*
salt, freshly milled black pepper
100g unsalted butter
1½dl port or madeira
1 ladle thickened veal juice or stock

1 tbs truffle, cut into thin strips
3 tbs firm unsalted butter

Garnish
4 artichoke bases, sweated in butter
salt, freshly milled black pepper
a squeeze lemon
12–16 tender green asparagus tips, cooked

Prepare the garnish and keep hot.

To cook Salt and pepper the *grenadins*, put them into a buttered sauté-pan and cook over moderate heat for about 10 to 12 minutes, depending on their thickness. Take out of the pan.

To make the sauce Deglaze the pan with the port or madeira. When the liquid has reduced slightly pour in the thickened juice or stock and reduce by half. Add the strips of truffle, then stir in the firm butter which should melt without boiling to thicken the sauce.

To serve Reheat the *grenadins* in the sauce for about 5 minutes. Arrange on a heated metal dish, coat with the sauce and garnish with the reheated artichoke hearts filled with asparagus tips.

Suggested wine Red Bouzy or a good red bordeaux.

RESTAURANT DROUANT ★ ★
PARIS 2e: PLACE GAILLON

VEAU MARENGO

Sautéed veal with fresh tomato sauce garnished with glazed onions and fluted mushrooms, croûtons and herbs.

For 8 people

2kg shoulder of veal
1kg breast of veal
4 tbs unsalted butter
3 tbs oil
250g carrots, finely chopped
250g onions, finely chopped
3 tbs sifted flour
½l dry white wine (reduced for 5 minutes before use)

½l veal stock
3 cloves garlic, squeezed through the garlic press
1 bouquet garni
1 tbs mixed herbs finely chopped

Garnish
12 small glazed onions
a squeeze lemon
unsalted butter

salt, freshly milled black	12 fluted mushrooms,
pepper	blanched in very little water
6 tomatoes, skinned, seeded	8 croûtons of white bread, cut
and softened in oil (without	into heart shapes and fried
overcooking)	

Divide the meat into pieces weighing 50 grams.

Heat 3 tablespoons of butter and 2 tablespoons of oil in a sauté-pan. Colour the pieces of meat over moderate heat so that they are evenly golden all over. Take out and keep hot. Add the remaining butter and oil. Put in the vegetables and brown lightly, stirring together. Put back the meat, heat through and sprinkle the flour over it. Stir well to allow the flour to colour lightly, then pour in the wine and veal stock. Add the garlic and bouquet garni as soon as the sauté is boiling steadily.

To cook Cover the pan and cook for $1\frac{1}{2}$ hours over moderate heat.

To serve Arrange the pieces of meat in a deep dish, with the garnish round it. Reduce the sauce slightly and pour over the veal Marengo and the garnish. Dust the vegetables with mixed herbs.

Suggested wine Beaujolais.

CHEZ MICHEL * *
PARIS 10e: 10 RUE DE BELZUNCE

RIS DE VEAU NORMANDE
Sweetbreads braised with apples. The cooking liquid is deglazed with cream.

4 veal sweetbreads	4 Cox's apples, peeled, cored
unsalted butter	and cut into quarters
salt, freshly milled black	$\frac{1}{2}$l double cream
pepper	2 tbs brown veal stock
	$\frac{1}{2}$dl calvados

To cook the sweetbreads Leave to soak for 2 hours in fresh water with a few drops of vinegar; rinse thoroughly under running water. Wipe and blanch them for 10 minutes in boiling salted water. Skin the sweetbreads, removing any little pieces of bone, fatty bits or pieces of cartilage so that they are quite clean.

To cook Butter liberally a heavy-bottomed sauté-pan large enough to take both the sweetbreads and the apples. Put the sweetbreads in first, dot with pieces of butter and season with salt and pepper. Crown with buttered paper and put the pan into the oven for 10 minutes, turning and basting the sweetbreads at intervals. Then spread the apples round them; cover with the cream, add the veal stock and put back into the oven at 190°C, 375°F, to cook the apples and reduce the cream for about 10 minutes or a little longer.

The sweetbreads should be lightly golden, the apples tender and the cooking liquid reduced. Check the seasoning. Take the pan out of the oven, pour over the calvados, which you have heated in a ladle, set light to it and take the dish to the table with the spirit still flaming.

Suggested wine A light red burgundy or a red bordeaux.

JOSEPH
PARIS 8e: 56 RUE PIERRE CHARON

RIS DE VEAU JOSEPH
Sweetbreads in cream, their cooking liquid deglazed with vermouth, madeira and brandy; served with Creole rice.

For 4 people

750–800g sweetbreads
4–5 tbs unsalted butter
salt, freshly milled black
   pepper

Sauce
2 tbs dry Noilly Prat vermouth
2 tbs madeira
2 tbs cognac

¾l fresh crouble cream
1 tsp nutmeg, grated
1 tsp potato starch, diluted in 1
   tbs cold water

To cook Blanch the sweetbreads for 3 to 5 minutes, depending on size. Run under cold water and wipe dry.

Melt the butter in a good heavy copper or enamelled cast-iron sauté-pan, put in the sweetbreads and cook for 12 to 15 minutes, covering the pan for the last 5 minutes. Salt and pepper them; take out and keep hot on a heated metal dish.

To make the sauce Deglaze the pan with the mixture of vermouth, madeira and cognac, and boil for 2 to 3 minutes. Add the cream and nutmeg away from the heat, then reduce for 10 minutes.

Dilute the potato starch and add it to the sauce, off the heat. Beat with a whisk and put back over the heat to thicken. Adjust the seasoning if necessary and pour, very hot, over the sweetbreads. Serve immediately with Créole rice (see p. 293).

Suggested wine A white burgundy such as Corton Charlemagne.

The same recipe from this restaurant may be used for veal kidneys, Use the same weight of trimmed kidneys for 4 people. Add to the sauce 1 teaspoon of powdered paprika and 1 tablespoon of strong Dijon mustard.

HÔTEL DU MIDI *
LAMASTRE (ARDÈCHE)

RIS DE VEAU BRAISÉ À LA CRÈME

A delicate recipe for sweetbreads on toast with a cream and mushroom sauce.

For each person

1 sweetbread
100g unsalted butter
1 onion, finely chopped
1 carrot, finely chopped
salt, freshly milled black
   pepper
1 sprig thyme
1 bay leaf
1dl white wine
1 slice white toast, crusts
   removed

Mushrooms
100g mushrooms

3 tbs water
juice of ½ lemon
1 tbs unsalted butter
salt, freshly milled black
   pepper

Sauce
3 tbs water
1 tbs unsalted butter
1dl cream
3 tbs cognac

Garnish
slivers of truffle
2 puff pastry crescents
   (optional)

To cook the sweetbread Blanch for 3 to 5 minutes, then refresh under cold running water. Drain and wipe with a cloth. Remove any tubes or waste pieces clinging to the sweetbread.

Heat half the butter in a small sauté-pan and stew the onion and carrot fairly quickly; add the thyme and bay leaf then put in the sweetbread. Lightly brown all over, over moderate heat, adding the rest of the butter. Season with salt and pepper. Pour over the white wine and braise, covered, for about 18 to 20 minutes, keeping an eye on the sweetbread, which is fragile. The white wine should be completely reduced by the end of this cooking time. Take out the sweetbread and keep hot on the buttered toast, which has been kept warm on a metal dish. Cover with paper and a lid.

To cook the mushrooms Slice thinly and cook separately in a small saucepan with the water, lemon juice and the butter, divided into small pieces. Add salt and pepper.

The sauce Put 3 tablespoons of water and 1 tablespoon of butter into the pan in which the sweetbread was cooked. Heat and deglaze the sauté-pan, and strain the juices into a small saucepan. Add the cream, boil for a few seconds, stirring with a whisk; add the cognac, flambéed in a ladle, and finally the mushrooms and their juices.

Heat the finished sauce, stirring all the time. Check the seasoning and coat the sweetbread with the boiling sauce.

Optional Garnish with a few slivers of truffle and 2 little crescents of puff pastry.

Suggested wine A dry white wine such as Pouilly Fuissé or Pouilly fumé.

TAILLEVENT ★ ★ ★
PARIS 8e: 15 RUE LAMENNAIS

RIS DE VEAU LAMENNAIS

Braised sweetbreads, the sauce thickened with cream and enriched with truffles and mushrooms.

For 2–3 people
2 sweetbreads
2 tinned truffles, cut into thin
   strips
1½dl dry white wine
juice from the truffles
½l double cream

Braising base
2 medium carrots
3–4 tbs unsalted butter
200g mushrooms, caps only,
   sliced thinly

To prepare Soak the sweetbreads in cold water for 1 to 2 hours. Blanch them for 5 minutes; drain in a sieve and refresh thoroughly under cold water. Gently soften the carrots in butter in a small sauté-pan, adding the mushrooms and continuing to cook, covered for 4 to 5 minutes. Place the sweetbreads and truffles on this bed of softened vegetables.

To cook the sweetbreads Braise them over moderate heat and pour in the white wine and truffle juice. Reduce by a third, then add the double cream and cook gently, still covered, for 20 minutes, turning the sweetbreads from time to time. Take out and keep warm on a metal serving-dish.

To make the sauce Let the cream reduce a little more, check the seasoning and coat the sweetbreads with the sauce and the garnish. Cut each sweetbread into 3 or 4 thick slices at the table.

Suggested wine A really good white burgundy or a good, light red bordeaux.

LAURENT ★
PARIS 8e: 41 AVENUE GABRIEL

RIS DE VEAU RÉGENCE

Whole sweetbreads, braised, served in a rich sauce consisting of port, cream, mushrooms, truffles and little pieces of foie gras.

For 4 people

2 pairs sweetbreads, soaked

Braising base
4 tbs unsalted butter
2 carrots, chopped
2 onions, chopped
1 stick celery
1 sprig thyme

Braising liquid
½dl red port
1dl very dry white wine
1½dl veal or chicken stock,
   reduced and skimmed
salt, freshly milled black
   pepper
Sauce
½ cup fresh double cream

125g mushrooms, chopped and
   stewed in butter
a squeeze lemon
1 slice *foie gras*, chopped

Garnish
4 slivers truffle

To prepare Put the sweetbreads into cold water, bring to the boil and blanch for 3 to 4 minutes. Refresh under cold running water. Trim, removing the tubes and rough parts.

To cook Melt 3 tablespoons of the butter in a sauté-pan with a lid and add the vegetables, spread in a layer. Add the thyme. Sweat the vegetables, stirring with a wooden spoon or spatula, then put the sweetbreads on top. Add the remaining tablespoon of butter and braise the sweetbreads for 5 to 6 minutes; add the port. Reduce a little; pour in the wine and continue to reduce for about 3 minutes. Pour over the stock, season lightly with salt and pepper and cook, covered, for 30 to 35 minutes. Take out the sweetbreads, arrange in a deep round metal dish and keep warm, covered.

To make the sauce Reduce the sauce in the pan by three-quarters. Add the cream and reduce again until the liquid has thickened slightly. Add the mushrooms, lemon juice and pieces of *foie gras*, if you are using it. Check the seasoning. The sauce should be thick enough to coat a spoon lightly.

Lay a sliver of truffle on each sweetbread and coat with the sauce.

Suggested wine A white burgundy such as Chablis or Meursault.

AUBERGE DU PÈRE BISE ★ ★ ★
TALLOIRES (HAUTE-SAVOIE)

FEUILLETÉS AUX RIS DE VEAU
These sweetbread pastries are the best of their kind for flavour and lightness.

For 8 people

2 pairs sweetbreads, each
   weighing 800g
100g unsalted butter
parsley, thyme, bay leaf
shallots
salt, freshly milled black
   pepper

½l very dry white wine
1 glass sherry
150g mushrooms, chopped
a squeeze lemon
600–700g half-puff pastry (see
   p. 356)
1 egg yolk to glaze
3 tbs fresh double cream

To prepare Blanch the sweetbreads and plunge into cold water. Braise them in most of the butter, adding parsley, thyme, bay leaf and shallots in small quantities. Season with salt and pepper. Pour in the white wine and sherry. Allow to reduce a little. Let the sweetbreads cool; skin them carefully and dice them.

Soften the chopped mushrooms in the rest of the butter. Season with salt and pepper and add a squeeze of lemon. Remove the mushrooms and reserve their cooking liquid.

To make the velouté sauce Make a very light roux. Pour in the cooking juices from the sweetbreads and mushrooms. Make the half-puff pastry (6 turns, see p. 356) in the quantity given. When it has been left to stand roll out to a suitable thickness. Allow about 60 grams of pastry (keeping 25 grams for the lid) for each *feuilleté*, and 100 grams of the filling of *velouté* sauce, sweetbreads and mushrooms. Fill the centre of each *feuilleté*, sealing the lid by brushing with water. Glaze with the egg yolk diluted in a drop of water. Decorate the surface with the point of a knife. Cook in a moderate oven, 175°C, 350°F, for about 20 minutes.

Suggested wine A light red bordeaux.

HÔTEL TERMINUS *
ARNAY-LE-DUC (COTE-D'OR)

PAIN DE RIS DE VEAU À L'ANCIENNE

This is not a true sweetbread 'loaf' because a veal quenelle mixture holds the sweetbreads together. It makes a subtle and elegant entrée which will satisfy even the most demanding guests. The sauce, deglazed with port and cream, admirably finishes the dish.

For 6 people

2 sweetbreads, each weighing
   325–350g
1 sprig thyme
½ bay leaf
a pinch coarse salt, freshly
   milled black pepper
larding bacon
1 truffle
1 carrot, chopped
1 onion, chopped
unsalted butter

Panada
½dl water
a pinch salt
1 tbs unsalted butter
50g flour

Quenelle mixture
250g veal, cut from the eye of
   the fillet
100g unsalted butter
2 eggs
salt, freshly milled black
   pepper
grated nutmeg

Sauce
2dl red port
2 heaped tbs double cream
truffle trimmings

Garnish
mushroom vol-au-vents

To cook the sweetbreads Soak the sweetbreads in water with a few drops of vinegar. Wipe them dry and blanch them by putting them into a saucepan of cold or tepid water which completely covers them. They must not be heated at all at this stage. Add the thyme, bay leaf, pinch of coarse salt and one twist of the pepper mill. Bring gently to the boil and cook for 3 minutes.

Rinse the sweetbreads under cold running water and wipe them dry. Trim and, using a larding needle, lard them with strips of larding bacon and stick with the trimmed truffle, cut into small sticks.

Sweat the carrot and onion in butter in a small casserole. Braise the sweetbreads on top of these vegetables, covered, in a moderate oven for about 20 minutes. Take out the sweetbreads; peel them carefully, cut into large pieces and reserve. Leave the braising base and cooking butter in the casserole.

To make the panada Pour the water into a saucepan and add the salt and the butter. Bring to the boil. Then add the flour and whisk until the mixture thickens. Work with a wooden spoon or spatula, drying the panada out over low heat. Take the saucepan off the heat and leave to cool. Meanwhile prepare the *quenelle* filling.

The quenelle filling Dice the veal and put through the mincer. Pound the veal in a bowl (or mortar), and incorporate the panada. Then add first the butter, then the unbeaten eggs one by one, salt, pepper and nutmeg, stirring them in with a wooden spoon or spatula. Work vigorously and taste for seasoning. This makes a veal *quenelle* filling.

To make up the 'loaf' Spread a layer of the *quenelle* mixture in a buttered rectangular mould followed by a layer of diced sweetbread. Repeat until all the ingredients are used up, finishing with a layer of *quenelle*. Take care to fill the corners of the mould properly.

To cook Put the mould into a pan of water. When the water begins to shudder transfer to a moderate oven, about 165°–170°C, 330°–340°F. The water in the pan should boil gently but continuously for 45 minutes.

To make the sauce Reheat the casserole containing the braising base and buttery cooking pieces and deglaze with the port. Reduce for a moment and scrape any particles off the bottom with the flat of a fork. Add the fresh cream and chopped truffle trimmings. Adjust the seasoning. Strain the sauce through a piece of muslin, heat and pour into a sauceboat.

To serve Turn out the 'loaf' on to an oval dish and serve with the sauce. Garnish the dish with small round pastry cases filled with mushroom *duxelles*.*

Suggested wine Chassagne Montrachet, Meursault, or Corton Charlemagne.

RESTAURANT HENRI-IV *
CHARTRES (EURE-ET-LOIRE)

ROGNON DE VEAU GRILLÉ EN PAUPIETTE, SAUCE BÉARNAISE

Kidney is at its best grilled. In this recipe the veal kidney is wrapped in a very thin escalope of veal. Inside this envelope the kidney keeps all its moisture. Béarnaise sauce goes perfectly with it.

For 2 people

1 good veal kidney
salt, freshly milled black
  pepper
2 tbs unsalted butter
2 escalopes of veal, cut very
  thin

Stuffing
150g mushrooms
2 shallots, finely chopped
1 tbs unsalted butter
2 tbs double cream
1 tbs parsley, very finely
  chopped
salt, freshly milled black pepper

To cook Trim the kidney of any fat and season it. Sauté rapidly in a frying-pan in the butter without cooking it through. Cut in half lengthways.

Cook the mushrooms *en duxelles* * with the rest of the ingredients for the stuffing. Salt and pepper the escalopes on a carving-board and place half the cooked *duxelles* mixture on each. Place a half kidney on top of one and roll up the escalope, tying it up with four bands of string. Repeat with the other escalope.

Brush with melted butter using a pastry brush and put the prepared paupiettes under the grill, turning half-way through.

To serve Remove the paupiettes to a heated metal dish and cut away the string. Serve with a dish of fried chipped potatoes and Béarnaise sauce (see p. 353) in a sauceboat.

To eat Do not unroll the paupiettes but cut them in slices. The kidney will be moist and pink.

Suggested wine A rosé from the Loire or from Anjou.

LEDOYEN * *
PARIS 8e: CARRÉ CHAMPS-ÉLYSÉES

ROGNONS FLAMBÉS LEDOYEN

Kidneys flambéed in armagnac in a sauce flavoured with mustard and enriched with cream.

For 4 people

4 good veal kidneys
4–5 tbs unsalted butter +
4 knobs butter
2 tbs strong Dijon mustard
salt, freshly milled black
  pepper

½dl red port
1dl armagnac *or* cognac
4 tbs fresh double cream
100g strained duck liver purée
juice of half a lemon
boiled potatoes

Trim the raw kidneys of any fat, removing the thin skin in which they are enveloped. Colour them whole in 4–5 tablespoons of butter in a sauté-pan for 2 or 3 minutes. Reserve the butter and the blood that has seeped out of the kidneys. Take out the kidneys and cut into large pieces, taking care to remove the sinewy core.

In a sauté-pan containing the reserved butter add the extra knobs of butter, and sauté the kidney pieces over moderate heat without letting them go hard. While they are cooking add the mustard, salt and pepper. Shake the pan and mix well with a wooden spoon or spatula. When the kidneys begin to take colour, deglaze with the port and flambé them with the armagnac. Add the cream off the heat; then heat, stirring well. Add the duck liver purée.

Mix well, shaking the pan and scraping a wooden spoon continuously over the bottom to thicken the sauce without boiling. Adjust the seasoning if necessary and squeeze the lemon juice over the whole dish.

To serve Transfer the kidneys and their sauce to a deep round metal dish and serve immediately on very hot plates. Serve with a small dish of boiled potatoes.

Suggested wine A light red burgundy or a very good red bordeaux.

AUBERGE DE NOVES * *
NOVES (BOUCHES-DU-RHÔNE)

ROGNON DE VEAU PRINTANIER
Casseroled veal kidney. Deliciously simple, it is cooked in its own fat, flavoured with fresh tarragon and coated with herb butter. It is served in the earthenware casserole in which it was cooked, with steamed potatoes.

For each person

1 whole veal kidney, trimmed but with its thick coating of fat
2 small sprigs fresh tarragon
2 sprigs parsley
salt, freshly milled black pepper

Sauce
1 dl dry white wine

2 tbs mixed parsley, chervil and tarragon, finely chopped
1 tbs strong Dijon mustard
4 tbs fresh unsalted butter
salt, freshly milled black pepper
a squeeze of lemon (optional)

To cook the kidney Put the kidney, surrounded by its own fat, into a small earthenware casserole and brown over high heat, without using any other fat. Add the sprigs of tarragon and parsley and cook, covered, for about 20 minutes, turning the kidney and making sure it does not become dry. Salt and pepper the kidney, then remove from the casserole and keep warm.

To make the sauce Remove the sprigs of tarragon and parsley from the casserole. Pour in the white wine to deglaze the juices, add the finely chopped herbs and reduce until nearly dry. Add the mustard, away from the heat, beating with a whisk; then over moderate heat add the butter, in pieces, whisking rapidly to thicken the sauce. Season with salt and pepper and add a squeeze of lemon if liked.

To serve Remove the fat from round the kidney but do not cut the kidney. Put it back into the casserole, cover with the sauce and heat carefully without boiling. Serve the kidney whole in the casserole. When it is ready to be eaten and is cut on a heated plate it will be juicy and pink and have a delicious aroma.

Serve with steamed potatoes.

Suggested wine Tavel rosé.

LÉON DE LYON *
LYON (RHÔNE)

ROGNONS DE VEAU COLLIOURE
(This recipe was awarded the Diploma of the Académie Culinaire de France)
The kidneys are cooked on a vegetable base with anchovies for which Collioure is famous.

For 4 people

4 pink veal kidneys, surrounded by their fat
5 tbs unsalted butter
2 carrots, very finely chopped
2 onions, very finely chopped
2 shallots, very finely chopped
1 clove garlic, unpeeled
½ dl dry white wine (preferably Pouilly Fuissé)

12 anchovy fillets, chopped and carefully pounded or put through a blender
salt, freshly milled black pepper
2 tbs parsley, finely chopped
4 pieces toast, fried in butter and dried on absorbent paper

In a well-buttered pan (use about 3–4 tablespoons of the butter) braise the kidneys, covered, on the bed of chopped vegetables and the garlic. Take out while they are still pink inside. Remove the fat. Continue cooking the vegetables stirring them from time to time, until they begin to go brown, then deglaze with the white wine. Leave to reduce by half.

Put the kidneys into a small casserole (copper if possible) with the rest of the butter, the finely chopped shallots and pounded anchovies. Season and stew gently, stirring from time to time. Pour the reduced cooking liquid from the pan over the kidneys; heat again for a moment and add the chopped parsley. Serve very hot in the casserole with the toast on the side of the plates so that it does not become soggy.

Suggested wine Gigondas rosé.

LE GALANT VERRE *
PARIS 7e: 12 RUE DE VERNEUIL

ROGNONS DE VEAU GASCONNE
Kidneys cut into small pieces, flambéed in armagnac and served in a sauce strongly flavoured with shallots and mustard.

For 4 people

2 good veal kidneys, fat and nerves removed, cut into cubes the size of a small walnut
salt, freshly milled black pepper
100g small white mushrooms
4–5 tbs unsalted butter
4 tbs oil

a squeeze lemon juice
1 dl armagnac
1 tbs shallot, finely chopped
1 dl dry white wine
1 dl double cream
1 tbs strong Dijon mustard

To prepare Pepper, but do not salt the kidneys as this will make them harden during the cooking.

Clean the mushrooms and cut off the stalks on a level with the caps. Use them whole or cut into quarters, depending on how big they are. Stew them in 2 tablespoons of the butter and 1 tablespoon of the oil. Salt and pepper them and squeeze over a few drops of lemon juice.

Heat the rest of the oil in a sauté-pan, preferably copper, and rapidly sauté the kidneys for 3 to 4 minutes. Drain the oil from the pan, pour in the armagnac and flambé the kidneys. Take them out and keep hot in a deep metal dish.

To make the sauce Add the shallot and the rest of the butter to the pan; cook for 1 minute. Pour in the wine; boil steadily and reduce for about 2 minutes. Then, away from the heat, add the cream and mustard and mix well. Return to the heat to thicken. Add the mushrooms and their cooking liquid. When the sauce is warmed through put in the kidneys to reheat. Adjust the seasoning.

To serve Arrange the kidneys in a serving-dish covered with the sauce. Serve with potatoes sautéed in a mixture of butter and oil, well drained and dusted with parsley, in a separate vegetable dish.

Suggested wine Either white Meursault or a really good red bordeaux.

À L'ESCARGOT MONTORGUEIL *
PARIS 1er: 38 RUE MONTORGUEIL

ROGNONS DE VEAU LIÉGEOISE
A simple and delicious dish of kidneys, sautéed in butter. The cooking juices are deglazed with brandy and juniper berries which give a special flavour to the sauce. The kidneys are served with little fried potatoes.

For 2 people

2 veal kidneys
4 tbs unsalted butter

Sauce
1 tsp juniper berries
½dl good cognac
2 tbs veal stock, reduced

1 tbs unsalted butter
salt, freshly milled black
   pepper

Garnish
350g small potatoes, trimmed
   and rounded and fried
   separately in butter

To prepare Trim most of the fat from the kidneys, cut them in half across and pepper them lightly, but do not use salt as this will make the blood seep out as you cook them.

To cook Heat the butter in a small sauté-pan, copper if possible. Put in the 4 pieces of kidney and sauté them fairly quickly for 7 to 8 minutes, turning them half-way through. Place the kidneys in a flan tin, timbale mould or a deep metal dish and salt them. Pour over the butter in which they were cooked and surround with the small fried potatoes. Keep warm without further cooking, so that they do not harden.

To make the sauce Put the juniper berries into the pan and deglaze with the cognac, adding the veal stock. Boil for a few seconds then, away from the heat and stirring constantly so that lumps do not form, add the fresh butter. When it has melted, season and pour this delicious sauce over the kidneys. Serve immediately.

Suggested wine A light, very good quality bordeaux, Médoc either Saint-Julien or Pauillac.

HÔTEL ET CHALETS DE LA VERNIAZ *
ÉVIAN-LES-BAINS (SAVOIE)

ROGNONS DE VEAU SAUTÉS VERNIAZ

Sautéed kidneys, flambéed and served with their cooking juices deglazed with madeira and enriched with cream. Pilaff rice is a good accompaniment.

For 2 people

2 veal kidneys
salt, freshly milled black
  pepper
1 tbs oil
1 tbs unsalted butter
1 glass madeira
100g mushrooms, finely
  chopped and cooked with
  2 tbs unsalted butter

1 small glass cognac
2dl double cream
Worcester sauce
a squeeze of lemon juice
1 tbs chopped parsley

To cook Chop the kidneys and season with salt and pepper. Heat the oil and butter in a sauté-pan and fry them over high heat. Take out of the pan and keep hot.

Deglaze the pan with the madeira, put back the kidneys and add the mushrooms. Heat, pour over the cognac and flambé the kidneys. Then add the cream and reduce by half.

Check the seasoning and add a few drops of Worcester sauce and lemon juice.

To serve Serve the kidneys in a small serving dish with the sauce. Dust with parsley. Serve a metal dish of pilaff rice (see p. 294) separately.

Suggested wine A red bordeaux such as Graves.

BEEF

BARRIER ★ ★ ★
TOURS (INDRE-ET-LOIRE)

GRILLADES AU FEU DE BOIS

This is not exactly a recipe, rather an explanation of the technique used in a first-class restaurant for grilling red meat; the quality of the finished dish is directly related to the amount of care given to it.

For 4 people

1 rib of beef with bone, weighing 2kg (it must be well hung)

100g best unsalted butter, clarified
salt, very good freshly milled black pepper
1 bunch fresh watercress

Charcoal grill Prepare beforehand a fairly deep bed of glowing charcoal. While cooking is in progress do not let the fire flare up, but keep the charcoal glowing.

Clarified butter Warm the butter slowly in a heavy enamelled cast-iron saucepan or a frying-pan for eggs (in which case it is easier to skim the butter) and bring it gently to the boil. Skim the surface with a small spoon to remove all the froth. The butter will now look clear and 'decanted' and the impurities and 'whey', which tend to burn, will have disappeared. All that is left is the fat, which does not alter when it comes into contact with the fire during the grilling.

To grill Brush the meat with the clarified butter and place it on the grid over the glowing charcoal. As soon as the part touching the flames is browned and crisp, turn to allow the other side to grill. Be sure to keep basted by brushing with the butter while it is cooking. It should take about 20 minutes to cook the meat, since it is advisable to eat it underdone. With this method of cooking the meat loses its juices and goes dry if it is overcooked.

To serve Charcoal-grilled meat should be accompanied by fresh vegetables such as French beans, cooked in butter and sprinkled with finely chopped parsley, grilled half tomatoes or soufflé potatoes (see p. 279). Garnish the serving dish with a bunch of watercress (no dressing).

Suggested wine A fairly full-bodied Chinon or Bourgeuil.

AU BOEUF COURONNÉ *
PARIS 19e: 188 AVENUE JEAN-JAURÈS

PAVÉ VILLETTE ET CÔTE DE BOEUF

The suburb of La Villette in northern Paris is the meat capital of France. The excellence of these two recipes is due first to the exceptional quality of the beef, then to the choice of cuts and finally to the method of grilling over very hot charcoal.

For 6 people

Pavé Villette
1·8kg fillet of beef

Côte de boeuf
3 ribs beef, each weighing about 700g with bone

To prepare both recipes Season the beef with salt and freshly milled pepper, then brush with oil. Put the meat on the grid, turning it over halfway through the cooking time. Make a chequered pattern on both sides of the meat with a red-hot skewer. These cuts of grilled meat are best eaten very underdone or slightly underdone.

Arrange the meat on a warmed serving dish with a garnish of watercress (no dressing). Spread with parsley butter and sprinkle with very finely chopped parsley. Serve with souffléed potatoes (see p. 279).

Suggested wine Beaujolais.

AU COCHON D'OR * *
PARIS 19e: 192 AVENUE JEAN-JAURÈS

FILET DE BOEUF POÊLÉ VILLETTE, GARNITURE BOUQUETIÈRE

This method of pot-roasting beef in a covered braising dish on a bed of vegetables produces meat that is very tender and keeps all its juices.

For 4 people

1 piece fillet of beef weighing 1kg, seasoned with pepper
4 tbs unsalted butter
1 carrot and 1 onion, roughly chopped

Vegetables
200g carrots, shaped
200g turnips
350g cauliflower flowerets
unsalted butter

To prepare the vegetables Blanch the vegetables separately, making sure that they are kept a little firm. Sauté them in butter for a few minutes. Just before serving, season with salt and pepper.

To cook the meat Stew the carrot and onion in 2 tablespoons of butter in a small braising dish with a lid for 2 minutes, stirring. Place the fillet of beef on top and seal on all sides, then add the rest of the butter. Cover with the lid and cook over moderate heat for about 20 to 25 minutes, so that the meat remains underdone. Season with salt when it is cooked. Lift the meat out of the braising dish on to a carving board and leave for 3 to 5 minutes.

To serve Carve the fillet into slices and arrange these on a warmed oval metal serving dish. Garnish the edge of the dish with the vegetables, arranging them to form separate 'bouquets'.

Suggested wine A red wine with a good 'bouquet', such as Juliénas, Fleurie or Hermitage.

LA JETÉE *
SAINT-ELME (VAR)

FILET DE BOEUF SOUS LA CENDRE
Fillet of beef in a pastry case, stuffed with foie gras *and served with Périgueux sauce.*

For 4–6 people

1kg fillet of beef, trimmed (preferably top fillet)
100g goose or duck *foie gras*
100g truffles, brushed, peeled and cut into long strips

500g salted brioche pastry made with butter (see p. 358)
½l Périgueux sauce (see p. 350)

Cut a slit along the whole length of one side of the fillet, but without cutting right through. Soften the *foie gras* by kneading it and fill the opening with it. Sew up the slit so that the *foie gras* can't slide out. Stud the outside of the meat with half the little sticks of truffle, by using the sharp point of a knife to make a slit into which each piece of truffle can be pressed.

To cook the fillet Seal the meat in a hot oven, 215°–225°C, 420°–440°F, for 5 to 6 minutes. Leave the meat to cool. When it is barely warm, wrap it in the brioche pastry. Put the pastry-covered meat in a buttered baking tin and transfer to an oven pre-heated to 210°C, 410°F, for 35 to 40 minutes, reducing the heat during the second half of the cooking time.

To make the Périgueux sauce While the beef is cooking, prepare the sauce. It is based on a Madeira sauce made in advance from a basic brown sauce. The Madeira sauce should be carefully skimmed of scum and grease.

For the Périgueux sauce, add an infusion made by poaching 2 finely chopped truffles in 1 decilitre of madeira wine. To finish off the sauce, add half a decilitre of madeira and the diced truffle, taking care that it doesn't boil.

To serve Carve the pastry-covered fillet and arrange the slices on a long serving dish. Serve the Périgueux sauce separately in a sauce-boat.

Suggested wine A really good red burgundy or bordeaux.

HENRY-ROBERT *
SAINT-HONORÉ-LES-BAINS (NIÈVRE)

CÔTE DE BOEUF, SAUCE MARCHAND DE VIN
A rib of beef grilled on the bone and served with a garnish of fresh vegetables.

For 2

1 rib beef, well hung, weighing about 500g

Sauce
3 grey shallots, chopped
1 glass very good red burgundy or Beaujolais or Côtes-du-Rhône
¼l concentrated veal stock
150g unsalted butter
good freshly milled black pepper, salt

Vegetables
2 potatoes, shaped
4 carrots, shaped
2 turnips, shaped
2 artichoke bases
2 tbs *petits pois*
2 large cauliflower flowerets
2 tbs French beans cooked in water salted when boiling, until tender, but still slightly firm
1 tbs chopped parsley
150g foaming unsalted butter, seasoned

Grill the meat until it is cooked to the required degree according to taste, either over a charcoal grill or on a barbecue. The sauce and the vegetables should be ready by the time the meat has finished cooking.

To make the sauce Reduce the shallots and the red wine without fat. Add the veal stock and then allow to thicken by whisking in the butter, salt and pepper.

Vegetable garnish Arrange the cooked vegetables round the edge of a round serving dish, alternating the colours and filling the artichoke bases with the *petits pois*. Moisten with the foaming seasoned butter and sprinkle with parsley. Keep warm.

To serve Carve the beef into slices on a carving board and arrange the slices (and the bone) in the centre of the garnished serving dish. Serve immediately.

Suggested wine A good red burgundy or a Beaujolais or a Côtes-du-Rhône.

RESTAURANT DE LA PYRAMIDE * * *
VIENNE (ISÈRE)

PIÈCE DE BOEUF À LA ROYALE

This was a favourite dish of Marius Guillet, owner of the Lyon bistrot 'Le Mal Assis' and a close friend of Fernand Point the famous proprietor of the 'Pyramide'. This boeuf mode Royal *is interlarded with pork fat and ham, flambéed, then braised in champagne and beef consommé. It is served cold in its own jelly, which is perfectly delicious.*

For about 12 people

3kg very tender top beef rump
7 strips pork fat, lightly seasoned with salt and freshly milled black pepper
6 strips ham
4–5 tbs butter
1 tbs oil
3 good-sized carrots
3 large onions
¼l good quality cognac
1 bottle extra-dry champagne
enough very good beef stock, reduced and with fat removed to cover most of the meat

3 boned calves' feet, blanched and rinsed in cold water
300g pork fat, blanched and rinsed in cold water
8 good fresh tomatoes, skinned, seeded and roughly chopped
6 cloves garlic
a bouquet garni* (parsley, chervil, sprigs of thyme, a sprig of fresh tarragon in season and 1 very small stick celery)
2 tbs black peppercorns

To prepare Interlard the meat with the strips of pork fat and ham. Tie up, put in a large braising-pan with the onions and carrots and brown slowly in the oil and butter until it is evenly coloured. Pour in the cognac and set it alight, shaking the pan and turning the meat over. When the flames have died down pour in the champagne and add the beef stock which should cover most of the meat. Add the calves' feet, the pork fat, tomatoes and garlic.

When the liquid is boiling steadily add the bouquet garni and the peppercorns.

To cook Cover with greaseproof paper and seal the pan hermetically. Place in a moderate oven, 170°–180°C, 335°–350°F, and cook for $2\frac{1}{2}$ hours. The liquid should be simmering gently. Remove the pan from the oven, lift out the piece of beef and drain well, then place it in a smaller braising-dish. Strain the liquid into a bowl, twice if necessary, and skim off the grease carefully. Now pour this juice with its delicious aroma over the beef in the second braising-dish, put the lid on and cook again in the oven for another $1\frac{1}{2}$ hours, basting frequently. When the meat is cooked to the point where it cuts the butter, drain it carefully and place it in an oval china terrine just big enough to hold it, so that the juice, which will have the consistency of a jelly, will completely cover it. Strain the jelly over the beef and place the terrine in the refrigerator for 24 hours.

To serve Serve cold, either turned out of the mould on to a dish or sliced in the terrine, with a green salad.

Suggested wine A burgundy or Côtes-du-Rhône.

AUBERGE DU MAIL *
AMBOISE (INDRE-ET-LOIRE)

COEUR DE FILET DE BOEUF EN CHEVREUIL, SAUCE GRAND VENEUR

This fillet is treated like a marinated piece of fillet of roebuck, roasted and served with Grand Veneur sauce, as with venison. The sauce, one of the most lavish in French cookery, is easy to make but requires a good deal of time and care.

For 10–12 people

2 pieces beef fillet, each weighing about 1·2kg, trimmed

Marinade
$\frac{3}{4}$ bottle really good red burgundy
wine vinegar, $\frac{1}{4}$ of the amount of burgundy
2 carrots, sliced
2 onions, thinly sliced
1 stick celery, chopped *or* 1 slice celeriac, diced
1 tbs black peppercorns
3 cloves of garlic, crushed
2 bayleaves
2 sprigs thyme

parsley stalks
2 tbs oil

Stock
at least 1kg lamb or mutton bones
2 carrots, chopped
2 onions, chopped
1 tbs tomato concentrate
1 branch thyme
1 bayleaf
cold water

Grand Veneur sauce
75g flour
2 tbs unsalted butter
2 tbs oil
100g pure recurrant jelly
$\frac{1}{2}$–$\frac{3}{4}$ cup double cream
a squeeze lemon

Garnish
little cubes of apple, 1cm each side

a few very small potatoes, trimmed to the shape of olives

To marinate the meat Marinate the 2 pieces of beef fillet for 48 hours in a marinade made from the ingredients listed, preferably in a deep earthenware bowl.

After 48 hours, remove the meat and wipe it. Drain the vegetables separately and reserve. Strain the liquid and reserve in a separate dish.

To make the stock Prepare this while the beef is marinating so that it will be ready for use. Put the bones, the carrots and the onions into a roasting-pan and brown them in the oven; then transfer them to a saucepan and cover with cold water, which should come up to a height of about 3 centimetres above the contents. Add the tomato concentrate, the thyme and the bay leaf. Boil rapidly for 15 minutes, skimming the surface, then leave to simmer very gently, uncovered, for 6 to 12 hours as convenient. It is important to maintain the level of liquid in the saucepan by adding extra tablespoons of cold water from time to time and skimming off the grease with a perforated spoon throughout the whole cooking time. During the last hour reduce the stock to 1 cup or $\frac{1}{4}$ litre. Strain and reserve.

To make the sauce Brown the vegetables, herbs and other flavourings from the marinade in a small frying-pan, so as to bring out their aromatic taste. Meanwhile, make a brown roux with the flour, butter and oil. Cook until the flour has become nut brown in colour, then leave to cool. Heat the liquid from the marinade to boiling point, then pour into the roux, whisking as you do so. Add the browned vegetables and flavourings and boil together for about $1\frac{1}{2}$ to 2 hours. Heat the reduced lamb stock and add to the sauce; simmer for about 30 minutes, then strain. To finish off the sauce, add the redcurrant jelly and the cream. Simmer gently for about 10 minutes, adding salt, freshly milled pepper and a few drops of vinegar or lemon juice, which go well with the redcurrant jelly.

The sauce must be thick, smooth and velvety, with a sweet-sour taste that goes well with marinated meat. It should be very well seasoned.

To cook the meat While you are making the sauce, roast the meat, previously oiled, in a very hot oven, 205°–215°C, 400°–425°F, for 25 to 28 minutes. It should be very underdone or slightly underdone.

Garnish Sauté the diced apples in butter and serve in little pastry cases or round the meat; they can also be alternated with small potatoes trimmed to the shape of olives and sautéed in butter until brown.

Serve the sauce very hot in a sauceboat.

Suggested wine A good red burgundy, such as Côte-de-Nuits, Corton or Chambertin.

HÔTEL D'ALSACE *
Rôtisserie des Ducs de Lorraine
SARREGUEMINES (MOSELLE)

CHÂTEAUBRIAND FLAMBÉ À L'ESTRAGON

A châteaubriand steak sautéed and flambéed with armagnac and served with a sauce made from shallots and tarragon sweetened with cream. The very best pepper, freshly milled, is an essential ingredient.

For 6 people

1 piece beef fillet, weighing
  1·2kg
2 tbs unsalted butter and 2 tbs
  oil, mixed
1dl armagnac
100g unsalted butter

2 tbs shallot, finely chopped
2 tbs tarragon, finely chopped
¼l concentrated veal stock
¼l double cream
salt, freshly milled black
  pepper
1 tbs parsley, chopped

Seal the fillet in a buttered and oiled frying-pan over high heat. Cook for about 15 minutes, turning it halfway through. Remove to a carving board and trim carefully, cutting away any fat. Return to the pan, add more oil and butter if necessary and heat through. Pour in the armagnac and set light to it. Lift the meat out of the pan and keep warm.

Sweat the shallot and tarragon in the 100 grams of butter in a small heavy-bottomed saucepan until they are almost a purée. Let them cook for a few seconds more, then moisten with the veal stock and reduce until almost dry. Finish the sauce by whisking in the cream until it thickens. Season to taste with salt and freshly milled pepper and then leave to reduce slightly.

To serve Carve the châteaubriand into nice thick slices and arrange these on a warmed oval dish. Strain over the sauce, sprinkle with parsley and garnish with fresh French beans and little fried sticks of potatoes.

Suggested wine A red burgundy such as Mazis-Chambertin, or a red bordeaux such as Château Margaux.

RELAIS GASTRONOMIQUE PARIS-EST ★
PARIS 10e: GARE DE L'EST

TOURNEDOS CURNONSKY

We can rely on the palate of that prince of gastronomes, Maurice-Edmond Saillant Curnonsky.

For 4 people

4 tournedos cut from a fine fillet of prime well-hung beef, each weighing 150–175g
160g clarified unsalted butter
salt, freshly milled black pepper

Sauce
the juices from the pan
3 tbs good cognac
4 tbs red port

1 small truffle, chopped
4 tbs *demi-glace* sauce (see p. 352)
2 tbs fresh unsalted butter

Garnish
2 tomatoes, cut in half and grilled
4 good slices beef marrow, poached and seasoned with salt and pepper

Fry the tournedos in the butter in a sauté-pan. Season and keep warm on a metal dish large enough to take all the trimmings, which should be cooked in advance.

To make the sauce Deglaze the pan with the cognac and port. Add the chopped truffle and the *demi-glace* sauce. Allow to reduce for a few seconds, then add the butter. Hold the pan just above but not on the heat and tilt it so that the butter melts but doesn't cook. Pour the sauce over the tournedos.

To serve On each tournedos place half a grilled tomato and on top of that a good slice of poached and seasoned beef marrow. Arrange round the edge of the dish some small shaped potatoes, tossed in butter, and some little croquettes of sweet corn, fried in breadcrumbs then arranged decoratively at intervals in little heaps.

Suggested wine Chambertin Clos de Bèze.

LES PALMES ET L'INDUSTRIE ★
CASTELNAUDARY (AUDE)

TOURNEDOS ROSSINI

A classic dish of the Twenties rarely found today on restaurant menus because of the high cost of the ingredients: a small piece of fillet of beef, a slice of foie gras, a thin slice of truffle. Fifty years ago these were served with Périgueux sauce. This recipe should satisfy even the most demanding guests.

For 4 people

4 slices fillet of beef, weighing about 200g each (*see note below*)[1]

2 tbs butter
1 tbs oil
salt, freshly milled black pepper

4 slices toast, fried golden
  brown in butter and salted
an 80g piece of tinned *foie*
  gras, sliced into four
1 truffle, very thinly sliced,
  fresh if possible (if tinned,
  reserve the juice)

Sauce
100g button mushrooms, very
  thinly sliced
3 tbs unsalted butter

1dl madeira
2 generous tbs double cream
2dl brown sauce
1 tinned truffle, chopped, or
  truffle trimmings (keep the
  juice from the tin)

To prepare the sauce Stew the mushrooms gently in the butter in a good thick saucepan, deglaze with half the madeira, add 1 tablespoon of the cream and leave to boil for about 3 minutes. Then add the brown sauce, the rest of the madeira, the chopped truffle and the truffle juice. Heat through to blend the flavours, then add the rest of the cream and keep warm.

To cook the tournedos Heat the butter and oil in a frying-pan and fry both sides of the tournedos quickly over high heat. They should ideally be served underdone, but cook them according to taste.

To serve Arrange the fried, toasted croûtons on a warmed metal serving dish and spoon 1 tablespoon of the sauce over each. Place a tournedos on each croûton, and on each tournedos a slice of *foie gras*, topped with a sliver of truffle. Cover the tournedos with the rest of the sauce and serve very hot.

Suggested wine A particularly good red bordeaux, such as Château Margaux.

[1] We do not agree with the weight of the tournedos, and are inclined to think that they should be between 120 and 125g. The tournedos should be round, fairly thick but small. This is a rich dish and it is better to finish it feeling that another two mouthfuls would be nice than to leave a third of it on the plate (*editor's note*).

LA PÉPINIÈRE
RIBEAUVILLE (HAUT-RHIN)

TOURNEDOS 1900

This recipe is somewhat similar to tournedos Rossini. It is a dish for people with healthy appetites, as each person is served with two small tournedos with a slice of foie gras *sandwiched between them. The sauce contains port and very finely chopped truffles.*

For 5 people

900g beef from the tail of the fillet, sliced into 10 tournedos each weighing 90g
unsalted butter
salt
5 slices white bread
5 round slices *foie gras*, the same size as the tournedos

1dl red port
$\frac{1}{4}$l unthickened veal or chicken stock
2 tinned truffles (keep the juice), cut into julienne strips

Cut the slices of bread to the shape of the tournedos, fry them in butter until golden, drain on absorbent paper, then sprinkle with salt. Arrange on an oval metal dish and keep warm.

To cook the tournedos Fry them in a frying-pan in very little butter over strong heat, keeping them underdone. Keep warm.

To make the sauce Drain the butter from the pan in which the tournedos were cooked, deglaze with the port, bring to the boil and strain into a good heavy saucepan. Add the veal or chicken stock and reduce it by a third, over even heat, skimming off the impurities as they rise to the surface. Add the truffle juice and reduce a little bit more. Finally add the little strips of truffle and heat through.

To serve Place the tournedos on the fried bread canapés at the last moment. A sandwich of two tournedos with *foie gras* in between goes on to each croûton, then the dish is put under a hot grill for 2 minutes. Remove, cover with the boiling sauce and serve very hot.

Suggested wine A château-bottled bordeaux or Moulin-à-Vent.

LA MARÉE ★ ★
PARIS 8e: 1 RUE DARU

TOURNEDOS 'CORDON ROUGE'

This tournedos is enriched with foie gras *and Parma ham. An interesting effect is achieved by using strips of red pepper to produce a crisscross pattern on top, instead of the usual branding with a red-hot skewer.*

For each person

1 thick tournedos weighing
  180–200g (*see note on* p. 240)
25–30g *foie gras*
1 extremely thin slice Parma
  ham
1 tbs unsalted butter
1 tbs oil
½dl cognac
½dl ruby port

1 tbs unsalted butter
1 or 2 tinned red peppers
  (according to size), wiped,
  seeded and cut into very
  thin strips
1 bread croûton the same
  shape as the tournedos, fried
  in butter until golden brown,
  drained on absorbent paper

Slit the tournedos along one side and slide the piece of *foie gras* into the opening. Interlard the tournedos with the Parma ham and tie it up with kitchen string.

Heat the butter and oil in a frying-pan over very high heat and sauté the tournedos until it is done to taste. Deglaze the pan with the cognac and port, then thicken by stirring in the butter, without cooking.

Remove the string from the tournedos and place it on the warmed croûton. Make a crisscross pattern on the surface of the tournedos with the prepared strips of red pepper, the same sort of pattern as you would make with a red-hot skewer. Now coat the tournedos with the deglazed juices from the pan.

Suggested wine Pomerol (Château Pétrus).

HÔTEL-RESTAURANT NOËL *
RÉALMONT (TARN)

TOURNEDOS AUX MORILLES

Tournedos served on croûtons. The juices are deglazed with madeira, which dresses up the meat and makes an attractive dish for dinner.

For 4 people

4 tournedos cut from a fillet of
  beef, each weighing about
  120–140g
4 bread croûtons the same size
  as the tournedos, fried in
  butter and salted
about 100g unsalted butter
1 tbs oil

400g fresh morels (or, as a
  substitute, button
  mushrooms sautéed in butter
  and sprinkled with lemon
  juice)
¼l concentrated veal stock
1 glass madeira

Heat about 4 tablespoons of the butter fairly slowly in a sauté pan and in it fry the croûtons until they are golden but not browned; remove them, drain them on absorbent paper and arrange them on a heated metal serving dish.

Clean the sauté-pan and heat in it a very small amount of butter and 1 tablespoon of oil over high heat. Sauté the tournedos very quickly until both sides are golden. Cook the steaks according to taste, remove them and place them on the prepared croûtons.

To cook the sauce Add 3 or 4 tablespoons of butter to the sauté pan and cook the morels, stirring them from time to time. Season them. Pour in the veal stock, bring it to the boil and add the madeira. Boil for 2 minutes, taste and adjust the seasoning if necessary; pour over the tournedos and serve.

Suggested wine A fairly full-bodied burgundy, heavy enough to overcome the taste of the madeira.

LE CHANZY *
ARRAS (PAS-DE-CALIS)

STEAK AU POIVRE

The steak is rolled in a special strong pepper, coarsely ground, called mignonette, *or failing this some other really good spicy pepper. It is fried, then flambéed. The sauce is deglazed with madeira and cream and is slightly reduced before being poured over the steak.*

For 2 people

1 steak cut from the fillet, 3cm thick and weighing 500g
2 tbs *mignonette* or spicy pepper

2 tbs fresh, unsalted butter
2 tbs cognac
2 tbs madeira
6 tbs fresh cream
1 bunch watercress

Lay the steak on a sheet of paper sprinkled with the pepper and press the steak gently into the pepper on both sides so that the pepper clings to the steak.

Heat half the butter in a sauté pan, copper if possible, and cook the steak quickly over high heat. When one side is done, add the rest of the butter and turn. Pour over the brandy and set light to it. When the flame has died away, remove the steak to a second sauté pan, which should be lightly buttered and heated until very hot; leave, covered, over very low heat.

To make the sauce Add first the madeira, then the cream to the first sauté pan, stirring continuously with a wooden spoon over very low heat until the sauce thickens to a good consistency.

To serve Carve the steak quickly in two and arrange the pieces on a warmed small metal serving dish, with a bunch of watercress for garnish. Strain the reduced sauce through a tammy and pour it over the steaks; serve on very hot plates.

Suggested wine A light, young Saint-Émilion.

AU DÉJEUNER DE SOUSCEYRAC *
SOUSCEYRAC (LOT)

TOURNEDOS AU POIVRE VERT

Fried tournedos coated with a sauce made of wine, cream, tomato and brandy. The sauce is light and smooth and the green pepper adds a special flavour, strong but fresh.

For 2 people

2 thick slices very good beef cut from the middle of the fillet
2–3 tbs olive oil

Sauce
3 tbs red wine vinegar
6 tbs good red bordeaux wine
1 tbs brown roux

4 tbs concentrated veal stock
½ fresh tomato, peeled, seeded and roughly chopped
2 tbs fresh cream
15 green peppercorns, well drained

To flambé
2 tbs unsalted butter
1 dl armagnac

To cook the meat Brush the steaks with oil. Pour the remaining oil into an iron sauté-pan and cook the steaks over high heat, turning them halfway through. They should preferably be left underdone, but cook according to taste. Transfer them to a heated oval serving-dish and keep hot. Season with salt.

To make the sauce Have all the ingredients for the sauce within reach and make it quickly so as not to keep the meat waiting any longer than necessary.

Pour off the oil from the pan. Deglaze with the vinegar and wine and then reduce to a glaze. Add the brown roux, the veal stock, the tomato, green peppercorns and the fresh cream, heating and stirring all the time. Boil rapidly for a moment or two.

[1]At this point in the recipe the steaks are flambéed (though this is optional). Add the butter and heat the armagnac. Pour over the dish and set light to it. Turn the tournedos so that they will be evenly flambéed, then drain the juices left from this operation into the sauce.

Pour the sauce over the steaks and serve immediately.

Suggested wine A red bordeaux such as Saint-Émilion.

---

[1] We think that it is a great pity to flambé top-quality tournedos, which will only dry out and toughen. We suggest the following method, which will produce a better flavour and will keep the meat tender. Flambé half a ladle of good armagnac in a kitchen ladle. When it has burnt well and reduced and the flames have died down, pour it boiling hot into the sauce (*editor's note*).

DOMAINE DE LA TORTINIÈRE ✶ ✶
MONTBAZON (INDRE-ET-LOIRE)

TOURNEDOS TOURANGELLE

Sautéed tournedos, their juices deglazed with madeira and enriched with a little piece of truffle. The dish is garnished with prunes stuffed with foie gras.

For 8 people

8 tournedos, each weighing 200g
salt, freshly milled black pepper
4 tbs clarified unsalted butter
32 prunes, steeped in warm tea to swell, then stoned and stuffed with _foie gras_ mousse

4 tbs madeira
1 small truffle, chopped, _or_ 2 small tsp chopped tinned truffle
1 small ladle veal stock, reduced and flavoured with madeira
1 generous tbs thick double cream

Season the tournedos with salt and pepper. Heat the clarified butter in a sauté-pan, preferably copper, and cook the tournedos until very rare, underdone or slightly underdone, according to taste.

Arrange the tournedos in the centre of a heated round metal dish with the prunes round them.

To make the sauce Deglaze the pan with the madeira, add the truffle, moisten with the veal stock and heat gently. Thin with the cream. Check the seasoning, which should be a little on the peppery side.

Pour the boiling sauce over the tournedos and serve very hot.

Suggested wine A light red bordeaux or burgundy.

LAPÉROUSE ✶ ✶
PARIS 6e: 51 QUAI DES GRANDS-AUGUSTINS

STEAK SAUTÉ LAPÉROUSE

Sirloin steak covered with a sauce made by reducing white wine with shallots and adding veal stock. It is served with creamed potatoes.

For 8 people

2·5kg sirloin, trimmed and carved into 8 thick steaks
unsalted butter and oil for cooking the steaks
300g shallot, finely chopped

4 tbs unsalted butter
½l white wine
½l thickened veal stock
4 tbs parsley, finely chopped
salt, freshly milled black pepper

Cook the shallot gently in butter in a small sauté-pan without allowing it to brown. Deglaze with the white wine. Reduce by half. Add the veal stock and reduce a second time by allowing it to simmer for about 20 minutes. Keep warm.

To cook the steaks Fry the steaks quickly in the butter and oil in another sauté-pan, preferably copper, over high heat, turning them once. Cook them to taste. Season with salt and freshly milled pepper.

To serve Heat the reduced sauce. Arrange the steaks on a heated long metal serving dish, strain the reduced sauce over and sprinkle each with chopped parsley. Serve with creamed potatoes (see p. 280).

Suggested wine Châteauneuf du Pape.

LA RÉSERVE *
PESSAC (GIRONDE)

ENTRECÔTE GRILLÉE À LA BORDELAISE

The steak must be grilled with great care. It is equally good served simply with shallot and parsley butter or with a delicious Bordelaise sauce, depending on the circumstances.

For 2–3 people

1 really good entrecôte weighing 1kg, brushed with oil and seasoned with salt

Shallot butter
3 tbs softened unsalted butter
1 tbs parsley, very finely chopped
1 tbs shallot, very finely chopped
salt, freshly milled black pepper

Bordelaise sauce (see p. 350)
2 tbs unsalted butter
1 tbs shallot, very finely chopped
1dl red burgundy
10 peppercorns, crushed
a good pinch thyme
1 ladleful *demi-glace* sauce (see p. 352)
75g beef marrow

To serve with shallot butter Grill the entrecôte on a bed of vine shoots or, failing that, over charcoal. Then burn a crisscross pattern on the meat with a red-hot skewer. Spread the meat with the shallot butter, which you have prepared beforehand by mashing all the ingredients with a fork.

To serve with Bordelaise sauce Grill the entrecôte as before. Stew the shallot gently in butter without allowing it to brown, then add the red wine. Add the pepper and thyme and reduce the sauce to a glaze, then add the *demi-glace*. Simmer for 10 minutes, then press through a conical sieve or a tammy.

Add the diced cooked marrow. Leave for 10 minutes over the heat but without letting it boil, and whisk in any of the melted marrow remaining on the surface. Stir the sauce with a wooden spoon and check the seasoning.

To serve Carve the meat in two. Garnish each piece with a good slice of hot cooked beef marrow, and either serve the meat covered with the sauce or serve the sauce separately.

Suggested wine Red bordeaux, red Graves or Médoc, Saint-Estèphe or Saint-Julien.

RELAIS DE PARME *
BIARRITZ AIRPORT, ANGLET (PYRÉNÉES-ATLANTIQUES)

ENTRECÔTE À L'OS, À LA BORDELAISE

Charcoal-grilled beef with beef marrow, shallots and a sauce named after the barrel-makers of Bordeaux.

For 2–3 people

a piece of entrecôte weighing
   about 1kg, trimmed
4 beef marrow bones
beef stock
3 tbs shallot, finely chopped
3 tbs unsalted butter

Tonnelière sauce
3 tbs shallot, very finely
   chopped
$\frac{1}{4}$l good red bordeaux
$\frac{1}{4}$l very concentrated veal stock
3 tbs unsalted butter
salt, freshly milled black
   pepper

To cook the meat Brush the meat with oil and place it on a grid or barbecue over a fire of vine shoots, which should be very red, fairly close to the flame so that the meat will seal properly. Cook the meat to the desired degree, according to whether it is liked very underdone, underdone etc.

To prepare the dish Poach the marrow bones gently in enough beef stock to cover them. Set aside in the stock and keep hot. Simmer the chopped shallot in the butter, without allowing it to brown. Reserve.

To make the sauce Heat the shallot and red wine and reduce almost completely. Add the veal stock and reduce by half. Add the butter in small pieces away from the heat, whisking the sauce until it thickens. Strain into a heated bowl or a metal sauceboat.

To serve Arrange the meat on a metal serving dish, which must be very hot. Spoon over the shallot and the marrow, which you should scoop out of the bones at the last moment. Serve the Tonnelière sauce separately. Everything should be kept very hot. The meat is carved at table and served on very hot plates.

Suggested wine Pomerol or Saint-Émilion.

AUBERGE DES TEMPLIERS *
LES BÉZARDS-BOISMORAND (LOIRET)

FAUX-FILET À LA BERRICHONNE

Thick steaks sautéed and covered with a special sauce based on wine and meat glaze, seasoned with garlic and shallots, scented with herbs and thickened with fresh chicken's blood.

For 4 people

4 pieces sirloin steak, each weighing 250g, trimmed

Garnish
150g fresh belly of pork, cut into small squares
200g very small onions, blanched in boiling water
75g unsalted butter

Sauce
6 cloves garlic, crushed
6 shallots, chopped
1 sprig thyme
1 bayleaf
a few stalks parsley
salt, freshly milled black pepper
½l very good red Sancerre (Pinot)
demi-glace (see p. 352)
4 tbs fresh chicken's blood

Heat the butter in a good, thick sauté-pan with a very flat base and sauté the pieces of pork in it. Add the blanched onions and stir well; when they are golden brown, remove them and place them on a serving dish with the little squares of pork.

To cook the steaks Cook the steaks in the same butter over high heat, turning them halfway through, until they are done to taste, then put them aside on the same plate as the onions and pork squares. Season with salt and pepper.

To make the sauce Drain some of the fat from the sauté-pan, then add the garlic, shallots, thyme, bay leaf and parsley stalks. Season. Pour in the wine and reduce rapidly by three-quarters. Add the *demi-glace* and whisk in the chicken's blood to thicken, taking care not to let the sauce boil. Heat the sauce through, check the seasoning, then strain over the steaks.

Serve very hot on warmed plates.

Suggested wine Red Sancerre (Pinot).

PRÉ AUX CLERCS ET TROIS FAISANS *
DIJON (CÔTE-D'OR)

RUMSTEAK AMOUREUSE À LA DIJONNAISE

A delicious sauce of mustard and cream is served with this steak, which may be garnished with a bunch of watercress and small Dauphine potatoes.

For 2 people

1 piece rump steak, weighing
    500g
salt, crushed black peppercorns
groundnut oil
1 tbs unsalted butter
1 tbs olive oil
½dl very good cognac

Sauce

3 tbs good dry white wine
1 tbs unsalted butter
1 tbs strong Dijon mustard
a tiny pinch crushed garlic
1 dsp fresh tarragon, finely
    chopped (or powdered dried
    tarragon)
3 tbs thick cream
salt, good freshly milled black
    pepper

To cook the steak Season the steak with the salt and crushed peppercorns and brush it with the groundnut oil. Heat the butter and the olive oil in a frying-pan and when very hot put in the steak. Cook until rare or medium, to taste, turning halfway through the cooking which must be done rapidly.

Draw the pan off the heat and flambé the meat with the brandy, heated in a ladle. Cut the meat into two pieces and arrange these on a heated metal dish.

To make the sauce Deglaze the pan with the wine, add the butter and bring to the boil for a few seconds and pour into a small saucepan. Add the garlic, tarragon and mustard, then the cream. Heat over very low heat, whisking, until the sauce is very hot, but don't let it boil.

Check the seasoning, adding salt and pepper if necessary, and pour the sauce over the meat.

Suggested wine Chambolle Musigny or Vosne Romanée.

STEAK TARTARE

True steak tartare is made from the meat of a freshly killed young colt which the Huns and Mongols used to put under their saddle to tenderise. With time, however, this dish has been adapted and steak tartare, made only with the best quality raw beef (filet or contre-filet), has become a classic French dish. America, on the other hand, has inherited the hamburger (cooked minced meat), a more civilized version of the steak tartare, which was imported by the Indians. Steak tartare is preferably a winter dish and is reputed to be an effective tonic against the cold.

RÔTISSERIE DE LA TABLE DU ROY *
PARIS 9e: 10 CITÉ D'ANTIN

STEAK TARTARE OR CANNIBAL STEAK (BASIC RECIPE)

Prime quality beef, finely minced, highly seasoned and flavoured, formed into the shape of a piece of steak and served raw.

For each person

220–250g absolutely fresh fillet of beef or sirloin, minced
1 egg yolk
a dash Worcester sauce
salt, freshly milled black pepper, mustard (either strong Dijon or English)

1 small tsp onion, finely chopped
1 tbs ketchup
1 tbs parsley, chopped
1 tbs capers
a squeeze lemon
1 tbs pure olive oil

Using a deep bowl, mix all the ingredients except the meat and the oil with a fork, or work them with a wooden spoon. Add the olive oil, and when the mixture is thoroughly blended work in the meat.

Serve the steak straight on to the plate, in the shape of a thick round disc. Decorate with a radish cut into a flower shape and laid on a slice of tomato, plus a bunch of watercress.

Garnish Chipped or soufflé potatoes.

Suggested wine Beaujolais-Villages or Brouilly.

RÔTISSERIE DE LA TABLE DU ROY *
PARIS 9e: 10 CITÉ D'ANTIN

STEAK TARTARE CAUCASIEN

This steak tartare has caviar in it and is the most delicious of all. Black caviar may be replaced by red.

220–250g basic steak tartare
2 slices hot, crisp toast, buttered
1 tbs caviar (red or black)

Spread a thick layer of steak tartare on half of each piece of toast. Then spread the caviar on the second half, with a squeeze of lemon. Sprinkle the toast with very finely chopped onions and the sieved yolk of a hard-boiled egg.

Suggested drink A red Côtes-du-Rhône, or vodka.

CHEZ PAULINE *
PARIS 1er: 5 RUE VILLEDO

BOEUF BOURGUIGNON

The most classic of French casseroles, always popular for a gathering of friends or for a family meal. Men are said to like it better than any other dish.

For 6 to 8 people

2kg shin of beef, cut into 4cm cubes
150g lean bacon
200g very small onions or button onions
400g button mushrooms, chopped into large pieces
4 tbs oil
50g pork rind
5 cloves garlic
80g flour

2 bottles good, fruity red wine (burgundy, Côtes-du-Rhône or Beaujolais), relatively young, about 5 years old
salt, freshly milled black pepper
1 lump sugar
1 bouquet garni (parsley stalks, bay leaf, sprig of thyme)
croûtons browned in oil
parsley

To cook the trimmings Melt the bacon in an enamelled cast-iron casserole. When it has turned colour add the onions and cook uncovered for about 15 minutes, stirring. Add the mushrooms, stir, cover the pan and cook over moderate heat for about 10 minutes.

Remove the solids with a perforated spoon and reserve, leaving the liquid in the bottom of the casserole.

To cook the meat Heat the oil in a frying-pan and brown the pieces of meat in it. When they are a nice golden brown lift them out of the pan with a perforated spoon and transfer to the casserole.

Heat the oven to a temperature of 165°–175°C, 325°–350°F.

Crush the garlic and mix with the meat. Heat the contents of the casserole gently, sprinkle with the flour and stir well. Transfer the casserole to the oven for about 10 to 15 minutes, stirring from time to time, until the meat is a good brown colour. Do not leave it for too long or it will toughen and go black.

Now add the red wine, season lightly with salt and pepper, add the lump of sugar and reheat. When the contents come to the boil add the bouquet garni. Stir and put on the lid. Transfer the casserole to the preheated oven and leave to simmer slowly for 3 hours, making sure that it simmers continuously.

Take the casserole out of the oven and put it on top of the cooker over very low heat. Add the reserved bacon, mushrooms and onions and heat through for about 15 minutes. Then skim any excess fat from the surface and transfer the whole dish to a heated metal serving dish.

Serve with golden, heart-shaped croûtons and a sprinkling of finely chopped parsley, plus steamed potatoes.

Suggested wine A burgundy or a Beaujolais.

LANGUE DE VALENCIENNES LUCULLUS

A smoked tongue, sliced, then reshaped; between each slice is foie gras *softened with butter and flavoured with port. The tongue is covered with a fine clear jelly flavoured with port.*

For 12 people

1 smoked ox tongue, weighing about 850g–1kg
400g *foie gras* from the Périgord region of France
200g unsalted butter

2 truffles (preferably fresh), chopped
1dl good red port
salt, freshly milled black pepper
½l good meat jelly, clarified and flavoured with port
1 truffle, sliced very thin

To make the foie gras mixture Mash the *foie gras* and butter together in a bowl with a fork, add the chopped truffles and season lightly with salt and pepper. Add the port. Work the mixture with a wooden spoon until you have a thin smooth paste. Reserve 2–3 tablespoons of this paste.

To prepare the dish Using a rectangular mould (known as a 'gutter mould'), restore the tongue to its previous shape by spreading each slice with the *foie gras* mixture so that it sticks to the next slice. When it is ready, wrap the whole in a piece of cloth, twisting the two ends. Press hard so that the tongue becomes well impregnated with the *foie gras* mixture. Remove the cloth. Use the reserved *foie gras* mixture to smooth over the whole surface. Decorate the tongue by pressing in the thin slices of truffle and glaze with the meat jelly, which should be warmed until it is the consistency of oil. Place in the refrigerator for 1 to 2 hours.

To serve Place on a long dish, decorating the edges with diced aspic.

Suggested wine Sherry or very dry champagne.

TRIPE

The preparation of tripe is a long and laborious process, and it takes a long time to cook, but it does not present any real difficulty.

The butcher will supply you with a bunch of tripes, that is to say the mesentery of an ox comprising the different parts of the stomach. To this must be added a little of the belly, the outer part of the stomach, known as the *gras double*. This is the fleshiest and also the most delicious of the various types of tripe.

If you buy tripe already washed, rinsed and blanched, you will be given a large chunk or a gelatinous roll which is sold in portions and by weight. They are supposed to be ready to eat if you warm them through in a sauce. But they often have a rather strong smell and may also have too much salt. We recommend that you should prepare them again yourself, as this will restore their freshness and bring out the best in them.

In Normandy they are cooked for 3 days (3 times for a minimum of 6 hours, or a total of 18 hours). The first recipe from the 'Aigle d'Or' at Pont-L'Evêque was worked out this way and has always (since 1925) attracted tripe lovers, but the recipe which follows and which gives a cooking time of 6 hours will be completely satisfactory. It is the 'Aigle d'Or' recipe shortened by 12 hours. Life eats up time and we must not let cooking eat us up; yet we have to maintain tradition while still saving precious time!

Before cooking Soak the tripe in a large bowl of cold water for 1 hour, changing the water every 15 minutes; or rinse well under running cold water for 15 minutes. Drain and then blanch twice, rapidly. Put the tripe, more or less covered with cold water, into a large stew-pot and bring slowly to the boil; boil for 6 or 7 minutes, then rinse under cold running water; repeat the operation a second time. Drain the tripe and it will be ready to cook; once cooked with the other ingredients they will have a fresh taste.

The choice of a cooking vessel is important. In Normandy they use a special earthenware pot with a very small opening called a *tripière*. Failing this, use an earthenware cooking pot for preference, which should have a lid that fits tightly. Before putting on the lid it is advisable to cut a circle of silver foil and lay this over the layers of beef dripping that will cover the tripe. Certain recipes tell you to seal the lid of the pot with a paste made of flour and water. In this particular case, no ingredient can be added while the cooking is in progress.

The idea behind this is to produce steam, which will make the tripe soft and smooth and keep them nice and white.

HOSTELLERIE AIGLE D'OR *
PONT-L'EVÊQUE (CALVADOS)

TRIPES À LA MODE DE CAEN
The finest Norman tripe that can be offered.

For 6 people

3kg tripe, bought cleaned and
    blanched
1 ox foot *or* 2 calf's feet
500g beef suet, in one piece
500g onions, 1 stuck with 6
    cloves
3 large sprigs thyme
4 bay leaves

1 tsp mixed spice
1 tbs juniper berries
150g bacon rinds, chopped
½l good dry white wine
½l beef stock, well seasoned
cold water if needed

200g carrots, cut into rounds	rock salt, freshly milled black
500g leeks, white parts only,	pepper
tied together	4 tbs calvados

To prepare Prepare the tripe as explained on page 253 and cut into strips 5 or 6 centimetres long, then into little squares measuring about 4 centimetres. Dip the ox foot into boiling water and then blanch for 6 or 7 minutes; rinse under cold running water, cut in half lengthways and then cut each half into 2 pieces. Cut some of the beef dripping into strips and flatten them; cut the rest into cubes. Boil the chopped bacon rinds for 5 minutes, then rinse under cold running water.

To cook Put the pieces of ox foot at the bottom of a tall earthenware stewpot with a lid. Arrange on top of them alternate layers of tripe, onions, herbs, spices and bacon rind. Pour over the wine and the stock and, if necessary, add water; the liquid should come 2 centimetres above the top layer of tripe. Cover the surface with the strips of beef suet, then cover with a piece of silver foil, shiny side downwards, and the lid. Place in an oven preheated to about 160°C, 320°F, and cook slowly and regularly for 3 hours; the temperature must remain constant and should not exceed 165°C, 330°F.

After the 3 hours, put the carrots and leeks into the pot, pushing them down into the stock. Do not waste time here and let the pot get too cool. If necessary add some beef stock or boiling water, seal the pot again and cook for another 2 hours.

Season with salt, add the calvados and cook for 1 more hour. During the last 15 minutes season with 3 turns of the pepper mill.

With the 6 hours of cooking now completed, remove the tripe with a perforated spoon and put it into a glazed earthenware casserole or a round china bowl with a lid. Strain the liquid into a saucepan, reserving the onions and carrots. Let the fat rise to the surface and skim it off carefully with a spoon; complete the process by laying sheets of absorbent paper on the surface until the liquid is quite free of fat. Check the seasoning; a squeeze of lemon juice can be nice.

To serve Garnish the tripe with a few onions and rounds of carrot. Heat the sauce and bring up to the boil a few times. The tripe should be served boiling hot, on burning hot plates.

Serve with a small dish of steamed potatoes. A compote of apples flavoured with lemon juice is less traditional but very pleasant.

Suggested wine A light young Beaujolais or a very dry Sancerre rosé, or a more fruity rosé from Provence. Incidentally, now is the time to indulge in a *trou normand*, a small glass of calvados taken in the middle of the meal to help the digestion.

LÉON DE LYON ★
LYON (RHÔNE)

GRAS-DOUBLE DE CHEZ LÉON

Gras-double *comes, like tripe, from the stomach of an ox. While
the tripe is the whole stomach and its contents the* gras-double
*is only the outside envelope of the stomach. It is fatty and
gelatinous but those who like it find it delicious. Butchers
generally sell* gras-double *cooked, ready for use. It is usually
found rolled up on itself like a large black pudding. It is then
cut into 7 or 8 millimetres thick and cut again lengthwise.*

For 4 people

1kg *gras-double*, well cooked
4 onions, finely chopped
unsalted butter

salt, freshly milled black
  pepper
a tiny piece garlic, crushed
1 tbs parsley, finely chopped
1dl white Pouilly wine
a squeeze lemon

Cut the *gras-double* into strips. Sauté over high heat in spluttering
butter so that it does not stick.

In a separate pan lightly colour the onions in butter, stirring
them until they begin to turn golden. Add them to the *gras-double*
and season with salt and pepper. Add the garlic and parsley and
deglaze with the white wine. Allow to reduce a little and stir.
Check the seasoning and transfer to an oven dish, to simmer for
a few more minutes.

Just before serving squeeze a few drops of lemon juice over.

Suggested wine Well chilled Pouilly Fuissé.

Dijon (gravure romantique)

PORK

GRILLADES DE PORC À LA DIJONNAISE

Dijon generally brings to mind mustard, and this recipe is for slices of pork grilled with strong Dijon mustard sweetened with cream and sharpened with gherkins, vinegar and shallots. It is a real man's dish, quickly made and appetizing.

For 4 people

4 slices pork fillet, each
   weighing 150g
2 tbs unsalted butter
1 tbs oil

Sauce
¼l double cream
2 tbs strong Dijon mustard
4 gherkins, thinly sliced
1 tbs shallot, finely chopped
1 tbs spirit vinegar
light seasoning of salt and
   pepper

To cook the meat Fry the pork in the hot oil and butter in a frying-pan for about 8 or 9 minutes, turning halfway through. Season with just a dash of salt and pepper. Drain carefully and arrange on a warmed metal serving-dish.

To make the sauce Mix together the cream, mustard, gherkins, shallot and vinegar in a bowl. Pour off all the fat left in the pan and pour in the mixture from the bowl. Boil for 2 minutes, stirring with a wooden spoon.

To serve Pour the sauce over the meat and serve very hot with chipped potatoes.

Suggested wine Beaujolais.

AU BOEUF COURONNÉ *
PARIS 19e: 188 AVENUE JEAN-JAURÈS

PIEDS DE PORC GRILLÉS

The trotters are one of the best parts of the pig; they are served with fried potatoes, apple sauce or green salad, and with strong mustard and gherkins.

For 6 people

6 pig's trotters, weighing about 500g each
200g lard
300g white breadcrumbs

Stock
1kg veal bones
1 carrot, cut in two
1 onion
1 sprig thyme
1 bayleaf
2 carrots and 2 onions, chopped
1 bouquet garni *
salt, freshly milled black pepper

To make the stock Put the veal bones, the halved carrot, the whole onion, the thyme and the bay leaf in a roasting-pan and brown in the oven, turning from time to time. Then place the browned bones, the carrots and the onions in a saucepan of water with the bouquet garni and salt and pepper. Cook for 20 to 25 minutes.

To cook the pig's trotters Add the trotters to the stock and simmer for $2\frac{1}{4}$ to $2\frac{1}{2}$ hours. Allow them to cool in the stock. When they are quite cold, drain and wipe them, brush them with a thin layer of melted lard and give them a good, even coat of breadcrumbs. Grill them over a bed of charcoal and crisscross them with a red-hot skewer.

Suggested wine Beaujolais.

HOSTELLERIE DU PRIEURÉ *
CHÊNEHUTTE-LES-TUFFEAUX (MAINE-ET-LOIRE)

ANDOUILLETTES DU PAYS GRILLÉÉS AUX AROMATES

An appetizing dish of grilled chitterling sausages served with a mustardy sauce; particularly good with steamed potatoes.

For 4 people

4 good chitterling sausages
2dl Saumur white wine for the marinade
1 tbs chopped herbs (parsley, chervil, tarragon and chives)
freshly milled black pepper

Sauce
2 shallots, finely chopped
unsalted butter
wine from the marinade, strained
1 tbs strong Dijon mustard
2 tbs fresh cream
1 tbs chopped herbs

Marinate the sausages in the white wine with the herbs and pepper.

To cook Remove the sausages, wipe them dry, brush with a little oil and put them under a red-hot grill. Cook them, turning frequently, until their skins are grilled and crusty and beginning to split in places.

To serve Arrange the sausages on a serving-dish and sprinkle with the herbs. Serve very hot – don't forget to warm the plates – with the mustard sauce and sautéed or steamed potatoes.

To make the sauce Stew a tablespoon of very finely chopped shallot in butter in a small saucepan. Deglaze with the strained wine from the marinade. Allow the sauce to reduce, then add the mustard, the cream and the herbs. Taste and add salt if necessary.

HÔTEL TERMINUS
ARNAY-LE-DUC (CÔTE-D'OR)

ANDOUILLETTES BRAISÉES AU ROSÉ DE MARSANNAY

Several generations of the Champmartin family have perfected this chitterling sausage braised in rosé wine from the Côte d'Or. This simple but perfect dish is served with flageolet *beans.*

For 6 people

6 pure pork chitterling sausages, made by hand, each weighing 180–200g
150g unsalted butter
1 shallot, finely chopped

½ bottle rosé de Marsannay
2dl brown stock, reduced by half
2 tbs parsley, finely chopped
salt, freshly milled black pepper

To cook the sausages Score them with the point of a knife and fry them gently in a frying-pan with one-third of the butter. Arrange them in a deep earthenware dish, lightly buttered.

To make the sauce Brown 2 tablespoons of the butter and the shallot in the same pan. Deglaze with the wine, reduce by half and add the reduced brown stock and half the parsley; season with salt and freshly milled pepper. Pour the resulting sauce over the sausages and braise them in a very moderate oven, 165°C, 330°F, for 15 to 20 minutes.

Remove the dish from the oven, add the rest of the butter, pour it over the sausages and sprinkle the surface with parsley.

Serve immediately, with a dish of *flageolet* beans sprinkled with chopped parsley.

Suggested wine The same rosé from Marsannay-la-Côte as you have used for braising the sausages.

RESTAURANT DE PARIS ★
LILLE (NORD)

JAMBON D'YORK EN CROÛTE

*A dish for all seasons that will provide a complete meal for 15–20
people, accompanied by Madeira sauce and spinach.*

For 15–20 people

1 ham, weighing about 7kg
bouquet garni★

Pastry
about 2kg half-puff pastry (6
   turns), ready to use (see p.
   356)
2 egg yolks

Garnish
3kg spinach
6 tbs unsalted butter
6 tbs fresh double cream
1dl Madeira sauce (see p. 350)

To cook the ham Soak the ham for 24 hours in a basin under a
very slowly running tap. Drain, place in a large stewpan and cover
completely with cold water. Simmer very slowly for 4 hours with
a large bouquet garni of thyme, bayleaf and parsley; the pan
should have the lid on and the water must boil gently all the time.

Remove the ham to a carving board and cut away all the rind
with a thin-bladed knife. Slice the ham, trim the slices and put
them together again to restore the ham to its previous shape. Dry
it carefully.

To prepare the pastry Wrap the ham in the pastry so that it is
completely covered, but leave a small hole to form a chimney.
Decorate with pastry leaves. Glaze the surface all over with 2 egg
yolks beaten with a few drops of water. Transfer to an oven
preheated to 190°C, 375°F, and cook for about 35 to 40 minutes,
until the pastry is cooked and a nice golden brown.

To prepare the garnish Blanch the spinach for 5 or 6 minutes,
then stew it gently in the butter and fresh cream. Serve with
Madeira sauce in two separate sauceboats.

Suggested wine Pomerol.

LE CLOS FLEURI *
SAINT-ÉTIENNE (LOIRE)

JAMBON CHAUD, DEMI-SEL

A ham with a true country flavour. It should be served very simply with onions and gherkins in vinegar, rye bread and fresh butter.

For 15 or 20 people
1 fresh ham, weighing 4–5kg
1kg rock salt

carrots, roughly chopped
onions, roughly chopped
thyme, rosemary, sage, savory,
    bay leaves

To prepare Choose a small fresh ham from a pig which has not been steam-blanched but treated according to a custom familiar in the Haute-Loire region but unfortunately disappearing. After slaughtering the pig is flamed on a bed of burning rye straw, which singes off the bristles and produces a smooth exterior, while giving a delicious flavour to the rind.

Pick over the fresh ham, remove the bone from the chump end, with rock salt, carrots, onions and herbs and let it stand for 4 hours.

Remove the ham from the marinade and wash in plenty of running cold water.

To cook Put the ham with plenty of water in a tall stewpot. Heat through and raise the temperature to 80°C, 175°F; the temperature is important. Cook the ham gently and evenly at that temperature, allowing 40 minutes per kilo.

To serve Serve hot, with small white onions in herb-flavoured vinegar, rye bread and fresh butter.

Suggested wine A red Coteaux de la Loire.

HÔTEL MODERNE *
CLUNY (SAÔNE-ET-LOIRE)

JAMBON PERSILLÉ

Ham flavoured with chopped parsley, served cold in its jelly.

For 20–25 people
1 lightly salted ham weighing
    4–5kg
pork rind
4 calves' feet

Stock
4l water

a pinch curry
1 large bouquet garni (thyme,
    bay leaf and parsley)
1 bottle good, young, dry
    white Burgundy
4 carrots, cut lengthwise
4 onions, 2 of them stuck with
    cloves

1 stick celery
1 sprig rosemary
2 leaves sage
6 coriander seeds
12 black peppercorns

Persillade
4 shallots, very finely chopped
2 cloves garlic, crushed
3 tbs unsalted butter

2 tbs parsley
2 tbs chervil
2tbs tarragon

Jelly
liquid from cooking the ham,
    strained and clarified
1dl cognac, flambéed
1 glass good red port
freshly milled black pepper (if
    needed)
a few leaves gelatine (if
    needed)

To prepare the ham Soak the ham for between 6 and 24 hours to eliminate the salt, according to the degree to which the ham has been salted, its quality and its origin. Prague ham has the most delicate flavour, but York ham is recommended for serving cold. The cooking time for Prague and York ham is about 15 minutes per pound. Hamburg or Westphalian hams need 20 minutes and should be soaked for between 12 and 24 hours.

A rule of thumb: cook the ham until the chump bone can be detached by hand while the ham is still warm.

To make the stock Boil the ingredients for the stock for 20 to 25 minutes (without salt) and remove from the heat.

To cook the ham Put the ham into a braising-dish or pot of suitable size, cover with cold water, bring to the boil, then pour away the water. Blanch a few pieces of pork rind and 4 calves' feet and rinse them in cold water. Pour the aromatic stock over the ham, add the pieces of rind and the calves' feet, cover with grease-proof paper and the lid of the pot and simmer for the time indicated. The ham should be well cooked. Remove the bone. Allow the ham to cool in the stock, then remove to a carving board.

To make the persillade Melt the shallots and crushed garlic in the butter, without letting them take colour. Mix with the herbs in a bowl and reserve.

To make the jelly Mix together the strained ham stock, the cognac and the port. Test the jelly by putting 2 or 3 spoonfuls on a saucer in the refrigerator. If the consistency of the jelly is not strong enough, soften the gelatine in cold water, wipe and add.

To finish the dish Remove the skin from the ham, leaving only a thin coating of fat, and line a large terrine with the fat from the ham. Cut the ham into fairly large pieces. Put a layer of ham into the terrine and cover evenly with a layer of *persillade*, then another layer of ham and another of *persillade*, finishing with a layer of *persillade*. Press the ham down well, then pour in the cooled jelly, which should be liquid but on the point of setting. Put in the refrigerator, where it will keep for several days.

To serve Turn out the ham and slice.

Suggested wine Mâcon blanc or Pouilly Fuissé.

HÔTEL DE LA CÔTE D'OR *
SAULIEU (CÔTE-D'OR)

JAMBON À LA CRÈME, DE SAULIEU

*This cream sauce from Saulieu is famous throughout the world.
This is a rich, savoury dish that you can offer to last-minute
guests if you have half an hour to spare.*

For 4 people

12 fairly thick slices cooked
  Morvan ham, about 60g
  each
200g button mushrooms,
  thinly sliced
salt, freshly milled black
  pepper
unsalted butter
1½dl very dry Chablis
3 tbs shallots, finely chopped

½l double cream
200g tomatoes, peeled, seeded
  and roughly chopped
⅓ cup grated Parmesan cheese

Beurre manié (optional) *
1½ tbs unsalted butter
2 tbs flour
a pinch of salt, freshly milled
  black pepper

Cook the mushrooms in a little water, with salt, pepper and a
walnut of butter, for 3 minutes. Remove the mushrooms and
reserve. Reduce the white wine, shallots, and the cooking liquid
from the mushrooms in a saucepan, and moisten with the cream.
Add the tomatoes and seasoning and boil for 5 or 6 minutes. If
the sauce is too thin, add the *beurre manié*.

Arrange the slices of ham in a deep metal dish, lightly buttered,
sprinkle with the mushrooms and cover with the sauce, then
sprinkle with the cheese. Glaze quickly under the grill, making
sure that the sauce doesn't boil.

Serve with rice pilaf (see p. 294) or pasta tossed in butter.

Suggested wine Volnay.

HÔTEL DE LA GARE *
MONTBARD (CÔTE-D'OR)

SAULPICQUET MONTBARDOIS

*This recipe for braised ham won the first prize in the regional
competition organized by the Touring Club de France in 1961.*

For 10–15 people

1 Morvan ham, or other good
  local ham, weighing 4–5kg
200g carrots
150g onions
4 tbs unsalted butter
1 bottle white burgundy (e.g.
  Chablis)
2l veal stock
1 bouquet garni
freshly milled black pepper

Sauce

1kg button mushrooms,
  thinly sliced
5 tbs unsalted butter
a squeeze lemon juice
salt, freshly milled black
  pepper
4–5 tomatoes (depending on
  size), skinned, seeded and
  roughly chopped
1l thick fresh cream

1kg *petits pois*, cooked
$\frac{1}{2}$l good cognac

To cook the ham Soak the ham for 24 hours to remove the salt. Wipe and cook in cold water in a large vessel over moderate heat for 15 minutes per 500 grams of ham. Lift out of the pan, remove the skin, trim the ham and place it on a bed of carrots and onions, lightly browned in the butter. Pour in the wine, then the veal stock. Add a bouquet garni of thyme, a bay leaf and parsley and season with freshly milled pepper. Complete the cooking. Reduce the liquid in a saucepan after you have removed the ham.

To make the sauce Simmer the sliced mushrooms in the butter; add a squeeze of lemon, salt and pepper and the tomatoes. Moisten with the reduced liquid from the ham, thicken with the fresh cream and cook for 15 minutes. Add the *petits pois* and the cognac. Taste the sauce and adjust the seasoning if necessary.

To serve Slice the ham and arrange the slices on a long dish. Cover with some of the sauce and serve very hot, with the rest of the sauce in a sauceboat. Possible accompaniments are leaf spinach, or small steamed potatoes in a vegetable dish.

Suggested wine A good Chablis or Meursault, well chilled, or a light red burgundy.

AU CANETON ★ ★
ORBEC (CALVADOS)

JAMBON MICHODIÈRE
A ham pie filled with sausage meat, dried and fresh fruit and served with tomato sauce.

For 4 people

4 thick slices ham, trimmed
1 onion, finely chopped
3–4 tbs unsalted butter
250g sausage meat
100g white seedless sultanas
100g prunes, stoned and
    roughly chopped

2 bananas, sliced thinly
2 dessert apples, sliced
200g half-puff pastry (see p. 356)
1 egg, beaten
2 tbs calvados
tomato sauce

Melt the butter in a sauté-pan over moderate heat and in it simmer the onion without letting it take colour. Add the sausage meat, sultanas, prunes, bananas and apples, mix together with a wooden spoon, then cover and leave to simmer gently for 20 minutes, stirring frequently.

    Butter a round ovenproof flan dish and spread over the bottom of it half the mixture from the pan. Arrange the slices of ham on top and then spread the rest of the mixture over the ham. Roll out the pastry and cut out a round piece big enough to fit over the dish. Lay it over the mixture, folding the edges back slightly towards the inside of the dish. Make a crisscross pattern on the pastry with the point of a knife after glazing it with beaten egg. Make a small hole in the centre of the pastry and transfer the pie to a hot oven, 190°C, 375°F, for about 25 minutes. Lower the temperature halfway through the cooking time.

During the cooking pour the calvados through the hole in the pastry, quickly replacing the dish in the oven. When the pie is a nice golden-brown, serve with a sauceboat of tomato sauce.

Suggested wine Rosé d'Anjou.

HENRY-ROBERT ★
SAINT-HONORÉ-LES-BAINS (NIÈVRE)

SAUPIQUET DU MORVAN
Escalopes of ham in Béarnaise sauce with truffles, Madeira and demi-glace *sauce.*

For 4 people

4 slices ham the same thickness as escalopes, each weighing about 180 to 200g and carved from a ham cooked on the bone
4 tbs clarified unsalted butter

Béarnaise sauce (see p. 353)
3 small sprigs tarragon
2 shallots, chopped

parsley stalks
1 glass white burgundy, Aligoté
freshly milled black pepper

To thicken and add to the sauce
2 egg yolks
125g unsalted butter
1 truffle, chopped
1 glass madeira
2dl *demi-glace* sauce (see p. 352)

Gently warm the ham escalopes in clarified butter in a sauté pan, allowing them to go very slightly golden in colour.

Make a Béarnaise sauce by reducing the ingredients, then thickening the resulting mixture with the egg yolks and butter.

Reduce the chopped truffle and madeira almost completely. Add the *demi-glace*. Thin the Béarnaise slightly by whisking the resulting mixture in gradually over very moderate heat.

To serve Arrange the slices of ham on a serving-dish and cover with the sauce.

Suggested wine A really good white burgundy.

GAME

ITHURRIA *
AINHOA (PYRÉNÉES-ATLANTIQUES)

CAILLES AUX POMMES EN L'AIR
Apples are very good with quail.

For 4 people

8 quail, ready for cooking
2 tbs oil
7–8 tbs butter
1dl madeira
2dl veal stock *or* 1 chicken
stock cube, dissolved and
brought to the boil in 2dl
water

4 good firm apples, preferably
Golden Delicious, cut into 6
pieces and rubbed with a cut
lemon
2 pinches caster sugar
freshly milled strong pepper
8 slices white bread, fried in
butter until golden and set
aside on absorbent paper

To cook the quail Heat the oil and half the butter in a sauté-pan
and sauté the quail, turning them, for about 3 minutes. Then
cover the pan and cook over low heat for about 5 minutes. Take
out the quail and keep hot, covered.

Deglaze the pan with the madeira, add the veal stock, bring to
the boil and put back the quail; cover and leave to simmer for
8 to 10 minutes. Quails take about 16 to 20 minutes to cook,
depending on their tenderness.

To cook the apples In a separate pan sauté the apple quarters in
the rest of the butter over high heat. Add the caster sugar, pepper
lightly and turn. Once they are a nice golden colour take off the
heat and leave covered. The apple should be soft but not mushy.

To serve Arrange the quail on the reheated croûtons on a heated
metal dish. Coat with the strained sauce, which must be very hot.
Arrange the pieces of apple round them.

Suggested wine Beaujolais Villages.

HOSTELLERIE DE LA POSTE ★ ★
(founded 1710)
AVALLON (YONNE)

BÉCASSE FLAMBÉE À LA RICHE

This exceptional eighteenth-century recipe is a precious document to be read by gourmets. It was intended for a gourmet bachelor.

For each person

1 woodcock, undrawn, with the head still on
4–5 tbs unsalted butter
½ glass really good red burgundy

peel of 1 lemon and a few drops lemon juice
3 tbs Fine Champagne or armagnac
salt, freshly milled strong black pepper
2 large knobs *foie gras*
2 slices bread, fried in butter

To cook Roast the woodcock in a generously buttered baking tin in a hot oven, 215°–225°C, 425°–450°F, for 12 to 15 minutes, basting and turning. Remove from the oven and reserve the cooking juices. In a saucepan boil the wine with the lemon peel. Reduce to a glaze and set aside for the moment.

Cut the head, legs and wings off the woodcock and reserve the intestines and the liver. Leave the breast fillets on the carcase; they will be lifted off later.

To make the sauce Put the head, legs and wings into the saucepan containing the reduced wine. Pour in the Fine Champagne or armagnac, heat and flambé. Deglaze with 1 tablespoon of the butter, heating as you do so, and add the cooking juices. Knead the finely chopped liver and intestines of the woodcock in a bowl with the salt, pepper and *foie gras* and a heaped tablespoon of the butter. Divide this mixture into two, spreading the first half on the fried croûtons. Keep warm.

Cut the breast fillets from the woodcock into escalopes, add to the pan to reheat, simmering, for a few seconds.

To serve Arrange the pieces of woodcock on the fried croûtons on a heated metal dish. Add the reserved liver mixture to the pan to thicken the juices, beating with a whisk over very low heat; add a few drops of lemon juice. Check the seasoning, particularly the pepper which is so necessary with woodcock. You will need at least 2 turns of the pepper mill. Pour over the woodcock. Serve on a very hot plate. The head is heated at the table over a candle and put on the plate when it has split.

Suggested wine Bonnes Mares 1961 or a red burgundy of a really good vintage.

HÔTEL DU GRAND CERF ∗
ÉVREUX (YONNE)

FAISAN À LA NORMANDE

A pheasant in cream with apples and Calvados — a typically Norman dish.

For 4 people

1 good tender pheasant, drawn and plucked
salt, freshly milled black pepper
unsalted butter
1 rasher barding bacon
2 shallots, finely chopped
½dl calvados
½l fresh double cream

2 large (or 3 medium) apples, peeled, cored, quartered and stewed to a purée

Garnish
2 half apples, peeled and baked in the oven with butter, salt and pepper
4 slices bread, fried golden in butter

To cook Season the inside of the pheasant with salt and pepper and insert a few knobs of butter. Interlard with the barding bacon and truss with string. Brown in a moderate oven in a well-buttered casserole or braising-dish, then add the chopped shallot. Leave the pheasant to turn an even gold colour, adding more butter and turning. Take the casserole out of the oven and put over low heat on top of the stove. Pour over the calvados and flambé, putting out the flames with the cream, off the heat. Heat, stirring well, and season. Put on the lid and cook for about 30 to 35 minutes.

To serve Strain the sauce with the puréed apples. Cut the pheasant into 4 pieces and arrange these on a dish garnished with the croûtons. Coat with all the sauce. Arrange the apple halves at each end of the plate as a garnish.

Suggested wine A red burgundy, such as Côte-de-Beaune or Mercurey.

HOSTELLERIE DU CERF ★
MARLENHEIM (BAS-RHIN)

FAISAN À LA VIGNERONNE

Roast pheasant with white and black grapes and croûtons spread with a paste made from the liver of the pheasant and foie gras. *The juices are deglazed with Alsatian wine enriched with cream and cognac and flambéed. The pheasant is served with sauerkraut and* spaetzlés *(fresh Alsatian pasta).*

For 4 people

1 *young* pheasant, wrapped in a piece of barding bacon, the liver reserved
150g unsalted butter
1 carrot, finely chopped
1 onion, finely chopped

Sauce
2dl Alsatian wine, preferably a riesling
1dl game stock
1dl fresh cream
½dl Fine Champagne
salt, freshly milled black pepper

a few drops lemon juice
1 bunch (250g) white grapes, peeled and pips removed
1 bunch (250g) black grapes, peeled and pips removed
2–3 tbs unsalted butter

Garnish
6 triangular croûtons
6 tbs unsalted butter
the pheasant's liver
2 tbs Fine Champagne
salt, freshly milled black pepper
1 tbs *foie gras*
lemon quarters

To cook Brown the pheasant in butter with the carrot and onion in a generously buttered casserole in a moderate oven, 165°C, 325°F, for 15 minutes, turning on all sides and adding more butter if necessary to prevent it drying out. Roast for 30 to 35 minutes, basting 2 or 3 times. Cover with a piece of buttered greaseproof paper towards the end of the cooking time if necessary, to retain the moisture.

To prepare the croûtons Meanwhile, fry the croûtons in 3 tablespoons of the butter and drain them on absorbent paper. Sauté the liver quickly in 2 tablespoons of the butter, pour over the Fine Champagne and set light to it. Season with salt and pepper. Mash the liver and its juices with the rest of the butter and the *foie gras*, using a fork. Spread the fried croûtons with the mixture.

To make the sauce Lift out the pheasant and keep it hot. Deglaze the casserole with the wine and stock. Bring to the boil and reduce, then add the cream and lastly heat the Fine Champagne in a ladle, set light to it and pour it flaming into the pan. Check the seasoning, adding salt and pepper and a few drops of lemon juice to taste. Strain the sauce into a saucepan.

Stew the grapes in the butter for 2 or 3 minutes, then add to the saucepan with the buttery juices.

To serve Carve the pheasant, starting by cutting off the legs. Carve the breast into long flat slices. Arrange the pieces on a heated metal serving-dish and coat with the sauce and the grapes. Arrange the croûtons round the edge of the dish and garnish with the lemon quarters.

Serve with sauerkraut and *spaetzlés*.

Suggested wine A really good white riesling or a Pommard, according to taste.

MAISON PRUNIER *
PARIS 1er: 9 RUE DUPHOT

POULE FAISANE EN COCOTTE, SAUCE SMITANE
Sautéed pheasant with a sauce made with cream and flavoured with onion.

For 4 people

1 very tender hen pheasant ready to cook, seasoned inside with salt and pepper
unsalted butter
1 dl very dry white wine

Sauce smitane
1 large onion, finely chopped
2–3 tbs unsalted butter
1 dl dry white wine
2½ dl fresh double cream
salt, freshly milled black pepper

Celeriac purée
2 good celeriacs
potatoes
2 tbs double cream
2 tbs unsalted butter

Garnish
4 large croûtons, fried in butter and salted
lemon quarters
redcurrant or cranberry jelly

To cook Put the pheasant into a well-buttered heavy-bottomed casserole. Gently brown it all over, adding more butter if necessary. Put on the lid and sauté over moderate heat for about 30 to 35 minutes.

Take out the pheasant and keep warm under paper. Deglaze the pan with the wine. Strain the cooking juices into a bowl and skim off the fat. Reheat when ready to serve. While the pheasant is cooking make the sauce.

To make the sauce In a heavy-bottomed casserole soften the onion in the butter without allowing it to colour at all, for 2 to 3 minutes. Season well with pepper, pour over the wine and reduce until there is almost nothing left. Add the cream away from the heat and boil for 5 to 6 minutes to reduce. Put through a sieve, pressing well on the onion, and adjust the seasoning.

To make the celeriac purée Deeply peel 2 good celeriacs. Slice and cook in salted water; drain and purée in the blender. Add the same weight of mashed potato, puréed. Then add the double cream and the fresh butter, beating with a whisk. Adjust the seasoning.

To serve Carve the pheasant into 4 pieces.

Place the reheated croûtons in a deep, round warmed dish. Arrange the pheasant pieces on top of them and coat with the sauce. Garnish the edge of the dish with the lemon quarters. Serve with the celeriac purée and the redcurrant jelly or cranberry jelly in a separate dish.

Suggested wine A red bordeaux such as Graves.

AUBERGE DU GUÉ DES GRUES *
AU GUÉ DES GRUES (NEAR DREUX) (EURE-ET-LOIR)

LAPÉREAUX SAUTÉS AU ROMARIN ET AUX GIROLLES

A delicious fricassée of rabbit. Rosemary has a natural affinity with rabbit and chanterelle *mushrooms are the natural accompaniment.*

For 8 people

2 young rabbits, each weighing
  1·5kg, cut into pieces of
  equal size
groundnut oil

*Beurre manié**
1 tbs butter
1 tbs flour

Sauce
1 onion, finely chopped

3 shallots, finely chopped
3 tbs flour
$\frac{1}{2}$ bottle dry white wine
1l chicken consommé
2 sprigs fresh rosemary
a pinch curry powder
salt, freshly milled black
  pepper
$\frac{1}{4}$l fresh cream

Garnish
1kg *chanterelle* mushrooms,

cleaned and washed	1 shallot, finely chopped
carefully, plunged in boiling	1 clove garlic
water and wiped dry	1 tbs parsley, finely chopped
3 tbs unsalted butter	3 tbs oil

To cook Sauté the rabbit pieces in oil over high heat, using a copper sauté-pan. When they are lightly golden drain off the oil. Leave over the heat for a few seconds, almost without cooking, with the onion and shallot so as to impregnate the rabbit with their flavour. Dust with flour, stirring well with a wooden spoon or spatula to distribute and cook the flour evenly. Leave to colour a little; deglaze with the white wine, then pour over the heated chicken consommé. When it comes to the boil add the rosemary, curry powder, salt and pepper and braise covered, for about 25 minutes.

Meanwhile sauté the cleaned and blanched *chanterelles* in the oil and butter. Add the chopped shallot and the garlic and cook until the mushrooms are soft and a light golden colour which will take about 16 to 20 minutes.

Take out the rabbit pieces, arrange on a heated serving-dish and keep warm, covered.

To finish the sauce Strain the cooking liquid into a saucepan. Skim off the fat then heat and thicken with the *beurre manié*. Add the cream, check the seasoning and bring to the boil. Whisk and pour over the rabbit.

Decorate the rim of the dish with the *chanterelles*, which should be nice and hot and dusted with parsley.

Suggested wine Rosé, either Sancerre or from Provence.

LE GRAND VENEUR *
BARBIZON (SEINE-ET-MARNE)

CIVET DE LIÈVRE

This is a classic recipe for jugged hare. It is cooked in a good full-bodied red wine, not more than 5 years old, such as a burgundy, Côtes du Rhône or Chinon. This delicious dish is garnished with little squares of bacon, glazed onions, mushrooms cooked separately, croûtons and, for those with a good appetite, a dish of steamed potatoes.

For 6 or 8 people

1 good medium hare, preferably young, skinned and jointed	*Marinade*
	1 onion, sliced thinly
2 tbs unsalted butter	3–4 tbs cognac
2 tbs oil	2–3 tbs groundnut oil
2 whole onions, peeled	a sprig of thyme
200g lean bacon, cut into lardons, blanched, refreshed and wiped dry	1 bay leaf
	5 juniper berries
	Sauce
	2 tbs unsalted butter *or* lard
	3 heaped tbs flour
	½l red wine (burgundy, Côtes du Rhône or Chinon)

½l good thick stock, already
   reduced
salt, freshly milled black
   pepper
1 clove garlic
1 bouquet garni (parsley
   stalks, thyme and bay leaf)

4 tbs cognac, flambéed
   (optional)

Garnish
20 mushroom caps, lightly
   browned in butter, with salt,
   pepper and a squeeze of
   lemon
20 small glazed onions (see p.
   293)

To prepare Leave the hare pieces to marinate in the ingredients listed for 3 to 6 hours. Drain and wipe dry.

To cook Heat the butter and oil in a cast-iron or copper frying-pan. Put in the little pieces of bacon and the onions, and lightly sauté them. Put in the hare pieces and fry evenly, turning. Take everything out of the pan.

To make the sauce Put the butter or lard into the pan and heat, then add the flour and leave to cook over moderate heat, stirring continuously with a wooden spoon or spatula until the mixture turns nut brown. Pour in the wine; bring to the boil, whisk, then pour in the stock and stir thoroughly. As it begins to reboil put the pieces of hare back into the sauce and the onions and set aside the browned bacon pieces. Put in the garlic and the bouquet garni; season with salt and pepper, cover the pan and cook over a moderate heat for 2¼ to 2½ hours.

To serve Arrange the pieces of hare in a deep dish. They must be well cooked. Arrange the bacon pieces round them as a garnish with the glazed onions and the mushrooms. Strain the sauce over the whole dish adding, if liked, the flambéed cognac. Dust the garnish with parsley, spike with the reheated croûtons and serve with small steamed potatoes in a vegetable dish.

Suggested wine Red wine of the same kind as the one used for the sauce but perhaps a little older.

CHEZ ALBERT ★ ★
PARIS 14e: 22 AVENUE DU MAINE

RÂBLE DE LIÈVRE À LA CAUCHOISE

An old recipe from Caux. The hindquarters of the hare are cut just above the haunch to give 4 nice pieces for serving. Apple quarters sautéed in butter are served as an accompaniment.

For 4 people

hindquarters and saddle of a
    hare, weighing about 3 kg
fat bacon, cut into thin strips
unsalted butter

Marinade★
dry white wine
oil
vegetables
herbs
freshly milled black pepper

Sauce
½dl calvados
¼dl double cream
6 tbs chicken *velouté*★ *or*
    thickened white stock
1 tbs strong Dijon mustard

Garnish
4 medium (or 8 small) Cox's
    apples
3 tbs unsalted butter
a pinch salt
a pinch sugar

To cook the apples Peel the apples, cut them into quarters and sauté in the butter. Season with the salt, sugar and one turn of the pepper mill. Reheat when ready to serve.

To prepare the hare Trim the hare and bone the legs. Lard all the meat (saddle and thighs) with the thin strips of fat bacon, using a larding needle. Truss the legs under the back by winding round twice with a piece of string.

Marinate the hare for 12 to 24 hours, then strain the marinade into a bowl and set aside.

To cook the hare Carefully wipe the hare dry and spread with butter. Put into a roasting-tin in a very hot oven preheated to 215°–225°C, 420°–450°F, to brown all over, turning it. Heat the marinade liquid; add to the roasting-tin and continue cooking the hare, basting from time to time. The cooking time is 30 minutes per kilogram (usually, 45 to 50 minutes).

When the hare is cooked take it out of the oven and keep hot.

To make the sauce Deglaze the roasting-tin with the calvados, add the cream and reduce by a quarter, then add the *velouté* or stock to thicken the sauce and, finally, the mustard. Beat with a whisk, reheating over moderate heat. Check the seasoning.

To serve Cut the saddle into 4 pieces and arrange on a heated dish. Garnish with the apples. Strain over the sauce through a conical sieve or fine strainer.

Suggested wine A still Blanc de blancs from the Champagne district.

LE CHAPEAU ROUGE ★ ★
FEURS (LOIRE)

LIÈVRE BRAISÉ AU CHAMPAGNE

A hare cut into pieces then braised with vegetables, seasonings and herbs and moistened with champagne and dry white wine. The sauce is enriched with cream and thickened either with beurre manié *or with the blood and liver of the hare, added, without boiling, at the last moment.*

For 8 people

1 good hare, skinned and cut into equal-size pieces
salt, freshly milled black pepper
2 tbs oil
2 tbs unsalted butter
1 carrot
1 onion
2 shallots
1 head garlic, the cloves unpeeled
2 tomatoes, skinned, seeded and pulped

Sauce

1 small bouquet garni
50g bacon, plunged into boiling water, rinsed in cold water and cut into lardoons
2 tbs oil
2 tbs unsalted butter
salt, freshly milled black pepper
½dl cognac
½ bottle champagne
½ bottle dry white wine
½l double cream

To cook the hare Season the hare pieces with salt and pepper. Heat the oil and butter in a large copper sauté-pan and brown the hare pieces uniformly over moderate heat. Stew the pieces of bacon, the carrot, the onion, shallots, tomato and garlic in a frying-pan with the butter and oil.

When the pieces of hare are lightly golden deglaze with the cognac (don't set light to it) then add the champagne and the wine and reduce for 5 minutes over high heat. Turn the contents of the frying-pan into the sauté-pan with the hare and cook, covered, over moderate heat for 1¼–1½ hours, depending on the tenderness of the hare. About three-quarters of the way through add the cream, off the heat, then finish cooking. Remove the pieces of hare to a flan tin or shallow serving-dish and keep warm.

To make the sauce Reduce the sauce, carefully skimming off the fat. It may be thickened in two ways: the simpler is to use some *beurre manié*★ made with 2 level tablespoons of unsalted butter, whisked into the sauce. Alternatively the reserved blood and chopped liver of the hare may be mixed in a bowl and whisked into the sauce without being allowed to boil.

To serve Strain the sauce over the hare. Serve very hot.

To garnish Little glazed onions (see p. 293) and button mushroom caps stewed in butter. This dish may also be served with fresh noodles.

Suggested wine Extra-dry champagne or a Blanc de blancs from the Champagne district.

HOSTELLERIE DE LA FUSTE *
LA FUSTE PAR VALENSOLE (NEAR MANOSQUE)
(ALPES-DE-HAUTE-PROVENCE)

CIVET DE LIÈVRE AUX SENTEURS DE PROVENCE

A particularly tasty civet, *though this is not a classic recipe. The sauce, unthickened with starch, has all the scents and savours of the scrubland of Haute-Provence.*

For 8 people

1 good large hare, hung for a
  week
1dl olive oil
3dl cognac
bouquet garni*
1 whole head garlic
3–4 tbs fresh breadcrumbs, if
  necessary

Marinade
1 sprig each thyme, rosemary,
  sage
pèbre d'ail[1] savory
a few juniper berries
a few black peppercorns
1 whole head garlic
1 onion, chopped
2 carrots, chopped
2 bottles Châteauneuf-du-
  Pape

To prepare Skin and clean the hare, reserving the blood in a bowl. Take out the gall and reserve the liver. Cut the hare into chunks each weighing about 40g and put these pieces into a large earthenware dish with the herbs, the peeled cloves of garlic, the juniper berries, peppercorns and vegetables. Pour over the wine and put the dish in a cool place. Leave to marinate for 24 hours, stirring from time to time. Then drain the pieces of hare and wipe dry.

Heat the marinade in an enamel saucepan and allow to boil for a few minutes.

To cook Meanwhile, heat the oil in a large casserole and brown the hare pieces evenly over high heat. Pour over the cognac and flambé. Pour in the marinade from the saucepan, add the bouquet garni and the peeled cloves from the second head of garlic. Cover and cook for about $1\frac{1}{2}$ hours over moderate heat. Lift out the hare pieces one at a time, carefully removing any bits of herbs that have stuck to them, and keep hot in a ragout dish. Strain the cooking liquid through a conical sieve into the enamel saucepan and reduce by half.

To make the sauce Chop the raw hare's liver very finely and mix with the reserved blood. Add 3 tablespoons of the reduced cooking liquid to dilute the mixture and reheat. Thicken the sauce off the heat by slowly pouring the contents of the bowl into the reduced cooking liquid, whisking all the time with a wire whisk. If the sauce is still not thick enough add 3–4 tablespoons of fresh breadcrumbs.

To serve Coat the hare pieces with the sauce and serve with cooked prunes, cooked semolina cut into diamond-shaped pieces and steamed potatoes.

Suggested wine Châteauneuf du Pape.

---

[1] *Pèbre d'ail* comes from the Provençal *pèbre d'ase*, which means 'donkey pepper'. It is a type of mountain savory with a peppery taste and a delicious fragrance. It is found on the scrubland and hills of Haute-Provence (*editor's note*).

AUBERGE DE L'ILL ★ ★ ★
ILLHAEUSERN (HAUT-RHIN)

SELLE DE CHEVREUIL SAINT-HUBERT

Saddle of venison is best when interlarded and marinated, then roasted.

For 8 people

1 saddle venison, weighing about 2kg
10–12 thin strips fat bacon
salt, freshly milled black pepper
unsalted butter

Marinade
2 carrots
2 onions, chopped *en mirepoix*★
crushed black peppercorns
thyme, bay leaf
1 clove
1 bottle good, full-bodied red wine

Game stock
trimmings from the saddle
3 tbs unsalted butter
mirepoix from the marinade

Liquid
1 cup good meat stock, reduced
the marinade, reduced to 1 cup

Sauce
1dl cognac
¼l double cream
1–2 tbs redcurrant jelly
1–2 turns of the pepper mill

Garnish
8 russet apples, baked
cranberry jelly

The marinade Trim the saddle and interlard with bacon. Marinate in the ingredients listed for 12 to 24 hours. Drain and carefully wipe dry.

To make the game stock Sauté the trimmings from the saddle in butter, then add the *mirepoix* and cook, shaking the pan from time to time until everything is a nice golden colour. Pour over the reduced marinade and the meat stock. Simmer in a good heavy saucepan for about 1½ hours, skimming from time to time.

To cook the venison Place in a buttered roasting-tin and roast in a hot oven, 190°–200°C, 375°–400°F, for about 30 to 35 minutes, basting as soon as it has begun to take colour with butter that is just melted. Take out of the oven and leave for 5 to 7 minutes before carving.

To make the sauce Deglaze the roasting-tin with the cognac. Strain the game stock through a conical sieve into a saucepan. Add the deglazed juices, the cream, redcurrant jelly and pepper. Keep the sauce hot but taste before serving to check the seasoning.

To arrange Carve the saddle into slices and arrange these in the centre of a heated oval metal dish. Fill the baked apples with the cranberry jelly and arrange round the meat. Serve the sauce in a sauceboat.

Suggested wine In Alsace saddle of venison is always served with a Wasserstriwela. Elsewhere a really good red burgundy will go well with it.

HÔTEL TERMINUS *
ARNAY-LE-DUC (CÔTE-D'OR)

CÔTELETTES DE CHEVREUIL DUC DE BOURGOGNE

The marinated cutlets are sautéed in butter. The reduced marinade is the base of the sauce, which is enriched with cream. The dish is garnished with russet apples, sautéed in butter and flambéed in calvados.

For 6 people

8 venison cutlets, trimmed and marinated for 6 hours
unsalted butter

Marinade
2dl good red burgundy
½dl Fine de bourgogne
1 onion, cut into rings
1 carrot, cut into rounds
1 clove garlic
5 juniper berries
a bouquet garni*

Sauce
4 generous tbs fresh double cream

Garnish
russet apples
calvados
unsalted butter

Wipe the marinated cutlets with a cloth, then salt them and sprinkle them with freshly milled black pepper.

To cook Sauté the cutlets in butter over a fairly high heat, turning them half way through. They should remain pink. Arrange on a metal dish and keep warm.

To make the sauce Deglaze the sauté-pan with the marinade and its vegetables and reduce the liquid by about two-thirds over high heat. Add the fresh cream. Boil for 2 minutes, then check the seasoning.

To serve Strain half the sauce over the cutlets and the rest into a heated sauceboat. Garnish the dish with the russet apples, which you have peeled, sliced thickly, sautéed in butter and flambéed in calvados, then seasoned lightly with salt and pepper.

Suggested wine A really good burgundy, such as Corton, Chambertin or Richebourg.

VEGETABLES

AU BOEUF COURONNÉ *
PARIS 19e: 188 AVENUE JEAN-JAURÈS (LA VILLETTE)

POMMES SOUFFLÉES
The nicest accompaniment of all for beef. They always seem rather mysterious but they need only a little practice. The procedure of frying twice at different temperatures is essential.

> For 6 people
> 1kg large yellow Dutch
>   potatoes (white potatoes
>   won't puff)
> 1l groundnut oil
> salt
> a bunch watercress

To prepare Peel and wash the potatoes and cut them lengthwise into slices about 3mm thick; dry in a cloth or on absorbent paper.

To cook Heat half the oil in each of the two frying-pans, keeping the first at a lower temperature than the second. Toss the sliced potatoes, a piece at a time, into the first pan, which should be hot but not smoking. Take care that they do not stick together. Raise the heat gradually, stirring the potatoes all the time. Lift out with a perforated spoon and drain on a double thickness of absorbent paper. Work as quickly as possible, as souffléed potatoes must not be left standing long. Plunge into the oil in the second pan, which should be considerably hotter than the first, so that they swell up. Drain in a free-standing strainer lined with grease-proof paper. Sprinkle with salt.

To serve Arrange the souffléed potatoes at one end of a dish of meat, with the bunch of watercress at the other end.
Serve with *pavé Villette* (see p. 232), rib of beef or grilled steak.

LAPÉROUSE * *
PARIS 6e: 51 QUAI DES GRANDS AUGUSTINS

POMMES DE TERRE À LA CRÈME
Creamed potatoes to go with the steaks served in the special style of the Lapérouse restaurant in Paris.

For 8 people
1·5kg yellow Dutch potatoes (about 20)
½l milk
½l cream
50g unsalted butter
salt, freshly milled black pepper
2 pinches grated nutmeg

Put the unpeeled potatoes in cold water and cook. Test with the point of a knife to see if they are done. They should still be firm. Drain, peel, and cut into fairly thick slices.

Now put the potatoes into the seasoned boiling milk. Add the cream and the nutmeg. Leave to boil vigorously for 10 minutes so that the liquid is absorbed. The starch in the potatoes will thicken the mixture. Add the butter a little at a time, correct the seasoning if necessary and arrange on a metal vegetable dish.

L'AUBERGADE *
PONTCHARTRAIN (YVELINES)

GRATIN DAUPHINOIS
One of the many types of potato dishes browned in the oven, but this is a special recipe.

For 4 people
500g raw potatoes, peeled, wiped and sliced
¼l milk
50g unsalted butter
salt, freshly milled black pepper, grated nutmeg
¼l cream
1 clove garlic
50g grated Gruyère cheese

Bring the milk to the boil in a pan large enough to hold the potatoes. Add the butter, salt, pepper and nutmeg, then the potatoes and the cream. Stir slowly with a wooden spoon, lifting the potatoes up as you do so. Cook for 30 minutes.

Pour the contents of the saucepan into a buttered earthenware dish, which you have prepared in advance by rubbing the sides with a clove of garlic cut in two. Sprinkle the surface with the grated Gruyère. Transfer the dish to a moderate oven, 165°–170°C, 330°–350°F, for about 40 to 45 minutes. If the surface is not a good golden colour, place under the grill for about 3 minutes.

L'OUSTEAU DE BAUMANIÈRE ★ ★ ★
LES-BAUX-DE-PROVENCE (BOUCHES-DU-RHÔNE)

GRATIN DAUPHINOIS

This is an exceptionally fine recipe. The cooking in a bain-marie prevents the cream from curdling. The cream from the cooking is drained off three-quarters of the way through and replaced by fresh cream and the gratin is returned to the oven to finish cooking. Then it is dusted with grated Gruyère and a little nutmeg and put under the grill to brown. Cooked in this way the gratin dauphinois is particularly smooth.

For 4–5 people

1·5kg potatoes, peeled, cut into very thin slices (like crisps), rinsed in cold running water and dried carefully in a cloth

2 cups double cream
75g freshly grated Emmenthal cheese
salt, freshly milled pepper
a tiny pinch of grated nutmeg
1 clove garlic

Put a thin layer of cream into an earthenware *gratin* dish rubbed with a cut clove of garlic. Follow with a layer of potatoes, and then add salt and pepper and sprinkle with the grated cheese. Repeat, finishing with a thin layer of cream but no cheese.

Cook this *gratin* in a pan of boiling water. First bring the water to the boil on top of the stove, then transfer to a moderate oven, 165°C, 350°F, for 35 to 40 minutes. Take great care not to let the potato get too hot.

Remove the dish from the oven, drain off the cream thoroughly by tilting the dish and cover the surface with the remaining cup of cream. Return to the pan of water in the oven for 15 to 20 minutes to finish the cooking.

About 5 minutes before serving, dust with grated cheese and a little nutmeg and place under the grill, still in the *bain-marie* so as to glaze the surface. Serve immediately.

This *gratin dauphinois* is the ideal accompaniment for grilled lamb or lamb *en croûte*.

Suggested wine Rosé from Provence or a white Côtes-du-Rhône.

AUBERGE DU PÈRE BISE ★ ★ ★
TALLOIRES (HAUTE-SAVOIE)

GRATIN SAVOYARD

*A classic potato dish found all over Savoy. It goes beautifully
with mountain lamb.*

For 6 people

1kg potatoes cut into slices
about ½cm thick
½l whole milk *or* ¼l
concentrated beef stock

6 tbs unsalted butter
1 cup Emmenthal, freshly
grated
salt, freshly milled black
pepper

Butter generously a fireproof dish (30cm in diameter). Pour in the
milk (or stock). Season with salt and pepper and boil.

Place a layer of sliced potatoes in the liquid, which they will
absorb. Sprinkle with a layer of grated cheese, and repeat with
another layer of potatoes and cheese. Cook on top of the stove
for 15 to 20 minutes, then transfer to an oven, preheated to
200°–210°C, 375°–400°F, for about 5 minutes or until golden.

MILLION ★
ALBERTVILLE (SAVOIE)

EMINCÉ DE POMMES DE TERRE AUX CHAMPIGNONS

A gratin *in which the potatoes are alternated with layers of mushrooms. To be served with roast lamb or beef.*

For 4–5 people

1kg potatoes, peeled and finely
   sliced, then dried in a cloth
250g mushrooms, cleaned and
   sliced, including the stalks
1 tbs oil
unsalted butter
salt, freshly milled black
   pepper

Melt the oil and 4 tablespoons of butter in an oven dish over heat. Remove from the heat and spread a layer of potatoes in the dish. Put back for a few seconds over a very high flame to seal them, then draw off again. Spread a layer of mushrooms and a few knobs of butter over the potatoes. Season with salt and pepper, then add another layer of potatoes dotted with knobs of butter, then a second layer of mushrooms and butter and a final layer of potatoes. Sprinkle the top with 4 tablespoons of softened butter, slightly melted (but not transparent).

   Cook in a moderate oven, 175°C, 350°F, for about 25 to 30 minutes or a little longer. Towards the end of the cooking time dot some more butter on the surface and cover with a piece of paper if necessary. The surface should be a light golden colour. Test with the point of a knife; if it goes in easily the *gratin* is cooked.

Suggested wine This depends on the meat that is to be served with the *gratin*, but a light red bordeaux is perfectly suitable.

LE GRAND HÔTEL ★
TENCE (HAUTE-LOIRE)

GRATIN DE POMMES DE TERRE À LA TENÇOISE

In this gratin *the taste of the Gruyère cheese dominates the potato.*

400g Gruyère cheese, cut into
   thin slices about 2–3mm
   thick
1kg large yellow potatoes,
   peeled, and cut into slices
   about 1cm thick

½l milk, boiled with salt,
   freshly milled black pepper
   and grated nutmeg, then left
   to cool
2 eggs

Arrange the sliced potato and cheese in a well-buttered *gratin* dish so that they are interleaved and overlapping like roof tiles with the cheese dominating the potato. Arrange in 1 or 2 layers depending on the size of the dish. Beat the eggs with the milk and seasonings and pour this mixture over the potatoes and cheese. Put the dish into a moderate oven, 165°–170°C, 325°–350°F and let the potatoes cook slowly for about 30 to 40 minutes, until the *gratin* is well browned and the potatoes tender.

This dish goes well with roast pork or lamb or hot ham.

L'OUSTEAU DE BAUMANIÈRE ★ ★ ★
LES-BAUX-DE-PROVENCE (BOUCHES-DU-RHÔNE)

MOUSSELINE DE POIS FRAIS

Excellent with roast lamb or lamb en croûte *and with roast or braised veal. The peas need not be very tiny; in fact large ones make the smoothest and lightest purée.*

For 4–5 people

2kg fresh peas
1 small carrot
2 white onions
1 sprig thyme
1 leaf sage

1 large knob unsalted butter
1 cup fresh cream
salt, freshly milled black pepper
1 tbs unsalted butter, cut in pieces

Put the peas into a saucepan containing enough boiling water to cover them completely, bring back to the boil and salt lightly with coarse salt. Add the carrot, onions, thyme and sage and cook until the peas are tender, taking care not to overcook. Taste to make sure. Remove the carrot, thyme and sage. Put the drained peas and onions through a vegetable mill, then give this purée a couple of turns in the blender, adding the knob of butter, the fresh cream, salt and pepper.

Heat the purée in a saucepan over a pan of boiling water, continuing to beat with a hand whisk, adding the butter a little at a time. Do not allow to boil. The purée should be light and frothy.

This dish is very good with *gigot d'agneau farci en croûte*, a recipe from the same restaurant (see p. 210).

CHEZ GILDO *
PARIS 7e: 153 RUE DE GRENELLE

FETTUCINE ALL'ALFREDO

Nothing seems easier to make than Italian-style pasta, but there are a few rules that must be observed.

For 6 people

500g tagliatelle, preferably
fresh
200g unsalted butter

100g Parmesan, grated
100g Emmenthal, grated
salt, freshly milled black
pepper

Cook the pasta in a large (4–5 litre) saucepan of boiling salted water.

Cooking time 2 minutes for fresh pasta, 7 minutes for dried pasta. It should be cooked but still firm. Tagliatelle is ruined if overcooked.

Drain a little without removing all the moisture. Return the pasta to the pan over very low heat. Add half the butter, the cheese, then the rest of the butter, stirring rapidly. Do not allow to boil. Add two turns of the pepper mill.

Transfer to a heated metal vegetable dish and serve immediately, very hot.

Suggested wine A rosé from the Dolomites.

AUBERGE DES MAURES *
SAINT-TROPEZ (VAR)

ARTICHAUTS À LA PROVENÇALE

An hors d'oeuvre that is peculiar to Provence and should be made with young artichokes from Provence. The artichoke is first cooked in water, then in olive oil flavoured with herbs, onions and a little garlic. In early spring when artichokes are very tender virtually all the leaves can be eaten. Unfortunately they are seldom found in England.

For 6 people

6 small or medium-sized
tender artichokes
2 lemons, cut in half
salt
2 onions, cut into rings
3 cloves garlic, crushed in a
garlic-press
1 sprig thyme
1 bay leaf

2dl light olive oil, not too
strong
6 tbs water
2 tbs parsley, finely chopped
a squeeze of lemon
chopped parsley

Trim the artichoke leaves by about 3–4cm. Trim the bases carefully and sprinkle with lemon.

Fill a large stew-pan with water, adding salt and lemon. Bring to the boil and cook the artichokes until they are three-quarters done. Take out and drain, turning them upside down. Arrange the artichokes in a small earthenware frying-pan (or an enamelled cast-iron one). Add the onions, distributing them evenly, and the thyme and bay leaf. Sprinkle with oil, add the water and cook covered over moderate heat until the artichokes are very tender. Add the garlic after 10 minutes. The total cooking time should be 20 to 25 or 30 minutes, depending on the tenderness of the artichokes. Sprinkle with oil so that the garlic is thoroughly coated. Once cooked the artichoke should look very well done, almost pickled. Test by pulling off a leaf which should come away very easily.

To serve Drain the artichokes, arrange in a deep china dish and decorate with a few of the onion rings.

Strain the cooking oil, which should be clear, into a bowl. Add a squeeze of lemon, a little salt and 2 turns of the pepper mill; whisk and sprinkle each artichoke with 1 or 2 tablespoons of this dressing. Decorate each artichoke with a good pinch of chopped parsley.

Serve with farmhouse bread and butter.

Suggested wine A rosé from Provence.

LE VENDÔME *
AIX-EN-PROVENCE (BOUCHES-DU-RHÔNE)

ARTICHAUTS VIOLETS À LA BARIGOULE

A wholly Provençal dish. The artichokes are stuffed with mushrooms, anchovies and ham, then cooked with olive oil, dry white wine, garlic and thyme from Provence. As they are very well cooked and very tender the whole artichoke can be eaten. They may be cooked in advance and reheated and are also delicious cold.

For 4 people

6 artichokes from Provence, young and tender
1 large onion, finely chopped
1 large carrot, sliced
1 dl olive oil
1 sprig thyme
1 bay leaf
4 cloves garlic, squeezed through a garlic press
a very little salt, freshly milled black pepper
½ l white wine
1 lemon

Stuffing
250g mushrooms, chopped *en duxelles**
6 anchovy fillets, finely chopped
250g sliced ham, very finely chopped
100g lean bacon rashers, cut into lardoons 3cm long

To prepare the artichokes Cut off the stalks and remove the lower leaves by pulling them off by hand. Cut off the tops of the leaves with scissors. Cut out the choke. Wash the artichokes in plenty of water with a few drops of lemon juice in it. Turn upside down, drain well and dry.

To make the stuffing Mix the ingredients thoroughly in a bowl and taste for seasoning. Stuff the artichokes with the stuffing, covering each one with a strip of bacon.

To cook Lightly colour the onion and carrot in the oil in a casserole. Add the thyme, bay leaf and garlic. Place the stuffed artichokes upright on top of the vegetables. Season lightly. Pour over the white wine and water, which should come up to the top of the artichokes, bring to the boil, put on the lid and continue boiling for about 40 minutes or until the artichokes are tender and the cooking liquid is thick and smooth. Reduce if too thin.

To serve Arrange the artichokes in a deep round dish. Add a squeeze of lemon to the sauce and pour round the artichokes.

Suggested wine Château Simone.

HOSTELLERIE ALSACIENNE
MASEVAUX (HAUT-RHIN)

FONDS D'ARTICHAUTS AUX MORILLES

An elegant way to use dried morel mushrooms. They are cooked in cream and used to fill fresh artichoke hearts.

For 8 people

16 medium-sized artichokes
1 lemon
salt
200g dried morels, soaked in
    water for a few hours
    beforehand
1l fresh double cream
salt, freshly milled black
    pepper

*Beurre manié**
2 tbs unsalted butter
2 tbs flour

Garnish
16 puff-pastry crescents
1 bunch watercress, without
    seasoning

To prepare and cook the artichoke hearts Remove the leaves by snapping them off with your hand. Cut carefully round the bases, and cook them in boiling salted water, with the lemon, for about 25 minutes. Drain, pull out the choke and trim the bases. Keep warm, covered with a piece of paper.

To prepare and cook the morels When the morels have swelled properly from the soaking, cut off the sandy stalks and wash several times in plenty of running water to get rid of any trace of sand. Wipe them. Cook for about 20 minutes in the cream, seasoned with salt and pepper.

To arrange the dish Take out the morels. Thicken the cream with the *beurre manié*★ and add a squeeze of lemon. Arrange the artichoke bases on a dish. Fill with the morels, spoon over the thickened cream and top with a hot crescent made of puff-pastry. Garnish the dish with the bunch of watercress and serve.

Suggested wine A dry white Riesling or Sancerre.

LE PRIEURÉ ★
VILLENEUVE-LÈS-AVIGNON (GARD)

AUBERGINES À LA PROVENÇALE
They may be served either by themselves, hot or cold, or with a fricassée of chicken, roast veal or pork or a plain omelette.

For 4 people	salt and freshly milled black pepper
3 aubergines	olive oil
coarse salt	2–5 cloves garlic according to taste
1kg tomatoes	
a pinch sugar	2 tbs parsley, finely chopped

To prepare the aubergines Cut the unpeeled aubergines lengthwise into slices about 1cm thick. Put in a dish or on a board, slit with the point of a knife, sprinkle at intervals with coarse salt to draw out their moisture and leave for about 30 minutes to drain. Wipe with a cloth and rub to remove the salt.

Heat the oil in a frying-pan, add the aubergines, spreading them out so that they are covered with the oil and fry gently, turning, until cooked. Take out and drain off all the cooking oil.

To prepare the tomatoes While the aubergines are cooking, skin, seed and pulp the tomatoes. Cook them in olive oil in a frying-pan until just soft, then leave to reduce over a very moderate heat with the garlic and chopped parsley for 45 to 50 minutes.

To finish the dish Arrange the aubergines in an earthenware dish and pour over a thick layer of the tomato purée to cover them. Reheat in the oven for a few minutes, or serve cold.

Suggested wine A rosé from Provence, well chilled.

AUBERGE DE NOVES * *
NOVES (BOUCHES-DU-RHÔNE)

RATATOUILLE PROVENÇALE

A dish of summer vegetables, flavoured with herbs and garlic and softened in oil. It can be served hot or cold and will go equally well with roast veal or pot-au-feu. It is delicious with poached eggs on top and left-over ratatouille makes a good filling for an omelette.

For 10 people

1kg aubergines, peeled, seeded and chopped
500g courgettes, chopped
500g green peppers, diced
light olive oil, not too strong
3 onions, very thinly sliced
750g tomatoes, peeled, seeded and crushed
salt, crushed black peppercorns
1 bouquet garni* (thyme, bay leaf, parsley, tarragon)
1 head garlic, with the cloves skinned and crushed
2 tbs tarragon, finely chopped

Pour a thin layer of oil into a small earthenware or enamelled cast-iron frying-pan and lightly fry the aubergines, courgettes and green peppers, one after the other, taking them out as they are done and putting them in a dish.

Pour off the cooking oil, wipe the pan, then pour in a thin layer of fresh olive oil. Put back the vegetables, adding the onions, tomatoes, bouquet garni, crushed garlic and crushed peppercorns. Salt lightly. Cover the pan and cook over low heat for 1 hour, keeping an eye on it and stirring from time to time. Add another 1 or 2 tablespoons of oil if necessary and 2 or 3 tablespoons of boiling water, but take care not to make the whole mixture too watery. Halfway through the cooking stir in the chopped tarragon.

Serve hot or cold in a deep dish.

Suggested wine Red Châteauneuf du Pape.

L'ARTOIS *
PARIS 8e: 13 RUE D'ARTOIS

CHOU FARCI CORRÉZIEN

A very popular rustic dish that tastes of the countryside. It may be served in the casserole in which it is cooked.

For 4–5 people

1 good cabbage, absolutely fresh
½l beef stock

Stuffing
300g sausage meat
300g boiled beef, finely chopped with a knife
4 beet or chard leaves, blanched for 5–6 minutes, then finely chopped with a knife
2 eggs

100g fresh white bread, finely chopped
4 tbs beef stock
4 thin rashers fat bacon
salt, freshly milled black pepper

Pull the leaves off the cabbage, keeping them whole. Cut out the hard core and slice away the hard ribs with a knife. Blanch the leaves for 10 minutes.

Butter generously a round cast-iron or earthenware casserole with a lid. Line the bottom and sides with cabbage leaves so that they overlap a little with no spaces left between them. Spoon a layer of stuffing on them, then add another layer of cabbage leaves, repeating the process until all the stuffing is used up. Finish off with a slightly thicker layer of cabbage leaves. Cover the surface with the rashers of bacon and leave uncovered. Put into a moderate oven, about 165°C, 350°F, for 15 minutes to turn the bacon golden. Pour over the hot stock, put on the lid and continue cooking for about another 1¼ hours. Remove the lid for the last 10 minutes, add a few dots of butter and place under the grill to brown the surface.

Serve by itself or with a *pot-au-feu* or roast pork.

Suggested wine Beaujolais or Cahors.

EYCHENNE ★
SAINT-GIRONS (ARIÈGE)

CASSOULET ARIÉGEOIS

A southern dish which, though simple, can compete with the famous bean stews of Toulouse and Castelnaudary.

For 4 people

250g white haricot beans
200g pork rind, cut into little pieces, blanched for 5 minutes and rinsed in cold water
200g shin of pork
200g lean bacon, boiled and rinsed in cold water

200g sausage
2 pieces goose meat
2 carrots, chopped
2 onion, chopped
3 cloves garlic
4 tomatoes, peeled, seeded and cut into quarters
a bouquet garni★
white breadcrumbs

Put the beans into a pan of cold water and bring to the boil. After 5 minutes cooking, throw away the water. Put the beans into a big saucepan of hot water. Add the pork rind, the various meats, the vegetables, garlic, tomatoes and bouquet garni.

When the beans are tender but not mushy, transfer the whole dish to an ovenproof casserole or earthenware dish. Correct the seasoning if necessary. Sprinkle with breadcrumbs. Put into a low oven, 150°–165°C, 300°–325°F and simmer for 2 hours.

Suggested wine Corbières.

RESTAURANT DE LA PYRAMIDE ★ ★ ★
VIENNE (ISÈRE)

ÉPINARDS À LA MODE DE CHEZ NOUS

New leaf spinach cooked in butter, served on large croûtons with ham and coated with a sauce thickened with egg yolk and served very hot. Fernand Point used to say that the flavour of spinach was improved if a pinch of sugar was added in addition to the usual seasoning.

For 4 people

1kg young, tender spinach
4–5 tbs unsalted butter
a pinch sugar
a pinch salt
1 very small piece grated nutmeg
freshly milled black pepper

Sauce
¾l Béchamel sauce (see p. 347)
5 tbs double cream
salt, freshly milled black pepper, nutmeg
3 egg yolks

Croûtons
5 large slices bread, fried in
   butter until golden
4 tbs butter
5 small thin slices ham

To cook Blanch the spinach in plenty of rapidly boiling water for 5 to 6 minutes, salting the water as it comes back to the boil. Rinse under cold running water and squeeze dry.

Put the butter into a sauté-pan over moderate heat. Add the spinach and stir continuously for 4 or 5 minutes, so that the butter is absorbed by the spinach. Season with a pinch of sugar and salt, a very small piece of grated nutmeg, and freshly milled black pepper.

Fry the croûtons in butter until golden, then garnish with the slices of ham, trimming with scissors to fit. Spoon a fifth of the spinach on to each croûton.

Make the cream sauce, thicken with the egg yolks and keep warm.

To serve Arrange the garnished croûtons on a warmed metal dish. Spoon some sauce over each croûton and serve very hot.

AUX LYONNAIS *
PARIS 2e: 32 RUE SAINT-MARC

SALADE DE PISSENLITS AU LARD
No oil is put on this dandelion salad. It is mixed at table with the hot fat bacon.

For 4–6 people

500g young dandelion leaves *or*
   2 heads chicory
1 clove garlic, peeled and cut
   in half
wine vinegar

salt and freshly milled black
   pepper to taste
250g pork fat *or* unsmoked
   bacon, diced
1 hard-boiled egg, shredded

Wash the salad in several lots of water to remove any earth or insects lodged in the curly edges. Sort through the leaves, cutting off the bottom and keeping only the best part.

Rub the salad bowl with the cut clove of garlic, then put in the salad and sprinkle with two good shakes of vinegar.

Soften the lardoons for about 10 minutes in a small buttered frying-pan. Pour all the contents of the pan over the salad and decorate by sprinkling with the shredded egg-yolk.

Suggested wine New Beaujolais.

EDITOR'S RECIPES

OIGNONS GLACÉS

Tiny onions trimmed to an equal size, cooked in very little water with salt, freshly milled black pepper and butter until all the water is absorbed.

Carefully peel the onion without cutting off the base so that it does not fall apart. Using a pointed knife cut a deep cross in the bottom so that the cooking liquid can penetrate right to the centre.

In a *small* saucepan, in which the onions fit closely together, sauté them in butter until they turn slightly yellow, adding a little more butter if necessary. Then add stock or water so that they are barely covered. Season with salt and freshly milled black pepper. Simmer, covered, for about 20 minutes, adding a pinch of sugar at the end of cooking time.

The onions are cooked when the liquid has reduced to a syrupy consistency.

The same method may be used for glazed carrots or turnips.

RIZ CRÉOLE, RIZ À L'INDIENNE

Rice is difficult to cook properly and the instructions must be strictly followed.

The rice is cooked in a large quantity of boiling salted water.

Cooking time 12 to 14 minutes, followed by rinsing under cold water and drying out in the oven for about 15 to 20 minutes.

Seasoning Use 1 teaspoon of coarse salt to each litre of water. The rice must never stick together through overcooking; the grains should be dry and separate.

To cook Do not wash the rice, but pour it slowly in a steady stream into the boiling salted water. Stir once to prevent it sticking to the bottom of the pan. Leave to cook without a lid for the time given.

Run under the cold tap to remove the starch and drain. Spoon into a buttered dish but do not pile up. Transfer to a moderate oven, lifting the grains with a fork every 5 minutes to dry those on the bottom. The rice will continue to swell as it absorbs its own moisture.

RIZ PILAF

For 4 or 6 people

1 cup Caroline rice
3 tbs oil
2 tbs onion, finely chopped
2½ cups veal or chicken stock
    or water

Heat the oil in a heavy-bottomed saucepan and cook the onion gently until it is soft but not brown. Add the rice and stir with a wooden spatula or spoon until it turns milky and becomes very lightly coloured. Pour over the heated stock, stir and cover as soon as it boils. Cook, covered, in a moderate oven for about 18 minutes.

The stock should have been absorbed and the rice will be completely cooked, with each grain separate. It can be left for 1 hour or more without becoming a solid mass.

HÔTEL BEAU-RIVAGE ★ ★
CONDRIEU (RHÔNE)

TARTE AUX POIRES, CHAUDE

A flaky pastry pear tart, served with fresh cream.

For 6 to 8 people

500g half-puff pastry (see p. 356), left to stand and chilled
3 tbs caster sugar
5 good firm pears, peeled and rubbed with a cut lemon to prevent discoloration

2 pinches vanilla powder
3 tbs unsalted butter
1 cup fresh double cream

Line a flan-tin with the pastry. Prick with a fork. Fill with the sliced raw pears, letting them overlap. Dust with the sugar and vanilla powder and dot with the butter.

Transfer to a hot oven, 190°–200°C, 375°–400°F, then lower the heat to finish cooking at 165°–170°C, 325°–340°F, for a total of 25 to 30 minutes' cooking time.

Turn out the tart and serve hot, with a bowl of fresh cream or Chantilly cream flavoured with vanilla and sugar.

Suggested wine A white Côtes-du-Rhône, preferably Condrieu.

RELAIS BASQUE
ORGON (BOUCHES-DU-RHÔNE)

TARTE AU CITRON

A tart made of crumbly pastry and filled with lemon cream flavoured with a little orange juice. The tart is filled before cooking.

For 6 people

Sweet short-crust pastry (see p. 356)
180g flour
100g unsalted butter
a pinch of salt
50g sugar
2–3 tbs water

Lemon filling
200g caster sugar
5 eggs
100g warmed unsalted butter
3 lemons
1 orange

Make the short-crust pastry. Roll out to a thickness of about 4 millimetres, then butter a flan tin and line with the pastry.

To make the filling Beat the sugar and eggs together in a bowl, then add the butter and the peel of one of the lemons. Work well with a whisk, then add the juice of the lemons and the orange. Beat again, then pour the mixture into the tart.

RESTAURANT DEMONCY ✶
DORMANS (MARNE)

TARTE AUX FRAMBOISES

The tart is baked blind, filled with fresh raspberries, coated with raspberry jelly and decorated with Chantilly cream.

For 6 people

500g raspberries, freshly
  picked
4 tbs raspberry jelly
200g fresh double cream,
  whipped with sugar
Sweet short-crust pastry (see p.
  356)
250g flour

100g sugar
vanilla powder
150g unsalted butter
1 egg
2 tbs water

Make the sweet short-crust pastry with the above ingredients (see p. 356). When the dough is smooth, wrap it and put it into the refrigerator to stand.

Line a flan tin with the pastry and bake blind in a hot oven 175°C, 350°F, for about 15 minutes. Leave to cool.

Turn the pastry out of the tin and put on a serving-dish. Fill with as many raspberries as can be pressed into it.

Heat the raspberry jelly in a small saucepan, stirring well to melt.

Coat the raspberries thickly with it and decorate with the Chantilly cream, using a forcing bag.

Suggested wine Still champagne or another very dry white wine.

LA POULARDE ✶ ✶
MONTROND-LES-BAINS (LOIRE)

TARTE PANACHÉE MIRLITON

An upside-down tart made with fruit in season. This recipe uses caramelized apples and half-apricots with a mixture of eggs, icing sugar, powdered almonds and cream.

For 8 people

1kg apples, peeled, cored and
  sliced
150g unsalted butter
200g lump sugar
½dl dark rum
400g sweet short-crust pastry
  (see p. 356)

12 apricot-halves from a tin,
  well drained

Mirliton cream
4 eggs
150g icing sugar
150g powdered almonds
½l double cream

To cook the apples Put the apples into a saucepan with the butter and sugar and heat, stirring all the while. Cook until they are lightly caramelized and flambé with the rum. Leave until cold.

Line a flan tin with the pastry, rolled out fairly thick. Prick the pastry. Arrange the sliced apples on it, with the apricot halves on top. Cook in a moderate oven, about 165°C, 325°F, for 35 to 40 minutes.

To make the Mirliton cream While the tart is cooling prepare the cream. Work the eggs with the icing sugar, stir in the powdered almonds and whisk, adding the fresh cream. Pour the mixture into the tart so that it covers the whole surface. Put back into the oven to cook slowly at the same temperature for 20 to 25 minutes.

To serve Turn the tart out on to a round dish lined with a paper doily, dust generously with icing sugar and serve warm.

Suggested wine A well-chilled Sauternes.

LE BERLIOZ
PARIS 16e: 135 AVENUE MALAKOFF

TARTE FAÇON TATIN

There are many versions of this tart invented by the Demoiselles Tatin from the famous restaurant of Lamotte-Beuvron. This one from the Berlioz restaurant is easy to make and melts in the mouth. We recommend that a special copper mould should be used.

For 6 people

1·5kg soft apples, preferably medium-sized Golden Delicious, peeled, halved and cored
3 tbs unsalted butter
4 tbs caster sugar

Sweet short-crust pastry (see p. 356)
200g sifted flour

140g unsalted butter
1 egg
1–2 tbs cold water
a pinch salt
1 level tbs caster sugar

Caramel roux
6–8 lumps sugar
a squeeze lemon juice

To prepare Make the pastry, roll it into a ball and chill in the refrigerator.

To cook Spread the butter over the bottom of a round copper mould and sprinkle with the caster sugar. Heat over low heat until the butter melts and the mixture caramelizes slightly. Arrange the apple halves on top, side by side and close together. Cook over low heat on top of the stove for about 1½ hours, until the apples are completely soft and their juice and the butter and sugar are beginning to run over the edge of the tin.

Remove from the heat and leave to cool; the tin should be barely warm.

Preheat the oven to 190°C, 375°F. Roll out the pastry to fit the tin and lay it over the apples, turning the surplus over to form a fat roll round the edge of the tin. Feather the rim and transfer to the oven. Bake for about 15 to 18 minutes, until the pastry is lightly coloured and comes away from the sides of the tin.

To serve Take the tin out of the oven, leave to cool and turn out, upside down, on to a round plate or dish. Smooth and arrange evenly the apples with a fork. Make a light brown caramel in a small saucepan with the sugar lumps moistened with water and a squeeze of lemon juice, cooked until they take colour. Pour the caramel, which should be soft and smooth, over the apples, smoothing the surface immediately with a metal spatula or the flat of a knife.

Serve warm.

Suggested wine A mellow white bordeaux such as Barsac.

GRAND HÔTEL DES CADETS DE GASCOGNE
CASTELJALOUX (LOT-ET-GARONNE)

TOURTE GASCONNE
An apple pie flavoured with armagnac.

For 6 people

400g flaky pastry (6 turns, see p. 356), ready to use
1 egg yolk
500g apples, peeled and sliced
4–5 tbs caster sugar
2dl armagnac

a few drops orange-flower water
vanilla powder
icing sugar

Roll out the pastry into 2 rounds. Line a tart-tin with one of them and spoon into the centre the apple slices, which you have previously macerated in the sugar and armagnac, with the orange-flower water and vanilla. Do not put the apples too near the edge. Moisten the edge and cover with the second round of pastry, pressing together to seal. Trim the edges and leave to stand for a few minutes to avoid shrinking. Glaze the surface with egg yolk beaten with a drop or two of water.

Cook the pie in an oven preheated to 175°C, 350°F, for about 35 minutes, keeping an eye on it. Lower the heat during the cooking if necessary.

When the pastry is cooked and the surface golden, take the pie out of the oven and make a small hole in the top. Pour in the armagnac and sugar mixture, which you have cooked for a few moments until it forms a syrup.

To serve Dust the surface with icing sugar and serve warm but not hot.

Suggested wine A semi-dry white bordeaux.

FRUIT TARTS AND FRUIT SWEETS

FEUILLETÉ CHAUD AUX FRUITS DE SAISON

A flaky pastry tart filled with seasonal fruit and coated with a red fruit syrup flavoured with kirsch.

For 10 people

1kg half-puff pastry, made with 500g flour and 400g butter (see p. 356)
1 egg yolk
strawberries, raspberries *or* quartered pears poached in water
1½ cups redcurrant syrup, flavoured with kirsch and raspberry liqueur

Make the pastry and leave to stand in the refrigerator.

Divide the pastry into individual *galettes* (girdle cakes) 3 or 4 millimetres thick or else make one big one. Leave to stand again for 20 minutes. Glaze the surface with egg yolk and cook in an oven preheated to 190°–205°C, 380°–400°F, for about 16 to 18 minutes.

To serve Fill the *galettes* with the fresh fruit and coat with the warmed syrup.

Suggested wine Either champagne or Monbazillac, chilled on ice.

To cook Cook the pastry with the filling in a moderate oven, 160°C, 350°F, for about 30 minutes. Eat hot or cold. Dust with icing sugar before serving.

Suggested wine A dessert wine such as a Muscat or a Frontignan, or a white port.

AUBERGE DU GRAND SAINT-PIERRE ★ ★
LES HAIES À CHARMES, DOURLERS (NORD)

TARTE AU MELON
This unusual and delicious tart tastes like one made with well-cooked, very sweet apricots.

> fine brioche pastry, ready to
>   use (see p. 358)
> 1 nice ripe Cantaloup melon
> 100g caster sugar
> powdered vanilla

Line a flan-tin measuring about 22 centimetres in diameter and 5 centimetres in depth with the pastry.

Scoop out the seeds from the melon, chop and remove all the skin. Put the pieces into an enamel saucepan with the sugar and vanilla powder. Cook for 10 to 15 minutes, then remove the melon pieces, reserving the liquid.

Drain the melon well. Arrange on the pastry as you would any fruit such as apricots. Leave to settle for about 1 hour, then transfer to a very hot oven preheated to 205°–215°C, 410°–425°F, for about 15 minutes. Remove the tart which is now ready to eat.

Suggested wine Normally no wine is drunk with this tart but a very light red wine would do if desired.

AUBERGE DU VIEUX PUITS ★
PONT-AUDEMER (EURE)

DOUILLONS DE POMMES À LA NORMANDE

*Norman apples wrapped in puff pastry and baked in the oven.
They are served with fresh cream and apricot jam.*

For 6 people

250–300g half-puff pastry
 (turned 6 times) (see p. 356)
1 egg white to seal the pastry
1 egg yolk beaten with a drop
 of water to glaze
a pastry brush

6 Normandy apples: skinned,
 cored and rolled at once in a
 mixture of 6 dessertspoons
 caster sugar and 2 tsp
 powdered cinnamon

To prepare Keep the pastry in the refrigerator until you are ready to use it. Then roll out to a thickness of 2 millimetres. Cut out 6 squares of equal size and six small diamond shapes which will make the leaves.

Place each apple in the centre of a square of pastry. Wrap the pastry round, bringing the four corners together, and sealing them together with egg white at the top. Top with a pastry leaf, moistened to make it stick. Glaze the pastry with egg yolk and trace veins in the leaves with the blunt edge of a small knife.

To cook Bake on a baking sheet in an oven preheated to between 190° and 205°C, 375°–400°F, for 10 minutes, then when the pastry has risen, turn the oven down to 170°–175°C, 350°F, for another 20 minutes.

Serve warm with fresh cream and apricot jam.

HOSTELLERIE DES SANTONS ★ ★
GRIMAUD (VAR)

POIRES FARCIES DES SANTONS

For 6 people

6 large William pears, peeled
 and cut in half
150g preserved fruit, chopped
 en salpicon★
50g sultanas
2dl Alsatian kirsch
100g caster sugar

½l fresh double cream
125g fresh raspberries
½l vanilla ice cream

Sugar syrup
200g caster sugar
½l water
a pinch vanilla powder

Scoop out the centre of the pears with a vegetable scoop and remove the cores. Macerate the preserved fruit and sultanas in the kirsch for about 2 hours. Meanwhile poach the pear halves in a sugar syrup made with the ingredients listed. Cook the syrup before putting in the pears. Poach them very gently for about 15 minutes, so that they remain firm.

Drain the preserved fruit and put 1 small tablespoon or 1 teaspoon into each half-pear. Put the pears together again as though they had never been cut, sticking the halves firmly together and wrapping round with a strip of silver foil, which is removed before serving. Put the filled pears into the refrigerator.

To make the sauce Mix the sugar and cream together, squeeze the raspberry juice into the mixture, whisking a little to thicken, but *do not whisk as for Chantilly cream.*

To make up Spread the vanilla ice cream over the bottom of a chilled fruit dish. Arrange the pears on the ice cream base, sprinkle with the kirsch and coat with the raspberry sauce. Serve immediately.

Suggested wine Extra-dry champagne, chilled on ice.

MICHEL PEREIRE *
PARIS 17e: 122 AVENUE DE VILLIERS

CLAFOUTIS
This sweet, which originated in Central France, is usually made with wild black cherries. It is served in farmhouses at harvest suppers.

For 6 or 7 people	1 tbs unsalted butter
3 tbs flour	icing sugar
a pinch salt	
3 tbs caster sugar	*Fruit*
3 eggs	1kg stoned cherries (in season)
3½dl milk	*or* 1kg apples peeled and
1 tbs oil	thinly sliced (in winter)
1 tbs dark 54° rum	

Put the flour, salt and sugar into a bowl. Whisk in the eggs one at a time, then slowly add the milk, still whisking to make a light, smooth paste. Add the oil and the rum. Leave the paste to stand while you prepare the fruit.

To cook Butter a flan-tin 20 centimetres in diameter (it must be made in one piece and not with a movable base or the paste will seep out). Pour in the paste, press in the fruit and put into an oven preheated to 175°C, 350°F, to bake for 40 to 45 minutes. Lower the heat half-way through. Test if the *clafoutis* is cooked by sticking in the point of a knife or a trussing needle; it should come away clean. Take out of the oven and turn out when nearly cold. Dust with icing sugar.

To serve Cut in triangular wedges as for a tart.

Suggested wine A mellow white bordeaux.

PIC ★ ★ ★
VALENCE (DROME)

BAVAROIS PRÉSIDENT NIXON

A strawberry bavarois decorated with fresh strawberries.

For 6 people

To line the mould
½l thick cream, sweetened with
  2 tbs caster sugar
20g gelatine, dissolved and
  mixed with the cream

Decoration and filling
500g large fresh strawberries,
  macerated in 1dl kirsch and
  sweetened to taste with
  caster sugar

Bavarois mixture
3dl fresh strawberry purée,
  thinned down with 3dl at
  32°C, 90°F sugar syrup
juice of 2 lemons
20g gelatine, dissolved and
  strained through a cloth
½l fresh cream, whipped with
  2 tbs caster sugar and ½ cube
  crushed ice

Line a chilled 1½ litre *bavarois* mould with the cream and gelatine
mixture. Leave to set, then fill the mould with the *bavarois* mixture.
As soon as it starts to set press in a third of the macerated strawberries. Cover with a piece of plain paper cut to the same size as
the mould. Put into the refrigerator for at least three hours.

To serve Dip the bottom of the mould in warm water. Turn out
on to a round dish lined with a paper doily and surround with the
rest of the strawberries, keeping the biggest one for the top.

Suggested wine Very dry champagne, well chilled.

RESTAURANT DE LA PYRAMIDE ★ ★ ★
VIENNE (ISÈRE)

FRAISES DE MAMAN POINT
An unusually fresh tasting strawberry delight.

For 4 people

700g large juicy strawberries
250g caster sugar
1dl kirsch
1dl double cream, chilled
2 large white peaches

Put the strawberries through a blender to make half a litre (2 cups) of strawberry purée. Add the sugar, the kirsch and the cream. Mix lightly. Chill in the refrigerator.

Skin the peaches and cut into small pieces.

Serve the strawberry purée in champagne glasses decorated with pieces of peach.

Suggested wine Extra-dry champagne, chilled on ice.

L'ESCALE ★ ★
VARCES (ISÈRE)

DIPLOMATE
A sweet which is made in a mould and turned out to be served. The base is crème anglaise *lightly stiffened with gelatine containing crystallized fruits and flavoured with kirsch. The dish looks beautiful and may be served with an apricot or raspberry sauce, also flavoured with kirsch.*

For 10 people

½ cup fresh double cream, chilled
1 cup crystallized mixed fruit, diced and macerated in ½dl kirsch

Crème anglaise (see p. 359)
1dl milk
5 egg yolks
½ cup caster sugar

1 tsp powdered gelatine
¼ glass water
24 sponge-finger biscuits, to line the bottom and sides of the mould

Filling
½ cup apricot jam, put through the blender
½l kirsch

To prepare the gelatine Soften the gelatine in a bowl with the water. Drain. Put the bowl into a pan of boiling water and stir with a whisk over moderate heat until it is completely soft. Set aside away from the stove, leaving the pan in the bowl of hot water.

To make the crème anglaise Heat the milk to boiling point. Take off the heat. Beat the egg yolks and sugar with a hand whisk in a saucepan, preferably enamelled cast-iron, until the mixture whitens. Pour in the boiling milk, continuing to whisk, then heat over very moderate heat to thicken the cream. Stir continuously with a wooden spoon and don't let it boil. Add the dissolved gelatine away from the heat. Strain the cream into a bowl set in a container full of ice. Continue to work the cream until it thickens and begins to chill. Add the fresh chilled cream, stirring it in with a wooden spoon, then the crystallized fruits and the liquid in which they were steeped.

To fill the mould Put the apricot jam through a blender and spoon into a small saucepan. Add the kirsch and bring to the boil over very moderate heat, stirring all the time with a wooden spoon.

Line the base of a 3-litre *bavarois* or charlotte mould with a piece of greaseproof paper; then line the base and sides with the sponge fingers. Brush with the warm jam. Pour half the fruit and cream mixture into the mould and arrange a layer of sponge fingers on top. Pour in the rest of the cream and press down the top of any biscuits that rise above the top of the mould. Fill any gaps with biscuit crumbs.

Chill in the refrigerator for 4 to 5 hours.

To turn out Dip the base of the mould very quickly in some hot water. Turn the mould upside down on to a plate covered with a paper doily. Remove the greaseproof paper and return to the refrigerator before serving.

Suggested wine Sauternes, champagne or Vouvray.

LA VIEILLE AUBERGE
CASTELJALOUX (LOT-ET-GARONNE)

PÊCHES FLAMBÉES DEMOISELLE SOPHIE

A very effective recipe which is quickly made if the sponge cases are prepared in advance.

For 6 people

12 peach halves preserved in syrup, well drained and dried
1dl medium dark rum
2 tbs unsalted butter
icing sugar

Sponge cases
120g sponge-finger biscuits
2 eggs
30g caster sugar

2 cups warm milk
powdered vanilla
2 heaped tbs apricot jam

French pastry cream (see p. 359)
1 egg + 1 extra yolk
3 tbs sugar
1 tbs flour
1 cup vanilla-flavoured boiling milk
1 grain coarse salt
1 tbs medium dark rum

To make the sponge cases Put the eggs and the sugar into a bowl. Work together until the mixture will form a ribbon, then pour over the vanilla-flavoured milk and bring to the boil. Heat until it thickens and add the sponge fingers, broken up into little pieces. Stir well with a wooden spoon until the biscuits have absorbed the cream and turned to a porridge-like consistency. Now add the apricot jam. Divide the mixture between six small tartlet moulds (or ramekins), buttered and sugared. Cook in the oven in a pan of water for about 15 minutes. The sponge cases may be kept in the tartlet moulds in the refrigerator for 2 to 3 days.

To make the pastry cream Meanwhile make the *crème pâtissière*, using the ingredients listed above.

To prepare the dish Put 2 tablespoons of butter in a metal fireproof dish. Turn out the sponge cases on to this and coat each one with *crème pâtissière* (using about 1 tablespoon to each case).

Arrange 2 peach halves to form a dome on top of each. Dust generously with icing sugar. Place under the grill for a couple of minutes until golden.

To flambé Heat the dish containing the peaches, dust with 2 more tablespoons of icing sugar and put under the grill to glaze a second time. The peaches should be boiling hot. Heat the dish again, pour over the rum, set light to it and carry flaming to the table.

Suggested wine Very dry champagne, chilled.

LE MORVAN *
AVALLON (YONNE)

ANANAS CHAUD À LA MARTINIQUAISE

A hot dessert in which the pineapple, coffee and rum blend marvellously together. It is very quickly made.

For 4 or 5 people

8 good rings tinned pineapple
2 tbs unsalted butter
4–5 tbs caster sugar
¾ cup pineapple juice

1 tsp soluble coffee powder
½ cup white rum

Garnish
2 tbs slivered almonds, roasted on a baking-sheet until golden

Melt the butter in a frying-pan and stew the pineapple rings gently on both sides until soft. Add the sugar, pineapple juice and coffee powder and reduce until slightly caramelized. Add the rum and set light to it. Arrange on a round dish and sprinkle with the slivered almonds. Serve with almond *tuiles* or petits fours.

Suggested wine The rum and coffee would ruin the taste of good wine but a small glass of chilled punch might be amusing.

GÂTEAUX

CHEZ MÉLANIE *
RIEC-SUR-BELON (FINISTÈRE)

GÂTEAU BRETON
A thick galette flavoured with rum. Galettes are made all over Brittany; this is an exceptionally delicate one.

For 10 people

275g flour
225g sugar
a pinch salt
250g softened unsalted butter
6 egg yolks
1 small glass rum

To prepare Place 200 grams of the flour in a bowl and make a well in the centre. Put into the well the sugar, the salt, the softened butter, 5 of the egg yolks and the rum. Mix and then work well together as for short-crust pastry. Add the last 75 grams of flour. Form the dough into a ball with your hands.

To bake Butter a *moule à manqué**. Line it with the pastry rolled out to a thickness of 3 centimetres. Dilute the remaining egg yolk with a drop of water and brush over the gâteau. Make a crisscross pattern on the surface with a fork. Bake in a hot oven, 175°–190°C, 350°–380°F, for about 20 minutes.

Suggested wine A light red wine or a dry white one will go equally well.

AUBERGE DU GRAND SAINT-PIERRE ★ ★
LES HAIES À CHARMES, DOURLERS (NORD)

GÂTEAU AUX NOIX ET AU RHUM

A walnut gâteau of pleasing appearance with white icing decorated with walnut halves.

For 12 people

half-puff pastry, ready to use
  (see p. 356)
unsalted butter
strained apricot jam

Walnut cream
250g walnuts, finely chopped
250g caster sugar
4 eggs, separated
100g unsalted butter, softened
3 tbs dark rum
1 tbs fresh double cream
vanilla powder

Line a buttered flan-tin with the half-puff pastry. Spread over a layer of apricot jam with a pastry brush.

Beat the sugar and egg yolks together in a bowl until the mixture whitens and will form a ribbon. Work this mixture with the walnuts, butter, cream, vanilla and rum. Whisk the egg whites until stiff with a pinch of salt. Fold carefully into the cream mixture.

Trickle the mixture over the pastry. Bake in a moderate oven 165°C, 330°F, until a golden crust forms on the surface, about 30 to 35 minutes.

To serve Leave to cool, then turn out. Spread with white icing made with icing sugar flavoured with rum. Decorate the icing with walnut halves.

Suggested wine A white bordeaux such as Sauternes or Monbazillac, chilled in the refrigerator, or a light champagne chilled on ice.

HÔTEL DEMONCY ★
DOUMANS (MARNE)

TURINOS

A sponge layer-cake with a filling of French pastry cream flavoured with rum and covered with a layer of almond paste.

For 8 people

Sponge mixture
4 eggs
120g sugar
160g sifted flour

Pastry cream
½l milk
1 vanilla pod
4 egg yolks
125g caster sugar
3 heaped tbs flour
½dl dark rum

Topping
300g almond paste
2 tbs rum

Bake the sponge in a square tin; turn out and leave on a wire rack to cool.

To make the pastry cream Cook the pastry cream (see p. 359) leave to cool and then flavour with the rum.

To make up the cake Cut the sponge horizontally into three and sprinkle each slice with a little rum. Spread half the pastry cream on the first slice, cover with the second slice, spread with the rest of the cream and cover with the third slice. Cover the surface of the cake with a layer of almond paste flavoured with rum, smoothing it with a spatula or the flat of a knife. Leave the almond paste to harden before cutting the cake.

Suggested wine Extra-dry champagne.

HÔTEL DE PARIS *
MONTE-CARLO (PRINCIPAUTÉ DE MONACO)

MILLEFEUILLE PRINCE ALBERT

A millefeuille *is undoubtedly one of the most popular of French pastries. The ingredients from which it is made, puff pastry and French pastry cream enriched with Chantilly cream, must be of the highest quality.*

For 4 or 6 people

600g very light puff pastry made with butter (see p. 356)
½l pastry cream (see p. 359)

2–3 tbs Grand Marnier
¼l double cream, whipped en Chantilly (see p. 359)
icing sugar

Roll out three rounds of pastry about 20 or 22 centimetres in diameter with a rolling pin; bake in an oven preheated to 205°C, 400°F.

Put the pastry cream in a bowl and flavour with the Grand Marnier, then carefully fold half the Chantilly cream into it.

To make up Spread the first round of pastry with half the cream mixture. Place the second round on top. Cover with the rest of the cream and then with the third round of pastry. Coat the sides of the *millefeuille* with the remaining Chantilly cream. Dust the top of the *millefeuille* lavishly with icing sugar.

Suggested wine Meursault or Sauternes.

LE GRAND VÉFOUR ★ ★ ★
PARIS 1er: 17 RUE DE BEAUJOLAIS

BÛCHE DE NOËL

A light sponge Christmas log flavoured with rum syrup and decorated with a chestnut and butter cream also flavoured with rum; it is served surrounded by marrons glacés.

For 6 people

Chestnut purée
400g chestnuts, skinned and
  peeled
¾l milk
10 lumps sugar
1 vanilla pod

Sponge mixture
3 egg yolks
500g caster sugar

1 level tbs baking powder
4 egg whites
250g sifted flour
¼l sugar syrup
1dl rum

Cream for decoration
the chestnut purée
unsalted butter, softened
5 tbs caster sugar
½dl rum

Decoration
10 *marrons glacés*

To make the chestnut purée Cook the chestnuts in the milk in a saucepan or enamelled casserole, with the sugar and vanilla pod.

To make the sponge mixture Meanwhile, work the egg yolks and sugar together in a bowl until the mixture pales and forms a creamy mass. Add the baking powder and egg whites (beaten until stiff with a pinch of salt) and sprinkle in the flour. Blend the ingredients well together to form a smooth paste.

To bake the sponge cake Butter a large rectangular baking sheet with raised edges, dust with flour and pour the mixture over it, smoothing and levelling the surface with a metal spatula or the flat of a knife. Put in an oven preheated to 165°–170°C, 325°–340°F, and bake for about 20 minutes. Add the rum to the sugar syrup, take the sponge out of the oven and sprinkle lightly with the syrup. Roll up immediately and place on a plate.

To make the cream This should be prepared while the sponge is cooking, and kept in the refrigerator. Drain the cooked chestnuts, put them through a fine sieve into a bowl and mash them to obtain a very fine, smooth purée. Weigh this and add the same weight of softened (not melted) butter. Blend well with a wooden spoon or spatula, adding the sugar and rum. Put into the refrigerator to chill. Decorate the log with this cream using a forcing bag with a rose nozzle. Decorate the log as the fancy takes you, imitating knots in wood and the lines of tree bark. Surround the Christmas log with *marrons glacés*.

Suggested wine Extra-dry champagne, chilled on ice.

LE TRINQUET *
SAINT-ETIENNE-DE-BAIGORRY (PYRÉNÉES-ATLANTIQUES)

GÂTEAU AUX AMANDES
This cake may be served for tea or as a dessert to accompany vanilla cream or chocolate cream.

For 10–12 people

20 very fresh egg whites
a pinch of salt
720g caster sugar
250g unsalted butter, softened
400g flour
a few drops lemon essence or
   the finely grated peel of 1
   lemon
50g slivered almonds

Beat the egg whites until stiff with a good pinch of salt. Carefully add the sugar, bit by bit, whisking. The mixture should change consistency, becoming creamier but firm. Then add, all together, the well softened butter, the sifted flour and the lemon juice or peel. Mix carefully so that the egg whites remain stiff. Pour the mixture into a well-buttered *moule à manqué*, about 22 centimetres in diameter. Sprinkle generously with the almonds.

Cook in a moderate oven, about 190°C, 385°F, for about 45 minutes. Test with the point of a trussing needle to see whether it is cooked. It should come out damp but clean.

Turn out the cake and allow to become cold before slicing.

Suggested wine If the cake is served as a dessert, dry champagne.

HÔTEL DE LA POSTE ★ ★
AVALLON (YONNE)

DOLCE BORGHESE

A Genoese gâteau filled with cream flavoured with different liqueurs.

For 8–10 people

1 Genoese* pastry (10cm thick, 25–30cm in diameter)

Meringue mixture
9 egg whites
300g sugar

300g unsalted butter
kirsch
Curaçao
raspberry liqueur

Icing
White icing flavoured with kirsch *or* chocolate icing

Cut the Genoese pastry horizontally into 4 slices.

To make the meringue mixture Gently warm the egg whites with the sugar. Take off the heat and whisk with a double whisk until completely cold.

Soften the butter with a fork. Pour the meringue mixture over a little at a time and blend well with the whisk, to make a very light butter cream.

Divide this cream into 3 equal parts in separate bowls. Flavour the first with kirsch; the second with Curaçao and the third with raspberry liqueur. Lay the slices of pastry on a plate. Sprinkle the first with kirsch and spread with a thick layer of the kirsch-flavoured cream. Place the second slice on top, sprinkle with Curaçao and spread with a thick layer of the Curaçao-flavoured cream. Repeat with the third slice, using raspberry liqueur and the raspberry-flavoured cream. Cover with the fourth slice. Smooth over any cream that runs down the sides with a metal spatula or the flat of a knife.

Ice the outside of the gâteau with white icing flavoured with kirsch or with chocolate icing. Leave to chill for several hours. Slice with a knife that has been dipped into boiling water.

Suggested wine Well-chilled Sauternes.

LE RIVIÉRA ★
'LE PIGONNET'
AIX-EN-PROVENCE (BOUCHES-DU-RHÔNE)

LA CARAQUE

This is a cake for people who love chocolate. It is a chocolate Genoese, filled with chocolate butter cream and iced with chocolate.

For 8 people

5 eggs
180g caster sugar
180g flour
60g sweetened cocoa powder

Filling and icing (for 1½ cups
 chocolate butter cream)
2 egg yolks
80g caster sugar
150g softened unsalted butter
a pinch vanilla powder
75g cooking chocolate, melted
3–4 tbs chocolate flakes

To make the Genoese Beat the eggs with the sugar in a large metal bowl (preferably copper) over low heat, whisking all the time with a double wire whisk, but not allowing the mixture to cook, until it has increased in volume and is a pale yellow cream. Then, off the heat, add the flour and cocoa mixed together, stirring slowly with a wooden spoon.

To cook Spoon the mixture into a buttered and floured *moule à manqué* and bake in a moderately hot oven, 190°C, 375°F (lowering to 175°C, 350°F) for about 30 minutes.

Filling and icing Mix all the ingredients, then work them together with a fork and beat them to obtain a perfect mixture. Refrigerate until you are ready to use. Cut the Genoese horizontally into 2 or 3 slices. Spread the chocolate butter cream on the slices with a palette knife. Put the cake together again and coat with the melted chocolate. Spread a little chocolate butter cream over the sides with the palette knife, and press the chocolate flakes gently into the cream with the palette knife.

 Slide the finished cake on to a dish covered with a paper doily.

Suggested wine Very dry champagne.

AUBERGE DU PÈRE BISE ★ ★ ★
TALLOIRES (HAUTE-SAVOIE)

GÂTEAU AUX FRAISES DES BOIS
A rich but subtle Genoese flavoured with kirsch and decorated with wild strawberries and Chantilly cream.

For 8 people

8 eggs
250g caster sugar
250g flour
1 dsp kirsch
1kg wild strawberries
250g Chantilly cream (see p.
 359)

To make the Genoese pastry Mix the eggs and sugar, then whisk over low heat. Add the sifted flour and work together. Pour the mixture into a buttered and floured cake tin and bake in a low oven for about 25 minutes.

Leave to cool, then cut horizontally into 3 slices. Sprinkle with a mixture of kirsch and 2 tablespoons of caster sugar dissolved in 2 tablespoons of water. Garnish two slices with wild strawberries and Chantilly cream.

To ice Cover with the last slice. Trickle over some white icing flavoured with kirsch. Decorate with Chantilly cream and wild strawberries.

Suggested wine Champagne or iced Sauternes.

AUBERGE DE L'ÉCU *
TRIE-CHÂTEAU (OISE)

GÂTEAU DE POMMES À LA CRÈME
An apple charlotte served with custard cream enriched with fresh cream and flavoured with kirsch.

For 6 to 8 people

8 Golden Delicious apples, peeled and thinly sliced
2 tbs water
2 tbs butter, cut into small pieces

75g sugar
1 vanilla pod
peel of half a lemon
6 eggs

Cook the apples in the water with all the other ingredients except the eggs until completely soft. Leave to cool, then put into a china bowl. Add the eggs, beaten with a fork as for an omelette, and mix well.

Butter a charlotte mould and fill with the mixture, tapping the mould on the table to settle the contents. Cut a piece of grease-proof paper to the size of the mould, butter it and lay it directly over the apples. Put the mould into a pan of water, bring the water to the boil on top of the stove, then transfer to an oven preheated to 165°–175°C, 325°–350°F, and cook for 50 minutes to an hour. The water should simmer gently throughout. Leave to cool.

Turn the gâteau out on to a round dish. Serve with a vanilla-flavoured custard cream (see p. 359). For every ½ litre of custard cream add 3 tablespoons fresh cream and 3 tablespoons kirsch.

Suggested wine A fruity Alsatian wine, well chilled.

PAUL CHÊNE *
PARIS 16e: 123 RUE LAURISTON

CHARLOTTE AUX FRAMBOISES

A sumptuous year-round sweet that may be prepared in advance.

For 10 people

250g caster sugar
250g unsalted butter
250g powdered almonds
2 liqueur glasses Cointreau
1½kg sponge finger biscuits
400g fresh (or frozen)
    raspberries

Raspberry sauce
400g fresh (or frozen)
    raspberries
5 tbs caster sugar
1 glass raspberry liqueur (or
    any fruit liqueur)

Purée the sugar, butter, powdered almonds and most of the Cointreau in a blender to obtain a light, frothy cream.

Soak the sponge fingers in the rest of the Cointreau in a bowl. Line the bottom and sides of a lightly buttered and sugared charlotte mould with sponge fingers, letting them overlap slightly. Fill the mould with alternate layers of almond cream, sponge fingers and raspberries. Finish off with a layer of sponge fingers, which will form the base of the turned-out charlotte. Put the charlotte into the refrigerator for 3 hours with a small weight (about 2 kilograms) on top so that all the charlotte ingredients are pressed well into each other.

Meanwhile prepare the raspberry sauce.

To make the raspberry sauce Heat the raspberries in an enamel saucepan with the caster sugar and the fruit liqueur. Boil together for a few minutes, then leave to cool. Pour into a sauce-boat.

To serve Turn out the charlotte and serve with the raspberry sauce.

Suggested wine Crémant de Champagne.

L'OASIS * * *
LA NAPOULE (ALPES-MARITIMES)

CHARLOTTE AU CHOCOLAT

For those who like chocolate, a classic chocolate charlotte.

For 8 people

250g unsalted butter
400g cooking chocolate,
    melted
5 egg yolks

100g sugar
10 egg whites, beaten until
    very stiff with a pinch of salt
20–22 sponge finger biscuits
a few *marrons glacés* or sugar
    violets, to decorate

| 100g chocolate to ice the gâteau | 3 tbs prepared coffee |

Soften the butter and mix with the warm melted chocolate, taking care it does not go oily.

Beat the egg yolks with the sugar until the mixture is pale in colour and will form a ribbon, then very gently mix the two preparations together. Lastly, gently fold in the very stiffly beaten egg whites.

Line a charlotte mould 10 centimetres high and 15–16 centimetres in diameter with the sponge fingers, then fill it with the chocolate mixture. Put in the refrigerator for at least 3 hours to set so that the charlotte can be turned out. Turn out and cover with the icing chocolate, melted with the coffee. Decorate with a few *marrons glacés* or sugared violets.

Suggested wine Sauternes.

HÔTEL DE LA POSTE
DOMFRONT (ORNE)

CHARLOTTE AFRICAINE

A classic chocolate dessert, served with vanilla sauce. Suitable for a winter dinner-party, it can be kept for a few days in the refrigerator.

For 8 people

1½dl rum
3dl cold water
1dl kirsch
about 30 sponge finger biscuits
icing sugar
Chantilly cream (optional)

Chocolate mousse
250g chocolate
250g butter

4 eggs, separated
80g caster sugar
a pinch salt

Vanilla sauce
6 egg yolks
125g caster sugar
½l milk
vanilla powder or 1 vanilla pod

Mix the rum, water and kirsch together, preferably in a deep dish. Dip the sponge fingers quickly into this mixture, without letting them go soft. Line a charlotte mould 16 to 18 centimetres in diameter and 12 to 14 centimetres high with the sponge fingers. Start by lining the bottom of the mould with sponge biscuit fingers cut in two, one end of each cut to form a point, arranging them point inwards to form a rose shape covering the whole surface. Then line the sides with whole biscuits, placed upright and slightly overlapping.

To prepare the chocolate mousse Work the chocolate with the butter in a heavy-bottomed saucepan over very low heat, taking care that the butter does not go oily. When the mixture is smooth add the egg yolks and sugar whisked well together until they have frothed up and turned white.

Beat the whites until stiff with a pinch of salt, then fold carefully into the chocolate mixture. Pour the chocolate mousse into the charlotte mould so that it comes half-way up. Sprinkle over a thin layer of chopped and steeped sponge fingers and then finish filling the mould with the rest of the chocolate mousse. Cut the sponge fingers level with the top of the mould; crumble the extra pieces and sprinkle over the top of the mousse. This last layer of biscuits will make a base for the turned-out mousse.

To make the vanilla sauce Work the egg yolks with the sugar in a heavy-bottomed saucepan. Bring the milk to the boil, add the vanilla flavouring and pour carefully into the pan, whisking all the time. Put the saucepan over low heat and stir with a wooden spoon or spatula scraping the bottom of the pan thoroughly and covering as much of the surface as possible, until the mixture thickens. Take care not to let it boil. Continue to stir off the heat, then leave to become completely cold. Pour into a sauceboat and put in the bottom of the refrigerator until ready to use.

To serve Turn the charlotte out on to a dish or fruit bowl. Dust with icing sugar. Decorate if wished with Chantilly cream squeezed through a forcing bag with a decorative nozzle. Serve with the vanilla sauce.

Suggested wine Champagne, chilled on ice.

AUBERGE DE FRANCE *
AVIGNON (VAUCLUSE)

CHARLOTTE AUX NOISETTES ET AU MIEL DE PROVENCE
A light hazelnut-flavoured Bavaroise cream moulded in sponge fingers.

For 6–8 people

22–24 sponge fingers
4 egg yolks
130g caster sugar
3 tbs honey
4dl milk

15g fine leaf gelatine
$\frac{1}{4}$l fresh cream
80g hazelnut praline*

Line the bottom of a charlotte mould 10 centimetres high and 15–16 centimetres in diameter with sponge finger biscuits cut in two and with the ends trimmed to a point. Arrange with the sharpened end pointing inwards to form a rose shape. Then line the sides with the remaining whole sponge fingers, letting them overlap slightly. Let them come up above the top of the mould.

To make the Bavaroise cream Beat the egg yolks with the sugar and honey in a bowl for about 5 minutes, until the mixture will form a ribbon. Pour over the boiling milk and beat with a whisk, then add the gelatine, which should have been soaked and softened in cold water.

Put the cream into a saucepan over low heat and allow to thicken, stirring continuously with a wooden spoon or spatula, then take off the heat and continue to stir until it is cold. Whisk the cream into Chantilly (see p. 359).

As soon as the Bavaroise cream is nearly cold and has the consistency of oil, fold in three-quarters of the Chantilly cream and then the praline. Pour the mixture into the prepared charlotte mould. Bend the tops of the sponge fingers over the cream and cover the surface with sponge-finger crumbs. This layer of biscuit crumbs will serve as a base when the mould is turned out. Put the mould into the refrigerator for at least 2 hours. Turn out on to a round dish lined with a paper doily. Decorate with the remaining Chantilly cream squeezed through a forcing bag and a few hazelnuts browned in boiling sugar.

Suggested wine Muscat, well chilled on ice.

HÔTEL BOURGEOIS ★ ★
PRIAY (AIN)

ÎLE FLOTTANTE AUX PRALINES

A dessert as light as it is subtle and even more attractive if you can get pink pralines.

For 6 people

120g granulated sugar
8 egg whites
a pinch salt
400g caster sugar
150g pralines, roughly chopped

Custard cream
6 egg yolks
120g caster sugar
½l milk
1 vanilla pod *or* vanilla powder, to taste

Make a smooth custard cream (see p. 359) with the above ingredients.

Leave to cool then put into the refrigerator.

Caramelize the mould with the granulated sugar and reserve.

Beat the egg whites until stiff with a pinch of salt. Fold in the sugar as soon as the whites have thickened, then the pralines. Fill the caramelized mould with this mixture. Cook in a pan of shuddering water in a moderate oven, 165°–175°C, 325°–350°F, for about 20 minutes.

To serve Turn out the 'floating island' into a bowl or deep dish, taking care to let the caramel flow. Leave to cool completely, then pour over the custard cream. This dessert can be kept in the refrigerator for 1 or 2 hours.

Suggested wine Extra-dry champagne, chilled on ice.

PANCAKES AND FRITTERS

CHEZ ALBERT ★ ★
PARIS 14e: 22 AVENUE DU MAINE

CRÊPES FARÇIES ARMORICAINES
Savoury pancakes, filled with a subtle mixture of small pieces of lobster, mushrooms and cream. The stuffed pancakes are covered with cream sprinkled with Gruyère and browned in the oven.

For 4 people

8 salted pancakes, cooked in the usual way and kept warm on a plate over a pan of boiling water

Filling
200g cooked lobster meat, chopped
150g rice cooked *à la créole* (see p. 293), well drained and dried in the oven

60g large mushrooms, chopped into very small pieces (but larger than for a *duxelles*★)
2 tbs *velouté*★
½l double cream
4 tbs lobster bisque (see p. 12)
3 tbs cognac
2 heaped tbs grated Gruyère

To make the filling Sweat the mushrooms in a saucepan. Add 4 tablespoons cream, allow to reduce a little; add the velouté and the bisque and leave to boil for 5 minutes.

Put the rice and lobster together in another sauté pan, moisten with the cognac and warm through. Set light to the mixture and add to the other pan. Mix carefully and leave to cool.

To cook Lay the pancakes flat and fill them with the lobster filling. Roll up into cylinders, lay in a deep well-buttered oven-proof dish and coat with the remaining cream. Dust generously with the grated cheese and transfer to a moderate oven, 175°C, 350°F, for about 15 minutes. The top should be a nice golden colour. If it isn't sufficiently coloured, place under the grill for a few minutes.

Suggested wine Well-chilled Muscadet.

JACQUES COEUR *
RENAISON (LOIRE)

CRÊPES AUX CHAMPIGNONS ET AUX FOIES DE VOLAILLES
Very thin pancakes, browned in the oven.

For 4 people

250g mushrooms, chopped *en duxelles**
1 small shallot, very finely chopped
3 tbs unsalted butter
6 chicken livers, trimmed and chopped

4 wafer-thin slices ham
½ cup fresh cream
grated nutmeg
50g grated Gruyère
salt, freshly milled black pepper
4 salted pancakes, cooked and kept warm on a plate over a pan of boiling water

To prepare the filling Stew the mushrooms and shallot in the butter in a pan over fairly high heat until soft but not browned. Remove the pan from the heat and add the chicken livers. Heat through, stirring vigorously with a wooden spoon so that the livers cook without drying up. Season the stuffing with salt and pepper and spoon into a bowl.

To stuff the pancakes Spread the pancakes out on a board; place a slice of ham on each and spoon over enough of the filling to cover. Roll the pancakes into cylinders and arrange them in a buttered oven dish. Coat with cream, grate over a little nutmeg, and sprinkle with the grated cheese. Put into the oven, preheated to 205°–225°C, 400°–425°F, long enough to reheat the pancakes and quickly brown the topping.

Suggested wine Renaison rosé.

AU CHAPON FIN ★ ★
THOISSEY (AIN)

CRÊPES PARMENTIER

Potato pancakes to be served with roast beef or lamb. This is a simple and quick recipe, the secret being to leave the mixture to settle for at least an hour, as with pancake batter.

For 4 people

3 large potatoes
⅓l milk
2 heaped tbs flour
6 eggs

2 heaped tbs fresh cream
salt, pepper, grated nutmeg
250g clarified unsalted butter,
  for cooking the pancakes

To prepare the pancakes Put the potatoes in a stew-pan filled with cold salted water, bring to the boil and cook until tender. Sieve them, then moisten with the heated milk until you have a fairly thin purée. Season, beat with a whisk and leave to cool. Now add the flour, then add the eggs whole one at a time, mixing them in with a wooden spoon, but do not stir. Add the cream.

Leave the batter for 1 hour.

To cook Heat 2–3 tablespoons of clarified butter in a flat frying-pan, as for an omelette. When it is very hot pour in a scant table-spoon of the batter. The pancakes will form themselves. Turn over with a wooden spoon and they are ready.

CHEZ LA MÈRE BLANC ★ ★
VONNAS (AIN)

CRÊPES VONNASSIENNES

Potato pancakes which may be served as a main dish with a salad. They are also very good with roast beef or with sautéed chicken or with ham.

For 6–8 people

500g potatoes suitable for
  mashing, peeled
boiling milk
2 heaped tbs sifted flour

3 tbs double cream
6 eggs
salt, freshly milled black
  pepper, grated nutmeg
175–200g clarified unsalted
  butter, well skimmed

Cook the potatoes in a little salted water until tender. Drain carefully. Put through a blender or mash to a purée. Thin with boiling milk, stirring with a wooden spoon. The purée should remain of a fairly thick consistency. Leave until really cold.

Add the flour, working it in thoroughly, then the cream and lastly the eggs, stirring them in with a wooden spoon one by one, without beating. The mixture should be very slightly runny.

To cook the pancakes They will be easier to cook if the batter has been left to stand for 15 to 30 minutes. Stir before using.

Heat 2–3 tablespoons of clarified butter in a small flat-bottomed frying-pan. Trickle in 1 tablespoon of the butter and the pancakes will form themselves. Turn, then slide out almost immediately. They are now ready.

Suggested wine As these potato pancakes are intended to be served with a main dish use the wine suggested for that dish.

HÔTEL DE LA BOULE D'OR *
BARBEZIEUX (CHARENTE)

CRÊPES LANDAISES
These pancakes are filled with sausage meat, lightly smoked raw ham and cèpes. *They are served coated with tomato sauce.*

For 4–6 people (depending on whether it is served as a first course or main dish)

Batter
280g sifted flour
3 eggs
¼l milk
¼l warm water

Filling
125g lightly smoked raw ham, chopped into little squares
200g *cèpes* (or ordinary cultivated mushrooms), chopped
1 small onion, very finely chopped
100g sausage meat
1 clove garlic, finely chopped

1 tsp parsley, finely chopped
a little salt (remember that the ham and sausage meat are already salted)
4 tbs oil for cooking the filling

Tomato sauce
¼l concentrated veal or chicken stock
1dl dry white wine
250g tomato concentrate
1 onion, very finely chopped
1 clove garlic, crushed
1 bouquet garni* (thyme, bay leaf, parsley)
3 tbs oil
3 heaped tbs flour

To make the batter Mix the flour and salt together in a bowl, gradually adding the milk and beating with a whisk, or put through the mixer. Leave to stand for 2 to 3 hours. (If there are any lumps in the batter, put it through a fine sieve.) Then cook the pancakes and keep warm on a plate over a pan of boiling water.

To make the filling Mix all the ingredients for the filling in a bowl, heat the oil in a frying-pan, add the filling and cook for 15 minutes, stirring with a wooden spoon. Taste and correct the seasoning if necessary.

To stuff the pancakes, lay them out flat and fill each with 3 tablespoons of the filling. Fold the edges over the filling and roll up.

Arrange the pancakes side by side in a deep buttered dish. Make the tomato sauce as described on p. 355, adding a nut of butter. Coat the pancakes with the sauce and heat through.

Suggested wine A well-chilled rosé. The tomato will not agree with too good a wine.

LORRAND-BARRE ★ ★
LES PONTS-NEUFS (CÔTES DU NORD)

CRÊPES BRETONNES

These inimitable Breton pancakes are made on special pancake irons. The trick is to spread the batter very, very thinly and cook the pancakes for only 30 seconds, without turning.

For 5–6 people (about 20 pancakes)

4 eggs
4 rounded tbs sifted flour
50g clarified unsalted butter
50g groundnut oil
a pinch salt
a pinch sugar
$\frac{1}{2}$l milk

To make the batter Break the egg into a bowl, add the flour and work together to form a smooth paste. Add the butter, oil, salt and sugar. Stir with a wooden spoon for 4 to 5 minutes. Add the milk a little at a time, to thin the batter. Beat well with a whisk and leave to stand for at least 4 hours.

To cook Lightly oil a griddle or heavy cast-iron pan. Heat until very hot. Put into a ladle the equivalent of $2\frac{1}{2}$ tablespoons of the batter and spread it as thinly as possible on the hot griddle (the batter should be transparent), using a small squared-off metal spatula to level it out. In Brittany a special iron is used. Cook over very high heat for just 30 seconds. Remove the pancake with a metal spatula or spoon, dust with vanilla-flavoured icing sugar and fold into a triangle.

If you like you can flavour the pancakes with a few drops of spirit or liqueur, such as rum, kirsch, cognac, Cointreau, Grand Marnier or anisette, or with a dessertspoon of orange marmalade.

Recommended drink Bottled cider.

AU CAPUCIN NORMAND *
MEGÈVE (HAUTE-SAVOIE)

CRÊPES NORMANDES AU CALVADOS

Apple pancakes flambéed in calvados.

For 5 people

Batter
125g sifted flour
1 whole egg + 1 yolk
a tiny pinch fine salt
1 dsp caster sugar
¼l warm milk
125g clarified unsalted butter

2 Cox's apples, peeled and cored, finely chopped and sprinkled with a little lemon to prevent them going brown
1½dl calvados

To make the batter Put the flour into a bowl with the eggs, the salt and the sugar. Whisk in the warm milk until the mixture is fairly thick. Keep whisking for 2 minutes, add half the clarified butter and leave to stand.

To cook the pancakes Butter two small, very shallow pancake pans with a teaspoon of butter and sprinkle a tablespoon of minced apple over the bottom of the pan. Brown lightly with a pinch of sugar, stirring all the time, then cover with a thin layer of batter. Turn the pancake halfway through in the usual way, taking care to slide a nut of butter under the second side.

Turn the pancakes out on to a warm metal dish as soon as they are cooked, allowing them to overlap. Dust with a little caster sugar, sprinkle with the warmed calvados, flambé and bring to the table.

Suggested wine A dry white wine such as Sancerre or Muscadet.

HÔTEL DU CHEVAL BLANC *
VIRE (CALVADOS)

CRÊPES CHEVAL BLANC

A slice of brioche steeped in crème anglaise *flavoured with vanilla and rum, placed between two thin soufflée pancakes and glazed in the oven. The pancakes may be flambéed in rum.*

For 4 people (8 pancakes)

Sweet pancake batter (see p. 357)
150g flour
2 eggs + 2 yolks
a pinch salt
1 tbs caster sugar
milk
rum
3 tbs clarified unsalted butter

When ready to use add
1 tbs fresh double cream
3 egg whites, beaten until stiff with a pinch of salt

4 slices round brioche
¼l *crème anglaise* (see p. 359) flavoured with vanilla and rum
unsalted butter

Leave the batter to stand for an hour or so, then add the cream and beaten egg whites.

Steep 1 slice of brioche in the *crème anglaise*. Put 1 tablespoon of melted butter into a small omelette pan, heat, then spread over a thin layer of pancake batter. Place the slice of brioche on top, then cover with more of the batter. Put the pan into an oven preheated to 175°C, 350°F, until glazed and golden.

Proceed in the same way with the other slices of brioche.

To serve Transfer the pancake brioches to a warm, buttered dish. Serve as they are, dusted with icing sugar, or flambé them in rum. Don't pour the rum over the pancakes but between them, then take the dish to the table before setting light to them. Sprinkle with more rum.

Suggested wine A light dry champagne, well iced.

RÉGENCE-PLAZA, HÔTEL PLAZA-ATHENÉE ★
PARIS 8e: 25 AVENUE MONTAIGNE

CRÊPES MONTAIGNE
Pancakes filled with French pastry cream and praline and covered with a mixture of French pastry cream and Chantilly cream, dusted with flaked almonds and glazed in the oven.

For 2–4 pancakes

Batter
250g flour
50g sugar
a pinch fine salt
5 egg yolks
1dl double cream
3 tbs cognac
about ½l milk
50g clarified unsalted butter

Filling
praline★ (1 nut per pancake)
12–15 tbs French pastry cream

Coating
1 cup French pastry cream
½ cup *crème anglaise* (see p. 359)
½ cup Chantilly cream (see p. 359)
3 tbs kirsch
2 tbs flaked almonds
icing sugar

Make the pancake batter and leave to stand. Cook the pancakes and fill them with the pastry cream and the praline. Fold each pancake into a triangle and place in a deep buttered dish. Mix together the ingredients for the cream coating to cover the pancakes. Spread over the pancakes. Sprinkle the flaked almonds over them and dust with icing sugar. Brown lightly under the grill.

Suggested wine Dry champagne.

LE FESTIVAL
CANNES: LA CROISETTE (ALPES-MARITIMES)

CRÊPES SUZETTE

Pancakes flambéed in Curaçao and Grand Marnier. The sauce is delicious and highly flavoured. The sort of dessert that is certain to be a success.

For 4 people

12 small thin pancakes made with sweetened pancake batter (see p. 357)
caster sugar

Orange butter sauce
100g unsalted butter, softened with a fork
50g caster sugar
3dl orange juice (preferably tinned)
½dl Curaçao liqueur

1 orange, peeled, sliced and chopped (with no trace of rind, pips or pith)

To flambé the pancakes
3 tbs caster sugar
the prepared orange butter
1dl cognac
1dl Grand Marnier

Make the pancakes and place each one as it is ready on a plate over a pan of boiling water.

Mix the ingredients for the orange butter sauce in a bowl, then carefully fold in the pieces of orange. Reserve.

Light a spirit-warmer at the table. Melt the sugar in a small iron or copper pan without letting it caramelize. Add half the orange butter, allow to melt and mix well, but don't let it boil. Dip the pancakes one at a time in this very hot butter until they are well coated, turn them, fold them into triangles and place them on the hot dish. Continue until all the pancakes, and the orange butter, have been used up. If any orange butter is left over, pour it over the pancakes. Sprinkle the pancakes with the cognac and the Grand Marnier, tilt the plate so that the flames can spread and flambé, dusting with the caster sugar. Turn the pancakes over with a fork and arrange them side by side at the other end of the dish. Sprinkle with the sauce from the dish and serve each person with three pancakes on warmed dessert plates.

HÔTEL RITZ ★
PARIS 1er: 15 PLACE VENDÔME

CRÊPES ROXELANE

A dessert for a grand dinner party. The pancakes are filled with a soufflé mixture exquisitely flavoured with lemon and Curaçao. They are dusted with icing sugar and patterned with a red hot skewer just before serving; they are served with melba sauce.

For 3 people (makes 6–7
   pancakes)

Batter
100g flour
a pinch salt
1 level dsp caster sugar
about 2½dl liquid (half milk
   and half water)
2 eggs
50g clarified unsalted butter

French pastry cream (see p. 359)
¼l milk
2 tbs caster sugar
30g (2 heaped tbs) flour
3 egg yolks

Soufflé mixture
2 egg yolks
grated peel of 2 lemons
1dl Curaçao
6 egg whites
a pinch salt

Melba sauce
300g redcurrants
300g raspberries
3–4 tbs caster sugar
3 tbs Curaçao

To prepare Prepare the batter and leave to stand. Prepare and cook the pastry cream in an enamelled cast-iron saucepan. Add the first three ingredients for the soufflé mixture to the pan and heat gently, whisking all the time. Beat the egg whites with the salt in a separate bowl until very stiff, then fold very carefully into the soufflé mixture.

To cook Make 6 pancakes. Fill with the soufflé mixture and arrange in a butter metal dish. Transfer to a preheated oven, 190°C, 375°F, for 7 minutes; remove. Dust the dish with icing sugar and marble the pancakes with a red-hot skewer.

Melba sauce Sieve the fruit. Collect the juice and any pulp clinging to the outside of the sieve. Add sugar and flavour with Curaçao. Beat well, then chill in the refrigerator. Serve with the pancakes.

Suggested wine Dry champagne, well chilled.

BRASSERIE DU NORD *
LYON (RHÔNE)

BUGNES LYONNAISES

This is by no means a light dessert, but bugnes *go down wonderfully at a party for ten-to-fifteen-year-olds. The alcohol flavouring can be replaced by orange-flower water.*

For 10–12 people

500g sifted flour
5g salt
40g caster sugar
4 egg yolks
100g unsalted butter, cut into
  pieces

½dl fresh cream
2 tbs kirsch or rum
1l groundnut oil
icing sugar in a sugar-sifter

To make the batter Put the flour into a bowl with the salt and sugar and mix well. Make a well in the centre of the flour and slide in the egg yolks, then the butter, cream and flavouring. Draw in the flour from the sides of the well with a wooden spoon and work into the centre until the mixture forms a mass. Then work with the hands until it becomes a firm dough. Roll into a ball and chill in the refrigerator.

Take out of the refrigerator and divide into little balls, each weighing about 50–60 grams. Roll out to a thickness of about 2 millimetres and, using a serrated pastry wheel, cut across into pieces so as to make 4 to 5 strips of pastry.

To cook Toss the *bugnes* into the very hot oil in a deep fryer. As soon as they are a nice golden colour (not browned), drain completely.

Serve on a dish covered with a paper doily. Dust with icing sugar. The *bugnes* can be served hot or cold and may also be eaten with redcurrant jelly.

Suggested drink For a children's party, choose fruit juice; otherwise a light rosé.

SOUFFLÉS

SOUFFLÉ AU CITRON

A light dessert which makes a pleasant ending to a good dinner.

For 6 people
French pastry cream (see p. 359)

3 egg yolks
80g caster sugar
powdered vanilla
2 heaped tbs flour

$\frac{1}{4}$l boiling milk
6 lemons
250g caster sugar
$\frac{1}{4}$l egg white
a pinch salt
icing sugar

Peel the lemons thinly with a vegetable peeler, avoiding the pith, and chop the peel very finely. Blanch in boiling water for 5 to 6 minutes, then cool and drain. Put the peel into a heavy enamelled cast-iron saucepan, add the sugar and moisten with enough water to cover the sugar. Add the juice of 3 of the lemons only, stir once with a wooden spoon and cook over very moderate heat until the mixture is the consistency of jam.

Leave to cool, then stir into the cooled pastry cream. Whisk the egg whites with a pinch of salt until very stiff, and fold in the lemon mixture little by little, carefully lifting and turning the mixture with a wooden spoon.

Pour the soufflé mixture into a buttered soufflé dish, the sides dusted with sugar, and transfer to an oven preheated to 205°C, 400°F, lowering the heat immediately to 190°C, 375°F. Leave the soufflé to rise, then lower the heat a little more (175°C, 350°F) for the rest of the cooking time. The soufflé will take about 25 minutes in all. Dust the top with icing sugar and serve immediately.

Suggested wine Chilled Sauternes.

LA TRUITE
PARIS 8e: 30 RUE DU FAUBOURG-SAINT-HONORE

SOUFFLÉ NORMAND

An apple and macaroon soufflé based on French pastry cream, flavoured with calvados.

For 6 people

Pastry cream (see p. 359)
100g sugar
3 egg yolks
45g flour
¼l boiling milk
a large pinch vanilla powder
2 tbs calvados
3 egg yolks
6 egg whites
a pinch salt

1 good apple, peeled and sliced
 thinly
caster sugar
2–3 tbs unsalted butter
2 slightly stale macaroons,
 crumbled

Make the French pastry cream, using the proportions given above. Once cooked it should be thick. Leave to cool, whisking from time to time. Add the calvados and the 3 egg yolks one after the other.

Meanwhile, beat the egg whites with a pinch of salt until very stiff. Add 2 tablespoons of this mixture to the pastry cream to thin it down, then very carefully fold the whole of the pastry cream into the egg whites a little at a time, lifting and turning from the bottom with a wooden spoon.

To prepare and cook the soufflé Roll the apple slices in caster sugar and fry in the butter in a small frying-pan. Pour half the soufflé mixture into a buttered metal soufflé dish or copper charlotte mould, lightly dusted with sugar. Arrange the apple slices and crumbled macaroons on top and then finish filling the dish with the rest of the soufflé mixture until it is three-quarters full. Transfer to an oven preheated to 200°C, 400°F, for about 18 to 25 minutes, lowering the heat to 180°C, 375°F, after a few minutes, then, towards the end, to 175°C, 350°F, if necessary.

When the soufflé has risen properly and is a nice golden brown with a good head, take it out of the oven. After a few seconds dust the top with icing sugar and serve immediately.

Suggested wine A dessert wine such as white bordeaux, Sauternes (or Barsac) or a dry or medium-dry champagne, well chilled.

HÔTEL DU CHEVAL ROUGE ★ ★
MONTOIRE-SUR-LE-LOIR (LOIR-ET-CHER)

SOUFFLÉ GLACÉ AU CHOCOLAT
A cold, uncooked soufflé that can be kept in the refrigerator.

For 6 people

4 egg yolks
80g sugar
6g gelatine
175g eating chocolate

$\frac{1}{4}$l fresh double cream
4 egg whites, beaten with a
   pinch salt until stiff
$\frac{1}{2}$ cube ice, crushed
icing sugar

Put the egg yolks into a large bowl. Cook the sugar in a saucepan until it reaches the 'ball' stage (see p. 366). Whisking all the time, trickle the boiling sugar slowly over the egg yolks and continue to whisk until the mixture is cold. The eggs will have swelled and will be lightly poached.

Add the gelatine, which you have softened in cold water and then warmed slightly. Melt the chocolate in 2 tablespoons of water and when it is quite smooth add to the mixture, whisking all the time. Stir in the fresh cream, which you have whipped up with the crushed ice, and, lastly, gently fold in the beaten egg whites.

Prepare a soufflé dish by tying round it a band of greaseproof paper protruding 3–5 centimetres above the top of the dish; tie with string and fasten with 1 or 2 pins to hold it firm. Fill the dish with the soufflé mixture so that it comes very slightly above the paper band.

Put into the refrigerator for 1–2 hours.

To serve Remove the paper band and the string. Dust the top with a layer of icing sugar. The part of the soufflé that comes up over the edge of the bowl will look like the risen top of a hot soufflé.

Suggested wine Vouvray, sparkling or still.

TAILLEVENT ★ ★
PARIS 8e: 15 RUE LAMENNAIS

SOUFFLÉ GLACÉ AU COINTREAU

A very attractive cold soufflé. It can be made beforehand and kept in the refrigerator.

For 4–5 people

Crème anglaise (see p. 359)
250g caster sugar
8 egg yolks
1l boiling milk
1 open vanilla pod

For the Italian meringue
8 egg whites
a pinch salt
$\frac{1}{4}$l water
500g caster sugar

$\frac{1}{2}$ cup crystallized fruit, finely chopped
$\frac{1}{2}$–1dl Cointreau, according to taste
1l fresh double cream, whipped until very light

Garnish
icing sugar
glacé cherries, halved
a few strips angelica

Crème anglaise Make a *crème anglaise* using the above ingredients. Put through a fine metal sieve, stir for a few minutes with a wooden spoon then leave until really cold.

Italian meringue Using a double-looped wire whisk, whisk the egg whites with a pinch of salt in a copper bowl until really firm. Cook the sugar with the water, until you have a syrup that registers 32°C, 90°F on the sugar thermometer. Trickle the boiling sugar syrup steadily over the egg whites, whisking hard all the time. This will poach the eggs and change their consistency.

Leave to cool, then fold in the cold *crème anglaise*, the candied fruit, the Cointreau and the whipped cream.

Tie a band of greaseproof paper or foil round a china soufflé dish to form a collar protruding about 7–8 centimetres above the top of the dish. Fasten with a couple of pins. Pour in the soufflé mixture until it comes 5–6 centimetres above the top of the dish. Put the soufflé into the refrigerator.

When you are ready to serve, remove the paper band. The iced soufflé will look like a hot soufflé. Dust the top with the icing sugar and decorate with the cherries and angelica.

Suggested wine Very dry champagne.

LAPÉROUSE ★ ★
PARIS 6e: 51 QUAI DES GRANDS-AUGUSTINS

SOUFFLÉ LAPÉROUSE
One of the lightest and most delicate of soufflés.

For 8 people

French pastry cream (see p. 359)
8 eggs, separated
240g caster sugar
60g flour
¾l boiling milk

1 vanilla pod
150g praline
2dl rum
100g crystallized fruit, finely
    chopped and macerated in a
    little of the rum

Prepare the pastry cream, using the proportions given above. Add the praline, the rum and the crystallized fruit.

Beat the egg whites with a pinch of salt until very stiff and gently fold in the pastry cream, using a spatula or wooden spoon.

Butter the sides and bottom of a soufflé dish and sprinkle with sugar. Pour in the soufflé mixture.

To cook Cook in a moderate oven, 175°C, 350°F, for 20 to 25 minutes. When the soufflé has risen and is golden brown with a good head, dust with icing sugar and put back into the oven to caramelize.

Suggested wine A chilled Sauternes.

LA TOUR D'ARGENT ★ ★ ★
PARIS 5e: 15 QUAI DE LA TOURNELLE

SOUFFLÉ AUX VIOLETTES IMPÉRIALES
A soufflé with Grand Marnier, garnished with sponge fingers, steeped in the same liqueur and with crystallized violets.

For 4 people

French pastry cream (see p. 359)
4 egg yolks

45g caster sugar
25g flour
1½dl boiling milk
15g butter

1dl Grand Marnier
4 egg whites
a pinch salt
2 sponge finger biscuits,
   broken into small pieces and
   dipped in Grand Marnier
   just before using

1 tbs crystallized violet petals
icing sugar
2 tbs whole crystallized violets

Make the pastry cream, which is the soufflé base. Whisk the egg yolks with the sugar in an enamelled saucepan, preferably a cast-iron one, add the flour and mix well. Pour over the boiling milk and beat over moderate heat until the mixture boils. Remove the pan from heat and continue to beat, then add the butter to the cooled pastry cream and flavour with half the Grand Marnier.

Using a double-looped wire whisk, whisk the egg whites with a pinch of salt until very stiff. Mix 2 tablespoons into the pastry cream, then fold the whole of the cream into the egg whites, lifting and turning the mass with a wooden spoon or spatula.

Spoon a layer of soufflé mixture on to the bottom of a buttered soufflé-dish sprinkled with sugar. Scatter pieces of sponge finger and violet petals over it. Cover with a layer of soufflé mixture, then another layer of broken sponge fingers and violet petals; finish with the rest of the soufflé mixture and cook in a moderate oven preheated to 160°C, 325°F, for about 12 minutes. Then quickly dust the top of the soufflé with icing sugar and glaze quickly in a hot oven, about 200°C, 400°F, for 2 to 3 minutes. Take out the soufflé and scatter over the whole violets.

To serve Place the soufflé in a large round serving-dish on a napkin folded into a circle. Surround with a few bunches of violets.

Suggested wine Very dry champagne, well chilled on ice.

RELAIS DE L'EMPEREUR ★ ★
MONTÉLIMAR (DROME)

SOUFFLÉ LOETITIA
A vanilla soufflé with crystallized fruit, flavoured with kirsch and served with vanilla ice-cream and hot chocolate sauce. A rich, very grand sweet.

For 4 people

Soufflé mixture
¼l French pastry cream (see
   p. 359) made in the following
   proportions:
   125g caster sugar
   3 egg yolks
   30g flour
   25g potato starch

a salpicon★ of preserved fruit
   (oranges, cherries, melon,
   pears), diced very small
3–4 tbs kirsch, for steeping the
   fruit
7 egg whites, whipped until
   very stiff with a pinch of
   salt
2 egg yolks

| ¼l milk, boiled with a vanilla pod | 10g potato starch icing sugar |

To make the pastry cream Work together the egg yolks and the sugar in the saucepan until the mixture whitens. Add the flour and potato starch and then pour over the boiling milk (having first removed the vanilla pod), whisking all the time. Bring to the boil, still whisking, to thicken the mixture. Draw off the heat immediately and continue to beat. Add the egg yolks and the potato starch.

Beat the egg whites until very stiff, then carefully fold in the pastry cream a little at a time, lifting and turning with a spatula or wooden spoon, but without stirring.

To make the soufflé Half fill a soufflé dish or charlotte mould (buttered and dusted with caster sugar) with half the mixture and add the well-drained macerated fruit, piling them lightly on top. Finish filling the dish to about 3½ centimetres below the top so that the soufflé can rise. Transfer to an oven preheated to 205°C, 400°F and immediately lower the heat to 190°C, 375°F. Leave the soufflé to rise, reducing the heat again, if necessary, for the last 10 minutes, to 175°C, 347°F. The total cooking time should be about 25 minutes. Dust with icing sugar 5 minutes before the end of the cooking time.

To serve The soufflé must be served straight from the oven. Serve with scooped-out balls of vanilla ice cream and hot chocolate sauce.

Suggested wine Very dry champagne, chilled on ice.

RESTAURANT PIERRE *
PARIS 1er: 10 RUE DE RICHELIEU

OMELETTE SOUFFLÉE, FLAMBÉE AU RHUM

A light, fluffy omelette which makes the perfect sweet after a simple meal such as cold meat and salad.

For 4 people	about 2 tbs unsalted butter
6 eggs, separated	1dl dark rum
75g caster sugar	2 tbs sugar to finish
a pinch salt	

Heat a skewer, which will be used to pattern the omelette, over a gas flame.

Whisk the egg yolks and sugar in a bowl until the mixture forms ribbons.

Using an untinned copper egg bowl, whisk the egg whites with the salt until really stiff. Mix the egg yolks carefully into the whites with a spatula or wooden spoon.

To cook Heat the butter in a flat-bottomed ovenproof frying-pan until it is very hot, tilting the pan to grease the sides as well. Pour the mixture into the pan. Transfer to a moderately hot oven, 165°–170°C, 350°F, for about 6 to 7 minutes.

To serve Turn the omelette out on to a warmed metal dish and dust with the sugar. Decorate by scoring with the hot skewer in a crisscross pattern.

To flambé Heat the rum, pour over the omelette, light and serve flaming.

Suggested wine A light dry champagne.

ICE-CREAMS AND SORBETS

HÔTEL EULER ⋆
BASLE (SWITZERLAND)

MOUSSE AU KIRSCH DE BÂLE

Vanilla ice-cream with whipped cream, flavoured with kirsch and decorated with chopped glacé cherries, served in a tall champagne glass.

For each person

3–4 chopped glacé cherries
½dl kirsch
2 scoops vanilla ice-cream
3 tbs thick fresh cream,
    whipped into a Chantilly
    (see p. 359)
½ glacé cherry to decorate

Soften the vanilla ice-cream slightly and whisk with the cream. Add the cherries and flavour the mixture with the kirsch in which the cherries have been steeped. Put into the freezer compartment of the refrigerator for about 2 hours.

To serve Fill a tall champagne glass with the kirsch mousse. Decorate with a rosette of whipped cream topped with the half cherry.

Suggested wine Very dry champagne or white wine, chilled on ice.

LEDOYEN ★ ★
PARIS 8e: CARRÉ CHAMPS-ÉLYSÉES

SOUFFLÉ GLACÉ AUX FRAISES

An extremely subtle strawberry ice, delicious with small meringues.

For 12 people
½l fresh strawberries, pulped
  and puréed in the blender

Sabayon
20 egg yolks
1l 30° sugar syrup

To prepare Whip up the *sabayon* by whisking the egg yolks and the sugar syrup in an untinned copper bowl over moderate heat until the mixture increases in quantity and will form ribbons. Remove from the heat and continue to whisk for 2 to 3 minutes. Then, still whisking, add the strawberry purée and leave until completely cold.

Whip the fresh cream in a separate bowl with a double-looped wire whisk, over a receptacle containing ice cubes. Fold the whipped cream into the chilled *sabayon*. Spoon into moulds lined with greaseproof paper and place in the freezer compartment of the refrigerator for at least 12 hours.

To serve Turn out on to a dish covered with a paper doily.

Suggested wine Very dry champagne, well chilled.

RESTAURANT DE LA MER
SAINT-GUÉNOLÉ (SUD-FINISTÈRE)

SOURBET PLOUGASTEL

Plougastel strawberries are famous and the sorbet which bears their name is exquisite.

For 6 people

750g very fresh strawberries
⅓l 18°C sugar syrup
juice of half a lemon
¼l fresh double cream, well
  whipped until light and
  chilled in the refrigerator

Cook the sugar syrup and leave to go cold. Put 500 grams of the strawberries through a blender. Mix the strawberry purée into the syrup, add the lemon juice, then leave the mixture for a few hours to set in a rectangular mould packed round with ice cubes in the freezer compartment of the refrigerator.

Turn out on to a dish lined with a paper doily. Cover the sorbet with the whipped cream, smoothing it over with a metal spoon or spatula. Decorate the surface and the edge of the dish with the rest of the strawberries. Serve with *langues de chat* biscuits.

Suggested wine Dry champagne.

MOULIN DU KNAGY *
STEINNBRUN-LE-BAS (HAUT-RHIN)

GLACE AUX NOIX
The crowning touch to a grand dinner-party. A very subtly flavoured ice-cream, served with caramel sauce.

For 6 or 8 people

1l milk
½l fresh cream
1 vanilla pod or vanilla
    powder
12 egg yolks
300g sugar

200 green walnuts
50g blanched almonds, finely
    chopped

Caramel syrup
250g sugar
1dl water

Heat the milk, cream and vanilla in a heavy saucepan until boiling.

Work the egg yolks with the sugar in an ovenproof dish until the mixture is pale in colour and will form a ribbon.

As soon as the milk mixture boils pour it gently over the egg and sugar mixture, whisking all the time. Return the mixture to very low heat, stirring continuously until the cream is thick enough to coat a wooden spoon or spatula. It must not boil.

Remove from the heat and strain through a sieve into a bowl. Add the walnuts and prepared almonds, still whisking. Leave to infuse until completely cold. Then put through the finest mesh of the vegetable mill, twice if necessary, or else put the walnuts and almonds through a mixer or blender so that they are completely crushed.

Leave to set in an ice-cream tray in the freezer compartment of the refrigerator for at least 6 hours until the ice-cream is firm enough to be turned out without collapsing.

Serve the ice-cream with caramel syrup.

Caramel syrup Cook the sugar and water until the 'crack' stage is reached. Pour ¾ litre of water very carefully over the burning sugar, taking great care not to burn yourself. Cook for 15 minutes. To test whether the syrup is the right consistency, put a drop on to a cold plate; it should neither harden nor spread too quickly.

Suggested wine In Alsace, a Muscat; elsewhere Meursault or dry champagne.

ALBERT 1ER ET MILAN *
CHAMONIX (HAUTE-SAVOIE)

MONT BLANC GLACÉ
Vanilla ice-cream, Genoese gâteau with rum, chestnut cream and whipped cream, all served in an ice-cream coupe.

For each person

1 cup vanilla-flavoured
   Chantilly cream (see p. 359)
2 heaped tbs chestnut cream

1 slice Genoese gâteau (see
   p. 312), flavoured with rum
   and cut into finger shapes
1 scoop vanilla ice-cream

Mix together 1 tablespoon of Chantilly cream and 2 of chestnut cream; put in the freezing compartment of the refrigerator.

Place the scoop of ice-cream in a coupe and cover with the fingers of Genoese gâteau arranged to form a crown. Using a forcing bag with a fluted nozzle, pile the remaining chestnut cream on top of the Genoese fingers to form a dome shape. Finish off with a small dome of Chantilly cream so that the whole dessert looks like Mont Blanc.

Suggested wine Barsac or Sauternes chilled on ice or a light champagne.

ITHURRIA *
AINHOA (PYRÉNÉES-ATLANTIQUES)

COUPE STÉPHANE
Vanilla ice-cream with chocolate sauce, grilled almonds, Chantilly cream and a meringue shell.

For 6 people

1l well-flavoured vanilla ice-
   cream

Chocolate sauce
½l milk
150g good unsweetened
   powdered chocolate
125g caster sugar

2 tbs cornflour, diluted in a
   little cold milk
a pinch powdered cinnamon

Decoration
20g shredded, grilled almonds
15g bitter chocolate, flaked
6 small, soft meringue shells
½l Chantilly cream (optional)

Boil the milk, chocolate and sugar together, stirring with a wooden spoon or spatula. Pour the diluted cornflour into the boiling chocolate mixture, whisking vigorously until it thickens. Remove from the heat, add the powdered cinnamon and stir.

To serve Place 2 scoops of vanilla ice-cream in each of 6 champagne glasses. Coat with the hot chocolate sauce and sprinkle with roasted almonds and chocolate flakes. Place a meringue on top of the ice-cream and, if wished, decorate with the Chantilly cream (see p. 359).

Suggested wine Extra-dry champagne Mumm Cordon Rouge or Piper-Heidsieck.

LA CARAVELLE
CASTRES (TARN)

COUPE GLACÉE CRÉOLE
A dessert which is simple to prepare and is delicious.

For 1 person

1 heaped tbs chestnut cream
1 tbs fresh double cream
1 scoop vanilla ice-cream

3 tbs hot melted chocolate
Chantilly cream (see p. 359)
1 tbs almonds flaked, grilled
1 *marron glacé*

Mix the chestnut cream with the fresh cream, without blending completely. Put this mixture into a champagne glass. Place the scoop of ice-cream on top. Cover with the hot chocolate. Decorate the sides with Chantilly cream, using a forcing bag with a fluted nozzle. Sprinkle with the grilled almonds. Lastly top with the *marron glacé*.

Suggested wine A mellow or slightly sweet white wine, such as Gaillac or a bordeaux from Graves or Barsac.

LA VIEILLE MAISON ★
CHARTRES (EURE-ET-LOIR)

GLACE NELUSKO
Coffee ice-cream, flavoured with Fine Champagne and served with hot chocolate sauce.

For 8 people	*Chocolate sauce*
300g sugar	250g chocolate tablets
12 egg yolks	50g butter
1l milk	3–4 tbs water
3–4 tbs soluble coffee extract	
3–4 tbs Fine champagne	

Put the sugar and the egg yolks into a heavy-bottomed saucepan, preferably enamelled cast-iron, whisk over low heat, then gradually add the boiling milk. Poach gently without allowing the mixture to boil, then take off the heat and leave to cool, still stirring continuously with a wooden spoon or spatula. Add the coffee extract and the Fine Champagne.

Once the cream is completely cold, spoon it into an ice-cream tray and place in the freezing compartment of the refrigerator for a few hours.

To prepare the chocolate sauce Melt the chocolate with the water over the heat, without boiling. Take off the heat and add the butter, working it in with a wooden spoon or spatula. The sauce should be runny.

To serve Turn out the ice-cream on to a fruit-dish, first making sure that it is quite firm. Serve with the hot chocolate sauce in a sauceboat.

Suggested wine Sauternes or Monbazillac.

CHÂTEAU SAINT-PHILIPPE *
SAINT-NICOLAS-DE-LA-BALERME (LOT-ET-GARONNE)

PARFAIT AU CAFÉ
The perfect coffee ice.

For 2 people	1 small cup very strong coffee
350g caster sugar	1l fresh cream
1 glass (1·2dl) cold water	½ cube crushed ice
6 egg yolks	

Put the sugar with the water in an untinned copper preserving-pan. Cook to the 'ball' stage.

Put the egg yolks into a copper bowl and pour over the boiling sugar in a thin thread so that the eggs are not cooked but just very lightly poached, whisking them hard all the time with a double-looped wire whisk, so that they froth up and whiten.

Ideally two people should make this dessert: one pours the boiling sugar over the eggs while the other whisks vigorously. Add the cold coffee, which will cool the mixture.

Whip the cream in another copper or cast-iron bowl with the crushed ice until light and frothy. Gently work the cream into the mixture in the first bowl. Put into a slightly damp ice-cream tray (rinse it in cold water and drain but do not dry).

Put into the freezing compartment of the refrigerator for 6, 12, or better still, 24 hours. Lay the ice-cream tray down on a fruit dish lined with a paper doily. Wipe a cloth dipped in hot water over the outside of the mould, then squeeze dry. The *parfait* will slide out by itself.

Serve with *petits fours* or ice-cream wafers.

Suggested wine A Sauternes chilled on ice if a sweet wine is required, or else Meursault, as its nutty taste goes well with the coffee flavour.

HIÉLY * *
AVIGNON (VAUCLUSE)
MERINGUE GLACÉE AU CHOCOLAT ET AUX AMANDES
A rich and very effective dessert. A meringue layer-cake filled with a pralin ice-cream flavoured with chocolate.

For 8 people

Meringue (3 rounds)
8 egg whites
a pinch salt
300g caster sugar

Ice-cream
10 egg yolks
300g caster sugar
1l boiling milk
200g unsweetened cocoa

Pralin
100g lump sugar
100g almonds

To make the meringue Using a double-looped wire whisk, whisk the egg whites with the salt in a round, untinned copper bowl until they form stiff peaks. Fold in the sugar with a wooden spoon or spatula, turning and lifting the egg white mixture as you do so. Divide the mixture into 3 equal parts and pour each into a round cast-iron meringue tin 20 centimetres in diameter. Smooth over the surface. Dry out in a very low oven, 90°–100°C, 200°F, for about 1 hour. The meringues must not take colour but should be dry and creamy white.

To make the ice-cream Whisk the egg yolks and sugar vigorously and continuously until the mixture whitens and will form a ribbon. Pour in the boiling milk flavoured with the cocoa-powder.

To make the pralin Blanch the almonds. Melt the sugar with water. Cook until it forms a golden caramel. Toss the almonds into the caramel and cook for 10 minutes over low heat. Pour the mixture on to an oiled marble slab and leave to cool completely.

344

Crush the resulting mass and grind in an electric coffee grinder a little at a time, giving 2 or 3 turns of the grinder each time. Then mix three-quarters of the *pralin* into the chocolate ice-cream.

To make up the layer-cake Turn out the meringues. Make up the layer-cake by taking a round of meringue and spooning a layer of ice-cream on top. Add the second round of meringue, spreading a second layer of ice-cream on to it and finish with the third round of meringue. Sprinkle the top and sides of the gâteau with the remaining *pralin* and put back in the freezer until you are ready to serve.

Suggested wine Sauternes chilled on ice or, if something drier is preferred, an extra dry champagne, also chilled on ice.

SAUCES APPENDIX

CENTRAL HOTEL ET RÔTISSERIE DE LA CRÉMAILLÈRE
NANTES (LOIRE-ATLANTIQUE)

BEURRE BLANC NANTAIS
'White butter' is a speciality of Lower Brittany. It goes with all grilled fish or fish poached in a court-bouillon.

For 2 people

2 tbs wine, white Muscadet (or very dry white wine: Sancerre or Loire)
2 tbs wine vinegar
1 tbs shallot, finely chopped
crushed black peppercorns
Separately:
2 tbs cooking liquid from fish, sole or turbot. reduced

100g fine quality unsalted butter, divided into small pieces and kept very hard or cold
Salt, freshly milled white pepper
1 heavy casserole
1 hand whisk

In the casserole, over a high heat, reduce: wine, vinegar, shallot and pepper until hardly a tablespoonful of liquid remains. Leave to cool and add the fish reduction.

Heat the reduced liquids in the casserole with 2 tablespoons butter, beginning to whisk. Continue whisking, hard and regularly, without stopping, adding all the butter in little pieces. Do not allow to boil. The butter should not be melted (transparent) but should stay white and opaque, at a temperature of 80°C, 175°F. Beginners may find it easier to work over a *bain-marie*.

Suggested wine Muscadet for a fish dish with white butter.

L'ESCALE
VARCES(ISÈRE) NEAR GRENOBLE

MAYONNAISE ANDALOUSE

This mayonnaise is served with the fresh salmon pâté from the same restaurant.

1½ cups good, firm mayonnaise (see page 354) made with lemon juice but no vinegar

Add :

3 sweet red peppers, tinned, well drained and dried and put through the mixer

¾ cup double cream whisked with:

1 tsp crushed ice
1 tbs bottled tomato ketchup
1 tbs bottled Worcester sauce
1 tbs cognac
salt, freshly milled black pepper
powdered paprika
pinch of cayenne pepper

Mix the ingredients in the order listed and serve in a sauceboat.

AU VIEUX PORT
LE LAVANDOU (VAR)

LA ROUILLE

A strong sauce spiced with hot red peppers. A pretty, reddish orange colour, it is served as an accompaniment to fish soups, bouillabaisses and sometimes bourrides.

2–4 clove garlic
2 small red chilli peppers
1 tbs crumb of bread dipped in a little fish bouillon or bouillabaisse, then pressed to extract liquid

2 tbs oil
2 dl fish bouillon or bouillabaisse

Put 2–4 cloves garlic, according to taste, into a mortar (preferably of marble or earthenware) with 2 small hot red peppers.

Crush together finely with a wooden pestle until completely broken down and amalgamated.

Add a small piece of bread soaked in a little fish bouillon and squeezed dry of all liquid. Continue to mash with the pestle until a paste is formed. Then add in a fine thread the equivalent of 2 tablespoons of oil, working with a wooden spatula and dilute this paste with about 2 decilitres of fish bouillon or bouillabaisse.

If the sauce is not a strong enough colour one may add 1 teaspoon of tomato paste diluted with 1 teaspoon olive oil.

RESUMÉ OF DEFINITIONS AND METHODS

White Sauces

BÉCHAMEL   Base of all white sauces
Method White roux: butter + flour – 2 tbs butte·· – 2½ tbs flour.
To moisten 2½ dl boiling milk.
Add Salt, freshly milled white pepper, grated nutmeg.
Enrich with 1 tbs fresh unsalted butter away from the heat.

MORNAY   White sauce with cheese
Method Béchamel sauce + 2 tbs grated Gruyère or ½ tbs grated parmesan.
Add 1 tbs fresh unsalted butter or 2 tbs cream, away from the heat.

CREAM SAUCE   White sauce enriched with cream
Method Béchamel sauce with the following ch··nges:
To moisten Only 2 dl boiling milk + 4 tbs fresh double cream.
Add Salt, freshly milled white pepper, grated nutmeg.

SUPRÊME   White sauce with a rich liaison
Method Béchamel sauce.
Liaison 2 egg yolks – 4 tbs fresh double cream.
Add Salt, freshly milled white pepper – a few drops of lemon juice.

VELOUTÉ   A 'blond' sauce moistened with bouillon (chicken, meat or fish velouté)
Method A blond roux: butter + flour – 2 tbs unsalted butter – 2½ tbs flour, cooked together until lightly golden.
To moisten 3 dl hot bouillon (chicken, meat or fish).
To cook 30 minutes constant boiling, adding ½ dl *cold* bouillon in spoonfuls during cooking, skimming off all the impurities which float to the surface from time to time.
Add A little salt, the bouillon being already salty – freshly milled white pepper.

CHICKEN VELOUTÉ
Method Blond roux – 2 tbs butter – 2½ tbs flour + white chicken stock.
To moisten 2½–3 dl chicken stock for 4 people or 5 dl for 6–8 people.

FISH VELOUTÉ
Method As above but moisten the blond roux with fish bouillon.

AURORE   Velouté sauce with tomato
Method 2½ dl velouté + 2–3 tbs (according to degree of concentration) tomato paste.
Add Parsley stalks – mushroom peelings – 3 tbs fresh double cream. Strain the sauce through a conical sieve.

FINANCIÈRE
Method 2½–3 dl chicken velouté.
Add 3 tbs finely sliced mushrooms, softened separately in butter – squeeze of lemon – adjust seasoning.
Garnish Veal quenelles, veal sweetbreads, pitted green olives, blanched

and refreshed.

Optional $\frac{1}{2}$ dl madeira – fresh double cream. Adjust seasoning again.

NANTUA   A special sauce for crayfish and quenelles de brochet

Method Cream of velouté sauce made with 4dl of Béchamel or velouté sauce as required – 2dl fresh cream. Reduce to 5dl. Strain.

Add 1dl double cream without allowing to boil, salt, freshly milled black pepper, pinch of grated nutmeg.

Garnish 125g good crayfish butter, do not boil – 20 small crayfish tails cooked in a court bouillon.

AMÉRICAINE   Special sauce for shellfish

Method To make a *sauce à l'américaine* first cook a lobster in the following manner:

1 lobster weighing about 750g.

Give it a good bang on the head to make it unconscious, using a hammer or rolling pin. Split the head carefully keeping the liquid, coral and creamy particles from the inside. Break off the claws, crush the shell. In a pan, preferably a copper one, heat:

2 tbs oil and 2 tbs unsalted butter.

Put in the lobster pieces, claws and head. Stew them quickly over a high heat until they are uniformly browned, then take out and set aside. Into the same pan put:

3 tbs unsalted butter – 1 crushed clove garlic – 12 grey shallots finely chopped – 1 carrot cut *en brunoise*.

Stew the vegetables, stirring with a spatula until browned at the edges, then put back the lobster. Add:

4 skinned and crushed tomatoes – 1$\frac{1}{2}$dl very good quality white wine – a pinch of salt – a pinch of cayenne pepper.

Cover and cook over a fairly high heat for 20 minutes. Meanwhile, crush the coral with:

3 tbs butter and set aside.

Take out the pieces of lobster and return the pan to a high heat. Add:

$\frac{1}{2}$dl cognac which should have been flambéed in a ladle and $\frac{1}{2}$dl good Madeira or sherry.

Allow to reduce slightly then add over a low heat the coral butter, a little at a time, the creamy parts and reserved liquid, whisking continuously. Lastly add:

$\frac{1}{3}$ fish velouté to $\frac{2}{3}$ sauce.

Adjust the seasoning and allow to thicken over a low heat. The sauce is finished. The lobster pieces may be served in the sauce.

CHASSEUR

Method Colour, without browning, in butter:

chopped mushrooms and chopped shallots.

Add flour and allow to turn pale golden. Moisten with:

dry white wine.

Leave to reduce by half. Add:

chicken bouillon – tomato – pinch of sugar – 1 whole clove garlic – salt – freshly milled black pepper – bouquet garni.

Leave to cook for 30–35 minutes. Garnish with slices of mushroom cooked separately with a very little water, knobs of butter, squeeze of lemon, salt and pepper.

Use With rabbit, fricassée of chicken or poached eggs on toast.

Mushroom Duxelles

CLASSIC DUXELLES

150–200 g button mushrooms, carefully cleaned, finely and evenly chopped – 2 small grey shallots finely chopped – 2–3 tbs unsalted butter.

In a small pan, over a moderate heat soften the shallot in butter, without colouring at all; put in the mushrooms. Cook for 3 minutes, stirring all the time to help the liquid to evaporate.

DRY DUXELLES

Clean and finely chop the mushrooms. Dry them by wrapping them in a clean cloth and, holding the cloth over the sink, twist the corners tightly together until the brown mushroom juices run out. Open the cloth and transfer the mushrooms to a small pan containing fresh unsalted butter.
To cook As for classic duxelles, with or without the shallots.

FUMET OF MUSHROOMS OR ESSENCE OF MUSHROOMS   To flavour a sauce

150–200g mushrooms carefully cleaned, washed and wiped. Remove stalks and slice finely – 1–2 tbs lemon juice – 5–6 knobs unsalted butter – salt, freshly milled black pepper.

Put the mushroom slices into a small enamelled pan with just enough water to cover, add lemon, salt, pepper and butter. Boil, uncovered for 4–5 minutes; this should draw out the vegetable liquid from the mushrooms. Strain the liquid through a sieve which will retain the mushrooms. Return the liquid to the heat and reduce to 2–3 tbs so as to concentrate the essence.
Use To flavour a thickened gravy or sauce.

Brown Sauces

BROWN SAUCE OR SAUCE ESPAGNOLE   Basic brown sauce

Basis of Madeira, Périgueux, Chevreuil and Bigarade sauces.
Method Brown roux. In a copper pan or small cast iron cocotte melt:
 2 tbs lard.
Add
 125g lean bacon cut into lardons – 2 onions cut in quarters.
Allow to take colour. Remove the bacon and onions. Add to the fat:
 $2\frac{1}{2}$ rounded tbs flour.
Cook gently allowing the flour to turn golden over a low heat, stirring all the time with a spatula to get a good all over colouring in 12–15 minutes.
To moisten $\frac{1}{2}$l good dry white Burgundy (or red Burgundy or Beaujolais. Leave to boil for 2 minutes, add:
 $\frac{1}{2}$l very good meat bouillon made with fresh veal or pork or chicken carcasses and giblets and the usual vegetables: leek, onion, carrot, celery and spices.
Seasoning A very little salt.
Add
 1–2 tbs (according to degree of concentration) tomato paste – 1 sliced carrot – 2 crushed cloves garlic – 1 bouquet garni.
Put back
 Bacon and onions.
To cook Minimum time: 2 hours on a very moderate heat, skimming occasionally, but $2\frac{1}{2}$–3 hours will give a better result. If cooking for the longer time use $\frac{3}{4}$l wine and $\frac{3}{4}$l bouillon, to make between $\frac{3}{4}$ and $\frac{1}{2}$l brown sauce. Strain through a conical sieve, pressing lightly.

BORDELAISE

Despite its name, this sauce is made with burgundy wine which, because of its higher alcoholic content, stands up to reduction better than bordeaux wine.

Method Reduce to a glaze in a hot oven:

1 bottle red Beaune wine (75cl) – 200g chopped shallots – a sprig thyme – 1 bay leaf.

To moisten 75cl chickened veal stock.

Add A pinch of mixed spice, salt and freshly milled black pepper.

Cook Over a moderate heat for 1 hour, skimming frequently. Strain through a conical sieve before using.

'Grande Cuisine' Sauces

MADEIRA SAUCE

Method Make a basic brown sauce: cook a mirepoix and add a brown roux to it.

Moisten with Enough dry white wine and bouillon to make $\frac{1}{2}$l brown sauce. While cooking add in spoonfuls:

1dl cold bouillon – 50g mushroom trimmings or chopped mushrooms – a little thyme – small piece bay leaf – 1$\frac{1}{2}$dl Madeira (just at the end of cooking) – freshly milled white pepper – salt, but only after tasting.

Cooking 35–40 minutes over a moderate heat, skimming from time to time.

PÉRIGUEUX SAUCE OR SAUCE PÉRIGOURDINE

Method Make a Madeira sauce; add an infusion of Madeira and chopped pieces of truffle and finally, $\frac{1}{2}$dl Madeira.

To make the Madeira infusion, sweat:

2 grey shallots finely chopped in 2 tbs unsalted butter, adding 25g fresh, unsmoked ham, shredded, minute piece of thyme and bay leaf.

Stew gently without colouring. Moisten with 1$\frac{1}{2}$dl Madeira and 1dl bouillon already reduced and carefully skimmed of any fat.

Reduce by half and put through a conical sieve.

Brush, wash and peel:

2 medium-sized truffles.

Reserve the skins. Dice the truffles and put aside. Poach the truffle skins in the Madeira infusion for 9–10 minutes. Leave to infuse, covered for 30 minutes. Strain the Madeira infusion, pressing hard and saving only the liquid. Skim off fat if necessary.

Add

$\frac{1}{2}$dl fresh Madeira and the reserved pieces of truffle.

Having left the pieces of truffle to infuse for at least 30 minutes (preferably 24 hours – this work may all be done in advance) add the Madeira infusion and pieces of truffle to the prepared Madeira sauce.

Editor's note This is one of the great sauces of French cuisine. Its preparation is lengthy but presents no problems. It cannot be simplified if one respects principles and tradition.

SAUCE POIVRADE Special pepper sauce for game and venison

Cook a mirepoix. Moisten with wine vinegar and very dry white wine. Add the same proportion of brown sauce, brown game stock and a little reduced game marinade. A very good pepper should be used.

Method Cook a mirepoix until soft (carrot, onion, celeriac, game or venison trimmings, thyme, bay leaf, parsley). Stew gently without colouring and moisten with:

2dl good wine vinegar – 2dl good very dry white wine.

Reduce to 1½dl of liquid. Add:
  1½dl brown sauce, 1½dl brown game stock and finally 1dl reduced game marinade.
Cook Over a moderate heat for 1½ hours, skimming from time to time.
Final addition 8 minutes before the end of cooking add:
  1 tsp very good crushed pepper.
Press through a sieve. If the sauce seems too reduced add:
  1–1½dl reduced brown sauce and 2–4 tbs well reduced marinade.
Simmer for a few minutes. If the sauce tastes a little too acid add:
  a pinch of caster sugar.
Strain once or preferably twice, through a conical sieve.

SAUCE CHEVREUIL   Special sauce for roast venison

Make a game stock with the trimmings from a haunch or saddle of venison, deglaze the roasting pan with Armagnac or cognac and a reduced marinade.
Method Trim the saddle and prepare with the trimmings a clear game stock (without thickening) which can be used either for a venison sauce or a grand veneur sauce.
For the game stock
  game trimmings – 1 carrot and 1 onion sliced – 1 *bouquet garni* – 1 stick of celery – 1l meat bouillon (preferably veal bone). Leave to simmer until reduced to 1½dl liquid.
Remove the saddle of venison, which should have been roasted in the oven, from the roasting tin leaving the juices in the tin. Deglaze with:
  1dl Armagnac or cognac – 1 tbs wine vinegar – ½dl reduced marinade.
Reduce for a few minutes.

SAUCE GRAND VENEUR   Same use as sauce Chevreuil

Make a brown roux, moisten with game stock and liquid from the marinade. Then add port or Madeira, cognac, flambéed, and finally fresh double cream.
Method Make a brown roux following the directions given under Brown Sauces.
Moisten with
  4dl unthickened game stock.
Add
  2dl liquid from the marinade.
Reduce by half. Strain through a conical sieve or muslin.
Final additions
  1½dl port or madeira – ½dl cognac, flambéed – 4 tbs fresh double cream.
Warm the sauce, mixing, without allowing it to boil. If wished it may be strained a second time.

SAUCE BIGARADE   For roast or sautéed duck or duckling

Make a caramel sauce (sugar and vinegar) and add it to a thickened brown sauce or stock. Finally add orange juice, slice of lemon and sliced orange zests.
Method Caramel sauce: in a saucepan, preferably a copper one, cook to a blonde caramel:
  1–2 lumps of sugar – 1–2 tbs wine vinegar.
As soon as the caramel is a good golden colour dilute it by adding little by little:
  2dl very hot thickened brown stock
scraping with a wooden spoon. Boil for 5 minutes.
Add
  The juice of 1 pressed orange – 1 squeeze of lemon – the rind of 2 oranges peeled very fine, cut into strips, blanched, refreshed and wiped dry.
Plus
  1dl good Madeira.

Optional
   ½dl cognac flambéed.
Adjust seasoning after tasting the sauce.

SAUCE DEMI-GLACE   To give body to sauces, bouillons and other cookery preparations

Make brown sauce (basic brown or sauce Espagnole) and add to clear veal stock which has been reduced separately and again together.
Method For ½l of demi-glace.
Reduce together by half:
   ½l thickened brown stock and ½l clear veal stock already reduced.
Never use salt. Demi-glace may sometimes have a small proportion of tomato added to it. Stored in jars in the refrigerator it will keep for 2 weeks.

MEAT GLAZE   To strengthen the flavour of sauces and certain dishes

A very slow reduction of clear brown stocks, meat or game; which, by being reduced, should coat a spoon. It should be strained through a conical sieve at least twice: during reduction and at the end of the process. It will solidify when cold and can be kept in a sealed pot in the refrigerator for 2–3 weeks.

STOCKS   Bouillons or gravies used to moisten sauces

(1) White Stock:
Chicken bouillon Whole chicken or carcase or giblets and raw chicken bones are used to make white stock. It should not be coloured.
Addition Chopped vegetables and spices.
(2) Clear Brown Stock:
Also called brown veal stock or veal gravy.
Coloured meat bouillon Veal bone or knuckle or piece of a leg of veal, browned in the oven.
Method Put the veal bones which have been browned in the oven into a saucepan with a piece of lean beef (pot-au-feu). Moisten with water or ½l dry white vine and ½l water.
Garnish The usual vegetables for pot-au-feu, seasonings and spices.
Use To moisten brown sauces.

Whisked Sauces

HOLLANDAISE

A whisked sauce with a base of egg yolks bound with an acid reduction and butter added little by little. The proportions of butter to eggs is 50–60g maximum per egg yolk.
Ingredients
   3 egg yolks – 150–180g unsalted butter, divided into small pieces – 1 tbs lemon juice – 1 tbs cold water – freshly milled white pepper – salt.
Method Put the lemon juice, cold water and the egg yolks into a small heavy bottomed saucepan. Break up the egg yolks with a whisk, add 30g butter and 2 turns of the pepper mill. Put the saucepan into another larger pan of hot water over a very low heat and whisk continuously until the butter becomes completely absorbed. Beat in a further 30g of butter and continue adding the butter little by little until it is all absorbed and the sauce is dense and homogeneous. The sauce should be light and thick enough to coat a spoon. Taste to adjust seasoning, add salt, squeeze of lemon and pepper as needed.
Use To coat poached eggs, artichoke bases and fish cooked in court bouillon.

TO KEEP HOLLANDAISE SAUCE

This is the method used by restaurants if the sauce has to wait. In order to be able to keep Hollandaise Sauce hot without separating add at the start of the operation a small quantity of white roux, potato starch or arrowroot. The eggs, being supported by the starchy element, will withstand a higher temperature and have less chance of curdling.

Two methods Add to the egg yolks, in the butter, before whisking:

1 tbs well thickened velouté or proceed as follows:

3–4 tbs boiled and cooled milk – 1 small tsp potato starch, arrowroot or other starch – 2 egg yolks – 150g unsalted butter – lemon juice – salt, pepper.

In the pan, while still cold, mix together 3 tbs milk, the starch, egg yolks, 25g unsalted butter, lemon juice, salt and pepper. Put the pan into a bain-marie or on to a very, very low heat. Whisk the sauce, adding the butter in small pieces whisking all the time as in the previous recipe.

This Hollandaise Sauce may be re-heated over a moderate heat. It must be done with care and must be whisked continuously.

SAUCE MOUSSELINE
(ALSO CALLED SAUCE CHANTILLY)

Ingredients

2–2½dl Hollandaise Sauce – 100g fresh double cream.

Method Whisk the cream until firm and incorporate into the Hollandaise just before serving. Adjust the seasoning.

Use For asparagus, artichokes, avocado pears, and fish cooked in court bouillon.

Whipped cream may also be added in this way to a cold sauce. Mayonnaise so treated is enriched and lightened.

SAUCE BÉARNAISE

This sauce is made in much the same way as Hollandaise but its basic ingredients are different, consisting of a reduction of good wine vinegar and shallot with added aromatic herbs among which fresh or dried tarragon is essential (one sprig). Proportions are:

60g unsalted butter – 1 egg yolk;

180g butter – 3 egg yolks (serves four);

250g butter – 4 egg yolks (serves 5–6).

For the reduction

1dl good wine vinegar – 3 grey shallots, chopped – 1 tbs tarragon leaves – 1 sprig thyme – a small piece of bay leaf – small sprig of chervil – crushed white peppercorns, salt.

Method Put the ingredients for the reduction into a small saucepan, preferably of enamelled cast iron, and reduce to 1½–2 tbs of liquid. Strain, pressing down well. Pour the liquid back into the pan; put in the egg yolks, break them up with a fork and add 1 tbs of butter. Start to beat in a bain-marie or over a very moderate heat whisking continuously adding all the butter bit by bit in small pieces. The process is the same as for Hollandaise Sauce. Adjust seasoning.

Use For poached eggs, sweetbreads and grilled meat.

SAUCE CHORON

Method Make a Béarnaise sauce and add:

1–2 tbs tomato paste.

Its acidity may be counteracted by 1 pinch sugar.

Use Grilled fish, poached eggs, veal chops.

SAUCE VALOIS

Method Make a Béarnaise sauce and add 1 tsp for 4 persons, or 1 tbs for 6 persons of:

meat glaze or demi-glace sauce.

Allow to melt into the Béarnaise, whisking.
Use Eggs in pastry, tournedos, sweetbreads.

Cold Sauces

MAYONNAISE A sauce whisked with oil
It is based on egg yolks and mustard.

Essential instructions Never refrigerate any of the ingredients; cold is the enemy of mayonnaise. Slightly warm the whisking bowl before using. Keep all ingredients at an even room temperature.

Ingredients
2–3 egg yolks – 1 tbs mustard – 3–4g salt – freshly milled white pepper – about 3dl groundnut oil – 1 dsp wine vinegar or 1 tbs lemon juice.

Method Put the egg yolks, mustard, salt and pepper into the well warmed dried and heavy bowl. Mix with a wooden spoon to bind the ingredients together, then leave for 40–50 seconds. Begin whisking the sauce adding the oil drop by drop and then in a thin stream until it is incorporated. As the sauce gains body the oil may be poured in a thicker stream. Add vinegar or lemon juice to sharpen.

Mayonnaise must not be kept in the refrigerator. It has a different flavour according to whether groundnut or olive oil is used; olive oil has many followers. Both oils may be used together ($\frac{2}{3}$ groundnut to $\frac{1}{3}$ olive). Mayonnaise made with olive oil has a tendency to be slightly more fluid. Walnut oil is a speciality of Savoy, Quercy and the Périgord region. Mayonnaise made with walnut oil goes well with winter salads: endives, celeriac, apples, beetroot and also with potato salad.

AÏLLOLI MAYONNAISE
Make a classic mayonnaise. Add 1 or 2 cloves crushed garlic, according to taste. Taste to check seasoning.
Mayonnaise sauce with garlic.

Ingredients
3–6 cloves garlic according to taste.
Crush garlic in a garlic press. Pound in a mortar with a few drops olive oil. Add:
2 egg yolks.
Whisk up the sauce in the mortar either with a spatula or a whisk pouring on the oil in a thin, then stronger, steam.
3dl oil.
Season with salt, freshly milled white pepper and add a squeeze of lemon.

Vinaigrette Sauce Seasoning for a salad, containing:
mustard, oil, wine vinegar, salt and freshly milled black pepper.
Beaten with a fork for 1 minute. Fresh, finely chopped herbs are optional.

SAUCE TARTARE
Same principle as mayonnaise but with a base of hard egg yolks and the addition of gherkins, chopped capers, mixed herbs and cream to finish the sauce.

Ingredients
3–4 hard boiled egg yolks – 1 tsp mustard – salt, freshly ground white pepper – 3–3½dl groundnut oil – 2 small chopped gherkins – 1 tbs chopped capers.
or
1 tbs chopped chervil and tarragon – 1 tbs chives finely cut with scissors or green parts of spring onion – 2 tbs fresh double cream.

Method Rub egg yolks through a strainer into a bowl. Mix with mustard, salt and pepper working with a wooden spoon. Whisk with oil in the same way as for mayonnaise (above) and when thick add either the gherkins and capers or mixed herbs. Bind with the cream and mix well.

SAUCE VERTE

Mayonnaise coloured with watercress and spinach juice and flavoured with fresh herbs.

Ingredients
$\frac{1}{4}$l good firm mayonnaise sharpened with lemon juice – 50g spinach leaves – 50g watercress leaves – 50g parsley, chervil and tarragon, finely chopped.

Method Blanch the watercress and spinach for 2 minutes. Put into a colander, refresh, drain and dry without squeezing too much. Put the spinach and cress into a spotlessly clean cloth and twist to squeeze out the green juice into a bowl. Whisk this, little by little, into the mayonnaise. Adjust the seasoning, adding salt, freshly milled white pepper and lemon juice if necessary.

Use To go with cold lobster or salmon cooked in *court-bouillon*. Or any fish cooked in *court-bouillon*.

FONDUE DE TOMATE

500g–1kg tomatoes, peeled, seeded and pulped – 1–2 onions – butter and oil – 1 bouquet of thyme and bay leaf – salt, freshly milled black pepper.

Gently stew the onion in the mixture of butter and oil. Immediately add the tomatoes and spices. Cook over a very moderate heat stirring from time to time (cover if necessary) until the tomatoes are very soft. The cooking time can vary from 20–30 minutes according to quality and quantity of tomatoes.

Butters

CLASSIC BEURRE BLANC

Reduce almost to a glaze:
1dl very dry white wine, usually Muscadet since 'white butter' comes from Nantes, or $\frac{1}{2}$dl white wine vinegar with 1 dsp grey shallot, roughly chopped. Add: crushed white peppercorns.

Strain this reduction into a heavy pan, pressing down well. Thicken over a moderate heat by whisking in 150g fresh unsalted butter in pieces. Add a squeeze of lemon, according to taste, and salt.

The sauce should be opaque.

CRAYFISH BUTTER

Cook the crayfish, shell them and set aside the tails. Completely crush the shells, heads, pincers and eggs etc. by pounding in a mortar. Put back to cook in the crayfish cooking liquid and leave to reduce over a high heat until you have 8 tbs of liquid. Strain through a metal strainer saving everything which sticks to the outside of the strainer. Pound the crayfish tails separately with butter to make a cream and work into the liquid and crayfish residue. Finish by putting the whole through a mixer. Use to enrich a sauce or fill tartlets. Same process for shrimp or prawn butter.

BEURRE MANIÉ   See glossary

BEURRE CLARIFIÉ   See glossary

BEURRE EN POMMADE

50g unsalted butter.

Put into a bowl. If straight from the refrigerator allow to reach room temperature, but do not heat. Mash with a fork against the sides of the bowl until softened but still thick. Before using whisk into a homogeneous mass.

Use Butter cream to fill cakes, butter for snails, herb butter for steaks.

PASTRY APPENDIX

SHORT-CRUST PASTRY (Pâte brisée)   Simple, for savoury tarts and quiches

Ingredients

200g sifted flour – 5g salt – 125g unsalted butter – about 3–4 tbs cold water.

SWEET SHORT-CRUST PASTRY (Pâte sablée)   For fruit tarts, sweet pies and desserts

Ingredients

200g sifted flour – 3g salt – 1 tbs caster sugar – 130g butter – 1 whole egg, mixed with 1–3 tbs cold water.

RICH SHORT-CRUST OR LINING PASTRY (Pâte à foncer)   For tarts and pâtés

Ingredients

200g sifted flour – 10g salt – 60g unsalted butter + 40g lard – 1 whole egg – 3–5 tbs water.

Method (Identical for the 3 types of pastry.) Sift flour into a bowl, add the salt (or salt and sugar) and the fats cut into pieces. Using one hand or a fork with wide prongs, work lightly and quickly until the mixture becomes 'sandy' in texture. Test by rubbing between the finger tips. Pour in the liquid, water or egg and water according to the type of pastry. Work the mixture lightly together by hand until it forms a compact mass which will not separate. Roll into a ball and leave to stand for at least 1 hour in the refrigerator. The latter is essential in order to stretch and firm up the dough before use.

PUFF PASTRY (Pâte feuilletée)

Puff pastry turned six times takes 3 hours to make, including preparation of pastry and allowing it to stand.

The different operations involved are: making the dough, buttering the dough and turning the dough. Puff pastry needs to be turned 6 times and should stand for 40 minutes between each turn and for 1 hour after the last turn.

Rough puff or flaky pastry method is easier and may be used for most things which need puff pastry.

HALF-PUFF OR FLAKY PASTRY (Pâte demi-feuilletée)   Quickest method

After 4 turns this pastry gives very good results for galettes, tarts and apéritif bouchées.

After 6 turns it rises as much and is as light as puff pastry. It is used for millefeuilles (Napoleons), pithiviers, vol-au-vents, or bouchées.

For 500g rough puff pastry:

200g sifted flour – 180g fat (i.e. either 180g unsalted butter or 120g butter + 60g margarine mixed) – 5g salt – 1dl, or very slightly more up to 1½dl maximum, water.

Method Put flour either into a large bowl or on a slab, making a well in the centre. Put salt into the well and mix. Add half the fat, i.e. 90g, cut into pieces. Mash with a fork or by hand, adding the water and working rapidly without trying to get a perfectly smooth mix. Form into a ball; dust lightly with flour; wrap in greaseproof paper and put to chill until the dough is firm.

Roll out a rectangle 1·5 cm thick on to a floured slab. Spread the rest of the butter over ¾ of pastry. Completely enclose the butter by firmly sealing together the edges of the dough using the rolling pin. Put into the refrigerator to stiffen for 30–40 minutes. Fold the dough in three to make two turns. Chill again for 20 minutes. Give it 2 more turns. Use the dough after the fourth turn or give it a further 2 turns (fifth and sixth) after leaving to stand, in the same way.

PANCAKE BATTER   Savoury

For about 12 pancakes.

Basic proportions

150g flour – 2 whole eggs – 2 tbs clarified butter – 1 pinch of salt – 3 tbs milk + cold water + 2 dsp light ale. This small quantity of beer acts as a raising agent.

Method Work all the ingredients together in a bowl in the following order:

flour, salt, eggs, milk and enough water to make a semi fluid consistency. Finish with beer if desired. Leave to stand for 1 hour.

PANCAKE BATTER   Sweet

A fine batter for about 12–15 pancakes.

Basic proportions

100g sifted flour – 1 pinch of salt – 1 tbs caster sugar – 2 egg yolks – 3 tbs milk and cold water to make a semi-fluid consistency.

Method The same method as for savoury pancakes adding the milk first then the water until the right consistency is obtained. Leave to stand for 1 hour.

The proportions may be doubled or even tripled to make the number of pancakes desired but the basic proportions must be the same.

CHOUX PASTRY

Classic proportions for about 25 choux.

¼l water – 80g unsalted butter – 130g sifted flour – 4 whole eggs + 1 egg white – salt – 1 pinch of sugar – 1 enamelled saucepan (preferably cast iron).

Method Put the water and butter into the saucepan and bring to the boil. As soon as the butter is melted and boiling point is pronounced, take the pan off the heat and pour all the flour in at one go. With a wooden spatula vigorously work the mixture until it forms a mass which will pull away from the sides of the pan. Return the pan to a moderate heat and continue working to dry out the pastry until a light film of pastry forms and covers the base of the pan.

Adding the eggs Remove pan from heat. Add the eggs one after the other, working vigorously with the spatula; add another egg only when the previous one is completely absorbed into the dough and so on. When all the egg yolks have been incorporated add one egg white, *unbeaten*, mixed in and absorbed like the whole eggs. Leave the paste to stand in the saucepan.

To cook Spread the choux either with a spoon, or squeezed out of a forcing bag, on to a lightly buttered baking sheet. They will probably be lighter if you use a spoon. Take care to space them sufficiently far apart as they double in volume when cooked.

Cook in a hot oven 200°–205°C, 400°–450°F, for about 20 minutes. The choux should be swollen, golden brown, crisp and light. Leave to cool on a baking rack.

BRIOCHE DOUGH

Brioche dough has many uses. This light, rich pastry may be buttery or only slightly buttered. According to the amount of butter used it will be a fluffy brioche or a plain brioche.

Forty years ago fluffy brioche often accompanied foie gras. At dessert it goes well with a chocolate cream or a coffee cream.

Plain brioches are served, individually, for breakfast. Plain brioche dough is also used for sausages and foie gras in a brioche, coulibiac of salmon and certain delicate fish pâtés. Round slices of brioche are used as canapés for chicken livers.

Ingredients

15g baking powder – 2 tbs tepid milk – 200g sifted flour – 125–400g unsalted butter – for fluffy brioche dough.

or :

100g unsalted butter for plain brioche dough – 2 whole eggs – 1 pinch of salt – 1 pinch of sugar.

Method In a bowl, preferably a metal one, dilute the baking powder with the warm milk, adding the salt and sugar. Add the flour and eggs beaten with a fork. Work the butter to soften it to the same consistency as the paste just made; divide it into small pieces and add it to the paste, kneading until it becomes 'elastic'. It is the right consistency when it no longer sticks to hands or bowl.

First rising (or proving) Form the dough into a ball. Place in a metal bowl (in the country it would be a wooden or earthenware one – the results are the same but the rising takes longer). Cut a cross in the top with scissors dipped in hot water. Dust with flour and cover with a perfectly clean folded cloth. Place the bowl in a warm place where the temperature will remain even and constant (25°–28°C, 75°–80°F), away from draughts (but not on the heat nor in the oven); leave to stand for 1–1½ hours until the dough has doubled in volume.

Second rising On the table, without removing dough from bowl, 'break' it by tapping lightly on the table. It will break apart of its own accord at the touch of your hand. Leave to rise a second time using the preceding method. For this second rising the temperature may be raised by a few degrees. When the dough is doubled in volume with an elastic consistency, carry it, without kneading, supporting it from beneath with your hands, to a buttered and floured tin. Tap the tin on the table to settle the dough well in. It should only come half way up the sides.

To cook Cook in a preheated oven at 190°C (375°–400°F) for about 25–30 minutes. The brioche should be golden.

For fluffy brioche Use same method but giving a third rising at 30°–32°C, 85°–90°F. Cut with a cross, working quickly and bake at 250°C (475°F).

CREAMS APPENDIX

CRÈME ANGLAISE OR VANILLA CREAM

A cream which is light in consistency, semi-liquid and cooked without boiling.

For ½l cream Work together in a cast iron enamelled saucepan:

   6 egg yolks and 150g caster sugar.

Boil

   ½l milk with 1 vanilla pod or 1 tsp vanilla powder.

Pour the vanilla milk, little by little, over the egg and sugar mixture, beating with a whisk. Put the pan on a moderate heat and beat first to boiling point without allowing to boil up. Stir smoothly all the time to prevent lumps forming. Take off the heat when the cream is of the consistency to coat the spoon; strain into a cream bowl and continue to mix as it cools.

CRÈME CHANTILLY

In a large bowl mix:

   ½l fresh double cream with 2 tbs (unpasteurised) milk. Add 1 crushed ice cube.

Place the bowl in another receptacle filled with ice and beat energetically with a balloon whisk, lifting the mixture well to aerate, until the cream doubles in volume and becomes fluffy. Then add:

   125g caster sugar, little by little, working the mixture gently without beating.

CRÈME PÂTISSIÈRE

This is a cream of a certain consistency, obtained by adding flour. It includes a mixture of whole eggs and egg yolks, or egg yolks alone for a finer cream.

In a cast iron enamelled pan, work together:

   2 whole eggs + 3 egg yolks and 125g caster sugar.

Then add all at once:

   50g or 3–4 tbs sifted flour, according to whether a thick or thin cream is desired.

Beat with a whisk to obtain a smooth and perfect mixture. Pour over boiling milk flavoured with vanilla and beat hard to thicken. Put the pan back over the heat to cook the flour. The cream must be heated until it boils and bubbles on the surface. Beat vigorously and transfer to a bowl. Strain and add:

   1 tbs butter.

Beat with a whisk to help it cool. Use as it is or to fill pancakes or a genoese.

GLOSSARY

Aiolli (dish) A Mediterranean dish made of cod and other poached fish; carrots and boiled potatoes; various blanched vegetables and hard-boiled eggs. Aiolli sauce is served separately with it in a sauceboat.

Aiolli (sauce) Garlic mayonnaise (see Sauces appendix).

Bain-marie Method of cooking using two receptacles of different sizes. The first one, containing the food, stands in the second which contains boiling water and is in direct contact with the heat.

Bake blind, to To pre-cook a pastry case before filling with fruit etc. It is lined with greaseproof paper and weighted down with rice, beans etc. to keep its shape.

Bard, to To wrap a piece of meat, poultry, game or fish in a thin piece of very fatty bacon. The bard is tied in place with 2 or more lengths of string. Prevents very lean meat from drying out and/or shrinking while cooking.

Barquette Oval shaped tartlet made from sweet or savoury short-crust pastry or flaky pastry.

Beurre manié Mixture of equal parts of butter and flour crushed together with a fork and used as liaison or thickening for sauces, stews, etc.

Butter, clarified Butter cleared by heating gently until foaming, skimming well and then straining off the clear yellow oil which is used. The sediment (milk solids) is left behind.

Butter noisette Butter cooked until just golden – not browned or burnt.

Blanch, to To cook in boiling water for a few minutes. Removes bitterness, too strong taste, impurities etc. from vegetables, rinds, zest of lemon, etc. etc.

Bouquet garni Selection of herbs tied together or in a bag. Traditionally a sprig of thyme and parsley and a bay leaf. Used to flavour soups, sauces, etc. Always removed before serving.

Braise, to To cook covered in a braising pot, casserole dish, etc. in a low oven. The pot should be buttered, lined with blanched and refreshed pork rind and a layer of thinly sliced carrots and onions. Method used with meat, fish or vegetables.

Braising pot Any oven dish with a close-fitting lid preferably copper, cast iron or earthenware.

Breadcrumbs May be made fresh or bought in packets. To make: dry out stale bread in the oven and crush with a rolling pin. To make browned crumbs known as 'raspings', bake the crusts in a slow oven until golden brown then crush in the same way.

Brunoise, en Method of cutting vegetables, fruit, etc. They are shredded very small.

Chinois Fine metal strainer, pointed in the form of a chinese hat. Used to strain stocks, sauces, etc.

Clarify, to To make soup, jelly, etc. completely clear. Liquids are clarified by a process of filtering or decanting. Jellies are clarified by adding egg whites and a little green stuff, roughly chopped parsley for example, followed by boiling and filtering.

Confit Pork, goose, duck and turkey meat cooked completely covered in its own fat and preserved in a receptacle. Pork and goose confits are preserved in stone jars in South-west France, where they are frequently used in home cooking. Commercially, they are treated by the Appert method and tinned in their fat. For this the goose is divided into four quarters.

Consommé Clear concentrated meat or poultry broth or bouillon.

Court-bouillon A liquid made up of water, dry white wine (optional), wine vinegar, vegetables: carrots, onions, stick of celery, *bouquet garni*, spices, peppercorns, and coriander seeds. Used to poach fish.

Croûtons Slices of bread with the crusts removed cut into small squares, or triangles. Cut into little cubes for use with soup.

Toast them lightly, spread with butter, margarine or oil and lightly brown. Drain on absorbent paper before use.

Deglaze, to To dilute (with wine or cream or butter) the coagulated meat juices, etc. in the bottom of the baking tin in which food was cooked. Stir and scrape the bottom with a fork to make a liquid gravy.

Reduce if necessary to bring to the right consistency and adjust seasoning. With juice from a roast add 1 tbs butter, away from the heat, allowing the butter to melt before straining gravy.

Duxelles Mushrooms and shallots, very finely chopped and stewed in hot butter for a few minutes without colouring. (See also Sauces appendix page 349.)

Farce Meat, fish, vegetables, etc. minced, seasoned with herbs and spices; usually bound with an egg or an egg yolk. Sometimes includes white bread soaked in milk or bouillon and drained.

Flambé, to To heat alcohol, pour it over the food while cooking, light it and stir until flame goes out.

Fleuron Little crescent of puff pastry used to garnish a dish.

Fondant icing Method employed in making patisserie. Cook the sugar to the 'ball' stage, work on a slab with a spatula until it is very smooth and white. Flavour with kirsch or rum. Used to ice cakes and pastries.

Fumet Liquid preparation used to enhance the flavour of stocks and sauces. Made by boiling up and reducing meat, poultry, game or fish trimmings or mushrooms, with clear soup, wine and water.

Garnish That which surrounds or decorates a dish; vegetables, shellfish, fleurons, croûtons, etc.

Genoese Light cake which may be eaten as it is or divided into 3 horizontally and filled with cream, jam, etc.

In a bowl, preferably copper, using a balloon whisk, beat the following ingredients over a moderate heat:

4 whole eggs and 125g caster sugar (until volume doubles and mixture will form a ribbon) then add, in small quantities, 125g sifted flour and 50g melted warm butter. Pour into a *moule à manqué* 4·5–5·5 cm high. This may be lined with greaseproof paper. Cook in a moderate oven 165°–175°C (350°–400°F).

Glaze, to (1) Put a dish under a hot grill to brown the surface rapidly.

(2) Dust with icing sugar and put under grill just long enough to caramelise the top.

(3) Mixture of egg yolk and 3 drops water brushed on pastry, etc. to give a golden surface when cooked.

Grâtiner, to To dust surface of a dish with breadcrumbs and/or cheese and put in oven or under grill to brown.

Julienne Vegetables cut into matchstick-sized strips. Also means a dish of several vegetables. Similarly you can have a *julienne* of truffles.

Lard, to To insert small strips of fatty larding bacon into very lean meat with the aid of a larding needle.

Liaison Thickening or binding agent of which there are several kinds.

Roux Simple roux, white roux, and brown roux are considered liaisons.

Beurre Manié (See above.)

Starches Potato starch, rice starch, arrowroot and cornflour – all diluted in cold water.

Cream and *seasoned egg yolks* mixed with a fork away from heat are used as liaison for sauce suprême.

Macédoine Dish of mixed vegetables or fruit, diced.

Marinade Preparation in which to marinate (see below).

Marinate, to To steep, without completely immersing, a piece of raw meat, poultry, game or venison in a mixture of wine or alcohol usually flavoured with spices. The pieces should be turned several times during the course of marinating which may take from 2–3 days for meat and game and 3–5 days for venison.

Mirepoix A mixture of vegetables, chopped *en brunoise* to which a little finely diced ham may be added.

It is cooked over a moderate heat in butter and oil in a small pan with a lid for about 30 minutes, stirring from time to time.

Mortar Marble, wooden or porcelain bowl used for pounding food, which is done with a pestle.

Moule à manqué Round tin mould with a raised edge about 5–6 cm high.

Mould, savarin Crown or ring shaped mould for serving rice, fish mousse or moulds held together by jelly.

Mousseline A very light quenelle made from pounded raw fish and same quantity of double cream, worked together over ice.

Mousseline, sauce See Sauces Appendix.

Panada (French: *panade*) Flour based mixture used to thicken and bind quenelle stuffings.

Panada Pâte à choux Put 3dl water, 50g melted butter and salt into a saucepan. Bring to the boil and pour in, all at once, 150g sifted flour; mix. When it has thickened, dry the mixture out over a moderate heat, like choux pastry, mixing with a spatula until the mixture shrinks from the sides of the pan and forms a film over the bottom. Pour on to a plate, cover with buttered paper and leave to cool before using.

Panada à la Frangipane Put 125g sifted flour and 4 egg yolks into a heavy saucepan. Mix well with a spatula then add 100g warm melted butter beating with a whisk. Gently pour over 2½dl boiled milk; then, still whisking, bring to the boil. Leave to cook for 1–2 minutes. Season with salt, pepper and nutmeg. Cool in the same way as Panada Pâté à choux.

Paupiette Thin slice of meat or fillet of fish, stuffed, rolled and tied up.

Poach, to To cook in a liquid which is barely boiling.

Potatoes – Dauphine Make a potato purée, well seasoned with pepper and nutmeg. At the same time prepare a choux paste. Mix the two in equal proportions. Form into balls the size of a nut and cook in deep oil or fat, boiling. Take out when brown all over and drain with a draining spoon on absorbent paper. Dust with salt and serve immediately.

Potatoes – Gaufrettes Potatoes cut into thin slices with a mandolin slicer. They are lattice cut by cutting the first slice in one direction and the next slice in the opposite direction. Fried in hot oil as for Dauphine potatoes.

Pralin Put into a copper frying-pan equal weights of caster sugar and almonds or any unskinned nuts. Stir over the heat with a spatula until the sugar begins to brown and caramelise. Pour out on to a marble slab. Leave to harden completely and cool. Then grind to powder in an electric coffee grinder.

Quenelle A mixture made up of white meat or fish, pounded with equal weight of double cream and a base called a *panada* (see above) which contains flour to thicken.

Refresh, to To put under cold running water to stiffen and restore colour to blanched green vegetables, etc.

Reduce, to To boil up a liquid, sauce, wine, cream, etc. to diminish the volume; may also be done by prolonged simmering.

Reduction Reduced liquid (see above).

Roux Mixture of butter and flour cooked for a shorter or longer time depending on colour required: thus white roux, blond roux, brown roux.

Sabayon A foamy and light dessert cream. May be served hot or cold. Continuously whisk 100g caster sugar, 3 egg yolks or 2 yolks and 1 whole egg, with 3dl Port or Marsala or sweet white wine. Work over a bain-marie or very low heat without boiling, until the mixture swells and becomes fluffy. Flavour with Curaçao, Kirsch or Cognac.

Sabayon for meat Egg yolks beaten with good white wine over a moderate heat until they are fluffy and double in volume. Add a few spoons good meat juice, salt and pepper.

Salpicon Various ingredients uniformly diced, e.g. *salpicon* of truffles; *salpicon* of preserved fruit, etc.

Sauté, to To cook in a frying pan in fat or oil, shaking pan to make ingredients jump (French: *sauter*), thus cooking elements from the bottom evenly.

Sorbet Fruit, or fruit juice and water ice. The mixture is held together with a drop of egg white, just broken with a fork. 1 egg white to each litre of sorbet. May be flavoured with fruit liqueur before being frozen.

Sugar syrup 1 kg sugar + $\frac{1}{2}$l water for syrup at 32°C, 90°F; 1 kg sugar + 1l water for syrup at 25°C, 75°F.

Stages:

Thread stage Wet the fingers in cold water. Pour a little sugar syrup on to a plate and when cool pick up a drop between finger and thumb – it should form a thread between them. Temperature or degree of cooking: 106°C, 225°F.

Ball stage Prolong cooking from thread stage and make the same test. This time it should form a resistant ball between the fingers. Temperature or degree of cooking: 118°C, 240°F.

Crack stage Ball stage. Dip index finger, well wet with cold water, into syrup off the heat and a fine film should adhere, which hardens immediately and when bitten should crack. Temperature or degree of cooking: 125°C, 260°F.

Skim, to To remove fat or scum from surface of a soup, sauce, boiling liquid, etc.

Sweat, to Cook over moderate heat with butter or fat but absolutely no liquid, for a short time; usually done with green vegetables to soften them.

Suprêmes The two white breasts of chicken or turkey.

Velouté See Sauces Appendix.

Zest Outside skin of citrus fruits used in cooking and pâtisserie making. Grated with a grater it flavours cakes or creams. Should be cut off with a vegetable knife (with *no* pith) cut into strips and blanched before use with duck for orange or lemon duck.

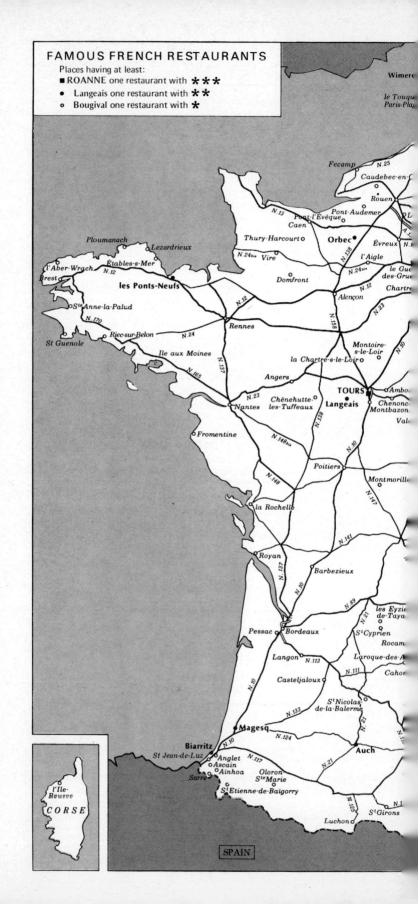

FAMOUS FRENCH RESTAURANTS

Places having at least:
- ■ ROANNE one restaurant with ✴✴✴
- ● Langeais one restaurant with ✴✴
- ○ Bougival one restaurant with ✴

Wimere

le Touqu
Paris-Pla

Fecamp N.25
Caudebec-en-C
Rouen
N.13 Pont-l'Évêque Pont-Audemer
Caen LC
Thury-Harcourt Orbec Évreux N.
N.24bis Vire l'Aigle
Domfront N.24bis le Gue
des-Grue
Alençon Chartre
N.138 N.23 N.
Ploumanach Lezardrieux
l'Aber-Wrach Étables-s-Mer
Brest N.12
les Ponts-Neufs N.12 Rennes Montoire-
s-le-Loir
St Anne-la-Palud N.158 la Chartre-s-le-Loir
N.170 Riec-sur-Belon N.24 Rennes
St Guenole Ile aux Moines Angers TOURS Ambo
N.137 Chênehutte- Langeais Chenonc
N.165 les-Tuffeaux Montbazon
N.23 N.138 Val
Nantes N.10
Fromentine N.148bis
Poitiers
N.148 Montmorill
la Rochelle N.147
N.141
Royan Barbezieux
N.137
N.10 les Eyzie
de-Taya
N.89 N.21
St Cyprien
Pessac Bordeaux Rocam
Langon N.113 Laroque-des-A
Cahor
N.111
Casteljaloux
N.10 St Nicolas- N.21
de-la-Balerme N.
N.133
Magesq
N.124
Biarritz Auch
St Jean-de-Luz N.10 Anglet N.117
Ascain N.21
Ainhoa N.
Sarre Oloron
Ste Marie
St Etienne-de-Baïgorry N.125 N.1
St Girons
Luchon

l'Ile-
Rousse
CORSE

SPAIN

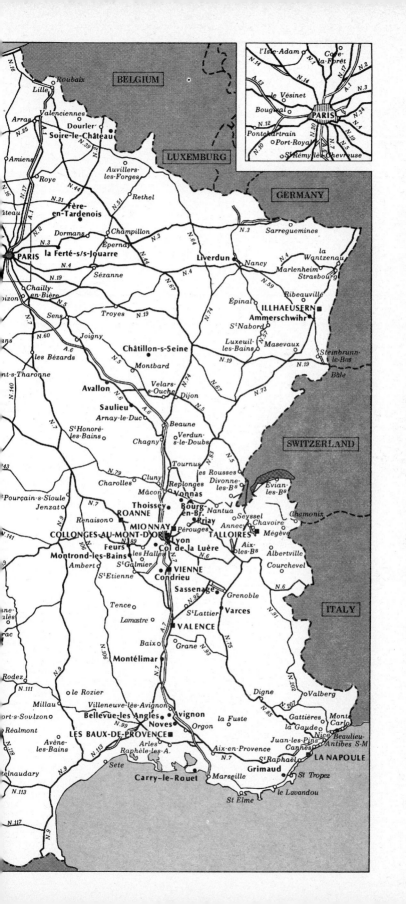

Saulieu
N.6
Arnay-le-Duc
A.6
N.74
Beaune
Chagny
N.80
Verdun-s-le-Doubs
N.5
N.83
SWITZERLAND
Tournus
N.83
les Rousses
Cluny
N.79
N.75
Divonne-les-Bains
Evian-les-Bains
Charolles
Replonges
St Jean-de-Gonville
N.5
Mâcon
Bourg-en-Bresse
N.84
N.506
Thoissey
Vonnas
Nantua
Seyssel
Chamonix
ROANNE
N.6
A.6
N.83
Priay
Annecy
Chavoire
N.201
Mégéve
N.82
Pérouges
MIONNAY
TALLOIRES
Feurs
les Halles
COLLONGES-AU-MONT-D'OR
N.504
N.201
N.508
Albertville
Montrond-les-Bs
Col de la Luère
Lyon
Aix-les-Bains
St Galmier
N.6
N.90
St Etienne
A.47
Condrieu
VIENNE
N.85
Courchevel
N.6
Tence
N.7
A.7
St Lattier
Sassenage
N.90
Grenoble
Varces
Lamastre
N.533
N.92
VALENCE
N.86
N.7
Grane
N.75
Baix
Montélimar

0   km   50

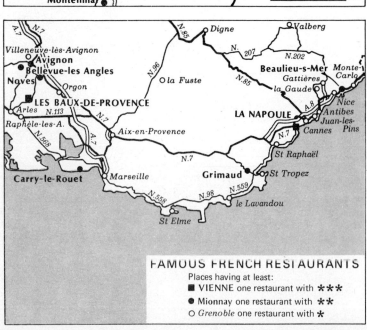

A.7
N.7
Digne
N.85
Valberg
Villeneuve-lès-Avignon
N.207
N.202
Avignon
N.96
Beaulieu-s-Mer
Monte-Carlo
Bellevue-les-Angles
la Fuste
N.85
Gattières
Noves
Orgon
la Gaude
Nice
Arles
N.113
LES BAUX-DE-PROVENCE
A.8
Antibes
Raphèle-les-A.
N.7
LA NAPOULE
Juan-les-Pins
N.568
Aix-en-Provence
N.7
Cannes
A.7
St Raphaël
Carry-le-Rouet
Marseille
Grimaud
St Tropez
N.7
N.559
N.558
N.98
le Lavandou
St Elme

FAMOUS FRENCH RESTAURANTS

Places having at least:
■ VIENNE one restaurant with ★★★
● Mionnay one restaurant with ★★
○ Grenoble one restaurant with ★

Regional Index

Flanders, Artois, Picardy

FLANDERS

ARTOIS

PICARDY

Paris

PARIS 1er

PARIS 2e

PARIS 4e

PARIS 5e

PARIS 6e

PARIS 7e

LA BOURGOGNE★
Œufs en Meurette — 30

LA BOULE D'OR★
Quiche Lorraine — 19
Soufflé au citron — 329

LE GALANT VERRE★
Rognons de veau gasconne — 228

CHEZ GILDO★
Fettucine all'Alfredo — 285

LE VERT BOCAGE★
Tarte à la tomate — 21
Filets de soles Vert Bocage — 122

PARIS 8e

LASSERRE★★★
Filets de soles homardine — 127
Canard braisé à l'orange — 186

MAXIM'S★★★
Potage Billy By — 13
Sole Albert — 133
Poulet au vinaigre de Xérès — 163

LEDOYEN★★
Soles soufflées à la mousse
de homard — 126
Rognons flambés Ledoyen — 225

LUCAS CARTON★★
Cassolette de queues
d'écrevisses à la Nantua — 94
Rouennais à la Rouennaise — 199

LA MARÉE★★
Aiguillettes de saumon Turenne — 113
Turbot à la moutarde — 138
Tournedos 'Cordon Rouge' — 241

RÉGENCE PLAZA HÔTEL

PLAZA-ATHÉNÉE★
Crêpes Montaigne — 325

TAILLEVENT★★★
Terrine de brochet Curnonsky — 45
Ris de veau Lamennais — 221
Soufflé glacé au Cointreau — 332

ANDROUET★
Feuilleté au Roquefort — 64
Salade Bernoise — 68

L'ARTOIS★
Soles Isidore — 121
Chou farci corrézien — 290

FOUQUET'S★
Médaillons de veau Alexandra — 216

JOSEPH
Ris de veau Joseph — 219

LAURENT★
Ris de veau Régence — 221

CHEZ MAX★
Thon frais braisé à la tomate — 150

LA TRUITE
Soufflé normand — 330

PARIS 9e

RÔTISSERIE DE LA TABLE DU ROY★
Steak Tartare or
Cannibal steak — 250
Steak Tartare Caucasien — 250

PARIS 10e

CHEZ MICHEL★★
Potiquet de moules farcies — 80
Ris de veau Normande — 218

RELAIS GASTRONOMIQUE

PARIS-EST★
Homard à la New-Burg — 83
Tournedos Curnonsky — 239

PARIS 14e

CHEZ ALBERT★★
Rable de lièvre à la Cauchoise — 274
Crêpes farcies Armoricaines — 319

PARIS 16e

LE VIVAROIS★★★
Timbale de coquilles
Saint-Jacques au Noilly — 79

LE BERLIOZ
Tarte façon Tatin — 297

LE GEORGE SAND★
Œufs Bragance — 29

JAMIN★
Œufs brouillés au homard — 32
Fois gras de canard aux raisins
de Smyrne — 48

PAUL CHÊNE★
Charlotte aux framboises — 315

PARIS 17e

LE CHALUT★
Timbale Normande — 81

CHEZ DENIS
Bouchées d'huîtres Denis — 73

MICHEL PEREIRE★
Clafoutis — 302

PARIS 19e

AU BŒUF COURONNÉ★
Pavé Villette et Côte de bœuf — 232
Pied de porc grillés — 257
Pommes soufflées — 279

AU COCHON D'OR★★
Filet de bœuf poêlé Villette,
garniture Bouquetière — 232

DAGORNO★
Filets de soles Dagorno — 122

PARIS 20e

RELAIS DES PYRÉNÉES
Oulliat or Tourri — 16
Confit d'oie comme en Béarn — 55
Confit d'oie à la Basquaise — 56

Ile-de-France

Champagne

Alsace, Lorraine

ALSACE

LORRAINE

Normandy

Britanny

Burgundy

AUBERGE DE NOVES★★
  Noves
  Rognon de veau Printanier   226
  Ratatouille Provençale   289
LEI MOUSCARDINS★
  Saint-Tropez
  Langoustes à la crème   86
  Capoum farci   144
LA BONNE AUBERGE★
  Antibes
  Coquelet sauté Provençale   167
LE FESTIVAL
  Cannes
  Crêpes Suzette   326
LE PROVENCAL★
  Juan-les-Pins
  Pollo Pépitoria   168
  Gigot au Pistou   209
LA POULARDE★
  Nice
  Rougets à la Sauvage   149
  Capilotade de poulet paysanne 180
SAINT-MORITZ★
  Nice
  Soufflé au fromage brioché   65
HÔTEL DU ROY RENÉ
  Aix-en-Provence
  *Brochettes de rognons et de foie
  de veau à la Provençale*   59
LE RIVIÉRA★
  Aix-en-Provence
  La caraque   312
LE VENDOME★
  Aix-en-Provence
  Brandade à l'huile d'olive   151
  Artichauts violets à la Barigoule 286
LE DIABLE VERT★
  Raphèle-les-Arles (near Arles)
  *Carré d'agneau grillé au feu
  de bois*   209

L'AUBERGE★
  L'Ile-Rousse
  Pâté de merles   39

L'ESCALE★★
  Carry-le-Rouet
  Moules grillées à la Provençale 71
MICHEL (Brasserie des Catalans)
  Marseille
  Bouillabaisse   7
  Bourride   21
RELAIS BASQUE
  Orgon
  Piperade   32
  Tarte au citron   299
HOSTELLERIE DES SANTONS★★
  Grimaud
  Poires farcies des santons   301
LA JETÉE★
  Saint-Elme
  *Brochettes de moules, sauce
  Provençale*   62
  Filet de bœuf sous la cendre 233
AUBERGE DES MAURES★
  Saint-Tropez
  Artichauts à la Provençale   285
HOSTELLERIE DE LA FUSTE
  La Fuste par Valensole
  (near Manosque)
  Truites aux amandes   102
  *Civet de lièvre aux senteurs de
  Provence*   275
AUBERGE DE FRANCE★
  Avignon
  *Charlotte aux noisettes et au
  miel de Provence*   317
HÔTEL DE PARIS★
  Monte-Carlo (Monaco)
  Volaille grillée Hôtel de Paris 153
  Millefeuille Prince Albert   309

CORSICA

Guyenne, Gascony, Béarn
GUYENNE

Bordelais
SPLENDID HÔTEL★
  Bordeaux
  Confit d'oie Sarladaise   55
LA RÉSERVE★
  Pessac
  *Brochettes de ris de veau à
  la Diable*   60
  Coq sauté au vin de Graves   159
  Entrecôte grillée à la Bordelaise 246

Périgord
HÔTEL DE CRO-MAGNON★
  Les Eyzies-de-Tayac
  Oeufs cocotte aux truffes   29
  Truites farcies aux fines herbes 104

Quercy
SAINTE-MARIE
  Rocamadour
  Omelette aux truffes   34
AU DÉJEUNER DE SOUSCEYRAC★
  Sousceyrac
  Tournedos au poivre vert   244

Rouergue
LE RÉGENT★
  Rodez
  *Confit d'oie Grand-Mère en
  boîte*   57
  Foie d'oie en boîte   58

GASCOGNE

HÔTEL DE FRANCE★★
  Auch
  Foie gras frais du Gers   51
  Steak de canard au poivre vert 194

AGENAIS

GRAND HÔTEL DES CADETS DE
GASCOGNE
  Casteljaloux
  Tourte Gasconne   298

NOTES